DATE DUE

ROBBER BARON

JOHN FRANCH

Robber Baron

THE LIFE OF

CHARLES TYSON YERKES

UNIVERSITY OF ILLINOIS PRESS

URBANA AND CHICAGO

Library of Congress Cataloging-in-Publication Data
Franch, John, 1967–
   Robber baron : the life of Charles Tyson Yerkes / John
Franch.
      p. cm.
   Includes bibliographical references and index.
   ISBN-13: 978-0-252-03099-4 (cloth : alk. paper)
   ISBN-10: 0-252-03099-0 (cloth : alk. paper)
   1. Yerkes, Charles Tyson, 1837–1905. 2. Capitalists and
financiers—United States—Biography. 3. Street-railroads
—Illinois—Chicago—Finance.
I. Title.
HG172.Y47F73   2006
388.4'2092—dc22   2005034416

Contents

Acknowledgments

This book could not have been completed without the aid of Paul Hadley; Phil Costello and Jeanie Childs, of the Archives Department for the Clerk of the Cook County Circuit Court; Martin Tuohy, of the National Archives—Great Lakes Region; Laurie Matheson, of the University of Illinois Press; and last but certainly not least, the members of my family. I also wish to thank William Maher, Chris Prom, Ellen Swain, and Debbie Pfeiffer, of the University of Illinois Archives; Winton Solberg; John Horachek; Eric Mogren; James Norris; James Barrett; Richard Burkhardt; Owen Covick; Polly Wharram; and Barbara Posadas. Many other people and archival institutions made this book possible and I thank them for their assistance.

1 *The Inner Light*

On a mild winter morning in 1872, a horse-drawn carriage thundered to a stop before the massive iron gate of Philadelphia's fortress-like Eastern State Penitentiary. A pair of burly deputy sheriffs wearing diamond stickpins on their shirtfronts emerged from the carriage followed by two more men. Entering the jail through an opening in the gate, the deputies led the grim-faced duo to a drab reception room. A clerk precariously perched on a high stool then began to interrogate the younger of the two prisoners—a handsome, muscular man with a neatly trimmed mustache and prematurely graying hair.

"What is your name?" the clerk asked.

"Charles T. Yerkes, Jr."

The clerk recorded the information in an enormous book that nearly covered his desktop.

"What is your age?"

"Thirty-four."

"What is your profession?"

"I am a broker."

Using a pine ruler, the clerk's assistant then measured the prisoner from head to toe.

"Five feet, nine inches," the assistant coldly announced.

The prisoner next emptied his pockets, and placed their contents on the desk: shirt studs, a railroad ticket, and $5.60 in change.

The clerk wrote in his book the broker's crime: Larceny. The sentence: Two years and nine months. And the date: February 10, 1872.

The other man then went through the same routine. He happened to be Joseph Marcer, ex-treasurer of the City of Philadelphia. After shedding their well-tailored suits for coarse gray uniforms and gray caps, the two unfortunates were hustled away to tiny cells seven feet wide and sixteen feet long sparsely furnished with an iron bed, a clothes rack, and a stool. Only months before, Prisoners 7126 and 7127 had possessed great wealth and position but now they did not even own a name.[1]

Yerkes would rebound in a big way from this disaster, becoming a street railway magnate of international fame and the founder of an observatory. Marcer would have a different future. "To a Philadelphian," a journalist wrote in 1905, "it could not but seem strange in the odd twistings of our fates, that . . . Yerkes was wielding the power of a multi-millionaire, while his comrade in the Eastern Penitentiary, the City Treasurer with whom he consorted in the misuse of public money in Philadelphia, was lying in an obscure grave after years of humble toil in a municipal clerkship. How oddly the paths of men diverge!" F. Scott Fitzgerald once said that there were no second acts in American lives. Charles Tyson Yerkes, though, was an American who would have a second—and a third—act before the curtain fell on his dramatic life.

———

In 1842 Charles Dickens had visited the Eastern State Penitentiary, famous worldwide for its "humane" system of solitary confinement, and pronounced it "a most dreadful, fearful place." His opinion of Philadelphia—the site of the penitentiary—was not much more favorable. He found the city to be "dull and out of spirits." The birthplace of the Declaration of Independence and the Constitution, Philadelphia had basked for a time in the glory of its past. As late as the 1790s the city continued to command the gaze of the nation, playing host to President George Washington and his cabinet. During those years, Secretary of State Thomas Jefferson and Secretary of the Treasury Alexander Hamilton battled over the future of the nation. In 1800, Philadelphia lost its political place in the sun to Washington, D.C., the nation's new capital. When the Erie Canal was completed in 1825, New York City captured the bulk of the Great Lakes trade and quickly eclipsed Philadelphia as the country's chief commercial center. Following this long streak of bad luck, the City of Brotherly Love "dwindled regretfully into a provincial town with memories." The clock on its tower solemnly tolling the hours, Independence Hall stood in the city's heart as a monument to those memories.

In his *American Notes* Dickens brilliantly captured the mood of this city so haunted by its past. Reaching his Philadelphia hotel late at night, the great author observed from his room's window "a handsome building of white marble, which had a mournful ghost-like aspect, dreary to behold." Expecting to see the next day throngs of people crowding the building's steps, he instead discovered that "the same cold cheerless air prevailed." Later asking the name of the mysterious structure, Dickens learned that it "was the Tomb of many fortunes; the Great Catacomb of investment; the memorable United States Bank." The recent closing of this bank, the novelist was informed, had "cast a gloom on Philadelphia, under the depressing effect of which it yet labored." Charging that it was a monopoly dangerous to democratic government and individual liberty, President Andrew Jackson—heir to Jefferson's legacy—had waged war on the United States Bank and its aristocratic custodian Nicholas Biddle. Jackson eventually succeeded in toppling Philadelphia's last important bastion of national influence.

Venturing out into the city of 250,000 inhabitants, Dickens was struck by the straightness of its streets. "It is a handsome city, but distractingly regular," the author remarked. "After walking about it for a hour or two, I felt that I would have given the world for a crooked street."[2] Laid out in rigid checkerboard fashion between the winding Delaware and Schuylkill rivers, Philadelphia's street plan conformed to its Quaker founder William Penn's desire for order and harmony. Though perhaps hard on the eyes, the city grid made it easy for the newcomer to get to his or her destination.

Straight rows of plain red and black brick buildings lined the nineteenth-century city's straight streets—a monotonous scene broken only by an occasional church steeple. The Scotchman Thomas Hamilton maintained that before the visitor had gotten halfway through the city "he [felt] an unusual tendency to relaxation about the region of the mouth, which ultimately terminate[d] in a silent but prolonged yawn."[3]

Many newcomers to Jacksonian-era Philadelphia judged its people to be as dull as its streets. "The first idea which strikes you when you arrive at Philadelphia is that it is Sunday; everything is so quiet, and there are few people stirring," a European noted in 1838. But one young man, newly arrived from the Ohio countryside, witnessed a bewildering amount of activity on the city's avenues that year. Jay Cooke, who would gain international fame as the "financier of the Civil War," furnished his brother with a wide-eyed account of the human carnival that daily paraded before him:

> What an odd mixture of incidents and sounds form a city life! The first thing in the morning that is heard is the rattling of the omnibuses, coaches, drays, ice carts, etc., over the pavement. This continues from daylight to sunset and after. "Sweep, oh!" "Fine Peaches!" "Hot Corn!"

"Coal, Coal, oh!" "Scissors to grind!" "Fine melons and apples!" "Hot Muffins!" etc., etc. Next comes up an organ grinder and hauls up before your door and, unless you throw a bucket of water upon him or something else as bad, he'll torment you with a jumble of tunes for half an hour and draw a crowd of gaping urchins about your door. Next comes perhaps a fight or a carriage running away and perhaps amidst all this confusion the startling alarm of fire breaks on the ear and crowds of firemen and engines, with bells ringing and loud clamor, flock towards the burning buildings. It is impossible to have any peace until about nine o'clock and then you can enjoy yourself.[4]

As he looked out of his office window at the bustle on the city streets below, young Jay Cooke may not have been aware that certain of these thoroughfares marked off rigid social as well as geographic boundaries. Market Street, Philadelphia's chief east-west artery, separated the city's upper-most class from the less "proper" elements. "Market Street is the northern boundary of fashionable residences," one visitor explained. "The fashionable inhabitants of Chestnut, Walnut and Spruce streets which lie to the south of that line, will scarcely recognize as compeers families living to the north of it." Some of these "fashionable" or "proper" Philadelphians could trace their ancestry back to the city's earliest years, but most attained upper-class status during the Revolutionary period. By the 1830s the lines had been sharply drawn and few outsiders could expect to ever gain admittance into the ranks of Philadelphia's elect. "There is no American city in which the system of exclusion is so rigidly observed as in Philadelphia," a foreigner remarked in 1833.

While Market Street marked off the latitude of Philadelphia's aristocracy, Broad Street, the city's major north-south thoroughfare, determined the longitude. A majority of the city's upper class lived east of Broad, clustered about Washington Square, until the 1840s, when a mass migration occurred. Well before Horace Greeley offered his famous bit of advice, Philadelphia's social leaders began heading west—west of Broad, that is—and settled in the area around Rittenhouse Square.[5]

Charles Tyson Yerkes, Jr., grew up in a world far removed from the latitude and longitude of Rittenhouse Square. He was born and reared near Franklin Square in the city's northeast quarter, a region "outside the pale" as far as fashionable Philadelphians were concerned. The young Charles, in fact, did not even reside in the City of Philadelphia, but instead lived just outside of its limits in a largely working-class industrial suburb known as the Northern Liberties. In 1840 this district of 34,474 inhabitants served as a gateway for Irish and German immigrants, who found work in the area's various factories. Plagued by high crime rates, the Northern Liberties and the several other large Philadelphia suburbs were, according to one observer, "infested with a set of the most graceless vagabonds and unmitigated ruffians." These youthful "ruffians" often belonged to one of the numerous gangs that roamed the city, groups with such ominous names as the Killers, the Blood Tubs, and the Deathfetchers.[6]

Such an urban environment was by no means a typical one for a Yerkes. Anthony, the founder of the Yerkes family in Pennsylvania, arrived in America around 1700 from Germany. He served for a time as a burgess in Germantown, near Philadelphia, and in 1705 married Sarah Watts, the widow of an eminent Baptist pastor. Four years later Anthony purchased 300 acres in what would become Moreland Township, about fifteen miles north of the City of Brotherly Love. Generations of Yerkeses would live and die on this hilly tract of land, diligently cultivating its rich soil season after season. Only two members of the Pennsylvania branch of the family abandoned the country for the city during the entire eighteenth century. One of these, Joseph Yerkes, a Quaker, established a private school in Philadelphia sometime before 1768 and during a thirty-year career gained a name for himself as one of that city's most accomplished teachers.

Silas Yerkes, Charles's grandfather, was a maverick like Joseph. He also left the country for the city and he was a Quaker as well, unlike most members of the largely Baptist Yerkes family. Arriving in Philadelphia in 1808 at the age of twenty-nine, Silas, a severe-looking man with a strong nose and piercing eyes, entered into business as a flour and feed merchant.[7] In the 1820s he fell under the spell of the charismatic Quaker preacher Elias Hicks. Hicks chided the largely urban and upper-class Quaker leadership for overemphasizing the Bible in their teaching. He argued that Quakers should rely on what was their traditional bulwark—the Inner Light—a "bit of divinity" lurking within everyone that furnished moral guidance. Hicks described the Inner Light as a "law of righteousness in every soul . . . clear and perfect," and argued that every person who "attends to this inward law has the will of God manifested to him." Quakers believed that an individual, unassisted by ministers or creeds, could achieve unity with God by tapping into this divine aspect of one's nature. While accepting the truth of the Inner Light, orthodox Quaker leaders believed Hicks's egalitarian teachings went too far, and would inevitably lead to a sort of religious anarchy.

Swept away by Hicks's magnetism and goaded by the arrogant Quaker leadership, the strong-willed Silas Yerkes—a "man of positive views"—and thousands of other mostly middle-class Friends separated from their Orthodox brethren and formed a Hicksite wing in 1827. The Society of Friends remained divided into these opposing camps until 1955. According to one scholar, the Hicksite branch appealed to those Quakers who wanted "freedom to follow their own individual bent in an atmosphere that is mildly religious and fiercely tolerant."[8]

Charles Yerkes, Sr., joined his father Silas in the Hicksite fold, though perhaps not as enthusiastically. Attracted by the lure of worldly wealth, Charles, Sr., sought business success rather than spiritual reward. Trained in Silas's feed store, he eventually obtained a job as a teller at a bank in Kensington, a suburb adjacent to the Northern Liberties. An organization man long before the term was invented, the elder Charles rose slowly but steadily up in the bank's ranks. In 1834, he married Elizabeth Link Broom, the daughter of a local merchant and granddaughter of a German immigrant who had fought in the Revolution. Their first son Samuel was born on November 27, 1834, followed three years later by Charles, Jr.

The young socially ambitious Charles Tyson Yerkes, Jr., had three strikes against him from the start. He grew up in the Northern Liberties among the "rabble," in the eyes of Philadelphia's aristocracy. His Quaker background only increased his isolation from the mostly Episcopalian members of the upper class. "The Quaker community . . . was effectively set off from the social group into which I was born as if between us there had been a Chinese wall," George Wharton, a "proper" Philadelphian, would recall. Finally, Charles's Hicksite ancestry separated him from the wealthy and socially important Orthodox Quakers. In Philadelphia, a bastion of conservatism, the Orthodox outnumbered the followers of Elias Hicks in both numbers and influence. Logan Pearsall Smith, an Orthodox Quaker, wrote that as a boy he believed the Hicksites to be "children of the Devil." He further remembered "climbing the wall that surrounded one of the Hicksite meetinghouses, and gazing in on those precincts with all the horror of one who gazes into Hell."[9]

Charles was born on June 25, 1837. It was not an auspicious time to enter the world. A severe depression gripped the nation. "All the merchants in N. Orleans except 4 have failed, nearly all are expected to fail in N. York, many of the best houses have gone here, several of the public works have stopped, the working classes are thrown out of employment, and universal bankruptcy and confusion . . . seem impending over the country," the Philadelphia lawyer Sidney Fisher reported in April 1837. "Never before, in the history of our country have ruin and embarrassment been so extensive and so deeply felt."[10] The Whigs charged that President

Jackson, a Democrat, had triggered the depression by destroying the Second Bank of the United States—the only institution, they claimed, that could have smoothed the stormy sea of speculation before it overwhelmed the country.

The depression opened a violent era in Philadelphia's history.[11] In 1838 mobs burned down an abolitionists' hall and then attempted to do the same to a Quaker-sponsored shelter for African American orphans. Six years later violence again erupted. Swarming through the streets of Kensington in May 1844, nativist throngs set fire to churches and traded gunfire with Irish Americans during four days of rioting. The following July, a crowd equipped with a cannon laid siege to a Catholic church.[12] Clearly, during the years of Charles's childhood the City of Brotherly Love did not live up to its name.

The seven-year-old Charles may have noticed in 1844 the large unruly mobs parading through the streets of the Northern Liberties on their way to Kensington. But he probably remained quite insulated from the era's violence and from the effects of the economic downturn. His father earned a good enough income to rear his children in middle-class comfort—a salary that, indeed, allowed him to move his growing family to more spacious quarters every few years. Charles's first home stood at 126 New Market Street, one of the Northern Liberties' major arteries. This house may very well have been one of the famous so-called bandboxes— two-and-a-half-story cubes with only one room to a floor—which had been erected en masse in the district in the late eighteenth and early nineteenth centuries. A former occupant of a New Market Street bandbox confessed that life in such a structure held no "glamour." He elaborated: "The chief trouble with the bandbox was that you had no privacy. You not only knew what your neighbor had for dinner, but you heard all his conversation and knew all his business."[13]

In those early days, Charles knew his neighbors. George Yerkes, a brush manufacturer and Charles's uncle, lived next door while grandfather Silas resided one block away, where he operated a livery stable. Another uncle, the druggist Samuel Parry Shoemaker, also resided nearby with his two sons. All of these relatives were at the time comfortably middle class, but by no means wealthy. Samuel Shoemaker, for example, left an estate worth $6,142 upon his death in 1858—an amount approximately equivalent to $106,000 in today's money. Though largely a working-class suburb, the Northern Liberties contained a wide assortment of different people, including some self-described "gentlemen" of independent means. "Social and economic heterogeneity was the hallmark of the age," wrote the historian Sam Bass Warner, Jr. "Most areas of the new big city were a jumble of occupations, classes, shops, homes, immigrants, and native Americans."[14]

All of Charles's early homes lay within a few blocks of the Delaware River. In the winter Philadelphia youths skated on the frozen Delaware, sometimes gliding as far as Camden, New Jersey, a foreign shore. There was "always a kind of Russian carnival on the ice," the author Charles Godfrey Leland recalled, "oxen sometimes being roasted whole, and all kinds of 'fakirs,' as they are now termed, selling doughnuts, spruce-beer, and gingerbread, or tempting the adventurous with thimblerig." In the summer, Charles could watch the majestic masted ships gliding past, their wide sails billowing in the breeze. He also must have noted with amazement the constant bustle on the Delaware's wharves, where, "as far as the eye can carry, nothing is seen but the masts and cordage of vessels, the puffing of steamers arriving and departing, and the struggling of draymen, porters, and sailors, engaged in the business of loading and unloading articles of commerce."[15]

When he was not roaming along the Delaware wharves, the youngster may have passed the time at his grandfather's livery stable. Charles loved horses—a passion that he shared with many other Philadelphia youths. "I am often amused at seeing the city boys, who having scraped together a few shillings, spend it in riding in a buggy or on horseback," Jay Cooke wrote to his brother. "A ride is considered one of the greatest luxuries in Philadelphia." Charles enjoyed the sensation of speed that a "ride" provided. He also admired the sleek grace of horses.

Even as a child, Charles seems to have been a devotee of the beautiful. The natural world especially appealed to him. Though in the process of being forever transformed into an industrial center, 1840s Philadelphia still retained some rural flavor. "Every house had its garden, in which vines twisted over arbours, and the magnolia, honeysuckle, and rose spread rich perfume of summer nights, and where the humming-bird rested, and scarlet tanager or oriole with the yellow and blue bird flitted in sunshine or shade," one resident remembered. "Then swallows darted at noon over the broad streets, and the mighty sturgeon was so abundant in the Delaware that one could hardly remain a minute on the wharf without seeing some six-foot monster dart high in the air, falling on his side with a plash." Flower-strewn meadows then closely surrounded Philadelphia, and even rare orchids and trillium could be found growing in pastures south of the city. Charles never forgot this Elysian paradise of his youth, which soon disappeared under the onslaught of industrialism.

Charles's life was changed forever on December 8, 1842, when his mother and her newborn infant died of childbed or puerperal fever. Only thirty-three years old, Elizabeth Yerkes contracted this common disease while giving birth under the supervision of Dr. Charles Noble.[16]

Coincidentally, only four days after Elizabeth Yerkes died, Dr. Oliver Wendell Holmes, father of the future Supreme Court justice, began an investigation of puerperal fever in his native Boston. After years of study, he would correctly conclude that the disease was infectious and spread to the patient by the doctor himself. Hundreds and thousands of women, he subsequently warned, are "liable to be poisoned in their beds by a pestilence that walks at noonday into their chamber—and charges it may be a guinea a visit for dispersing the deadliest of diseases to a young and innocent mother." Dr. Noble had in fact unknowingly infected Elizabeth Yerkes and her child with the bacteria that caused this "deadliest of diseases."[17]

In 1845, Charles's father remarried, taking as his second bride Margaret Patterson, the daughter of a grocer. Like his first wife, Margaret also was not a member of the Society of Friends. Quakers frowned upon those Friends who married out of the "order." Learning of this second infraction, the members of the elder Charles's Quaker meeting dispatched a committee to question the errant bank teller. Unsatisfied with the interview, the committee advised that the elder Charles be expelled from the Society.

The full meeting ratified the committee's recommendation on October 23, 1845.[18] Charles, Sr., discovered that even the strongly individualistic Hicksites expected rules to be followed.

Young Charles received a great deal of exposure to Quaker beliefs before his father's expulsion from the Society. An Irish journalist later discerned in Yerkes's face "that quietism which is and always remains the expression of the man or woman who has begun life amid the prolonged silences and the stern self-discipline and self-control of the Society of Friends."[19] Charles was taught early that one should lead a simple life free of outward display, that all people are equal in the eyes of God, and that being good means doing good. Most important, he learned every person possessed within himself or herself a divine essence—the Inner Light—that, if heeded, would lead one toward the correct path. Throughout his life, Charles believed in a sort of Inner Light, although his was a decidedly secular version. "I have a principle in myself that suggests what is right and what is wrong," he asserted in 1898. "When I make up my mind that I am doing the right, I continue to try to do it. If I feel I am in the wrong, I drop it very quickly, because life is too short to chase anything that you feel is going to be a failure. And a wrong will never be a success."[20]

Charles was also brought up to believe in the gospel of success. Quakers prized material success, seeing in it a sign of divine favor. Young male

Friends were instructed to be diligent, industrious, frugal, and orderly—values thought to be necessary for the attainment of wealth. Even in the earliest years of the Society's existence, Quakers had a reputation as shrewd and successful businessmen, thanks to their strong work ethic.

The public schools of the period preached the gospel as well. Self-made men, like Philadelphia's own Benjamin Franklin, were held up to students as role models. "In short, the way to wealth, if you desire it, is as plain as the way to market," Franklin had once written. "It depends chiefly on two words, industry and frugality; that is, waste neither time nor money, but make the best use of both." The public schools drummed such lessons into pupils' heads day after day. Attending such schools from the age of seven until seventeen, Charles was taught that successful men possessed certain virtues, such as thrift and industriousness, and that wealth—the chief mark of success—only came to those who worked hard for it. Failure was the fault of the individual in a nation where "the road to wealth, to honor, to usefulness, and happiness is open to all." The schools prepared students for a career of business achievement by stressing "useful knowledge"—reading, writing, and, in particular, arithmetic.

A product of his time, Charles always disliked novels. He maintained that "the time spent in the reading of novels is time very nearly wasted. There is almost no instruction to be got from them." He especially hated the "silly story of the girl that loves the man she can not have or the girl who has done wrong and for whose foolish errors sympathy is asked." (He admitted, however, that he enjoyed the historical romances of Sir Walter Scott.) True to his early education, Charles considered only science and history books to be useful and therefore worth reading.

Charles was pressured to succeed at an early age. His teacher at the Madison grammar school selected him and five other boys to take the Central High School examination.[21] Opened in 1838 as a "people's college," Central High stood at the pinnacle of Philadelphia's public education system. The goal of many of the grammar school students was to scale this pyramid and reach Central—a very difficult task, considering the fact that only one out of every fifty first-graders could ever hope to gain admission.

The biggest obstacle to scaling the pyramid was the notoriously difficult entrance exam, which 40 to 60 percent of students failed. This exam was designed to show whether a boy could read, write, spell, and do arithmetic. In late January 1852—during a spell of unseasonably warm weather—Charles and 159 other nervous yet hopeful boys began the two-week-long battery of exams, both written and oral.

Taking the tests in the late 1850s, one student deemed the "algebra examination utterly unfit for boys so little prepared as we are." Excelling in mathematics and the manipulation of numbers, Charles probably did well on the algebra exam but he must have found some of the other tests "utterly unfit." On Friday, February 7, he learned—perhaps to his amazement—that he had made the cut of 115 fortunate students, gaining admission to Central High with a score of 55. Though scoring rather low, Charles did better than thirty-six others who also passed. He had reason to be proud of himself and his feelings undoubtedly echoed those of another boy who, upon learning that he too had made the cut, pronounced it "The greatest day in my life."[22]

Located in the heart of Philadelphia two miles southwest of Charles's home, the Central High School in 1852 occupied a building three stories in height, with a blue marble front and a white marble Ionic portico. Though supposedly "opening its portals alike to the son of a President or a ploughman, a Governor or his groom, a millionaire or a hewer of wood," Central had in 1850 a student body of 514 that hailed overwhelmingly from the middle class. In Charles's particular group most boys came from such a background; twenty-seven students, in fact, had fathers who were either merchants or clerks. Working-class families often could not afford to lose the income generated by a high-school-age boy. The Central High student, after all, had little time for outside work. Beginning the morning by attending a Bible reading, the schoolboy filed at 9:00 A.M. into the first of the seven forty-five-minute classes he would have to attend that day. The freshmen had to remain in school until 3:00 P.M., unlike the upperclassmen, who were dismissed earlier.

In the words of Central's first principal Alexander Bache, the greatgrandson of Benjamin Franklin, the high school prepared students for "the pursuits of commerce, manufactures, and the useful arts."[23] An excellent eleven-member faculty, especially strong in science and mathematics, helped fulfill Bache's mission. During his first year, Charles took such eminently useful courses as algebra, composition, phonography (a form of stenography), and bookkeeping.

One instructor in particular seems to have impressed the struggling student. The thirty-five-year-old Ezra Otis Kendall took sophomores on a guided tour of the universe in a course entitled "Uranography." Owl-faced with a sharp, beak-like nose and prominent eyes, Kendall looked every bit the astronomy professor. A graduate of the Boston Latin School, he exuded an air of "uniform urbanity and geniality," and employed a "quiet, philosophical, thorough method" of teaching. Using as his text his own book also titled *Uranography*, the scholarly instructor whisked his pupils through the entire universe in only five months. Of course, the universe was much smaller in those days.

Kendall was probably more comfortable in the dark coziness of Central High's observatory than in the classroom's harsh spotlight. Located behind the school in a forty-eight-foot-high brick tower, the observatory housed an excellent six-inch refractor.[24] On occasional clear nights, Kendall allowed his students to invade the observatory's sacred precincts and peer through the telescope at Saturn's rings or Jupiter's moons.

Though small by today's standards, Central High's German-made refractor was an impressive telescope for the time. According to a contemporary scientist, the construction of the school's observatory "formed an epoch in the history of American astronomy, in consequence of the introduction of a class of instruments superior to any which had been hitherto imported." In 1854 only six other public observatories in the United States boasted larger telescopes. Topping the list, Harvard University owned the nation's most powerful refractor—one with a fifteen-inch diameter lens. Inspired by Ezra Otis Kendall into boyish flights of fancy, Charles Tyson Yerkes, Jr., dreamed of surpassing Harvard, of one day building the biggest telescope in the world.[25] For some, dreams have a way of coming true.

2 The Spoils of War

In 1840 the youthful Philadelphia banker Jay Cooke noticed in his customers "the same all-pervading, all-engrossing anxiety to grow rich, to snatch from the unwilling hand of fortune that which her caprice will never permit her to grant them." Money, he asserted, "is the only thing for which men live here."

The teen-aged Charles Yerkes shared this "anxiety," in common with many others of his generation. Dubbed the "Gilded Generation," those who were born between 1822 and 1842 "came of age in an era of economic swings, floodtide immigration, and a darkening national mood," write William Strauss and Neil Howe, the authors of *Generations*. Rejecting high-minded notions and spiritual matters, the members of the Gilded Generation worshipped at the altar of materialism. They were America's original conspicuous consumers. Those born in the latter half of the Gilded Generation were especially tenacious in their pursuit of monetary success. The railroad speculator Jay Gould was born in 1834, the financier J. P. Morgan in 1837, and the oil tycoon John D. Rockefeller in 1839. "Shortly before or very shortly after 1840 were born nearly all the galaxy of uncommon men who were to be the overlords of the future society," Matthew Josephson wrote of the men he christened the Robber Barons.

The members of the Gilded Generation were "commercial before they get out of their petticoats," a foreigner noted.[1] Charles Yerkes also displayed an acute commercial sense at an early age. He was, according to a biographical sketch, "an active young man, always desiring to be at the head of all schemes, whether it was mischief at school or a money-making project."

Money, not mischief, was on the mind of the eleven-year-old boy one Saturday afternoon in 1850. As he wandered along a Delaware River wharf, he noticed an auction sign in front of a commission house. Going inside, he discovered that the auctioneer was selling soap—boxes of the very brand his family used. "That will go cheap," Charles thought, and an idea suddenly struck him. "I straightaway ran to the corner grocery," he later recalled, "and after drawing from the grocer a promise to pay a certain price for as many boxes of that soap as I could furnish (he, of course, never dreaming I would supply them) I returned to the salesroom." Charles successfully bid for one box, and the bystanders were much amused at the spectacle. Their "laughter gave place to amazement when I bid in the entire lot of twenty-two boxes," Charles remembered with delight. He then sold the boxes of soap to the grocer for twice the amount he had paid for them. Upon learning how Charles had obtained the soap, the grocer remarked, "Well, I guess I could have done that myself!" "I guess you could have, too!" the budding capitalist responded. Charles later claimed the "making of this money so startled him that instead of being filled with the idea that money was easy to make, his great fear was that he might in some way lose it."[2]

This fear, however, did not stifle Charles's youthful eagerness to make money. With the idea of entering the business world, he left the Central High School in July 1854 after completing the two-year course. His academic performance had been less than stellar. He graduated with a 71.5 average, ranking seventeenth out of the twenty-five boys in his class. But his school years had been far from a total waste. He at least had learned some skills—especially bookkeeping—that would be useful in business, and, besides, a Central diploma opened employers' doors. Like eleven other boys in his graduating class, he chose to become a clerk—a popular occupation for middle-class youths just starting out in the mid-nineteenth-century world.

Thanks largely to his status as a high school graduate, Charles quickly secured a job as a bookkeeper and general office boy at James P. Perot and Brother, a commission house located on a Delaware River wharf. Financially backed by their wealthy father, James Perot and his brother Sansom bought and sold grain on the Philadelphia Corn Exchange. Charles embarked upon his first job with what he termed "trembling and fear." He later described the first impressions of a young boy just beginning in business. "The office or store or manufacturing establishment which he enters is a mystery to him," Charles recalled. "In all probability he has never been across the threshold of anything similar to it. He is as much a stranger to it as he would be to a far-off country, and, generally speaking, his mind has never sought its realms. He is entirely unsophisticated, everything being strange and unusual. . . . He has entered another life and an entirely new world dawns before him; the attainment of success in that life being his goal." The youthful seeker of success plunged uncertainly into this brave, new business world.

Charles already understood from his high school classes the basics of bookkeeping. He knew that the firm's account books should be kept in a manner that clearly showed the merchant "to whom he owes, and who owes him, what goods he purchased; what he has disposed of, with the gain or loss upon the sale, and what ready money he has by him."[3] The neophyte office boy quickly demonstrated that he had a knack for book-keeping, a flair for adding up large sums and making credits and debits balance. He received no salary the first year, considering it "a great privilege to be permitted to enter a first-class house to learn the business." But the novice bookkeeper performed his job so well he was given fifty dollars at the end of the year as a reward for good work.

As Charles daily huddled over the account books tallying figures, he could not help but notice that his firm's debts grew larger year after year while its earnings dwindled. In 1855 a credit reporter wrote that James P. Perot and Brother were "doing a moderate business with moderate means and fair credit." Two years later, the reporter observed that the two brothers "have not made much of late" and did not possess "hardly sufficient capital to manage their business with ease." Matters only worsened for the firm in succeeding months. "Rubbing along rather short of money" in August 1857, the partnership suspended business the following month after a financial panic caused commodity prices to tumble.[4]

Sharp and severe, the Panic of 1857 plunged the nation into economic gloom for several years. Like most of the country's cities, Philadelphia staggered under the financial blow. On September 25, the mighty Bank of Pennsylvania closed its doors, sparking a "fever of excitement" among depositors, who clamored for their money. Some bankers even called for police squads to fend off terrified customers desperate to regain their savings. The unemployed swarmed in the streets, appealing to the city government to provide assistance. "A nightmare broods over society," a Philadelphian lamented. "The City is still as a Sabbath day. The oldest, wealthiest houses are crashing down day by day. . . . Scores of thousands are out of work. . . . Bread riots are dreaded. Winter is coming. God alone foresees the history of the next six months." Philadelphia Mayor Richard Vaux responded to the outcry of the distressed, pumping up the local economy with an extensive public works program.

Charles did not greatly suffer from the effects of the financial panic. Though perhaps temporarily thrown out of work, he soon returned to his old job when James P. Perot and Brother resumed operations shortly after its suspension. While working at this firm, Charles learned more than how to keep books or how to trade in grain. For the first time he was given a glimpse of a world far removed from the middle-class gentility of his upbringing. Reputed to be "free and fast livers," James P. Perot and his brother Sansom showed Charles what money could make possible.[5]

While their freewheeling lifestyle certainly appealed to him, Charles did not particularly like the Perot brothers' line of trade. Since 1857 he had closely followed in the newspapers the rampaging "bulls" and "bears" on Wall Street. The panic of that year eliminated the stodgy old-guard investors from the Street, and set the stage for the emergence of a new breed of trader—"a younger race of financiers," in the words of the broker Henry Clews. Charles wanted to enter the financial arena and run with these young bulls (or bears). He wanted to become a stockbroker.

In the late 1850s brokers were increasingly in demand, especially needed by the new corporations to market their stocks and bonds. During the late 1700s Philadelphia led the way in the use of the state-chartered corporation as a means of funneling the savings of many investors into large private enterprises.[6] Corporations—legally sanctioned associations of investors—raised money by issuing two major kinds of paper certificates: stocks, which represented ownership in the firm, and bonds, which were interest-bearing loans. Able to pool the resources of a small army of investors, corporations commanded far more capital than the individual small businessman could muster. And more capital was needed to afford the expensive steam-powered machinery used in manufacture and transportation. Industrialism encouraged the growth of the corporation as a means of doing business.

As a child, Charles had witnessed the immense change wrought by industrialism. His neighborhood in the Northern Liberties harbored a wide variety of different factories, including Henry Disston's famous Keystone Works, the world's largest saw manufacturer. Every year new industrial plants arose, transforming the face of the neighborhood. In 1851 alone, three textile factories, a malt house, a machine shop, and a saw mill were all erected in the Northern Liberties.[7] The railroads and the other corporate agents of industrialism required brokers to help finance their vast designs. Charles was eager to oblige.

In 1859 he left James P. Perot and Brother, giving up the security of a $300 annual salary, and opened his own brokerage at 23 South Third Street. Charles, however, did not jump into the financial arena completely unarmed; his pockets were not completely empty. "I didn't begin life as the typical barefoot boy on the tow-path," he later admitted. "I had some money when I started—not a great deal but some." He had begun depositing money while only a boy in an account at the Philadelphia Savings Fund. His initial $5 deposit "grew from year to year," he recalled, "and when I was 21 years of age the money of which this was the foundation amounted to several thousand dollars invested in good securities." He also had inherited money from a deceased uncle, possibly Samuel Shoemaker, who died in March 1858.[8]

Charles's new office was located in the heart of Philadelphia's financial district. In the 1850s nearly 95 percent of the city's brokers had offices located on Third Street. "Stock-jobbers, note-shavers and speculators of all kinds congregated on Third street up as far as Market street," a city historian noted, "and the neighborhood was familiarly known as the 'Coast of Algiers.'" The Mecca of all these financial pirates lay only a block or two south on Third: the Philadelphia Stock Exchange, also known as the Board of Brokers. The Board occupied a second-floor room in the Merchants Exchange building, a distinctive Grecian Revival structure designed in 1834 by the noted architect William Strickland. One critic likened the Corinthian portico of the Merchants Exchange to "a crushed shot-tower, flattened and extended at the sides by some immense pressure, since removed."[9]

Founded in 1790, the Philadelphia Board of Brokers was the first stock exchange established in the United States. Its constitution in fact served as a model for the New York Stock Exchange, which opened in 1817. In its early years the Philadelphia Board specialized in the securities of governments, banks, and canal companies, but by the 1830s railroad stocks had become the "sweethearts" of the exchange. In 1846 the newly invented telegraph revolutionized the business of the Board, providing almost instant access to market-making or market-breaking information. Running the Board as if it were an exclusive gentlemen's club, the brokers prescribed strict rules of conduct to be observed on the trading floor. Members were fined if they addressed the chairman with their mouths full, if they used profane language (such as "devil"), if they wound the clock without permission, or even if they simply whistled. In keeping with its aristocratic tone, the Board's 150 brokers lounged sedately in plush armchairs while they bid on stocks, bonds, bank notes, gold, or silver for themselves or for customers. Occasionally, when members engaged in a big speculation or a financial panic swept the nation, the Board room became "resonant with the frantic shouts of the 'bulls' and 'bears.'"

Hoping to make money on a rise in stock prices, the bulls constantly battled the bears—speculators who sought profit from a fall in values. Whether a bull or a bear, a broker needed to have strong nerves and a cast-iron stomach, subject as he was to constantly fluctuating prices. "Above him hovers, day and night, a vast dark, formless shape, threatening ruin and penury," a Wall Streeter described the stock speculator's plight. "One day he is lifted to dizzy heights, the next, plunged into black depths. He is hurried through dark labyrinths through paths where a single step is destruction. He climbs on the edge of a sword to a fool's paradise, where he tastes joys brief as a dream, and in an hour is abased to the earth where he drinks the full cup of humiliation and want."[10]

While often speculators themselves, brokers earned their bread and butter from the commissions they obtained from customers. On the Philadelphia Board brokers charged a commission of twelve-and-a-half cents on each share they bought and sold (for shares selling over $10). Often furnishing "hot tips" on promising stocks, a commission-hungry broker enticed wary customers to take frequent plunges into the market. It didn't matter to the professional stock trader if the tip proved wrong since he still made money. "Buying and selling is the same to him, as he collects toll both ways," a journalist noted. Unsurprisingly, the general public tended to steer clear of the stock markets in the years before the Civil War, viewing the broker as a "sharper" who was "more intensely close to his own interests than to those of his friends."

Charles, however, did not start out as a stock trader. He first dealt in bank notes, which were used as currency in the antebellum years. Thousands of state-chartered banks issued in those days their own paper money or notes, the value of which varied from place to place. Notes issued by rural "wildcat" banks were often nearly worthless in Philadelphia. A holder of this sort of paper could go to a note broker, also derisively known as a "money-shaver," and receive gold or silver for it, but at a fraction of the notes' face value. The broker then sold the notes at a price usually far greater than what he had paid for them. This sort of business proved to be very profitable in the years before the Civil War, Andrew Jackson's defeat of the Second Bank of the United States having cleared the way for wildcat banks. "It was a grand time for brokers and private banking," Jay Cooke fondly recalled. Charles would have agreed. Probably tutored in the trade by his banker father, he prospered as a note broker. He earned $63 on the very day he opened his office's doors, and reported a profit of over $12,000 by the end of his first year in business.[11] At the tender age of twenty-one, Charles could afford to get married.

On the frosty evening of December 22, 1859, he wedded his childhood sweetheart Susanna Guttridge Gamble in the Episcopalian Church of the Nativity on Eleventh Street and Mount Vernon Avenue. Only one year younger than her husband, Susanna had grown up within a block or two of Charles's early homes. Her father, George Newton Gamble, had emigrated from Leicestershire, England, to the Northern Liberties, where he set up shop as a textile manufacturer. He died while Susanna was still a child, leaving his wife and family a considerable estate. Susanna's mother, also an English native, reared her four sons and two daughters in several different homes, eventually settling in the nearly rural outskirts of Philadelphia. Charles and his new bride also chose to reside outside the city's center, purchasing for perhaps $3,000 a nice home in North Philadelphia. Three stories high, the brick house contained many modern amenities, including gas heating, a cooking range, and hot and cold running water. To complete this picture of upper-middle-class comfort, Charles hired a maid to assist his wife in her daily chores. He could easily manage such a lifestyle, although in business for only a short time. In 1860 he owned $5,000 in personal property alone—an amount equal to $90,000 in today's money.[12]

"Early in 1860, arose in the political sky a cloud, at first, no larger than a man's hand," a Wall Street man recalled, referring to growing talk of secession among Southerners. "Every one saw it, but not so many looked at it with apprehension." In truth the nation had been split over the slavery question since its founding, with the North and the South long locked in an uneasy embrace. This sectional balance was threatened when the Mexican American War added a vast amount of new territory to the country. Would the new states be slave or free? Henry Clay attempted to address this momentous question with his Missouri Compromise, but it was already too late to paper over the problem. During the 1850s tension grew over the slavery issue, and by the end of the decade rumblings of discontent were increasingly heard in the South. This small cloud noticed by the Wall Streeter quickly developed into an ominous cumulonimbus, darkening the national landscape with the prospect of civil war. Even after Abraham Lincoln's November 1860 election as president, Philadelphia's business community continued to naively believe that a war might be averted.

During the long interval between Lincoln's election and his inauguration a financial panic gripped the country, as one Southern state after another seceded from the Union. Customers were then "afraid to make purchases on the Stock Exchange," Charles later remembered. Only once more in his life would he witness "such distrust of the business situation." Stock prices fluctuated wildly, at times buoyed by hopes of peace, at others depressed by talk of war. "Events which would have made a century prominent have been crowded into a few weeks," a journalist noted.[13] Uncertainty ruled the day.

Passing through Philadelphia on the way to his inauguration in Washington, President-elect Lincoln clarified matters. While addressing a large, buzzing crowd from the balcony of his room at the Continental Hotel, Lincoln pointed to Independence Hall and vowed that he would forever honor "the teachings of those holy and most sacred walls" where the Declaration of Independence and the Constitution had been written. "All my political warfare has been in favor of the teachings coming forth from that sacred hall," he solemnly declared. "May my right hand forget its cunning and my tongue cleave to the roof of my mouth, if ever I prove false to those teachings." The president-elect's listeners must have wondered how far he would go to uphold the Constitution and preserve the Union. On inauguration day—March 4, 1861—Lincoln made his course clear to all when he pledged to ensure "that the laws of the Union be faithfully executed in all the States."[14] The president would not allow the seceded states to remain outside of the Union. They would have to return to the fold, one way or another. A clash seemed inevitable. And it came on April 14, when Southern troops fired on Fort Sumter. The Civil War had begun.

The news of the attack on Fort Sumter sent shock waves through all Philadelphia. "With the first fire that was opened, all desire for conciliating the South seemed to have passed from the masses," a newspaper reported. Enormous crowds gathered in the streets nervously awaiting the latest war news, and thousands of men began to drill in militia companies amid a newly sprouted forest of red, white, and blue. Those who expressed support for the South did so at their own peril. When a youthful secessionist derided the American flag as "only a rag," his "nasal organ" was "violently peeled" by an outraged Union man.[15]

Charles Yerkes and the brokers on the Philadelphia Stock Exchange remained loyal to the Stars and Stripes. On April 16, 1861, two days after the fall of Fort Sumter, the Board of Brokers unanimously declared "their devotion to the Federal Union, to the Constitution, and to the Government acting under it." A few days later the Board backed up its pledge with money, voting to spend $3,000 of its funds "to maintain the honor of the national flag." Making an open display of their patriotism, the brokers on April 26 unfurled a huge Union flag sixty feet by thirty—the largest in

Philadelphia—outside their room in the Merchants Exchange. "Third Street, at the time, was lined with our citizens," a witness reported, "and as the Stars and Stripes floated out upon the breeze, cheer after cheer arose, the National anthem was sung, and the whole Board joined in the chorus." The brokers concluded the national anthem with a new stanza especially written for the occasion:

> And now on our soil, when vile traitors assail
> That glorious flag, by all nations respected,
> Defiant we fling its bright folds to the gale,
> And swear from rebellion it shall be respected!
> Yes! we swear to defend
> To the last bloody end,
> The Red, White and Blue, which in Union still blend:
> And that Star Spangled Banner in triumph shall wave
> O'er all the fair land of the free and the brave.[16]

While more than willing to offer the Union moral and financial support, Charles and many of his broker friends were not quite as prepared to put their lives on the line for the cause. (To be fair, a few Board members did serve under the Stars and Stripes and at least two, Henry J. Biddle and Richard W. Woolworth, died in battle.) The war, though, threatened to come to the brokers in September 1862. Following a string of brilliant military victories, the Confederate army under General Robert E. Lee moved northward toward the Pennsylvania border. On September 4 Pennsylvania Governor Andrew Gregg Curtin issued a proclamation advising "the immediate formation throughout the Commonwealth of volunteer companies and regiments." Six days later, with Lee's army continuing its advance, an alarmed Curtin ordered "all the able-bodied men of Pennsylvania to organize immediately for the defense of the State, and be ready for marching orders upon one hour's notice." Though the governor had requested 20,000 volunteers from Philadelphia, only 6,000 of that city's inhabitants answered Curtin's plea. "The enemy is at your very door, and yet many of you shrink from your duty," a Union soldier chided Philadelphia's men. "For God's sake, arouse from your lethargy before it is too late to preserve the heritage your fathers built up for you."[17]

Finally responding to the call, Charles on September 12 joined a regiment of the Home Guard under the command of Colonel John Newkumet, an "old German soldier." Organized to defend Philadelphia, the Home Guard attracted nearly 5,000 to its ranks in the hopeful early months of the conflict, but its membership quickly dwindled to a few hundred after the initial war enthusiasm waned. Charles enrolled as an adjutant in the Guard's officer staff. On the misty morning of September 16 he and the 800 other men in his regiment, "all governed by the same noble patriotic motive," journeyed via train 114 miles westward through rolling countryside to Harrisburg, the state capital. "When we reached Harrisburg, we found no preparations made to receive us," a member of the Guard recalled, and so they "concluded to pass on towards the scene of action."[18]

The "action" began early the next morning—when the Army of the Potomac commanded by General George McClellan met Lee's forces at Antietam Creek near Sharpsburg, Maryland. During the twelve hours of this fierce clash, 22,719 men were killed, wounded, or reported as missing in action. "No single day of this or any other American war would surpass that fearful record," one chronicler of the battle asserted. Krewson and William H. Yerkes, distant relatives of Charles, were among the many who fell on that bloody half-day. Krewson suffered a bullet wound in the side and William lost his right foot.

As the two armies maneuvered into position, Charles and the other members of the rag-tag Home Guard were marching toward Chambersburg, near the Maryland border. Wearing stiff-collared, single-breasted gray frock coats and gray pants brightened by a red, white, and blue rosette, Charles and his brother Guardsmen attracted the admiring gaze of townsfolk scattered along the fifty-four-mile route. While trudging through Carlisle's main square past the Greek Revival courthouse and the 100-year-old limestone-fronted First Presbyterian Church where George Washington had once worshipped, the perspiring, dust-streaked troops received "huzzas and cheers of the most enthusiastic kind." For the first and last time in his life Charles must have felt like a military hero. Reaching Chambersburg on the morning of the 17th, the weary Philadelphia men organized as the Ninth Regiment of the Pennsylvania Volunteer Militia, and then scrounged up quarters in local churches, schools, and warehouses.

Receiving its marching orders two days later, the regiment was dispatched to a camp two-and-a-half miles from Chambersburg "situated in a beautiful grove of oak trees, with corn and clover fields on each side." Apparently eager to see battle, "ready to go where most needed," the men expressed disappointment because they were not sent across the state border into Maryland. "So far as I can learn, there was not a man in the whole regiment who would have refused to cross the line," a member of the Ninth maintained. "The universal desire was to be of some aid to General McClellan, whose name ha[d] a talismanic power among all true patriots." The men did face some danger while settled in their pastoral retreat, a danger posed not by Confederate guns but rather by bad water, which caused "considerable sickness." This water, a victim explained, "[was] limestone, and produce[d] diarrhea and, of course, weakness."[19]

The miseries of camp life finally ended on September 25, when the Ninth was discharged from service.

Narrowly escaping action at Antietam, Charles dodged another bullet less than a year later when Lee invaded Pennsylvania. In late June 1863 Lee's army crossed into the state, and headed toward Harrisburg. Issuing several calls for emergency troops, Governor Curtin again received an underwhelming response, especially from the state's largest city. "Philadelphia has not responded," the governor complained. "Meanwhile the enemy is 6 miles this side of Chambersburg, and advancing rapidly."[20] On June 30— one day before the battle of Gettysburg—Charles, now a 1st lieutenant, joined many of his former comrades-in-arms, including Colonel Newkumet, in a new regiment, the Thirty-first. He could safely leave his brokerage and again play soldier for a few weeks as there was "nothing new to report in the Stock market." "The whole mind of the public is taken up with military matters, to the exclusion of all business matters," a financial journalist observed, "and many of those who take ventures on the Exchange are marching to drive the Rebels from the soil of the old Commonwealth."

By the time Charles and the other broker adventurers reached Harrisburg, the Union army had already accomplished that end, defeating the Confederates at Gettysburg. Enduring the boring routine of camp life for several weeks, Charles and the rest of his regiment were discharged from service on August 8 in what was a virtual replay of his previous military experience.[21]

Charles never in later life referred to his military "career," perhaps out of embarrassment, and resisted the temptation to embellish his wartime record, unlike others. One prominent politician, for instance, who had served in the Pennsylvania militia actually claimed (falsely, of course) that his regiment offered "the first serious resistance" to Lee's army, firing "the opening shots of the battle of Gettysburg." To his credit, Charles at least responded when his state was in danger. He and the other militia men "came forward at a moment when there was pressing need," wrote Samuel Bates, an historian of the Pennsylvania emergency troops. Perhaps because he had never seen a battle up-close, Charles was fascinated by war throughout his life. He collected exotic weapons and purchased paintings that glorified combat.[22] War and its instruments thrilled him, but only as an abstraction: something that could be displayed in a parlor or hung up on a wall.

If not a general on a battlefield, Charles was at least a "little Napoleon" on Third Street, and he quickly gained for himself a reputation as an "almighty shrewd" broker. The brokerage business prospered during the Civil War, riding on "a tide of prosperity" set in motion by massive government spending. Eager to reap enormous profits, people from all walks of life overcame their distrust of brokers and started to speculate. Brokers labored mightily throughout the year to keep up with their customers' orders. During the final two years of the war the Philadelphia Stock Exchange "experienced no cessation of business even in dog-days, and the telegraph lines from the sea-side resorts quivered with orders to buy and sell, from the opening until the closing of the board."[23] War had awakened the once sleepy Philadelphia Stock Exchange.

A rising tide of stock speculation lifted Charles only so far. His father provided a big extra boost. A "gentleman of the old school," the elder Charles had slowly but surely ascended the corporate ladder, rung by rung. Beginning as a lowly clerk at the Kensington Bank in the 1830s, he was promoted to cashier in 1852. Though viewed by some as a mere "glorified bookkeeper," the cashier often functioned in that era as a bank's chief executive officer.[24] Late in 1864, Charles, Sr., finally ascended to the top rung, becoming the Kensington National Bank's president.

As his status grew, Charles's father branched out into the social sphere. Early in 1863 he joined Philadelphia's "best men" in the Union League, an organization formed to provide "unqualified loyalty to the government of the United States, and unwavering support of its efforts for the suppression of the Rebellion." One member maintained that the Union League made patriotism respectable, sending a message to "rich and fashionable people that they would lose caste if they became Copperheads." Never exhibiting Copperhead leanings, Charles, Sr., in fact, belonged to a "radical" Union League faction favoring the formation of African American regiments. In June 1863 he, along with 265 others, signed a petition calling upon Secretary of War Edwin Stanton to raise "three Regiments of Volunteers of Colored Men, from this part of Pennsylvania, for the war."

Now mingling with Philadelphia's social leaders, the elder Charles had drifted far from his rural Quaker roots. A contemporary photograph shows the fifty-five-year-old bank president looking very un-Quaker-like, draped in an expensive frock coat hanging loosely about his thin frame. Sad eyes peer out from a deeply lined, weary-looking, almost Lincolnesque face, bordered by a small beard that blends into his necktie. His left hand clutches a shiny new top hat and his right weakly grasps a chair.[25] Drawing upon his father's social and financial clout, in early 1865 Charles opened a bank and brokerage at 20 South Third Street. His new business occupied a handsome four-story, flat-roofed brownstone that had cost

$33,000. Originally a dwelling, this structure had been remodeled in 1847 by the broker W. L. Hutchinson, who even added Egyptian Revival doors to provide "a not so subtle suggestion" of his "firm's sobriety." Late in January 1865 Charles proudly advertised his new firm in local papers:

C. T. YERKES, JR., & CO., BANKERS—
BANKERS,
STOCK AND EXCHANGE BROKERS.
GOLD, SILVER AND BANK NOTES
WANTED.
STOCKS AND BONDS OF ALL KINDS
SOLD ON COMMISSION.
20 South Third Street.

This notice appeared just below an ad for Drexel and Co., the powerful banking firm.[26] Charles quickly impressed the local business community with his money-making abilities. In 1866 a financial observer noted that Charles "does a fine business" and was "in excellent credit," estimating his worth at an astounding $100,000—roughly $1,057,000 in today's currency.

Shortly after launching his new business, Charles had reason for further celebration. On the night of April 9, 1865, Philadelphians learned that Lee had surrendered to General Ulysses S. Grant. The long, terrible Civil War was finally over, and the City of Brotherly Love rejoiced. "Men, women and children came upon the sidewalks and took part in the grand demonstration," a witness remembered. "By midnight the roar of cannon was added to the other demonstrations of joy, and it seemed as if every individual in Philadelphia felt called upon to add his voice to the general rejoicings." The following morning the party continued, even on the floor of the usually somber Stock Exchange. "The entire board" was on "a bender," a tipsy financial writer slurred, "Champagne very plentiful."[27]

Euphoria quickly turned to grief less than a week later when reports of Lincoln's assassination reached the city. "Strong and brave men wept as they read the news," a local paper reported, "and the gleam of rage was seen to sparkle in the eyes of the more excitable." Two days after the assassination, Philadelphians arose "to an almost continued line of black the entire length of all our streets," symbolic of the gloom that blanketed the city. The following Saturday tens of thousands assembled downtown to watch as Lincoln's body was transported to Independence Hall. Drawn by eight sleek black horses, the canopied hearse, its four plumes bobbing back and forth, rattled to its destination before a wall of silent mourners, followed by a long procession of prominent Philadelphians, including Charles's father. All through the night patient crowds waited in line to glimpse Lincoln's body as it lay in state at Independence Hall.

Thirty-two years later Charles visited Lincoln's final resting-place, his tomb at Springfield, Illinois.[28] As he gazed at the tomb's 100-foot-high marble obelisk, the fifty-nine-year-old streetcar magnate must have remembered that gloomy April evening when all of Philadelphia, it appeared, had turned out to mourn a dead president. Perhaps he also recalled a certain young banker whose future then seemed limitless.

3   Addition, Division, and Silence

In the years following the Civil War, businessmen continued to preach the gospel of self-reliance while increasingly seeking favors from government. Railroad men lobbied for land grants. Manufacturers sought high tariffs. Promoters vied for public utility franchises. Bankers battled for the right to market government bonds. The historian Vernon Parrington vividly described this postwar rush for governmental gold as "a huge barbecue" thrown for "all the important persons" of the era.

Charles also scrambled for a place at the barbecue table. The political boss and State Treasurer William Kemble provided the young banker with an admission ticket. Thirty-seven years old in 1865, Kemble was perfectly cast in the politico role. With a face reminiscent of the prototypical class bully, a disingenuous smile, and a bulging build, he looked like he had stepped out of a Thomas Nast cartoon. He also acted the part of a political boss, gaining a reputation as a scoundrel of the first magnitude. Not interested in ideology, he viewed politics as merely a pathway to personal wealth and power. "Put him through as you would me," Kemble once wrote to recommend an acquaintance planning a raid on the federal treasury. "He understands addition, division and silence." These three words neatly summed up Kemble's political creed. He was so unscrupulous even his friends couldn't trust him. Once, when Kemble opened a bank, he had difficulty persuading a crony to invest in it. "Well, do you think I am going to put any money in a thing that you run," the friend explained. "By God, I would wake up some morning and there wouldn't be a damned cent in the bank, and you would be gone, and all the money would be gone too."[1]

Charles met Kemble sometime during the Civil War, perhaps through his father. The two made an effective team. Charles offered Kemble his considerable business skill, including an uncanny stock-picking ability, and undoubtedly acted as a financial adviser to the treasurer. Charles also served as an important link between the political boss and the financial barons on Third Street. Kemble, for his part, gave the young financier access to the rich resources of the Pennsylvania treasury, occasionally depositing over $100,000 of state funds in Charles's bank.[2] With his considerable political clout, the treasurer also could "fix" any legislation Charles desired.

Kemble most likely helped Charles obtain a position as the agent of Philadelphia's city treasurer, the colorfully named Henry Bumm. Early in 1866 Bumm hired Charles to boost the market price of Philadelphia's bonds, then selling at only 90 percent of their face or par value. The city had issued $13,000,000 worth of these bonds in the preceding five years partly to cover war-related expenses, an amount piled atop an already existing $19,000,000 debt. Political corruption contributed to this massive financial burden, which was greater than that of the entire state of Pennsylvania. "Philadelphia politics in the years after the Civil War were as great a gamble as a crap game and about as honest as a pair of loaded dice," one observer asserted. Certain highly placed municipal officials (including Henry Bumm) were the winners in this "crap game." These "servants of the public" gobbled up taxpayer money, and lived luxuriously on the proceeds. Meanwhile, they increasingly paid the city's creditors in warrants or IOUs.

All too aware of this growing financial mess, investors began to fear that the city would soon not be able to meet the interest payments on its debt—a fear reflected in the sagging price of Philadelphia bonds. Enlisted by Treasurer Bumm, Charles undertook the Herculean task of restoring investor confidence in the city's credit. He first engineered a rise in the price of the bonds by "a judicious handling of the security on the stock exchange." Bumm then started selling bonds through Charles, who managed to keep their price above par. "To do this he was obliged to go into the market and take all amounts that might be offered," according to a biographer. The record of Charles's masterly performance was registered daily on the Philadelphia Stock Board, as the bonds rose steadily in value throughout 1866, peaking at 100 (par) in October after a ten-point ascent. Working a little financial hocus-pocus, Charles had within a year salvaged the city's credit. He continued in this role as an Atlas of the stock exchange, almost single-handedly holding up the price of city bonds, until 1871. He was well rewarded for his efforts. In addition to receiving a generous commission on all his purchases and sales, he was allowed to temporarily use the city bonds at his disposal.[3]

Charles also realized great profits from his dealings in city warrants. This system of IOU payments was a boon to politicians like Bumm and brokers like Charles. Instead of cash, the thousands of Philadelphia municipal employees received warrants as payment for their salaries. These warrants could be turned into cash at only a few specialized banking houses on Third Street—most notably the firm of Charles T. Yerkes, Jr., and Company. Charles did not pay off these IOUs at their full value; he purchased them at a 5 percent discount. He then sold the warrants on the exchange, often obtaining a fraction over their face value. Charles and his confederates in city hall then divvied up the excess among themselves.

Having gained a name for himself among Philadelphia financiers, Charles soon achieved statewide notice, again thanks largely to Kemble. In 1867 State Treasurer Kemble decided to make his "pile." He hatched a scheme to pay off a portion of the state's debt with newly created debt. The crafty politician proposed that the state issue $23,000,000 in bonds, the proceeds of which were earmarked to redeem long overdue loans. Persuaded by this Svengali of a state treasurer, the Pennsylvania legislature overwhelmingly passed Kemble's refunding plan early in February 1867.

The politico now set about springing his trap. "He had his arrangements all made with certain parties in Philadelphia who were to subscribe for the whole of the loan, and by skillfully manipulating it run it above par," a political insider explained. On April 1, 1867, the financial world learned the identities of these "certain parties." That day Kemble awarded $16,000,000 of the state bonds to Jay Cooke and Company, E. W. Clark and Company, and Drexel and Company, the three most influential bankers on Third Street. To the astonishment of the Philadelphia business community, the treasurer also allotted $2,000,000 of the bonds to an obscure banking firm—Charles T. Yerkes, Jr., and Company. Charles's connection with Kemble had once more worked wonders. The youthful banker and the other loan recipients did not pay anything for the bonds, despite the bids they tendered. "There was no money to pay down," an insider asserted, "and these men obtained control of the whole loan without being required to deposit a single dollar." Charles let Philadelphia know of his latest triumph in a newspaper ad that proudly declared:

NEW $23,000,000
SIX PER CENT LOAN
OF THE STATE OF PENNSYLVANIA
FOR SALE IN AMOUNTS TO SUIT PURCHASERS
C.T. YERKES, JR., & Co.,
No. 20 S. THIRD STREET[4]

The Drexel-Cooke-Clarke group eventually bought out Charles's $2,000,000 interest to prevent competition in the sale of the bonds. Making a good profit out of this deal, Charles always considered this "his first great venture." Meanwhile, Kemble's banker confederates, acting according to plan, sparked a rise in the market price of the new state bonds and "compelled persons who had a few hundred or thousand dollars to invest to pay a handsome premium before they could get the bonds." Kemble and his financier friends then pocketed a portion of this premium. Almost overnight the treasurer became a rich man.[5]

Charles soon found another political ally in the person of Robert Mackey, who was elected state treasurer in 1869. Mackey proved to be a "thoroughly accomplished political master," in the view of Alexander McClure, who ranked him the "greatest of all our Pennsylvania politicians." Tall, thin, almost emaciated, with stooping shoulders and a shuffling gait, Mackey was a consumptive who often endured coughing spells "so violent that it seemed impossible for him to survive." He muted the ever-present pain with whiskey, a bottle of which was always at his side.[6]

Alcohol wasn't Mackey's only weakness. He also had a gambling problem, and used state funds to speculate in stocks. The treasurer employed Charles, a man with the Midas touch, as his broker. An uncharitable observer claimed that Mackey and his allies in the so-called Treasury Ring hired the canny financier as their agent because he was someone "they had reason to repose trust [in], possibly because he was willing to wink at their rascalities and share the profits of their plunders." Charles, though, had performed a similar role for the previous two treasurers, including Kemble, and was therefore a logical choice for the position. Both Charles and Mackey found their partnership to be a profitable one. The new state treasurer deposited large sums into Charles's bank, receiving in return interest at the rate of 6 percent. Mackey, of course, also relied on his broker's business savvy when he plunged into the market with state money.

Elected to oversee the treasurer's accounts, the auditor general was the one state officer who could have put an end to Mackey's speculations. But the Civil War hero John Hartranft then filled that office and his hands were even deeper into the state cookie jar than Mackey's. In a two-year period Hartranft purchased nearly $700,000 worth of stock through Charles, tapping into the treasury to make good his debts. The auditor general even attempted to use the power of his office to aid his speculations. Learning from a subordinate that the state appeared to have a legitimate $100,000 claim against the Oil Creek and Allegheny Valley Railroad Company, Hartranft pressed the railway for this sum. Betting that the news of the claim would cause Oil Creek's stock price to plummet, he ordered Charles to sell short 100 shares of this security. Following Hartranft's orders, the broker arranged a future sale of Oil Creek at $40 a share, hoping to later purchase the 100 shares at a lower price and thus realize a profit for the auditor general. But this state officer's neatly laid plan went awry when the Attorney General F. Carroll Brewster ruled against the $100,000 claim. As a result, Oil Creek stock went up instead of down. Hartranft wrote Charles of the bad news on March 9, 1870:

> Dear Yerkes
> Buy as soon as possible 100 shares of Oil Creek and Allegheny Valley RR and then have my account, or rather have an extract made from my account, so that I can see the exact loss I have sustained on Oil Creek . . . The Atty. Genl. has given a decision against our settlement on Oil Creek, which takes the starch right out. I don't know what to say about buying Oil Creek as a future investment. If you think well of it you may buy. I think the chances are that it will go up, but as everything else is drooping but little can be expected from Oil Creek. What do you think of gold?

Relatively unsuccessful in their stock speculations, Mackey and Hartranft realized greater profit from their operations in state bonds. Taking a page out of William Kemble's playbook, they proposed early in April 1870 to pay off a piece of the state debt soon coming due. Edwin Lewis, a financial agent of the State of Pennsylvania, appointed Charles to "bid at the Brokers' Board" for the state bonds, as he was "the most competent man . . . to effect the transactions and purchases, and the one most likely to succeed." Employing another broker for what he termed ordinary business, Lewis reserved Charles for matters requiring "secrecy, or a talent of a particular order." The latter approached people who were known to hold large amounts of the loan and offered to pay them "anything they would take" for the bonds. Initially meeting heavy resistance, Charles bid up the bonds on the Board in the hope that higher prices might tempt the holders to sell.

This idea worked and in one month he purchased $459,000 of the state debt, earning a commission of one-quarter percent, or $1,147. The big money, though, wasn't in the commission. According to a prearranged plan, Charles sold a portion of these purchased bonds to the state treasury "at a considerable advance above the price paid for the same," dividing the resulting profits among himself, Mackey, and Hartranft. The two state officials reaped $5,643.42 on this tidy transaction. Careful to cover his tracks, Mackey warned Charles to keep the accounts of the operation "in so obscure a manner that it would be difficult, in case of an investigation, for it to be detected."[7]

The majority of Charles's customers weren't influential politicians. Charles Fitler, for example, was a twenty-something drug company manager who hired Yerkes as his broker in the autumn of 1867. Two years later, Fitler began buying gold "on margin," paying Charles perhaps 10 percent of the total purchase price. Manipulated by the shady financial genius Jay Gould, the value of gold skyrocketed in the late summer and early fall of 1869. As the price ascended to ever-higher levels, legions of outside operators like Fitler were tempted into the market, hoping to ride to fortune on the tail of a golden comet. Initially "somewhat successful," Fitler's speculations at one point showed on paper a $3,000 gain. Knowing his broker's love of horses, an exultant Fitler told Charles that he "intended to make him a handsome present of a colt called the Yerkes colt" when his profits reached $4,000. Consumed by glittering visions of wealth, the novice trader "extended" his speculations, and purchased more gold just before the comet crashed.

On September 24, 1869—"Black Friday"—Gould's titanic effort to control the value of gold collapsed spectacularly. That day the price of the precious metal fluctuated wildly, peaking briefly at 170 before plummeting to 134. Reportedly, one Philadelphia broker who lost a fortune in the crash was removed "from the bustling haunt of the money-changers, a raving maniac." Charles Fitler, the drug company manager, did not suffer such an awful fate. Watching his profits turn to losses overnight, Fitler instead merely found himself deeply in debt. "Mr. Yerkes wrote for margins which were not forthcoming," Fitler recalled, "and the thing then assumed an unpleasantness."[8] The broker never recovered his money.

Charles came to feel "the utmost contempt" for fortune-seekers like Fitler. "I defy any broker to show me any man who has dealt with him for two years or more—a 'ticker player,' as we used to say—who has come out of it with money," he later declared. The novice stock gambler almost always lost in the end. "The man who speculates has the percentage against him," Charles explained. "He must pay for commissions. He may make a slight percentage on a rise in stocks, but if the price drops he usually gets scared, and all his profits are gone, with an indebtedness staring him in the face. That's human nature, and I've seen it again and again."

Unlike Fitler, Charles initially made money out of his speculations— lots of it. The half year between December 1870 and June 1871 was, in Charles's words, "the most prosperous one of my business life." He later claimed "the profits on stocks purchased during that time had reached the sum of $129,085.50"—an amount worth roughly $1,650,000 in today's money. In July of that year he joined the ultra-exclusive New York Stock Exchange, plunking down $4,000 for his membership. In the "seething, whirling, roaring" Wall Street "maelstrom" a thousand brokers traded tens of millions of dollars' worth of securities in a single day.

Charles's business success did not go unnoticed. In 1871 a financial reporter estimated the young banker's credit at $250,000—$3,198,000 in contemporary terms—and called him "a shrewd financier, honorable and fully responsible for any and all contracts." Philadelphia's "best Bankers considered him as doing a good business and to be as good a man and as reliable as anyone on the street," another source maintained.

These bankers treated Charles as a depositor "in whom entire confidence is felt." The youthful broker was a familiar figure in most of Philadelphia's banks, even the mightiest of them all, Drexel and Company. Charles could boast of "an intimate acquaintance with the Drexels," and he frequently borrowed large sums from them. But his most active account was at the First National Bank. Often loaning Charles millions of dollars, the First National allowed him "special facilities, as a Broker of large means and business and of good credit and repute." Contrary to usual practice, this bank's officers even furnished him money "at or near the close of the business day if his business required it" with no other security than his personal check. Charles also enjoyed a friendly arrangement with his father's Kensington National Bank. Charles, Sr., the president of the bank, employed his son to collect money due from rural and New York City banks, and permitted him to use these funds for up to a week.[9]

In the late 1860s, Charles and his wife Susanna signaled their rising status by moving to the elite Twentieth Ward in North Philadelphia. Large numbers of the city's newly rich flocked to this ward after the war and erected "rememberable great houses with generous gardens embellished with enchanting greenhouses." Some of the most opulent homes lined the "almost European in visage" Broad Street, which was flanked by "two rows of great trees on one side and a single one on the other." Charles built a "rememberable" great house two blocks from Broad at 1535 Girard Avenue, next door to his father's residence. Costing $35,000, this handsome three-story brownstone mansion contained a parlor, a dining room, and two kitchens on the first floor; two chambers, a bath, a sitting room, a library, and a conservatory on the second; and four chambers and a bath on the third. The banker and his wife needed the extra space now that they had two children: Charles Edward, born August 25, 1863, and Elizabeth, born November 3, 1866. Charles and Susanna had planned to have a larger family, but four of their children died in infancy.

Charles's new address, 1535 Girard Avenue, was located far "beyond the pale of fashionable civilization," in the eyes of "proper" Philadelphians.[10] "Proper" Philadelphians still tended to dwell south of Market

Street, in the exclusive Rittenhouse Square neighborhood. According to a half-serious newspaper article, those social climbers who dared settle in the region north of Market became "lost in the wilderness beyond," and were "heedless until too late, of the clang of closing doors behind them, shutting them out forever from paradise."

Though living over a mile from Rittenhouse Square, Charles nonetheless found the gates of "paradise" open to him. He was not the typical nouveau riche gate-crasher who had accumulated a fortune on government contracts during the war and who expected immediate entry into the sacred precincts. His father was a rich and respected bank president and a member of the prestigious Union League. Charles himself had gained a sterling reputation as a skilled and trustworthy businessman, winning the esteem of such upper-class bankers as Anthony Drexel, Clarence Clark, and Henry Borie. He had a bewitching personality as well. "Polished, affable, courteous and suave, masterful yet gracious, Mr. Yerkes possessed in an extraordinary measure that almost hypnotic power of stealing away men's vigilance and influencing them against their judgment and convictions that people loosely describe as magnetism," an observer later noted. Wealthy, confident, and charismatic, the brown-haired, athletically built Charles also looked the part of a gentleman. He was strikingly handsome, his symmetrical face adorned by a well-groomed mustache, a strong nose, and a "wonderful pair" of piercing brown eyes, "searching eyes that seemed to read the very soul of the one on whom they were fixed."

Aided by these useful tools, Charles seemed to be on the verge of breaking into Philadelphia society. On January 3, 1870, he was elected an active member of the First City Troop, a cavalry company founded during the Revolution and one of Philadelphia's "major status conferring institutions," according to the historian E. Digby Baltzell. Initially organized as a military unit, the First City Troop evolved over the years into a socially exclusive club "maintaining a sense of upper-class cohesion."[11] Charles's entry into this citadel of the city's upper class marked an important step on the road to high social position.

By 1870 the Third Street financier was close to realizing his own particular version of the American dream. Beginning life as an outsider with three strikes against him, he had ascended on his father's shoulders to dizzying heights. The "paradise" inhabited by the city's social leaders seemed within his grasp, just above him. But instead of rising higher, he would fall. It was a long way down.

4 *Trial by Fire*

Visiting Philadelphia in 1905, the novelist Henry James discovered that the city "was two distinct things—a Society, from far back . . . the most genial and delightful one could think of, and then parallel to this, . . . a proportionate City, the most incredible that was ever organized all for plunder and rapine, the gross satisfaction of official appetite." Charles moved in both of these Philadelphia worlds. He daily conducted business with upper-class bankers belonging to James's "most genial and delightful" Society, and had finally won admittance into their ranks. He also formed alliances with certain local politicians, representatives of that other City "organized all for plunder and rapine"—politicians like City Treasurer Joseph Marcer.

A lawyer by profession, the light-haired, blue-eyed, diminutive Marcer had made a name for himself in the political arena, serving as the Philadelphia Common Council's president from 1867 until 1869. In this latter year the thirty-nine-year-old Marcer was elected city treasurer, a decision hailed by the local press. Marcer did not seek the city treasurer slot simply out of a desire to be active in public affairs. "The City Treasurership was the most lucrative political office of the day," one observer explained. "To the City Treasurer accrued all the interest on city deposits as perfectly legitimate spoils of office—legitimate, that is, from a politician's viewpoint." A city official could earn a bundle in an amazingly short period of time. The liberal Republican Alexander McClure recalled one nearly bankrupt man who, upon entering office, suddenly could afford to spend over $5,000 on a lavish party that featured "hundreds of canary birds summoned for the occasion to greet the guests with song."

A family man with two girls and one boy, Marcer probably did not indulge in such displays of conspicuous consumption. But he could have. As city treasurer, he amassed a considerable fortune in a breathtakingly short time. Several months after his 1869 election, he reported owning $10,000 in real estate and personal property. After only two years of service in the city treasurer's office, Marcer could boast a $60,000 net worth—a six-fold increase.

Charles helped make Marcer's fortune. Ever since 1866, when he had salvaged Philadelphia's credit, the banker had labored as the treasurer's agent, buying and selling city bonds and city warrants. Like his predecessors, City Treasurer Marcer relied on Charles to perform this important work. As he manipulated the flow of this river of public money, Charles frequently diverted a portion of the stream into his pockets and into those of Marcer and David Jones, the treasurer's chief clerk. Jones was no stranger to the city treasurer's office. He had served as the clerk of Henry Bumm, the treasurer who first appointed Charles a city agent. With "his intelligence and obliging disposition," Jones had then "rendered the business at the City Treasury easy and agreeable," according to the *Philadelphia Public Ledger*. Charles certainly found Jones to be "easy and agreeable" in the extreme.

In July 1870 Chief Clerk Jones offered to lend city money to Charles, who was not one to refuse such a gift. But there was one major problem: Every month a city council committee inspected the treasurer's accounts, and would most likely discover these loans of municipal money. As a way of getting around this difficulty, Jones instructed Charles to give him at the end of each month, just before the committee's inspection, a check for the amount borrowed. The chief clerk used this check to temporarily cover the deficit in the treasury. Then on the first day of the succeeding month Jones returned the municipal money to Charles. The clerk also allowed the broker to use city bonds as collateral for personal loans, but again required the account to be settled at month's end.

An "obliging disposition" won Jones far more than favorable newspaper notice. He divided with Charles the one-quarter percent commission the latter earned on his sales and purchases of city bonds. They padded this commission by also pocketing the difference between the bonds' actual sale price and a lower figure that was recorded in the city's account books. Marcer was well aware of the transactions in city bonds, having shared in their profits. According to Jones, Marcer realized about $400 per month from the bond sales.[1]

Strongly fortified by over $300,000 of borrowed city money, Charles embarked upon a colossal speculation during the summer of 1871. The success of this risky venture hinged on the outcome of a legal proceeding involving the powerful Pennsylvania Railroad, which then controlled a 6,000-mile transportation network stretching from Philadelphia to Chicago. The railroad, though, lacked one critical puzzle piece: an outlet into New York City, the country's business center. On June 30, 1871, the Pennsylvania finally secured this missing link when it leased sixty-six miles of New Jersey rail property, including the Camden and Amboy road. But certain disgruntled stockholders quickly obtained an injunction against the lease, and the matter was thrown into a New Jersey court.

Based upon inside information he had gleaned, Charles believed the court would decide in favor of the lease. He further expected that such a ruling for the Pennsylvania Railroad would spark a rise in the stock market. The "effect of the consummation of this lease," Charles boldly predicted, would be "to advance the price of the Pennsylvania and Camden and Amboy so very materially that it" would carry "the whole market with it." He was so confident of his prediction that he bought nearly $5,000,000 in stocks of "the best kind," mostly shares of the Pennsylvania, Camden and Amboy, and Reading railroads, borrowing the money from local banks. "These stocks had been purchased and carried by me on loans made on the security of the stocks themselves with the agreement that I should keep the loan below the value of the stocks," Charles later explained.

It was a tremendous gamble, but one promising tremendous reward. He would realize a healthy $50,000 profit on a paltry one percent gain in his stocks' value, and on a 10 percent rise a staggering $500,000—an amount surpassing his net worth. On this one throw of the die he could become a millionaire. Long a slave to his business, he finally might be able "to take life more easily."[2] He also would win the acclaim of his Third Street peers, who would forever honor him as "a bold and successful operator." But what if the market went down?

On Sunday night, October 8, 1871, the unexpected happened. A terrible fire engulfed Chicago, a fledgling metropolis of 300,000 located on Lake Michigan's western shore. The inferno ripped through the city's heart. Hundreds of Chicagoans raced to the lakefront, hoping to escape the towering wall of rolling flame. "Like an immense drove of panic-stricken sheep, the terrified mass ran, and rushed, and scrambled, and screamed through the streets," a reporter noted. In the end the conflagration claimed 300 lives, left 10,000 homeless, and destroyed $190,000,000 in property. The proud Florence of the West had been reduced in a few hours to rubble.

The telegraph, "the nerves of the mighty system of traffic now encircling the globe," almost instantly spread news of the fire across the nation. On the following day, October 9, stockholders reacted much like those Chicagoans fleeing the flames, and panicked. They feared the disaster would disrupt trade—Chicago being a major transportation hub—and so frantically unloaded their securities. "A conflagration in a great city, nearly nine hundred miles west of us, destroyed in an hour the equilibrium of our Stock and Money markets," a Philadelphia newspaper asserted, "and men on Third street saw their wealth melting away under the rapid depreciation of values, as did the unfortunate Chicagoans behold their stately stores and crowded warehouses swept out of existence by the flames."[3]

At first the "older and cooler" brokers on Third Street discounted the reports coming from Chicago, believing they were exaggerated. But by the afternoon of the 9th they had come reluctantly to accept the stories detailing the incredible destruction. At 1:00 P.M. the Stock Exchange's 150 members, including Charles, sat silently behind their desks, waiting for the Board president to open the bidding. "The countenances of all wore an anxious look, a feeling of nervousness and anxiety pervaded the usually self-possessed body," according to the *Philadelphia Inquirer*. At the ringing of the bell the president began calling the names of stocks, and pandemonium broke loose. A torrent of sell orders flooded the Exchange. "The president found it impossible to keep the members, now wild with excitement, in their seats," the *Inquirer* reported. "There was a grand rush from all parts of the chamber to the open space in front of the president's desk, and in this area the nervous screaming crowd swayed to and fro. 'Sell,' 'sell,' 'sell,' 'sell Reading,' 'sell Pennsylvania,' were the only words which resounded high above the din of the Babel of Mammon, now laboring under one of the mad convulsive fits to which it is liable." The stocks Charles owned were especially hard hit that afternoon. A whopping 49,000 shares of Reading Railroad stock were sold, depressing its price two-and-a-quarter points. Pennsylvania Railroad stock did even worse, falling two-and-a-half points.

This "absolute madness" continued on Tuesday, October 10. "Again there was a wild pressure to sell, the effort to get rid of stock being the principal business of all the operators," a newspaper remarked. "So eager were the efforts to sell and so overpowering the rush of business that the clerks were several times unable to keep a correct transcript of sales, and operations had to be checked until accounts could be straightened." Charles and his "bull" allies could do little to lift the falling tide of stocks. But he had to do something. His securities lost between 5 and 20 percent of their value in the days following the Chicago Fire.[4] The banks would soon call in his loans, Charles feared, unless he furnished more collateral to protect them from loss.

His fears were realized that Tuesday, when he received a telegram from New York's Drexel, Morgan and Company demanding payment of a $600,000 loan. Unable to pay this huge sum, an anxious Charles left his office at No. 20 South Third Street and walked a few doors down to No. 34, Drexel and Company's address. Housed in an imposing four-story Italianate structure, Drexel and Company was one of the world's greatest banks and run by "one of the country's most resourceful and successful bankers." Bald, with a mustache and a pleasant-looking face, the forty-five-year-old Anthony Drexel, "Tony" to his friends, was a major figure in the banking world, and yet "one of the most retiring and unpretentious of men." Inheriting control of the Philadelphia bank after his father's 1863 death in a railroad mishap, Anthony expanded his business empire seven years later when he opened Drexel, Morgan and Company in New York. (The "Morgan" in this firm was a young, ambitious financier by the name of John Pierpont.)

Well knowing that Drexel controlled this latter bank, which had called in his $600,000 loan, Charles pleaded with Tony to "be as easy as he could on him." The older banker realized his friend could not pay the amount demanded, but Charles's outstanding loans were too heavy to be simply shrugged off. In addition to the $600,000 New York debt, the young broker owed the Philadelphia firm $200,000. Making matters worse, Drexel had also personally loaned $95,000 to Charles. All of these loans were secured by stocks that had depreciated greatly in value. And Drexel believed that the market would go down even more. "My idea was that the Chicago fire had destroyed about two hundred millions of dollars and I couldn't see any future in speculative stocks," the banker said. He was particularly pessimistic about Pennsylvania Railroad stock, which he "thought would decline from the interruption of the trade with Chicago and the Great West."

Assuring Drexel he would soon emerge from his financial troubles, Charles, as charismatic as ever, convinced the powerful banker to give him more time to liquidate his debts. But Tony stressed that he wanted the money paid back as fast as possible, it not being his desire "to make a permanent investment with Mr. Yerkes." Drexel later explained why he gave Charles a break in this instance. "We could have sold out the stocks at once and paid the debt had we been disposed to have done so," he maintained, "but we preferred having Mr. Yerkes nurse his stocks along so as to get more for them and meet the market gradually—in other words we didn't want to slaughter his stocks."[5]

Narrowly averting ruin on one front, Charles soon faced more trouble on another. David Jones, the city treasurer's chief clerk, had watched in alarm as the stock market crashed. He had permitted, even encouraged, Charles to borrow $300,000 in city funds, and foolishly had not asked for collateral to secure this loan. Now the clerk feared that the money had been consumed in the financial firestorm. Haunted by visions of scandal and public disgrace, Jones visited Charles on Thursday, October 12, and demanded $150,000, or half of the loan amount, by the following Tuesday. "All right," Charles blandly replied.

The broker continued to put his faith in a rising market. He had some reason for hope: The New Jersey court had not yet ruled on the Pennsylvania lease, and a decision was expected any day. Borrowing huge sums from the First National Bank in particular, Charles purchased blocks of mostly railroad stocks in an effort to force prices up. But this financial Atlas couldn't hold on for much longer. The avalanche of sell orders on the Exchange threatened to crush him.

The monetary panic worsened on Friday the 13th. Thronging the gallery overlooking the Philadelphia Exchange, masses of terrified stockholders "called out the names of their brokers at the top of their voices and yelled out orders to sell." Desperate to be heard, some of these brokers jumped onto the Board president's desk and "screamed out their bids." According to one witness, the Exchange that "black" Friday presented an amazing spectacle: "a seething, vociferating mass of well dressed men, apparently bereft of reason and on the verge of some inexpressibly frightful disaster."

Charles at least could be pardoned for his behavior that day: He *was* on the verge of such a disaster. But he wasn't going down without a fight. On Saturday, October 14, Charles appeared on the Stock Exchange floor, leading one of two "detachments" of brokers determined to lift the market. The battle raged fiercely between the bulls hoping for a rise and the bears betting on a fall. Brokers "surged to and fro over desks and chairs, in their wild haste to buy and sell," a newspaper noted. "All courtesies and rules were forgotten." Greeting the depressing activities of their opponents with "hootings and groans," Charles and his fellow bulls managed for a time to send "prices up at a rate to deprive the dismayed 'bears' of the power of shouting." The bears, though, put up a stiff resistance, and soon set the pendulum swinging in their direction. But late in the afternoon Charles and his forces rallied, spurred on by the cheers of interested spectators in the galleries. The bulls carried the field that day, with all stocks selling higher at the close of business.[6]

Charles had won only a skirmish in what was a struggle for his very financial survival. Stocks had gone up, but their prices were still far below pre-Fire levels. He owed several local banks staggering sums, and in a few days he was expected to pay $150,000 to the city treasury. He needed money—and fast. For perhaps the first time in his life—and maybe the last—Charles Tyson Yerkes, Jr., panicked. It was a desperate man who traveled that Saturday the few blocks from No. 20 South Third Street to the city treasurer's office. Encountering David Jones, Charles told the chief clerk that he had purchased for the treasury $33,048.50 worth of city bonds, and then requested a check for that amount. The broker had stretched the truth. He had not yet bought those bonds. Unaware of this fact, Jones later gave a check for the $33,000 to Charles's errand boy, instructing him "to be very careful and not lose it." Charles followed up this fatal misstep with another. He confronted a woman customer, Rosemary Cooney, and demanded from her $1,000 in city bonds. Cooney eventually yielded to this demand, which, she charged, was backed by "force and arms."

All of Charles's efforts to avert ruin were useless. The curtain on the first act in his life closed the following Monday, October 16. A thick fog blanketed Philadelphia that cool autumn morning, enshrouding two men huddled together in discussion. Standing in the yard behind their adjoining Girard Avenue homes, Charles and his father talked about monetary matters. The elder Charles wanted his son to pay back the $22,000 in checks the latter had borrowed from the Kensington National Bank on Saturday. Wearing a mask of unconcern, the younger man said "that on Tuesday he would have plenty of money to take up the checks or many of them." The father would never have asked for the payment if he had known how desperate was his son's financial plight. Charles, though, "kept his business to himself and I never inquired much about it," the elder Yerkes later explained. He merely understood his son "was doing a very large business and required a great deal of money to carry it on."[7]

Leaving his father, Charles drove to his Third Street office in a covered carriage drawn by an expensive pair of horses. As he plunged through the billowing fog, the beleaguered broker must have wondered whether he was really on the road to ruin, really about to say goodbye to his life of luxury. His future was as unclear as the path ahead of his carriage.

Matters only became murkier when he arrived at No. 20 South Third Street. He learned that two banks had called in his loans, demanding immediate payment on a $150,000 debt. Not yet ready to give up, Charles scoured the local banks in a humiliating quest for money. He succeeded in scraping up only $25,000, borrowing it from the First National, his financial bulwark. Charles needed a further $125,000 to redeem the remainder of the called-in loan. If he could not obtain this amount, he would be forced to close his business. Charles's father arrived at this moment of crisis, and, finally learning of his son's dire predicament, agreed to assume the unpaid portion of the loan.

But, like the Chicago Fire that caused it, Charles's financial troubles could not be contained. Just as he put out one fire, another blaze, even more threatening, would spring up, and spread uncontrollably. While he and his father discussed the $125,000 loan, an agitated David Jones burst into the Third Street office. Jones wanted one-half of the money Charles owed the city: $150,000. He also called for the $33,000 in city bonds the broker said he had purchased, and for which he had received a check on Saturday. Ignoring the first demand, Charles blandly responded that his stepbrother Joseph, one of his clerks, "had the order [for the transfer of the city bonds] and would attend to it."[8]

Though disaster was now certain, Charles still refused to concede defeat. He acted as if this were an ordinary business day. At 11:30 A.M. he walked the two blocks to the Stock Exchange, where he nonchalantly discussed the day's trade with his fellow brokers. These astute financial operators had no idea that Charles was about to go under, though rumors of his difficulties had been afloat. The embattled broker carefully concealed his very real worry. He exuded confidence when speaking to Anthony Drexel. Charles "had assured me the day of his failure that he would get through," Drexel recalled. "He told me he was selling his stocks very nicely and was paying us up . . . and that he would liquidate all in a very short time."

Charles was fooling himself. When he returned to his office at 2:00 P.M., he finally yielded to the inevitable. The persistent Jones had again visited him just before he left for the Exchange, and again demanded the $150,000. Charles had perhaps hoped that the pesky chief clerk would simply go away, leaving him free to settle his financial affairs. But he now understood that Jones wasn't going anywhere. Charles simply could not meet the debt he owed the city. He had tapped dry all of the monetary resources at his disposal, and had even overdrawn $147,000 on his account at the trusty First National. He had only one choice left, and a very unpleasant one at that. He had to close his business. Notifying the First National not to pay his checks, Charles shut the doors of No. 20 South Third Street at 2:20 P.M.[9] Ironically, the skies cleared the very hour of his failure.

Word of Charles's suspension quickly spread across Philadelphia. The news hit with particular force on Third Street. The brokers there were stunned to learn that one of the Board's brightest stars—the "little

Napoleon" of Third Street—had fallen. "I thought at the time it was a mere temporary embarrassment," the broker George Fox said of Charles's failure, echoing the sentiments of many on Third Street. "I thought Mr. Yerkes was being troubled unnecessarily by people and that he would be all right in a day or two if they would let him alone."

Joseph Yerkes didn't realize "something was wrong" until 3:00 P.M., when he returned to the Third Street office from the Stock Exchange. Entering the office's back room, he noted four men crowded into that cramped, sparsely furnished space. The banker Clarence Clark was there, urging Charles to prefer him over other creditors. Charles's father was there, telling his son "not to do anything of the kind." And David Jones was also there.

The city treasurer's chief clerk had made his third visit to Charles's office that day, absolutely determined this time to recover the $150,000. As he waited in the front room, he overheard clerks murmuring, saying disturbing things about checks returned and transactions not fulfilled. The more he heard the more fearful he became that Charles was in "a precarious way." Reduced to a state of semi-panic, Jones nervously asked the broker "how it was with him" when the two finally met. Charles replied that "he didn't know." The clerk was terrified at this less than reassuring answer. "I hope you haven't failed," Jones blurted out. Charles coldly responded that "he didn't know how he was." Jones now realized that he wouldn't get the $150,000 owed the city. Thoughts of scandal, disgrace, and ruin must have flashed through his mind. Crumpling under the impact of this terrible mental blow, Jones broke into tears. If I don't get this money back I'll go to prison, the clerk cried. Pleading with an impassive Charles, he wanted to know what, if anything, the broker could do to salvage the situation. Jones, in desperation, then appealed for help to the financier's father, telling him that "this was a bad business of Charles." In response, the older man simply indicated to Jones that it was "unwise" to make this demand on his son at such a time.[10]

Charles's fall had been swift. Almost overnight his wealth, position, and power were wiped away. One day the Philadelphia financial community considered him as a "'money-changing' genius" whose word could be trusted, and the next as "a dishonest failure." What lesson, if any, did Charles take from this catastrophe? "The man who speculates will lose in the end, and I don't care how much money he has," the onetime avid speculator later declared. "When he starts that way a guardian should be appointed for him."[11]

5 Trial by Jury

In the days following his failure, Charles scrambled to pick up the pieces, struggling under the wreckage of his ruined fortune. He quickly moved to appease his biggest creditors: the bankers. He permitted them to sell the collateral they held on his loans. Charles unfortunately could not give much assurance to his creditors on the Stock Exchange. Vainly hoping that their stricken comrade would soon be back on his feet, these brokers fully expected to recover the $15,700 Charles owed them. They all "thought he was rich."[1]

But by October 18 the brokers finally learned that the "little Napoleon of Third Street" had met his Waterloo. That day the Stock Exchange's president Henry Gowan appointed a committee to find out whether Charles could fulfill his contracts. The rules of the Exchange required the suspension of a member unable to honor his obligations. Charles later angrily recalled that this rule, though "seldom or never carried into effect," was "put in force in my case." When visited by members of the committee, he refused to disclose to them his financial condition. They then asked him what he could or would do to satisfy his creditors. Deeply resentful of this interrogation by his former friends, Charles angrily responded that he "would do nothing." News of this reply "naturally gave rise to a great deal of indignant talk against Mr. C.T. Yerkes, Jr." He was promptly suspended from the Exchange. This decision seems not to have elicited any protest from the Board's unsentimental operators. Their attitude was revealed in a *Philadelphia Inquirer* editorial. "Those who fell in the memorable days from the 9th to the 18th of last month, are now regarded as little other than very weak concerns, which it was best to have out of the way," the *Inquirer* wrote in November. "Third Street is heartless in all matters pertaining to business in progress; there is neither time nor inclination for regrets or sympathy."[2]

The press also did not show any sympathy for the fallen broker, especially when it became known that he owed the city over $300,000. On the very day of his failure a *New York Herald* reporter, smelling a story, approached Charles for an interview. The "cool" broker, though, refused to grant an extensive one, merely confirming that he had failed and admitting that his affairs were in bad shape. "I have always had a 'horror' of being interviewed," Charles later confessed. His fear of the Fourth Estate was justified. The enterprising New York journalist managed to piece together a "highly sensational account" of the broker's dealings with the city treasurer. This story and subsequent ones triggered outbursts of indignation on local editorial pages. "This house of Yerkes & Co. was not worthy to be trusted with any of the public funds," the *Evening Bulletin* huffed, "and sensible men, acquainted with their mode of doing business, did not consider them worthy of it before their failure."

The publisher Henry Charles Lea shared this editorialist's outrage. As an eighteen-year-old, Lea had confessed to a love of nature's fury. "I love to watch any convulsion of Nature," he wrote in his journal, "and a tremendous thunderstorm is delightful, the more awful the better. It always creates a kind of opposition in me that raises my spirits and makes me feel better for hours afterward." By 1871 Lea had turned his penetrating gaze earthward. The scholarly publisher now delighted in political storms, often ones of his own making. A year earlier he had founded the Citizens' Municipal Reform Association to combat political corruption. "We were being most frightfully robbed," one Philadelphian recalled. "To demonstrate this was the work the Reform Association set itself to accomplish." Lea relished this role pitting him against political evildoers. The author of several works on the Inquisition once boasted that when he hit a man he liked "to hear him squeal." Lea resolved to take a decisive stand, this time against the persons responsible for looting Philadelphia's treasury.

On October 21 Lea and his reformer friends appointed a committee to investigate the "city treasury muddle." Three days later the patrician lawyer John J. Ridgway, Jr., the committee's chairman, delivered a scathing report. He recommended that the reformers seek from the district attorney bills of indictment "against the said Yerkes and the City Treasurer and all persons whom he shall discover to be implicated in the said misuse of the public funds."[3] District Attorney Furman Sheppard agreed to cooperate with Lea's men, and go after Charles and City Treasurer Joseph

Marcer. But Sheppard had to work quickly. His term as D.A. was set to expire in less than two weeks.

His successor would be William B. Mann, who had just won his fifth election to that office. Built like a grizzly bear and almost as hairy as one, with a bushy beard and a curled mustache, Mann was also a heavyweight in the Philadelphia political arena. No "man ever exercised more absolute power in the Republican Party in the city than that exercised by Mann," Alexander McClure maintained. First elected district attorney in 1856, Mann employed the large fees he earned to forge a strong political machine. After being unseated in 1868, he engineered passage of the so-called Registry Law that effectively disenfranchised Philadelphia Democrats. Aided by this notorious law, Mann again wrested control of the district attorney post. Though well past his political peak, he remained a formidable force. A vindictive man, he sometimes used the law to punish his personal enemies. "Everybody seems to fear Bill Mann," a journalist noted in 1872. "He is the great bugbear, the head devil that cannot be coped with by anybody."

For some unknown reason, Mann numbered Charles among his many enemies, and therefore delighted in the thought of the latter behind bars.[4] On October 25—days before he assumed the district attorneyship— Mann agreed to serve as Alderman Henry Huhn's lawyer. Huhn had endorsed Joseph Marcer as treasurer, and now faced possible financial embarrassment and political ruin thanks to Charles's failure. Intending to bring criminal charges against the broker, Huhn, accompanied by Mann, journeyed to City Hall and made an affidavit before Mayor Daniel Fox:

> October 25, 1871,—Henry Huhn, being duly sworn according to Law, deposes and says that Charles T. Yerkes, Jr., Broker, No. 20 South Third street, has embezzled funds belonging to the city of Philadelphia, to the amount of one hundred and forty-five thousand dollars, and deponent further charges said Charles T. Yerkes, Jr., with larceny as bailee of about the sum of thirty-three thousand dollars.
>
> HENRY HUHN

The allegations were, of course, serious. The embezzlement charge referred to $145,000 in city bonds Marcer had given Charles to sell. The broker had sunk the proceeds of these sales into private ventures. He used the bonds that he didn't sell as collateral for personal loans. The larceny charge was an even graver matter. On the Saturday preceding his failure, Charles had obtained from the city treasury a $33,000 check after falsely claiming to have purchased that amount of bonds.

After hearing Huhn's accusations, Mayor Fox ordered warrants for Charles's arrest. Returning to Third Street sometime in the afternoon, Charles learned that he was a wanted man. The news stunned him. He never expected to be arrested. He had tapped into city funds for his own personal use, but many other Philadelphia bankers had also done so. Escape was not a realistic option, especially for a man who hoped ultimately to reestablish himself in Philadelphia's business world. So Charles and his father trekked to the Central Police Station, and the latter posted a $50,000 bond for his son.[5]

Three days after his arrest Charles returned to the Central Police Station, where a hearing was held on the charges of embezzlement and larceny. Stepping out of the shadows, William B. Mann revealed himself as the real force behind the prosecution, not Henry Huhn. Though still days away from becoming district attorney, Mann took charge at the hearing, and presented a strong case against Charles. The crafty politico skillfully examined a parade of witnesses, including the obliging David Jones, Marcer's chief clerk. Mann had probably promised Jones immunity in return for his testimony. Fulfilling his end of the bargain, the clerk furnished the most damaging evidence against Charles. Jones charged that "there had been no return" for the $33,000 he gave the broker on October 14, all but actually saying that Charles had stolen the check. Clearly the clerk was going to be the star witness in the upcoming trial.

Some Philadelphians wondered why Charles was the only target in Mann's sights. "Everybody is ready to cry out against the broker, and he is arrested upon criminal charges and held in heavy bail to answer," the *Evening Bulletin* noted. "But is he alone, or even principally, the guilty party in this transaction. Clearly not."

Henry Charles Lea and many of his fellow reformers agreed with the *Bulletin.* They regarded "the prosecution instituted against the broker, Mr. Yerkes, as an effort to divert the public attention from more guilty parties, while those concerned may be able to 'fix' matters to suit themselves." The reformers suspected that one of the chief culprits was City Treasurer Joseph Marcer, who, they believed, formed "the centre of a ring too powerful to be attacked by the ordinary processes of the law." Even if an indictment of Marcer could be secured, Lea and his associates feared that the case would be dismissed well before any revelations were made that might "prove unpleasant to the ruling political clique of the city." The reformers nonetheless urged "in the interest of good morals" that municipal officials conduct a "searching" investigation of the City Treasurer's affairs, an inquiry which, they guessed, would "reveal a complicity in corruption in unexpected quarters that would startle the public."[6]

The Philadelphia City Council had in fact already appointed a committee to investigate the treasury muddle. The aldermen on this committee turned up evidence establishing "the fact that large sums of money belonging to the city were allowed to remain in C.T. Yerkes & Co.'s hands, without any security whatever of any value." Charles, the committee reported, had borrowed $300,000 of public money, with the approval of David Jones and possibly Joseph Marcer. He also had used for his own personal benefit $145,000 in city bonds, and had obtained on false pretenses a check for $33,048.51. In all, the broker owed the city a staggering $478,048.51. The investigating aldermen ended their report on a properly moralistic note: "The Committee cannot condemn in language too strong the misconduct of the City Treasurer and his chief clerk, David Jones, and the fraudulent acts of C.T. Yerkes & Co." John Bardsley, the committee's chairman, later demonstrated that he knew a thing or two about misconduct. In 1891, Bardsley would conclude his term as city treasurer with a term in the penitentiary, having been found guilty of embezzling municipal funds!

But that was twenty years in the future, and City Treasurer Joseph Marcer now squirmed in the public spotlight. He had hoped his influential political pals, especially Henry Huhn and William Mann, would get him off the hook. But Mann was not yet district attorney and could do little to help his friend. Furman Sheppard, the current occupant of that office, had allied himself with the reformers, and, with their aid, obtained indictments of Marcer and Charles on November 1. The Grand Jury agreed there was enough evidence to warrant a trial after hearing the testimony of several witnesses, including the ubiquitous David Jones. Drawn "with exceeding great care to prevent the action falling through any technical error," the bill of indictment charged Marcer and Charles with "conspiracy in cheating and defrauding the city out of the sum of $300,000." Henry Lea and his friends were proud of the instrumental role they played in securing these indictments. They called for a "speedy and energetic prosecution of the case," but not out of "a spirit of vindictiveness." The safety of the community, they declared, "demands that an example should be made which will serve as a warning for the future."[7]

William B. Mann did not share the reformers' high-minded notions of justice. He did not deal in such abstractions. He wanted to send Charles to prison, but for personal reasons. Mann's friend Marcer also would have to be sacrificed in order to appease an angry public opinion and to protect the Republican Party. Shortly after he entered office on November 6, District Attorney Mann took steps to ensure a successful prosecution. He decided to make the $33,000 check the centerpiece of his case against Charles. The evidence was clearest regarding this check. But there was one major problem. As matters then stood, Mann simply could not prosecute Charles for larceny. The latter had only been charged with embezzlement and conspiracy. Even worse from Mann's perspective, the bill of indictment did not even mention the $33,000 check. The district attorney quickly moved to correct the situation, convening a new Grand Jury, which obediently indicted Charles on four counts, including larceny. Mann set the trial for early December in the Court of Quarter Sessions.

The besieged broker was also under attack in the civil courts. On November 10 one of his creditors attempted to force him into bankruptcy, an outcome he desperately wanted to avoid. Once declared bankrupt by a judge, he would be legally required to surrender all his property to court-appointed administrators acting in behalf of his creditors. Any money he made, other than a small allowance, would go to these administrators for the payment of his debts. Charles had already taken measures he hoped might keep him out of bankruptcy court. On October 24 he had transferred most of his estate to Joseph Pile, a lawyer friend. Pile then, in his own words, "gave notice to all persons indebted to the Estate and . . . held interviews with large numbers of them." The lawyer managed to persuade some of these creditors to go easy, and even "expected to effect a settlement of many of the contested and desperate accounts."[8]

Despite the success of Pile's efforts, Charles still appeared to be headed into bankruptcy. Determined to avert this calamity, he decided to confront his creditors and beguile them with his charm. The showdown occurred on November 19 at No. 20 South Third Street. Charles did not face a friendly crowd. Many of the thirty-four creditors present at this meeting had lost their savings when his firm failed. The broker revealed for the first time the magnitude of this failure. He estimated his assets at only $250,000 and his liabilities at a whopping $850,000. After hearing these figures, the assembled creditors probably despaired of receiving any amounts from Charles. But the latter did have a proposition in mind. He vowed to pay, as soon as possible, 30 percent of his debt in cash and offered to take up the remainder in installments stretching over three years. Believing this proposal to be better than nothing, the creditors accepted the offer in a 29–1 vote, with four persons abstaining.

Charles also tried to reach a settlement with the City of Philadelphia and the Commonwealth of Pennsylvania, his largest creditors. The banker owed $478,000 to the city and $165,000 to the state. Robert W. Mackey, the sickly, whiskey-sipping state treasurer, had loaned Charles the latter amount, and now understandably wanted it back. Meeting with a Philadelphia City Council committee, Charles promised to surrender property valued at $229,000 to satisfy the claims of both city and state. The committee's members, including Mayor Fox and the banker John Welsh, looked favorably on Charles's proposal, and submitted it to the City Council for approval.[9]

Charles was edging his way back from the brink. Or so it seemed. He assumed a characteristic confident pose when speaking to an *Inquirer* reporter late in November. "You might say that I have a prospect of being able to carry out . . . the propositions made to my creditors, provided I am not interfered with in present arrangements by the bankruptcy proceedings or the Court of Quarter Sessions," he asserted. "My friends have been very kind in coming forward with pecuniary assistance in this matter, and with their assistance I will be able to make the payments proposed." When the reporter asked Charles whether this arrangement with his creditors would enable him "to resume business as heretofore," the broker gave a remarkably optimistic response. "Yes, sir," he said. "I have no fears as regards my ability in the future to put myself financially in as good a position as I ever was." Significantly, Charles did not suggest that he would regain his old *social* position.[10]

One door had closed, while another threatened to open. As he journeyed to the county courthouse on the frigid, sunny morning of December 5, Charles must have thought a great deal about that second door, the one that led to the Eastern State Penitentiary.

———————

Completed in 1867, the New County Courthouse cost only $34,500 to build and looked it. The two-story-high redbrick and granite structure squatted on Sixth Street in the shadow of Independence Hall. The courthouse's interior was as unimpressive as its exterior. Trials were held on the second floor in a courtroom only sixty feet long and seventy feet wide. Though small, this room suffered from terrible acoustics. "The best that can be done is to huddle together closely the judges, the jury, the counsel, and the witnesses," one observer lamented. Courtrooms in those days were "bare and dingy," according to the Philadelphia reformer George Norris. "There were no draperies, no marble or hardwood ornamentations, and the judges wore no gowns," Norris recalled. The writer Owen Wister put it more concisely: "In that day Justice still sat at Sixth and Chestnut Streets amid considerable squalor."[11]

Charles now sat amid this "squalor" at Sixth and Chestnut. He occupied a seat in the prisoner's dock, located in the center of the courtroom. Directly in front of him, Judge Edward Paxson presided behind a massive railed desk. Unfortunately for Charles, the judge was a close friend of William Mann. The elephantine district attorney stood on Charles's left, near the witness stand and jury box. Close on the right was his defense counsel E. Spencer Miller. Though a member of Henry Lea's Citizens' Municipal Reform Association, Miller had agreed to defend the disgraced broker. Behind Charles, a large crowd of spectators—brokers, lawyers, and merchants as well as "the usual number of 'bummers' attracted by idle curiosity"—fidgeted in long pews, eagerly awaiting the trial's beginning. The low early morning sun bathed the scene in a sea of yellow, adding a needed touch of color to the somber courtroom, with its black walnut furnishings.

Mann opened the case for the prosecution. Though an able orator, the district attorney had decided to put substance ahead of style during his presentation. He believed that a simple recitation of the facts in the case would have the greatest effect on the jury. Mann stated flatly that Charles had committed larceny when he obtained the $33,048.50 check from the City Treasury. The broker had received this check as reimbursement for the purchase of "a certain quantity" of city bonds. But Charles had never bought those bonds, Mann charged, and therefore had done nothing for the $33,000. He had in fact stolen the $33,000, the district attorney maintained.[12]

Following Mann's brief but effective presentation, E. Spencer Miller, Charles's defense attorney, addressed Judge Paxson. Miller wanted the judge to compel Mann to be more specific about his client's crime. Charles, after all, had been indicted on four counts: larceny, embezzlement, larceny as bailee, and embezzlement of money derived from a check. "Here are four distinct counts," Miller asserted. "I think the defendant should have the privilege of knowing exactly what he is charged with." Mann responded that the Commonwealth of Pennsylvania had "the right to pursue the course proposed—trying the defendant on the entire bill [of indictment]." The district attorney hoped to keep the jury's options open. Judge Paxson ruled in favor of Mann.

David Jones, the city treasurer's chief clerk, was the first witness for the prosecution. And he was more obliging than ever. Mann walked the clerk step by step through the events of October 14. Charles called at the treasurer's office that day, Jones recalled, and claimed to have bought $33,000 in bonds for the city. "Five minutes after he told me that, one of his employees came in with a bill," the clerk remembered. "I ordered a check for $33,048.50 to be drawn; I endorsed it and handed it to Mr. Yerkes' young man, and told him to be very careful and not lose it." Jones was later shocked to discover that Charles had not purchased the bonds—or so the clerk claimed. "The city has received nothing for this $33,048.50," Mann's star witness dramatically declared.[13]

In his cross-examination of Jones, the defense attorney Miller attempted to cast a shadow on the prosecution's seemingly clear-cut case. He first hoped to show that Charles had indeed been the city treasurer's broker and not some common thief. Jones admitted as much. "Mr. Yerkes has been the agent for selling and buying city loans since Mr. Marcer was City Treasurer," the clerk testified. Did Charles ever purchase city bonds as the treasurer's agent? Miller asked. "There have been times when Mr. Yerkes came and said it was necessary to buy city loans . . . to keep up the price," Jones replied. Charles had routinely performed this service for the treasurer, Miller argued, and may have done so in the days prior to October 14. But suppose the prosecution was right and the broker had not yet bought these bonds when he asked for the check? Could his request for the $33,000 still be justified? Miller labored mightily to provide this justification. He tried to demonstrate that Charles had often been paid *in advance* for city bonds, and intimated the $33,000 had simply been given for future transactions. Jones stubbornly refused to accept Miller's line of argument, and insisted that the money had been stolen. But the clever defense attorney had seemingly given the jurors cause for doubt.

Partly repelled by Miller on one front, District Attorney Mann moved to another. The district attorney suggested that Charles had also robbed the city of $145,000 in bonds entrusted to him for sale. The broker had indeed sold most of these bonds, Mann alleged, but he kept the proceeds and used the rest as collateral for personal loans. The testimony of John Hopkins, Charles's head bookkeeper, gave support to Mann's assertion. Hopkins admitted his boss had often used city bonds to secure personal loans.[14]

E. Spencer Miller now stepped up to bat, opening the case for the defense. Addressing the jurors, Miller boldly declared that for years every city official knew that "no man would accept the office of City Treasurer without the privilege of using the money for his own private gain." Only recently, he pointed out, the "City Councils were . . . asked to put a stop to this state of things, and refused to do so." The blame, Miller was suggesting, lay in a corrupt system rather than in particular individuals. Charles was caught up in this system. He had been employed by a number of city treasurers to purchase and sell bonds. "For all these transactions, settlements were exacted on the last day of the month and not before," Miller stressed. Charles had indeed borrowed city funds, but with the full approval of Chief Clerk David Jones. Such practices had become routine in the treasurer's office, and, according to the defense lawyer, had the sanction of custom. "Why, if this were thievery, it was a trap set by the people, by their public officers, by Councils who refuse to remedy it for the future," Miller argued.

The defense counsel next recited the events leading up to Charles's failure. Early in October the broker owed $300,000 to the city. Then disaster struck, the panic caused by the Chicago Fire "diminishing the value of stocks and of course diminishing the value of margins." Charles might have survived this catastrophe had Jones not demanded $150,000 on Monday, October 16, the attorney suggested. Expecting to settle his accounts with the city at the end of the month as usual, the broker was surprised by Jones's call. Charles simply could not afford the $150,000 during that period of financial crisis. "He stopped receiving payments," Miller concluded his narrative, "and knowing that the demand for $150,000 on Monday would be followed on Tuesday with a demand for a second $150,000, he stopped business." Charles then, according to Miller's account, was a victim of a corrupt political system and of a freak disaster. He had never intended to defraud the city, the lawyer maintained, and would have been able to pay back the city at the end of the month if only Jones had not interfered.

Miller tried to anchor his account on a solid factual foundation. Ex-City Treasurer Joseph Marcer was called as his first witness. Frail and of a nervous disposition, Marcer had succumbed to the strain of the last few months. A *New York Herald* reporter found the former treasurer to be a broken man, his voice trembling with emotion and tears rolling down his cheeks. Marcer certainly believed he was not guilty of anything. He later claimed to have had no knowledge of David Jones's loans to Charles, only learning of these transactions during the broker's trial.

Perched on the witness stand, Marcer told Miller that Charles normally settled his accounts with the city at the beginning of the month. "Did you make the settlements monthly because it would be inconvenient to settle every small transaction as it occurred?" the defense attorney asked. Mann objected to this question, claiming that it had nothing to do with the $33,000 check. Parrying the district attorney's thrust, Miller offered to prove that the monthly settlements had been a matter of convenience. Judge Paxson rejected Miller's offer, and sustained Mann. "I think the only way to try this case with justice to the Commonwealth and defendant is to stick to the issues," the judge ruled. This decision damaged Miller's case. He wanted to show that Jones had upset an established routine with his mid-month demand for money.

Undeterred by the judge's ruling, Miller next called David Jones as a witness. The defense attorney hoped to support his contention that Charles had been forced to the wall by Jones's demand for $150,000. But the chief clerk stubbornly refused to go along with Miller. Jones insisted that he had not asked for that amount on Monday, October 16. The clerk said that he had then requested only $75,000 or $100,000, and wanted it on Tuesday, not Monday.

Confronted by an obstructive judge and uncooperative witnesses, Miller closed the case for the defense without having proven his assertions. The clock stood at 8:45 P.M. An entire day and most of an evening had passed by—a short time to decide the fate of a man.

A Philadelphia Board of Brokers committee later provided support for Charles's case. Five brokers examined their former colleague's balance sheets and failed to "find any evidence of an intention to deceive or defraud." They believed Charles would have been able to meet all of his obligations had the Chicago Fire not occurred. "Mr. Yerkes allowed himself to be drawn into enormous ventures in the Stock market, with every prospect of success, and while in the act of reaping large profits, was suddenly arrested by the panic growing out of the Chicago fire, and forced to suspend," the committee asserted. This panic caused a tightening in the money market, and deprived Charles of his usual sources of credit. He had deposited city bonds as security for various bank loans, and, according to the brokers, "had there been no interruption to his usual manner of conducting his transactions with the City Treasurer his transfers would have been made." While careful to condemn this "reckless risking of borrowed money," the committee concluded that Charles was in fact a "victim of the vicious system of doing business which now so universally prevails."

The committee's report came about ten days too late to help Charles. Having heard the arguments on both sides, Judge Paxson issued to the jurors their marching orders. "The jury should give this case a calm, fair and impartial consideration, uninfluenced by any other cause than the law and the evidence," Paxson declared. "For every verdict rendered from a biased or partisan nature was a direct stab at our republican institutions. Far better that every dollar involved in this case should be thrown into the river than that the defendant should not receive fair and equal justice."

After delivering this stump speech, Judge Paxson instructed the jury on the law. If the jurors decided that Charles had not purchased the city bonds before receiving the $33,000 check, then he was guilty of larceny. If the jurors believed the broker had been an agent of the city when he stole the check, then he was guilty of the two embezzlement charges. Finally, if the jurors determined that Charles had been given the check for

a specific purpose yet "appropriated it to his own use," then he was guilty
of larceny as bailee. Of course, the judge added, if the jurors harbored reasonable doubts, then a verdict of not guilty must be rendered.[15]

At 9:05 P.M. the twelve men of the jury retired to deliberate. They were
escorted by the bailiff to a loft underneath the courthouse roof where,
according to one source, "unfortunate jurors shiver in winter and roast in
the summer." These "unfortunate jurors" certainly shivered in this narrow room that frosty December night when the outside temperature registered fifteen degrees. Perhaps in a hurry to escape the cold, the jury
returned to the courtroom in only twenty minutes. Charles and everyone
else in the room were ordered to stand. At 9:25 P.M. the foreman read the
verdicts.

> On the first count of larceny: Guilty!
> On the second count of embezzlement: Guilty!
> On the third count of larceny as bailee: Guilty!
> On the fourth count of embezzlement of money derived from a check:
> Guilty!

Though the jury recommended the mercy of the court, Charles must
have been devastated by the verdicts. Until this point he had probably
never believed he would really go to jail. But now the possibility of a prison
term had become a probability. Yet Charles still had some cause for hope.
He would be free until his sentencing hearing early in 1872, and might
somehow be able to fix matters before then. His lawyer also had not given
up, and had motioned for a retrial. But despite these bright spots, matters
were indeed bleak for the broker. He later confessed that "this was the
most trying period of his life." The "severe strain" he then endured was,
in his view, one "that few men could stand."[16]

State Treasurer Robert W. Mackey helped make life even more miserable for Charles. Mackey had convinced some banker friends to fill the
gaping $165,000 hole in the state treasury caused by Charles's failure.
Mackey now owed this sum to his cronies, and expected to squeeze it out
of Charles's estate. Realizing that the broker was no longer in a position
to settle his debts, the state treasurer petitioned in federal court for
Charles to be made a bankrupt. Judge Cadwalader granted Mackey's petition on December 14.[17] As a result, Charles's property was thrown into
the hands of court-appointed administrators. The broker had nothing left,
except his name and, at least for now, his freedom. Charles, though, had
no intention of doing time. He now had a plan.

6   Judgment Day

Not long after his trial, Charles managed to secure the support of the one man who could save him from a prison cell: Pennsylvania Governor John White Geary. The Civil War hero Geary's ambitions matched his six-foot, six-inch frame. He wanted nothing less than to be president of the United States. Political enemies, however, had unearthed a skeleton in his closet and the sound of the rattling bones threatened to drown out all talk of his presidential prospects. In return for a pardon from the governor, Charles agreed to furnish information that would neutralize Geary's principal enemies—Auditor General John Hartranft and State Treasurer Robert Mackey.

Acting according to this plan, Charles made out affidavits accusing his former clients Hartranft and Mackey of illegal speculation with public money. Appearing before Alderman William Dougherty on December 23, 1871, the broker swore

> That for some years past he has been acquainted with J. F. Hartranft, Auditor General of the State of Pennsylvania. That he has at various times purchased and sold stocks of different kinds, and carried the same with money belonging to the Commonwealth of Pennsylvania, which the said J. F. Hartranft has caused to be deposited with this deponent by the State Treasurer [Robert W. Mackey]. That this deponent did pay to J. F. Hartranft, Auditor General, on the 10th day of December, the sum of twenty-seven hundred ($2700) dollars, which sum was derived from profits on purchases of loans of the Commonwealth and sales of the same to the sinking fund, which sale was on the 29th day of April, 1870. That said deponent has also paid to said J. F. Hartranft various amounts

of money for profits arising from stock speculations with money deposited with this deponent by the State Treasurer at the instance of the said J. F. Hartranft.

The same day Charles made a similar affidavit against State Treasurer Mackey.[1]

Writing to an attorney on December 27, Geary indicated a willingness to pardon Charles. "I cannot see any reason for withholding executive clemency in the case brought to my notice this evening, if properly supported by the names of men of influence," the governor stated. Geary's enemies had long accused him of pardoning prisoners for a price, so he needed political cover before granting clemency. Charles eagerly obliged the governor. During the next few weeks, the businessman and his friends collected petitions of support for the pardon, obtaining the signatures of some of Philadelphia's most prominent and powerful citizens. Now assured that the move would be politically safe, Geary agreed to grant the pardon in a little over a month: on February 10, 1872—the day set for Charles's sentencing.[2]

So it was a confident man who strode into the courtroom that February morning. Charles's calm, optimistic manner stood in stark contrast to that of Joseph Marcer, who looked fearful and defeated. A crowd had again gathered, this time to witness the ultimate fate of the "unfortunate young men, who in an evil hour yielded to temptation."

Three judges sat before the bench on that mild winter morning. Edward Paxson, District Attorney Mann's friend, once more presided over the court, flanked by James Ludlow and Thomas Finletter. The judges first dealt with Joseph Marcer. Ruling in behalf of himself and two other justices not present, Paxson upheld the ex-city treasurer's conviction and refused a new trial. According to the judge, the facts showed that Marcer had, with full knowledge, illegally permitted Charles to borrow municipal money. "Stripped of its thin disguise, it was a scheme under color of law for Mr. Marcer to loan, and Mr. Yerkes to use, the money of the city of Philadelphia in the private business of the latter," Paxson declared. "The form in which it was done was not material. It was wholly unlawful."

The presiding judge now considered Charles's case. Deciding for the majority of the court, Paxson threw out three of the four counts in the indictment against the broker. Only one charge remained: the larceny of a $33,048.50 check. "For what purpose did the defendant get the check?" the judge asked. "He was upon the eve of failure. He had already hypothecated, for his own debts, the loan of the city placed in his hands for sale— he had unlawfully obtained $300,000 in cash as a loan, and it is reasonable to suppose that he could obtain nothing more from the city treasury by any ordinary means. Then it is that he goes there, and, with a falsehood upon his lips, obtains $33,000 more." Paxson sustained the jury's verdict on this one count.[3]

Judge Finletter delivered his opinion next. The "tall, thin, bloodless, and arbitrary" Finletter also happened to be independent-minded and he offered a dissenting view. He did not think the evidence in the trial proved Charles had stolen the check. "The verdict of the jury does not establish this fact," he asserted, "for the same jury, upon three other counts, found the defendant guilty without the semblance or shadow of evidence. How can we say that their conclusions upon the first count are unerring, when they so palpably erred upon the other counts?"

Judge Ludlow was even more critical of his colleagues than Finletter. Ludlow—"able and honorable, but quick tempered and very human"—believed that the majority ruling set a dangerous precedent. "In my judgment," he warned, "the doctrine now announced by the majority of the Court extends the crime of constructive larceny to such limits that any business man who engages in extensive and perfectly legitimate stock transactions, may, before he knows it, by a sudden panic in the market, become a felon. When a principle is asserted which establishes such a precedent, and may lead to such results, to say the least, it is startling."[4]

Following the reading of the opinions, Paxson pronounced sentence on the two condemned men. "Joseph F. Marcer, stand up," the judge ordered. The ex-city treasurer arose, "looking pale and nervous, and leaning on the back of his chair for support," according to a reporter. Paxson proceeded to lecture the doomed man, scolding him for his sins. "I do not desire to add to the pain of your position by any extended remarks," the judge began. "I cannot let the occasion pass, however, without expressing our emphatic condemnation of your offense. The misapplication of public money has become the great crime of the age. If not promptly and firmly checked, it will ultimately destroy our institutions. When a republic becomes honey-combed by corruption, its vitality is gone. It must crumble upon the first pressure."

Veteran political watchers in the audience must have been struck by Paxson's brazen hypocrisy. The judge, after all, had played an active part in what Alexander McClure called "the first general debauchery of the [Pennsylvania] Legislature" in 1855. That year twenty candidates—including one backed by Paxson—vied for the U.S. senatorship. The contest became a bidding war, and money was showered on legislators in a frantic effort to gain the prize. "The episode of legislative debauchery was the first in the history of the State in which the highest honors in the gift of the Commonwealth were made a matter of commerce," McClure stated.[5]

Paxson continued his harangue. After briefly chastising the public for its apparent indifference to political corruption, the judge again tore into his chief target, the ex-city treasurer. He saved his most dramatic oratory for last. "The people had confided to you the care of their money," Paxson intoned. "It was a high and sacred trust. You should have guarded the door of the Treasury even as the cherubim protected the Garden of Eden, and should have turned the flaming sword against everyone who approached it improperly. Your position as a member of the bar, and for some years as chairman of the Finance Committee of Councils, gave you ample opportunities of knowing the law. You have sinned against the light."

Paxson severely punished Marcer for his sins. He ordered the guilty man to pay a staggering $300,000 fine and sentenced him to a term of four years and nine months in the Eastern State Penitentiary. A collective gasp rippled through the audience when the harsh sentence was read. Some members of the crowd even stood up to get a glimpse of the "unhappy man" Marcer's reaction.

The judge then turned his attention to Charles, sitting next to Marcer in the dock. Paxson commanded the broker to rise. Charles did so. The "wealthy, handsome, and dashing Third Street broker," as one reporter called him, exuded confidence. From his "outward appearance it could not be told that he had such a fearful stake in the proceedings," another journalist noted with wonder. Charles's incredible poise had a simple explanation: He never expected to go to jail.

Judge Paxson addressed the financier. "Charles T. Yerkes, Jr., you have been convicted by a jury of your own selection of the offense of larceny," the jurist stated. "Your offense was one of more than usual gravity, the more so that the large amount of money which you obtained belonged to the city. . . . If your case points no other moral, it will at least teach the lesson, long needed at the present time, that the treasury of the city is not to be invaded and plundered with impunity, under the thin disguise of a business transaction, and that there is still a power in the law to vindicate itself and to protect the public."

Having disclosed the moral of the story being told that day, Paxson fixed Charles's punishment:

> The sentence of the court is, that you pay a fine of five hundred dollars to the Commonwealth for the use of the county, that you pay the costs of prosecution, and that you undergo imprisonment in the State Penitentiary for the Eastern District by separate or solitary confinement at labor

for the period of two years and nine months, and that you stand committed until this sentence is complied with.[6]

Charles drew another lesson from that day's proceedings, a lesson he
never forgot: The biggest criminals like Mann manipulated the law to
their own advantage, and used it to get back at their enemies. For him, that
was the only moral of this story. But he would have the last laugh, or so he
believed. Governor Geary had already drawn up a pardon. His friends had
witnessed the governor sign it. He was told that this document would be
waiting at the penitentiary's gates. Charles was so certain of freedom he
carried in his pocket a railroad ticket.[7]

Charles Tyson Yerkes, ca. 1886. Yerkes had a commanding presence. Observers were especially struck by his "searching eyes that seemed to read the very soul of the one on whom they were fixed." (*A Biographical History with Portraits of Prominent Men of the Great West*, 1894)

Yerkes, ca. 1895. (*Catalogue of Painting and Sculpture in the Collection of Charles T. Yerkes Esq.*, vol. 1, 1904)

Though he wore traditional Quaker dress, Silas Yerkes, Charles's grandfather, was a maverick. (*Chronicle of the Yerkes Family*)

Charles Yerkes, Sr., was expelled from the Society of
Friends after marrying a non-Quaker in 1845. When
this photo was taken (ca. 1865), he was president of
the Kensington National Bank in Philadelphia.
(*Chronicle of the Yerkes Family*)

The Eastern State Penitentiary in 1838. Convicted of larceny, Yerkes was imprisoned in this forbidding structure in 1872. President Ulysses Grant would help secure his release. (*Philadelphia: A History of the City and Its People*)

The Belgian dandy Jan van Beers rendered this image of Charles Yerkes, ca. 1892. According to critics, van Beers achieved such realistic likenesses by simply painting over photographs. (*Yerkes Collection*, vol. 2, 1904)

Mary Adelaide Yerkes, Charles's second wife, posed for this portrait by Jan van Beers, ca. 1892. Mary is accompanied by her pet poodle "Diamonds." University of Chicago President William Rainey Harper judged Mary to be the most beautiful woman he had seen in years. (*Yerkes Collection*, vol. 2, 1904)

A North Chicago Street Railroad Company cable train emerges from the LaSalle Street tunnel, ca. 1897. The tunnel was central to Yerkes's plans for modernizing Chicago's transportation system. He conceived the brilliant idea of running cable cars through the tunnel in order to avoid the traffic congestion on the Chicago River bridges. (*Yerkes System of Street Railways, 1897*)

A West Chicago Street Railroad Company cable train passes a power house on Jefferson and Van Buren streets. In 1887, Yerkes added the West Side's streetcar lines to his growing empire on rails. (*Yerkes System of Street Railways, 1897*)

7 Buried Alive

Charles realized something had gone horribly wrong only when he arrived at the very walls of the Eastern State Penitentiary. No pardon awaited him there, as Governor Geary had promised. Instead, two stocky deputy sheriffs escorted the befuddled broker and Joseph Marcer (who had been convicted of embezzlement) through an opening in the jail's twenty-seven-foot-high iron gate. "They are buried from the world for a long time, and perhaps forever," one witness intoned.

Charles learned later what had happened. District Attorney William B. Mann had intervened, disrupting the broker's scheme at the last minute. The vindictive district attorney despised Charles and wanted him behind bars. Using state Attorney General Frederick Carroll Brewster as his spokesman, Mann persuaded Governor Geary to withhold the pardon. The governor had little choice but to heed Mann's wishes. The latter politician had, after all, stolen the last election for Geary.

The grim granite-faced Eastern State Penitentiary sprawled over ten acres in the still largely rural North Philadelphia. Opened in 1829, the prison quickly became famous for its "humane" system of solitary confinement and attracted such notable early visitors as Charles Dickens and Alexis de Tocqueville. In most jails of that era prisoners had one or more cellmates, with solitude being reserved for only the most serious offenders. Reformers believed that solitary confinement coupled with mandatory labor would help bring about the convict's moral regeneration. "Thrown into solitude, he [the prisoner] reflects," de Tocqueville explained. "Placed alone, in view of his crime, he learns to hate it."

Dickens visited the penitentiary in 1842 and left with the firm conviction that the cure was worse than the disease. While there, the great author met several inmates, including a German man who had beautifully painted the walls and ceiling of his cell. With tears pouring down his cheeks, the prisoner—"a dejected, heart-broken, wretched creature"—openly wondered whether his sentence might be commuted. "I never saw or heard of any kind of misery that impressed me more than the wretchedness of this man," Dickens asserted. The novelist blamed the system of solitary confinement for the German man's misery. In ringing words he condemned the method of punishment that could reduce a person to such a state:

> I hold this slow and daily tampering with the mysteries of the brain, to be immeasurably worse than any torture of the body; and because its ghastly signs and tokens are not so palpable to the eye and sense of touch as scars upon the flesh; because its wounds are not upon the surface, and it extorts few cries that human ears can hear; therefore I the more denounce it, as a secret punishment which slumbering humanity is not roused up to stay.[1]

The Eastern State Penitentiary's mode of punishment was supposed to be harsh. Even the jail's outward appearance suggested the terror of solitary confinement. "The exterior of a solitary prison should exhibit as much as possible great strength and convey to the mind a cheerless blank indicative of the misery which awaits the unhappy being who enters within its walls," the jail's building commissioners decreed. The British-born architect John Haviland certainly followed the commissioners' orders, designing a dungeon-like structure that seemed more suited to the Middle Ages than the nineteenth century. The penitentiary's main entrance was especially intended to inspire dread in the newly arrived prisoner. "One's heart quickens as he enters this terrible place of punishment," a French tourist gasped. Constructed of huge granite blocks, the 200-foot-long Gothic front possessed a forbidding arched iron gateway and was surmounted by three imposing towers, the central one of which soared eighty feet high.[2]

It is not known how Charles reacted when he first set foot in the jail, but a reporter did record Marcer's initial response. The ex-city treasurer's face turned "ashy pale" as the massive gate clanged shut behind him. "He glanced at the solid masonry and then looked furtively at the great iron door through which he had just entered," the journalist wrote of Marcer. "Then a sigh escaped him and dropping his eyes on the stone pavement, he tottered off with the officer."

Flanked by two deputy sheriffs, the prisoners headed to Warden Edward Townsend's office, where they were examined. A clerk recorded their names, ages, and other vital statistics in a "great book." Following this examination, Charles and Marcer traded in their elegantly tailored clothing for the drab apparel of the penitentiary: gray trousers, gray jackets, and gray caps. They were then both given numbers—7126 for Charles and 7127 for Marcer—designations that would serve as substitutes for their names during the entire period of imprisonment.

A penitentiary official led these two now nameless men to their cells in the first block. Typically a convict's head was covered with a black hood to obstruct his or her view of the jail's layout, but it is likely that this procedure was waived for the "respectable" Charles and his companion. Like the spokes on a wheel, seven cellblocks radiated outward from a central octagonal building that functioned as a guard tower. The individual cells were large for that era (and even for ours): seven-and-a-half by twelve feet. They were sparsely furnished with an iron bed, a clothes rack, a stool, and a washtub. In the back of the cell two sturdy doors—one made of iron and the other of wood—opened out onto a walled exercise yard seven feet wide and eighteen feet long. Inmates were allowed to use these yards for an hour a day, weather permitting.[3]

By 1872 the Eastern State Penitentiary's much-vaunted system of solitary confinement had begun to break down. That year 596 convicts occupied only 550 cells; as a result, some prisoners had company. Penitentiary officials had replaced the "separate system" with what they called an "individual treatment system." Deputy Warden Michael Cassidy explained the latter phrase. "Each case is studied, its peculiarities noted, and the prisoner treated as his case warrants," he said. "We do not propose to treat them all alike. There are no two people alike." Cassidy believed that certain people were predisposed to commit crimes, people belonging to what he termed the "criminal classes." In the view of the deputy warden, most of the prison's middle- and upper-class inmates were not really criminals, even though they languished behind bars. "Bank embezzlers, clerks who lived too fast, bank presidents, cashiers, heads of institutions, all of that sort come to prison, and it is not fair to treat them like the fellow that comes from the slums," Cassidy stated.

Charles was not a criminal according to Cassidy's peculiar definition of the term, and consequently his keepers treated him more generously than they did the other inmates. For example, most convicts were allowed visitors only every three months while Charles could see relatives and business associates every week. Robert Laughlin, a fellow stockbroker, often saw the prisoner, "carrying delicacies and cheering him up with pictures of a bright future." Charles's wife Susanna visited so often she became known as "the prison angel."[4] Penitentiary officials also exempted Charles from the mandatory labor requirement.

Despite this favored treatment, Charles's prison experience was anything but pleasant. He had fallen far and had lost everything, including his freedom. At first undoubtedly shocked beyond words by the very fact of his imprisonment, Charles eventually assumed an attitude of resigned acceptance. His Inner Light sustained him during this trying time when days seemed to last an eternity, though officially beginning at dawn and ending at 9:00 or 10:00 P.M. Charles passed the long hours by "doing almost anything to keep my mind from my troubles," he later confessed. He often read in the afternoons and even studied telegraphy for a time. Crawling out into his narrow yard, Charles would spend one-half hour of each day building up his body with dumbbells and Indian clubs. Breakfast, dinner and supper were the major events in the inmate's life. The first and last meals often consisted of little more than corn mush, while dinner sometimes featured pork or even beef.

Charles settled uneasily into the monotonous routine of prison life. Placed within every cell, a printed copy of the penitentiary's rules daily reminded Charles of his lost individuality and independence. Among other injunctions, the regulations demanded the inmate to keep his "person, cell and utensils clean," to "obey promptly, all directions given," to "not make any unnecessary noise," to be "respectful and courteous" to the prison officials, and to observe the Sabbath day.[5]

Two politicians soon spearheaded an effort to free both Charles and Marcer. Auditor General Hartranft and State Treasurer Mackey were running scared. A doctor by the name of William Paine had gotten hold of Charles's affidavits and other documents exposing the pair's involvement in illegal stock transactions. The pesky doctor had already tried—unsuccessfully—to prod the Pennsylvania legislature into an investigation of the state officials' alleged crimes. And now he threatened to feed this information to the newspapers. Hartranft and Mackey hoped that, when freed, a grateful Charles would deny the genuineness of the affidavits and thus defuse the potential scandal.

John Hartranft particularly desired Charles's release. Simon Cameron, Pennsylvania's supreme political boss, had tapped the tall and handsome auditor general to succeed John White Geary as governor. With the election slated for that October—only months away—Hartranft could not afford to have his questionable speculative habits revealed to the Pennsylvania electorate. If scandal could be averted, the auditor general had an excellent chance to become governor. He could boast of an impressive war record that made him "the ideal volunteer soldier of the State."[6] Unfortunately, Hartranft had caught a strong case of speculative fever while auditor general and had used state money to bet on stocks and bonds. If Dr. Paine exposed Hartranft's dirty little secret, enraged Pennsylvania voters might very well throw their support behind Charles Buckalew, the Democratic candidate for governor.

Hartranft hoped Governor Geary would get him off the hook by pardoning Charles Yerkes, who alone could dispute the authenticity of Paine's documents. But the headstrong governor "expressed himself as decidedly unwilling to interfere with the due course of the law." His presidential ambitions having been torpedoed, Geary was not in the mood to be nice, especially to a political enemy like Hartranft.[7]

Hartranft's worst fears were realized when Dr. Paine leaked the incriminating information, including Charles's affidavits, to the crusading New York *Sun*. Hartranft's troubles increased in July 1872 when the Democrats nominated as their presidential candidate the eccentric newspaper publisher Horace Greeley, leader of a group of Liberal Republicans unhappy with the corrupt Grant administration.[8] The fusion of the Liberals and Democrats terrified the Grant Republicans, particularly those in Pennsylvania. Hartranft, their candidate for governor, needed all the votes he could get. Even in 1868, when the Republicans were "all united and enthusiastic," their Party carried Pennsylvania in the October elections by less than a 10,000 majority and only by "Super human exertions."

Already politically crippled by Paine's revelations, Hartranft faced even greater danger when the influential Philadelphia *Press*, published by the erratic and alcoholic John W. Forney, joined *The Sun*'s crusade. "Too many damaging facts have already been proved against General John F. Hartranft to admit of any further question in the minds of honest, conscientious voters as to his fitness for the Gubernatorial chair of Pennsylvania," the *Press* declared. "It has been established by the testimony of Yerkes, corroborated by Hartranft's own letters, that he was a party to corrupt and unlawful speculations with the State moneys."

This "floodtide of merciless criticism" nearly cost Hartranft his place on the ticket. In July the state's top Republicans, led by the political boss Simon Cameron, secretly gathered to consider the selection of a new candidate. Cameron's son persuaded the group to stick with Hartranft. The political leaders eventually accepted an alternative strategy—a rescue operation. Charles would be released from prison, and, as the price for his pardon, he would swear that the affidavits were forgeries, thus absolving Hartranft of any illegality. The situation was critical. In the view of many Regular Republicans, Charles held the key to the election of not only Hartranft but also President Grant.

Cameron assigned H. Bucher Swope, a Pittsburgh lawyer and federal officeholder, to implement the rescue plan. According to an unfriendly source, Swope "had experimental convictions as to the total depravity of mankind, and his work did not, therefore, conflict with any of the natural instincts of an honest man."[9] The lawyer met Charles in his cell, and guaranteed him a pardon if he would declare the affidavits to be false. One newspaper later painted a harrowing portrait of the "mental and moral tortures" the prisoner endured as he struggled between "hope and conscience, between the desire for liberty and a sense of duty not all extinct." But it is more likely that this was a journalist's touch of poetic license and that Charles readily assented to Swope's proposition. He desperately desired freedom, and undoubtedly would have made even greater sacrifices to secure that end. Charles soon signaled to Hartranft a willingness to go along with the scheme. "I have been extremely sorry that I have not been able . . . to assist you to deny the ingeniously contrived articles and false statements that have been published in the papers," the inmate wrote to Hartranft on August 27. "It is my earnest desire to alleviate all you have suffered by reason of matters in my office. I will take every opportunity of doing so."[10] In keeping with this promise, Charles began work on an elaborate document that would later do much to alleviate Hartranft's suffering.

Early in September an intrepid reporter visited the jailed man at the center of a political hurricane. When the journalist first arrived at Prisoner 7126's cell, he found Charles to be in "excellent spirits." Putting down the book he had been reading, the inmate warmly greeted his visitor, who happened to be an old acquaintance, and he promised to answer any questions. But when asked to give a history of the "unfortunate transaction" that had led to his imprisonment, Charles balked. "No, sir," the prisoner replied, "I do not want to say anything on the subject. There have been newspaper reporters and others to see me, and I have always refused to have any conversation with them, because I knew it was for the benefit of getting up some excitable article. . . . As a general thing, I am misrepresented in all I say and do. In fact I do not remember of but very few articles that I have seen in the newspapers since my complications have commenced which represented matters as they really were or anything like it. In fact some have been too ridiculous for any sane man to notice."

True to his bargain with Swope, Charles denied that Mackey and Hartranft had speculated with public money. The reporter then wondered how the prisoner accounted for all those newspaper articles maintaining otherwise. "Well, you know this is election time," Charles answered, with a candor that would later become customary, "and politicians or managers of political newspapers are not over scrupulous about what they say, who they injure or what material they manufacture so long as they can injure the opposite party and forward their own interest. . . . I would rather it had not been so, but it troubles me very little."

The newspaperman closed his interview with an expression of hope that the convict would soon be free. "I thank you for the kind wishes, and trust that they may be realized," Charles responded. "I have stopped hoping, and just lead this miserable life, waiting one day to see what the next day will bring forth."[11]

Charles, of course, had not really stopped hoping. Swope had after all promised him a pardon. But the lawyer crashed into a six-foot-six-inch-high obstacle. For months, efforts had been made to persuade Governor Geary to free Charles and Marcer. Many of Philadelphia's most influential citizens—including the banker Anthony Drexel, the lawyer John Bullitt, and even Edward Paxson, the judge who sentenced the men—supported the pair's release. Most amazingly, William B. Mann, the zealous district attorney and the man most responsible for Charles's imprisonment, now also favored clemency—not out of mercy, but simply for the good of the Republican Party: He wanted Hartranft to be elected. "There is almost unanimous opinion prevalent in the community that it is inhuman to keep these men longer in confinement," the *Philadelphia Inquirer* could say without exaggeration, "and that they are more sinned against than sinners." Yet Governor Geary steadfastly ignored all of these pleas. He knew that Charles, when released, would maintain the affidavits were forgeries, and thereby salvage Hartranft's faltering campaign. Still bitter over the failure of his presidential hopes, the governor absolutely had no desire to aid his rival Hartranft. He would pardon both Charles and Marcer but only *after* the October election.

But even the bull-headed Geary could not ignore the wishes of the president. Arriving in Philadelphia on the morning of September 26, Grant set up camp in the palatial Continental Hotel, the same place where Lincoln had stayed in 1861. For several hours the president conferred with Simon Cameron and Swope on the local political situation. As early as the previous June, Elihu Washburne, a close friend of Grant, had predicted that the twenty-nine electoral votes of Pennsylvania would decide the outcome of the presidential election. "I think our wise and controlling men in the Party should address themselves with great earnestness to the Pennsylvania situation," Washburne had advised Grant. "It is my deliberate judgment that if we lose the State in October we lose the Presidential election." Cameron also believed that "the fight" would be won in November only if Hartranft prevailed. The president's second term seemed to hinge on the success or failure of a major general whose battlefield exploits had once before given Grant a glorious victory. The president intended to ensure that history would repeat itself. Swope was dispatched to Harrisburg, armed with a presidential order commanding Geary to pardon Charles and Marcer.

Following their long conference, the drably dressed chief executive and Cameron strode out onto a hotel balcony. On the street below, a throng of businessmen greeted the two politicians with "deafening applause," and then serenaded them with a brass band. Grant, who looked "exceedingly careworn," smiled at this kind reception. He must have smiled even wider when he heard Cameron confidently predict to the crowd "that the State will elect Gen. Hartranft in October by 20,000 majority, and Gen. Grant in November by 50,000."[12]

H. Bucher Swope had the unenviable task of making certain Cameron's prediction came true. Traveling via train to Harrisburg early on the 27th, Swope presented the governor with the president's directive. Confronted with an order from the commander-in-chief, Geary—a good soldier—obeyed and signed the pardons. At 4:00 P.M. Edward Townsend, the Eastern State Penitentiary's warden, received word from the governor that a messenger was on the way to the jail. Two hours later Swope arrived at the prison's gates, accompanied by Philadelphia Mayor William Stokley, Colonel Lee, the governor's secretary, and John L. Hill, a city official. Entering the forbidding edifice, the four men made their way to the warden's office. "I have something important for you to read," Swope informed Townsend, and then gave the warden two documents. "Why, these are pardons for Messrs. Marcer and Yerkes, and they are all right," Townsend announced after a brief inspection. "Gentlemen, step this way."

The warden led the foursome to Cell Block One, where the prisoners were lodged. Joseph Marcer was the first to receive the good news. Genuinely surprised by the information, Marcer buried his head in his hands and wept with joy. His health had been shattered during this awful experience, and he couldn't believe that the nightmare was finally over. Charles, in contrast, had not "suffered much physically by his confinement" and looked "quite well and strong." Instead of crying, he laughed when he learned of his release. According to Townsend, Charles "cracked jokes and seemed in right good humor."[13]

The warden then read the pardon to Prisoner 7126. In this document, the governor carefully explained why he was granting clemency. Geary said he had received numerous letters from prominent persons asserting that Charles possessed "an irreproachable character as an honest and intelligent business man," and arguing that he had been unfairly "convicted of a crime for an act done by his clerk, in the ordinary routine of duties." The governor also claimed that 133 distinguished lawyers and thirty-four aldermen had expressed doubt as to Charles's guilt. Having fully defended himself against potential critics, Geary, "by virtue of the authority vested in me by the Constitution," pardoned Prisoner 7126 "of the crimes whereof he is convicted." After the warden finished reading the pardon, Colonel Lee handed it to Charles. "This is the Governor's own voluntary gift, uncoupled with any promise," Lee told the financier.

Charles exited the penitentiary, and plunged into the gloom of a warm, gray autumn evening. Waiting at the prison entrance, a smiling Robert Laughlin congratulated his freed friend, and offered him a ride in his carriage. Charles asked to be driven to his family's temporary new home on Nineteenth Street. Once there, the financier warmly greeted his loyal wife Susanna and his two children, nine-year-old Charles Edward and five-year-old Elizabeth Laura.

This emotional homecoming had to be cut short. Swope delivered on his promise, and now Charles had to fulfill his end of the deal. The latter knew what he was expected to do; the Pittsburgh lawyer had, after all, given him instructions during a half-hour conference in his cell. Shortly after his family reunion, Charles journeyed to the Continental Hotel, where Swope awaited him. The lawyer examined the document exonerating Hartranft and Mackey that Charles had prepared while still in prison.[14] Once satisfied of its contents, Swope sent the document to Clayton McMichael, publisher of the *Philadelphia North American.*

The following day—September 28—that newspaper printed Charles's literary masterpiece—a work of pure fiction. "In coming before the people with this explanation, which relates to the charges against General J. F. Hartranft, late Auditor General, and now a candidate for Governor of the State, and R. W. Mackey, State Treasurer, of having used through me the money of the Commonwealth in stock speculations, and for their private needs and benefit," Charles began, "it is my desire to make some plain statements which the public demand, and which I believe it not only their right to have, but my duty to them and myself to give." Charles went on to stress that he was making this statement out of a sense of justice. "While a victim has been made of me, dupes have been made of others by a few designing men, who used everything and everybody within their reach for the purpose of circulating and publishing assertions and statements which were false in the extreme, with the object of breaking down the character of General Hartranft, in the hope of thereby preventing his election," he alleged.

Pointing the finger of blame squarely at William Paine, Charles claimed the doctor had stolen from his office various letters and memoranda. He intimated that Paine had manufactured the affidavits in an attempt to discredit Hartranft. The clever financier next addressed the question of Hartranft's and Mackey's supposed criminal activities. He vehemently denied that the pair had ever used state money in private speculations. Hartranft, he said, had employed his own money in his speculative ventures while "Mr. Mackey never gave me an order to buy any stock for his or any other account." John S. Hopkins, Charles's former bookkeeper, supported these assertions in an affidavit quoted by the broker. "There is no entry [in Charles's account books] showing that either the State Treasurer or Auditor General ever derived any benefit from State deposits," Hopkins stated.

Charles closed this "remarkable production" in appropriately dramatic fashion. "It will be seen from the foregoing that a great fraud has been attempted," he intoned, "but I am happy to be in a measure the humble means of frustrating it. Of the originators of the bold plot I say nothing more, but leave them with the feeling that in their contemplation of the failure of their iniquitous schemes they have their just reward. Hoping I may not be again called before the public notice, I am, etc., Charles T. Yerkes, Jr."[15]

Splashed across the front pages of newspapers throughout Pennsylvania, Charles's defense brief enraged Hartranft's critics and delighted his supporters. "If an angel had come down from Heaven on purpose to testify in favor of General Hartranft, his adherents could not be more elated than they were on Saturday over Mr. Yerkes' statement," the *Press* acidly observed. "Yet Mr. Yerkes is not really an angel, and he did not come from Heaven, but from the penitentiary." For the pro-Cameron *Evening Bulletin*, on the contrary, Charles's statement completely cleared Hartranft of any crimes. "Thus is unraveled, exposed and frustrated the wickedest conspiracy ever organized against the character of an honest man and the credit of a great State," the *Bulletin* crowed.

The New York *Sun* expected Charles's defense to hurt Hartranft's election chances. "This desperate expedient will harm Hartranft far more than it will help him," that paper guessed, indulging in a bit of wishful thinking. "The honest voters of Pennsylvania will never stoop to pick up a candidate for Governor who has tried to make himself presentable at the polls by means of a whitewashing certificate furnished by a scoundrel who was let out of the penitentiary on the express condition that he would give it." But the *Sun* was wrong. Less than a week after this editorial appeared, Hartranft defeated Buckalew and won the Pennsylvania governorship by 35,000 votes. One month later Grant crushed Greeley at the polls.

While Grant had regained the presidency, Charles had simply regained his freedom. At least his surreal seven-month-long ordeal was finally over. He and Marcer, unfortunately, would never be able to entirely escape the penitentiary's shadow. In the words of the *Philadelphia Inquirer*, they had been "set apart from mankind, branded forever as convicted felons."[16]

8   Starting Over

There were many casualties of the brutal 1872 election campaign. A mentally and physically broken Horace Greeley died only weeks after his devastating loss. Early in 1873, an exhausted ex-Governor John White Geary succumbed to heart failure. And, disillusioned by their defeat and Grant's victory, the patrician leaders of the Liberal Republican revolt turned away from the political arena, leaving their Party securely in the hands of corrupt bosses like Simon Cameron. "I have always considered that Grant wrecked my own life, and the last hope or chance of lifting society back to a reasonably high plane," the reform-minded Henry Adams later wrote. "Grant's administration is to me the dividing line between what we hoped, and what we have got."

The events of 1872, of course, had not been kind to Charles either. The businessman nonetheless later tried to put a positive "spin" on the tragedy. "By the time I was thirty-five I had accumulated a fortune of some $1,000,000, which in those days was looked upon as a large fortune," Charles told an English journalist in 1901. "Then, by a stroke of ill-luck, I lost it all, and had to start the world over again. This, of course, is nothing extraordinary for Americans, who frequently make and lose half a dozen large fortunes before they finally consolidate their position. It also as frequently happens that adverse strokes of fortune prove a man's best friend, inasmuch as he comes out of each failure all the stronger for the lessons he has learned."

Charles had indeed taken away lessons from this "stroke of ill-luck." He had come to feel the utmost contempt for society and its major institutions: the political system, the courts, and the press. Never accepting his guilt, he believed that he had been a victim, a scapegoat conveniently put forward by opportunistic politicians to appease an angry and stupid public. He had been too weak to thwart his enemies. For the rest of his life, Charles was consumed by an almost pathological need for power—power that would give him mastery over his environment. He did not intend to become a victim again.

Charles's penitentiary experience also strengthened certain aspects of his nature. If he had cut moral corners before his imprisonment, he did so afterward with a vengeance. "Good society" would no longer admit him—an ex-convict—within its hallowed precincts, so he no longer felt bound by its rigid strictures. Before his jail sentence Charles had already displayed a strongly inner-directed personality, one that stemmed in large part from the Hicksite Quaker influence of his youth. Yet he had also aggressively sought the respect and praise of others higher up in the social sphere. His mishap showed him the folly of this boot-licking. Self-satisfaction would now be his chief aim. "I do things not from a sense of duty, but to satisfy myself," Charles averred in 1898. "If I do not satisfy myself I lose confidence in myself."[1]

Though all too aware that his social ambitions were now not likely to ever be realized—at least in Philadelphia—Charles had not given up on his hopes of business success. "I have made up my mind to keep my mental strength unimpaired," he confidently informed a newspaperman while still in prison, "and think my chances for regaining my former position, financially, are as good as they ever were." He had a long way to travel, and would have to start over again, almost from square one. A credit reporter succinctly described Charles's financial plight a year after his pardon. He "has no standing or credit in this market [Philadelphia]," the reporter asserted, and "has no means of his own." But this shrewd observer did not paint an entirely gloomy portrait. He pointed out that Charles was "really a very sharp man" who possessed "first rate business abilities." This talent had already made him a legend on Third Street. The brokers there suspected—half-seriously—that Charles had even reaped a fortune while behind bars.[2] If anyone could rebound from adversity, the brilliant financier was just the person.

He started slowly on the road to recovery. Shortly after his release, he escaped the scene of his recent troubles, and headed north to New Hampshire. Several years earlier, gold—embedded in quartz crystals—had been discovered on this tiny state's western border. "While it lasted, what a boom!" a local historian exclaimed. "It all centered on Lisbon, for the quartz was crushed in stamping mills there. In new hotels and coffee houses, saloons and even an opera house, the excited town welcomed the crowds of easy-money boys who poured in." Charles joined the throng of fortune-seekers who flocked to this mountainous, heavily forested region. With the financial backing of his father, he purchased a stake in the grandly named Electro Gold Mining Company. Journeying deep into the trackless wilderness, Charles assumed control of the mine and its operations. His golden expectations quickly turned to dross. The gold field in fact contained only small amounts of this precious metal. "Even in the genuine mines the veins, though rich on the surface, at a hundred feet or so down in the soil pinched out in slate," a historian reported. Charles and other investors eventually lost over $1,000,000 in the New Hampshire gold rush. While he had not enhanced his bank account, he had at least made a favorable impression upon the folks at Lisbon, who forever after counted "C. J. Yerkes" as one of their "notable sons."

This New Hampshire misadventure convinced Charles to stick with what he knew best: the brokerage business.[3] Before he could return to his old occupation, hc had to clear out of the way a major obstacle. As long as his estate remained deeply mired in bankruptcy court, he was legally required to pay most of his income to creditors. The estate's administrators had recovered only a small fraction of the $850,000 he owed. (His real estate holdings, including his banking house and coal mine, only fetched at auction a little less than $100,000.) With no hope of ever retiring this debt, Charles opted for another solution. Turning on his considerable charm, he attempted to persuade his creditors to support a petition releasing him from bankruptcy. He carried on this lobbying effort for nearly a year, shuttling back and forth between New Hampshire and Philadelphia, and finally captured the consent of a majority. His greatest triumph occurred in June 1873, when the Philadelphia Council canceled the $478,000 debt Charles owed the city. "To hold said indebtedness over him will prevent him from entering into business, and thereby inflict great injury to his family, without any advantage to the city," the Council's resolution stated. On October 3, 1873, Judge Cadwalader released Charles from the bankruptcy court's control.[4] He had won his freedom for a second time.

One man rose, while another fell. Only two weeks before Charles's victory, Jay Cooke suspended operations. The famous financier of the Civil War had dreamed a great dream: He hoped to link the Upper Midwest and the Pacific Ocean with a 2,000-mile-long railway line. The great banker, however, had lost his magical touch, and failed to market enough bonds to bankroll the construction of this road—the Northern Pacific. A desperate Cooke began pouring his bank's money into the line in an attempt to rescue it. Instead of saving the Northern Pacific, he wrecked his own banking firm. On September 18, 1873, he closed his company's doors for the last time.

Jay Cooke's failure stunned the economic world, partly because it came as a complete surprise. Best expressing this amazement, the Philadelphia *Press* called the news "a thunderclap in a clear sky." A severe financial panic followed closely on the heels of the Cooke disaster, and plunged the nation into an almost decade-long depression. This "financial tornado" quickly swept away many businesses, including the brokerage owned by Charles's two stepbrothers, the twenty-seven-year-old Joseph and the twenty-four-year-old Henry. Charles himself weathered the storm far better than his siblings. Taking advantage of a declining market, he ordered his broker to sell short a large quantity of stocks, and amassed a tidy sum in the process. Charles later claimed to have recovered "a good portion" of his fortune in this speculation, but in fact he gained about $25,000—only one-tenth of his previous net worth.

Charles used the $25,000 to resurrect his old brokerage firm, Charles T. Yerkes, Jr., and Company.[5] His plans met a serious hitch when the Philadelphia Stock Exchange refused to readmit him as a member. According to the Board's regulations, any member "who shall be declared a bankrupt shall ipso facto be suspended from the Stock Exchange; but a suspended member presenting a certificate of discharge . . . becomes eligible under the rules for re-instating suspended members." No longer a bankrupt, Charles had fulfilled this requirement, and was therefore eligible for reinstatement. Yet the members of the Exchange's governing committee rejected his petitions—on the grounds that his failure had not been a "fair one."

Since the Exchange would not permit him to buy and sell stocks, he decided to hire someone who could. And that someone was his friend John P. Bell, a "respectable and well connected" broker. A member of the Stock Exchange since 1857, Bell had learned the trade from Thomas Biddle, a scion of one of Philadelphia's most prominent families. Charles needed Bell to give his firm an air of respectability, while the financially strapped Bell required the $3,000 annual salary the new job provided.

With Bell as his front man, Charles tried to cultivate a new image for himself and his business. Once glorying in his reputation as a risk-taking and high-flying stock speculator, he now wanted to be regarded as a conservative, cautious broker. He later outlined his firm's new sober-minded policies. "We take no stock risks and accept only customers whom we know to have ample means for the lines of stock they operate in," Charles maintained. "We do not accept deposits on any terms. We borrow no money except [if] we give ample collateral and loan none except in the same manner."[6] His business's new location on Chestnut Street—in the middle of ultra-respectable "Bank Row"—signaled to the world that this was a different man with a different outlook.

———————

But old habits die hard and Charles soon began associating again with William Kemble, the notorious politician who had taught him addition, division, and silence. Not merely a shrewd political operator, Kemble was also a skilled manager of horsecar lines and, in his own way, a revolutionary. Hailed by some as "the improvement of the age," horsecars forever changed the way millions traveled within cities. More than that, they transformed the city itself, its shape and size. At first glance, horsecars didn't appear to be all that innovative. They were simply rectangular carriages that could accommodate several dozen persons pulled by horses along a railed track. Despite their simplicity, they represented a vast improvement over their predecessors, the omnibuses—horse-drawn coaches operated directly on the pavement without benefit of a track. The horsecars ran more smoothly than omnibuses, held far more people, and moved 30 percent faster—six to eight miles an hour.

First introduced in New York City in 1852 and six years later in Philadelphia, the horsecar came along at a crucial period in the development of the American metropolis. The cities' populations were mushrooming, swelled in large part by an influx of immigrants. Between 1840 and 1850, Philadelphia, for example, experienced a phenomenal 58.4 percent boost in its numbers, exploding from 258,037 persons to 408,762. During this era the boundaries of cities also expanded dramatically. In 1853 Philadelphia only occupied two square miles of territory; a year later the City of Brotherly Love added over 100 square miles to its extent through annexation, including the Northern Liberties, Charles's boyhood home.

The horsecar and its successors—the cablecar and the trolley—made this explosive urban growth possible. Before the omnibus and the streetcar, walking distances set strict limits to city size. Even mighty Rome in its heyday occupied only a little more than five square miles. Whether for good or ill, the streetcar helped uncork the genie of growth.

The streetcar also promoted the emergence of suburbs. Suburbs had existed almost since the inception of the city. These early suburbs, however, tended to be the exclusive province of the upper classes. But in the 1800s, the suburban movement became more widespread, thanks in no small part to the railroad and the streetcar. To some extent, these inventions democratized the suburb. As nineteenth-century cities grew and became congested, more and more people found that they could flee these urban centers. The horsecars and the railroad offered those who could regularly afford their fares an avenue of escape to "the pure air, gardens and rural pleasures" of the suburbs. Launching a modern trend, these mostly middle- and upper-class commuters increasingly worked in the city and lived in the suburbs.

By the 1860s millions of people were using the horsecar and Philadelphia investors were quick to take notice.[7] Haunted by "visions of wealth and fat dividends," hundreds of persons often assembled in front of horsecar company offices on days when stock was being offered. Charles himself took the plunge in the early 1860s and invested in a horsecar line —the Seventeenth and Nineteenth Streets Passenger Railway Company. Incorporated in 1859, this road passed six miles through some of the city's poorest *and* wealthiest districts, bridging Philadelphia's ever-widening class divide. In 1862 this railway company's stock rose dramatically, increasing from $3 to $10 per share. Impressed by this upward activity, Charles bought out the banker Francis Drexel's interest in the firm, and he eventually acquired enough stock to gain a seat on the road's board of directors. Subsequently serving as the Seventeenth and Nineteenth's secretary and treasurer, the young broker immersed himself in the line's financial operations under the watchful eye of Joseph Gillingham, the company president. Unlike some of Philadelphia's other horsecar firms, the Seventeenth and Nineteenth Streets Passenger Railway Company never became a big money-maker, and always produced only modest dividends. Charles's early career in the street railway field ended in 1871 with his failure, when he was forced to sell his horsecar holdings.

Charles's face wasn't always buried in the ledger book during his first decade in the streetcar business. He also promoted changes in the running of his road. However, in those early days of mass transit, progress came slowly. "I can see before me a plant that was run with one-horse cars, a driver, and no conductor, a pay box in the front end of the car where the passenger was required to advance and deposit his fare," Charles recalled. "I see that line changed to two horses and obtaining the dignity of a conductor to collect fares from passengers. That was a great improvement. And then we had straw in the bottom of the cars in winter—not overly clean, because we could not afford to put in fresh straw every day, but still this was a luxury—an oil lamp at each end of the car, which supplied the double purpose of lighting the car and showing the signal on the outside. We went at the rapid rate of six miles an hour when we could make it and keep on the track. The motion of the car was most agreeable to a person who desired to ride on the billowy waves. We see this changed so that the track was smooth, the straw in summer time was taken out, the floor always clean, and a stove giving comfortable warmth placed therein in winter time. This was advanced luxury."

Not everyone welcomed the advent of the horsecar. Charles remembered "very well" when the first street railway track was put down in Philadelphia: "The people tore up the track at night which the company had laid during the day, and it was not until after there had been several riots, and the authorities had awakened to the fact that the law must be sustained, that the company was able to finish the road."[8] Conservative property owners objected to the road's construction, expecting the noisy and "dangerous" horsecars to depreciate the value of their real estate. Other people believed the railway tracks would make the streets unsuitable for travel in private carriages. Reformers like Henry Charles Lea, though, had more valid criticisms of the streetcar firms. They feared the immense political power wielded by the managers of these companies, seeing in this power a threat to representative government itself. "Those corporations care only to make money," one Philadelphia man declared. "They are responsible to no one, owe no duty to the public, and are beyond its control."

William Kemble, Philadelphia's foremost horsecar operator, certainly didn't feel any duty toward the public. He was, according to one critic, "domineering, forceful, and absolutely contemptuous of public opinion." During the Civil War, Kemble had used his substantial political clout to wrestle from the Pennsylvania legislature a charter for a horsecar road— patriotically named the Union Passenger Railway Company.[9] Kemble undoubtedly did employ the "soul stirring word" "Union" in part for its public relations value, but he also chose it to suggest the scope of his ambitions. With monopoly on his mind, he intended to unite in one system Philadelphia's twenty-plus horsecar roads. The legislature got Kemble off to a good start, granting him the right to run his vehicles on forty-one miles of Philadelphia's busiest streets. The Union Passenger Railway Company quickly became one of the city's most profitable lines, carrying over 10,000,000 riders a year.

Kemble's aggressive drive for monopoly failed to please some of the Union Railway's more conservative directors, who were content to simply sit back and collect their big dividends. Following a "bitter quarrel" with these fogies, Kemble jumped ship, and left the Union in his enemies' control. In 1873 he formed a competing road—the Continental Passenger Railway Company. The Continental's nine-mile-long rail network "tapped the heart of the city, paralleled those of its great rival, the Union, and was equipped with better and more comfortable cars." Kemble eventually hoped to regain control of the Union, intending to make this line the nucleus of a unified transit system.

Kemble recruited Charles to aid him in his struggle against the Union Railway. In 1876 the horsecar magnate appointed Charles a Continental director. The broker welcomed this opportunity to return to the streetcar field, lured in part by the prospect of fabulous profits. Kemble offered Charles a large amount of the Continental's stock at the bargain basement price of $15 per share. The latter leapt at this offer. He eventually sold this stock for nearly seven times the purchase price. A banker later confided to a credit reporter that "Yerkes made $100,000 out of the formation of the Continental Passenger Railway Company, which gave him his present start."[10]

While working as a Kemble lieutenant, Charles came into close contact with two men destined to change his life—Peter A. B. Widener and William L. Elkins. This pair fully shared Kemble's belief in streetcar "traction as the big fortune right-of-way of the future." Both men had climbed "up the ladder" in true Horatio Alger fashion. The product of working-class parents—his father was a brick maker—Widener grew up in a Philadelphia district not far from Charles's boyhood neighborhood and attended the elite Central High School.[11] While laboring as a butcher during the Civil War, he received a contract from Simon Cameron's War Department to supply mutton to all the troops within a ten-mile radius of Philadelphia, a venture that netted him $50,000. In 1871, Widener was elected city treasurer to succeed Joseph Marcer. "It was the City Treasurership of Philadelphia that gave him his start," a commentator observed of Widener, "and it was out of his savings while in office that his gigantic street railway enterprises grew."[12] A West Virginia native, William Lukens Elkins also had a working-class background. Starting out as a grocery clerk, Elkins went on to operate a lucrative Philadelphia produce business, and, later, an oil refinery. In 1875 he joined hands with John D. Rockefeller, and subsequently sold out his refining interests to the "oil king."[13] The Philadelphian had new fields to conquer with William Kemble and Peter Widener.

Nicknamed "the traction twins," Elkins and Widener did in fact resemble each other. Both powerfully built, they possessed strong, bulbous noses, deep-set eyes, and "carefully trained" walrus mustaches. Elkins, however, was taller than his younger partner, and had more strands of hair covering his scalp. The West Virginia native's florid complexion and dapper manner of dress caused some to think—wrongly—that he was "a high liver." One newsman asserted that Elkins's most notable characteristic was his Sphinx-like silence. Yet the businessman did occasionally open his mouth. "He has a deep voice, which he uses with remarkable effect when he wants to inform a timid newspaper reporter that he does not want to be interviewed," another journalist discovered. Some observers suspected that Widener "carried" Elkins. According to these persons, the latter figure "was exceedingly hard-headed and close-fisted, slow, plodding, routine, and . . . would never have made his great success had it not been for Widener's support."[14]

However, it was William Kemble who in reality carried Elkins—and Widener—and even Charles to a certain extent. The ex-state treasurer had made these men part of his winning team, and coached them on how to run a street railroad. Kemble held very strong views on this subject. He strongly believed in economical operation, and kept a tight rein on his firm's costs. "We give the best accommodations of any city railway in the world, and at the lowest price, quality and distance considered," Kemble boasted in 1881. "This we can only continue to do by the most rigid discipline among our employees and the strictest economy." He sustained this "rigid discipline" by keeping his workers' wages at a low level, and by stoutly resisting unionization efforts.

Kemble also instructed his associates in the political side of the street railroad business. Ever since the 1850s politicians had controlled the fate of horsecar companies, advancing the interests of some and hindering those of others. The legislature created these firms and what the legislature gave it could take away. Kemble, a politician himself, was all too aware of this fact. He therefore actively aided political allies who promoted and protected his companies. "It is what I regard as higher than all Constitutions, that one good turn deserves another," Kemble once asserted.[15] True to this statement, he rewarded his friends both financially and politically. He appointed important politicians like Robert W. Mackey and Matthew S. Quay, a Cameron aide and future Pennsylvania boss, to his Continental Railway's board of directors. He also promised to deliver the votes of his many streetcar employees to friendly candidates.

The tough-talking Kemble sometimes resorted to cruder means to attain his political ends. He frequently employed bribery to persuade recalcitrant legislators to see his way. In 1873 he distributed 3,000 shares of Continental Railway stock to lawmakers, who returned the favor by passing a law granting the road the "outrageous" right to lay tracks on any street between Diamond and Lehigh in Philadelphia. Six years later Kemble again attempted to bribe politicians, but this time the dubious tactic nearly landed him in jail. After being sentenced to one year's imprisonment for bribery, he managed to wangle a pardon with the assistance of his friend Quay. When bribery didn't work, the streetcar operator pulled a club out of his big bag of tricks, and beat his legislative opponents into submission. In 1876, for example, he openly threatened to squash the nomination of a state attorney general who had dared to rule against his Continental road.

Kemble taught Charles, Widener, and Elkins to take a hard line against business as well as political rivals. He frowned upon any competitors who sought to overthrow his "empire on rails." Influenced by the example of the Pennsylvania Railroad, with its main line and numerous tributary branches, Kemble planned to build a streetcar network that functioned as an integrated "system." Under his grand scheme various subsidiary lines would radiate outward—octopus-like—toward the suburbs from a trunk line operating in Philadelphia's center. Transfers would be given passengers, allowing them to ride throughout the city for only one fare.[16] In the end, Kemble hoped to bind Philadelphians together with ribbons of steel. As a price for this progress, he wanted nothing less than a monopoly of the city's streetcar lines.

To achieve this ambitious aim, Kemble first had to regain control of the Continental's major rival—the Union Railway, which occupied many of the city's most important streets. He intended to make the Union the trunk line in his horsecar network. Kemble fiercely assailed his competitor, and used the parallel Continental road as his weapon. Quickly taking advantage of his railway's strategic position, Kemble attempted to attract Union passengers by offering faster and more frequent service. He even outfitted the Continental with horses of "a far superior character," and with cars that were "models of architecture and beauty." Failing to defeat the Union in this way, Kemble next tried to squeeze the life out of his antagonist. In 1879 his Continental line acquired control of the Seventeenth and Nineteenth Railway—Charles's old road—a move that gave Kemble mastery of all the central city's streets west of Broad (except Fifteenth). A chastened William McGrath, the Union's chief owner, accepted the inevitable, and early in 1880 sold his interest in the company to his opponent. The Continental Railway had served its purpose, and Kemble quietly leased that firm to the Union, which he now headed.

As a Continental Railway director in charge of the road's physical plant, Charles enjoyed a front-row view of Kemble's tactical maneuvers (and certainly played no small part in them). He had learned much from this street railway master, and would later put those lessons to use in Chicago. But Charles took issue with Kemble's final move. The broker believed the Continental's shareholders had not received adequate compensation under the Union lease. He felt cheated as a large stockholder in the company, and strongly protested to Kemble, Widener, and Elkins. This trio ignored Charles's complaints, and endorsed the lease, which was subsequently approved by the stockholders in an overwhelming vote.

The Union's "big three" did not appreciate Charles's disloyalty, and were unlikely to forgive him easily. As a result, Charles could no longer expect to be a part of Kemble's winning team. The broker's Philadelphia street railway career had come to a sudden end. Charles underlined this fact in September 1880 when he offered to the public $500,000 of Continental Railway stock.[17] Charles needed the proceeds of this stock sale. He had decided to leave Philadelphia—his home of forty-three years— and go west.

———————

Charles hoped to make a new start in the West. Domestic discord played a role in this momentous decision. He and his wife Susanna had grown farther apart, and by 1880 formed an "ill-assorted pair." They had endured a great deal of tragedy during their twenty-one-year marriage. In the decade of the 1860s four of their children had died in infancy, and early in the 1870s Charles lost his fortune and his freedom. Susanna had faithfully stood by her husband throughout his prison ordeal. "She was constant in her visits and bravely clung to him in the darkest hours of his troubles," one observer reported. Charles nonetheless drifted away from her. He desired a younger woman. "Mr. Yerkes valued women as he did pictures," a critic charged. "He picked them out because they were pleasing to the eye."

Charles certainly did value beautiful women. "It is true he had a weakness for women," an associate admitted. "Many times I have heard him say, 'God bless them all.'" Another acquaintance suspected that Charles even frequented "fast houses" in his youth, but later "when he got wealth and power, he was discriminating, and wanted 'mentality, as well as body.'" Indeed, Charles came to appreciate intelligence in women. Though by no means politically progressive, he strongly disagreed with the Victorian notion that a woman should merely be "the bright ornament in society, the tender companion of man." He believed that the "rudiments of a business education should be given to girls" to allow them to take care of themselves. "The ignorance of women in regard to business affairs is proverbial; in fact, I may say, it is stupendous," Charles once bemoaned. "As a class they do not seem to have the most remote idea of what business means."[18]

Yet Charles turned his back on his wife Susanna, a woman of "broad culture and brilliant conversational powers," and set his eyes on Mary

Adelaide Moore, an insecure twenty-two-year-old brown-haired beauty. Charles may have met Mary through her brother George, a broker. The daughter of a wealthy Philadelphia chemist, Mara—as she was nick-named—was the second oldest in a family of eight children. She enjoyed a reputation as the prettiest of the four striking Moore girls. Like a gardener sculpting a shrub, her domineering mother employed harsh techniques to enhance Mary's appearance. She strapped Mary in braces every night to prevent her daughter from becoming round-shouldered. "They [the braces] cut me and hurt me, but my mother insisted upon me to keep the things on," Mary bitterly remembered. She nonetheless later credited her mother for helping make her figure as "lithe and supple as an acrobat's." Mrs. Moore also forced Mary to sleep on "a low, hard, hair pillow" to pre-vent "the skin of the face from being pushed forward and wrinkling up."

Mary's face, with its haunting green eyes, especially captivated observers. "Her eyes are the most remarkable feature," the famous jour-nalist Viola Rodgers gushed in 1906. "They are of that wonderful greenish gray which Juliet's are supposed to have had, and which are Bernhardt's greatest boast. They are wide and ever changing in color, with the pupils dilating with every emotion." Even William Rainey Harper, the scholarly University of Chicago president, was impressed by Mary's appearance, calling her "the most gorgeously beautiful woman I have seen for years."

Charles was not attracted to Mary merely because of her beauty. He found in her many other enticing qualities: kindness, generosity, and a passion for life. She also shared his love of art, and, like him, enjoyed lux-urious living. Mary understood his status as a social outcast better than most; her parents also had never won the acceptance of Philadelphia's upper class. Perhaps most important, Mary possessed a boundless faith in Charles's future and encouraged his great ambitions. Harboring dreams of her own, she ultimately hoped to break into "good society." Mary would pursue this goal tenaciously; she had an iron will, as Viola Rodgers found out. "An expression of helplessness rather than strength predominates," Rodgers noted of Mary, "though at times an imperious quality sweeps over which is strong, masterful—masterful in the manner of a hunted fawn brought to bay and making a bold effort for freedom."[19]

Early in 1881 Charles himself made a bold effort for "freedom." He planned to divorce his wife Susanna and take Mary as his new bride. His friends warned him against making such a move, telling him that he was "nearing a dangerous shoal." Charles coolly shrugged off these objec-tions. Leaving behind the intolerance and conservatism of Philadelphia, the financier headed to the Dakota Territory, where new frontiers beck-oned—and where divorces could be obtained easily.

9 The Phoenix

Charles spent most of 1881 in Fargo, Dakota Territory. While waiting for his divorce to become final, he settled into the role of "Colonel" Yerkes, Fargo's foremost booster. He speculated in land, built city blocks, and even spearheaded the Dakota Territory's first agricultural fair. But Fargo did not offer a big enough field for Charles's colossal ambitions, and so in November 1881 he and his new bride journeyed to the mighty young city on the shores of Lake Michigan—Chicago.

Charles and Chicago were seemingly linked by fate. He emerged into the world the same year Chicago was incorporated as a city. His old life ended when flames consumed the town in 1871, severing "with ruthless hands the bonds of history and precedent." Both the financier and the city would rise from the ashes, stronger than ever.

Chicago was, according to Theodore Dreiser, a "city of over 500,000, with the ambition, the daring, the activity of a metropolis of a million." In the decade after the fire the city's population had doubled, jumping from roughly 300,000 to 600,000 persons. Hundreds of thousands flocked to Chicago in search of their share of the elusive American dream. "The adventurous, practical as well as wishful, were setting out for it from nearly every land—Iceland to Africa," one witness reported. "It was a new gold or hope-rush, such as California knew in '49, the Klondike in 1908." Many of these adventure-seekers were drawn to Chicago because of its newness, because it "was the only great city of the modern world born after the steam-engine, and never under the shadow of feudal land tenure or folkways." Encrusted tradition did not bar anyone's way in Chicago. The metropolis was the ultimate fantastic creation of a freewheeling capitalistic society nurtured on the gospel of success. "Here . . . throbbed the true life—the true power and spirit of America; gigantic, crude with the crudity of youth, disdaining rivalry; sane and healthy and vigorous; brutal in its ambition, arrogant in the new-found knowledge of its giant strength, prodigal of its wealth, infinite in its desires," the novelist Frank Norris declared.[1]

The city drew its strength from its location in a rich agricultural region on the shores of Lake Michigan. In its early days the city linked the factories of the East with the farms and forests of the West by means of waterways. Canals soon gave way to the railroads, and the town quickly became the junction point of the nation. By 1880 Chicago was the home of between twenty-five and thirty railroads. It stood at the head of a 25,000-mile-long iron highway that "brought the people of even the remotest hamlets into close business and social relations with the metropolis." Chicago ruled over a vast empire that controlled the destinies of millions. In the words of the journalist E. W. Lightner, the city was "the crowned king devil of trade."

The throbbing heart of this great trading engine occupied an area only one square mile in size—a tiny fraction of Chicago's thirty-six-square-mile total extent. This compact central district was fenced in by the murky Chicago River on the west and north, and by Lake Michigan on the east. Within this cramped space much of the city's business was conducted. Here one could find Chicago's chief financial, mercantile, and political institutions. Tens of thousands daily commuted to this downtown area—by train, by carriage, by horsecar, or on foot—to work in tall edifices, to shop in palatial stores, or simply to see the sights.

Even well-traveled foreigners came away impressed with the central city's architecture. "The business streets are lined with handsome massive houses, some six or seven stories high, substantially built, sometimes of red brick with stone copings and elaborate carvings, while others are built of that creamy stone which reminds one of the Paris boulevards," the very British Lady Duffus Hardy remarked.[2] Amazingly, this area lay in ruins only a decade before. Occasional vacant lots strewn with "piles of smoke-blackened bricks" were the sole relics of the Great Fire.

The Chicago scene did not captivate all visitors. Like Dickens before him, Rudyard Kipling toured America and recorded his impressions of the Western nation. Also like Dickens, Kipling saw little that he liked. He especially hated Chicago. "I have struck a city—a real city—and they call it Chicago," the twenty-four-year-old author wrote in 1889. "The other places do not count . . . This place is the first American city I have encountered . . . Having seen it, I urgently desire never to see it again."

Kipling walked the congested streets—"long and flat and without end"—and was horrified by the spectacle that surged before him. "I had never seen so many white people together, and never such a collection of miserables," he reported. Most faces in the crowd bore somber expressions. Other observers also noticed this fact. "The business-men generally have a hunted, driven, tired appearance, as if pushed beyond their powers," Bessie Bramble, a Pittsburgh woman, asserted. "They look as if engaged in a great and arduous struggle for wealth—as if they knew that without money they were nobodies—without lots of cash there was no fun, no enjoyment, no nothing. Their brows are furrowed with thought and their faces wrinkled with care while yet only in the middle age. Life seems to them not so much a pursuit of happiness as a great fight and arduous scramble for cash, and place, and power."

Mrs. Bramble's observations were on the mark. Chicagoans seemingly outdid other Americans in their worship of the almighty dollar. According to the novelist Henry Fuller, Chicago was "the only city in the world to which all its citizens have come for the one common, avowed object of making money." The language of business invaded seemingly every nook and cranny of the metropolis. Kipling discovered in his hotel lobby a crowd of "barbarians" chattering "about money and spitting about everywhere." Even during opera performances, brokers could be overheard discussing the latest Board of Trade news. "Why could not men leave their business outside, why must the jar of commerce spoil all the harmony of this moment," a character in Frank Norris's *The Pit* wonders in despair.[3] "Almost everything is on a financial basis in Chicago," Charles himself would later lament.

Chicago residents were proud of their brash, young city, sometimes irritatingly so. During his brief sojourn in the metropolis Kipling hired a cab driver to reveal the "glory of the town for so much an hour." The novelist quickly became disgusted with the cabbie. "He conceived that all this turmoil and squash was a thing to be reverently admired," Kipling wrote in amazement. The guide showed the befuddled author "canals, black as ink, and filled with untold abominations," dragged him into a saloon that had a floor covered with coins, and escorted him down "business blocks, gay with signs and studded with fantastic and absurd advertisements of goods." To hear Kipling tell it, he barely survived this awful experience. "I spent ten hours in that huge wilderness, wandering through scores of miles of these terrible streets," he maintained, "and jostling some few hundred thousand of these terrible people who talked money through their noses."

Kipling's ordeal was not over when he parted company with the cab driver. He soon bumped into another boastful Chicagoan, a man "full of figures." This person bombarded Kipling with a barrage of statistics demonstrating the city's business might: "Here they turned out so many hundred thousand dollars' worth of such and such an article; there so many million other things; this house was worth so many million dollars; that one so many million more or less." This litany was too much for the Englishman. "It was like listening to a child babbling of its hoard of shells," Kipling complained. "It was like watching a fool playing with buttons."

Yet the city's economic numbers were indeed impressive. In 1880 local manufacturers employed 79,391 people, paid out $34,646,812 in wages, and produced goods worth nearly $250,000,000. In the United States only New York and Philadelphia topped these figures. The metropolis's burgeoning industrial strength was even written in the sky. The pollution billowing from the stacks of thousands of coal-burning factories coalesced into a cloud that could be seen for dozens of miles away. Hamlin Garland poetically described the smoke cloud as having "a shape like an eagle, whose hovering wings extended from south to east, trailing mysterious shadows upon the earth." An Italian observer trapped within the city wondered whether there were "celestial spaces" beyond the smog.[4]

E. W. Lightner called Chicago "the earth's sublimest illustration of the fiendish spirit of modern civilization." For him, the city was a "fascinating hell" marked by "the clash and clatter and roar of the strife of man with man and woman with woman for place and preference, for sticks and coals, for bread and bones." In this young metropolis, the gap between the rich and the poor had already become an unbridgeable chasm. "The extremes of wealth and poverty . . . are startling, are appalling when one considers that it's a new city and in a new country," the editor of an Indianapolis newspaper remarked in 1888. "It's but a step from Michigan boulevard to South Clark Street, but what a gulf yawns between them."

Waves of immigrants from Southern and Eastern Europe began to arrive in the early 1880s, swelling the ranks of the poor. These newcomers tended to settle in a "poverty belt" that ringed Chicago's central business district. Here could be found the notorious tenements—multistory houses a health official deemed as "unfit for habitation by civilized people." As early as 1878, there were 4,896 tenement houses in Chicago. Infectious disease took a heavy toll in the poverty belt. In 1882, a staggering one-half of the children of Chicago died before reaching the age of five.

Charles had not gone to Chicago because it was a paradise spot. He decided to settle in the city precisely because of its unregulated and chaotic growth. The financier had been impressed by one economic fact about Chicago in particular. Sometime during the fall of 1880 he learned that "while almost every steamer from England brought a shipment of gold, none of it remained in New York, but was sent West, principally to this city." During the period of the late 1870s and the early 1880s, an increasing number of Western banks began depositing their money in Chicago institutions, abandoning their long ties to New York. Shortly after he stumbled across this information, Charles journeyed for the first time to the fledgling metropolis. Armed with a letter of introduction, he met Lyman Gage, the eminent cashier of the First National Bank—the man perhaps most qualified to speak about the city's financial position. Gage told Charles that his bank alone held over $20,000,000 in deposits. This statement staggered the broker; he knew that the biggest Philadelphia bank carried only $7,000,000 in deposits. Charles came away from his interview with Gage absolutely convinced that Chicago was on the way to becoming a major financial center, one that might eventually rival New York itself.

One year later, Charles and his new wife Mary had moved to the city where all the gold was going. While they looked for a residence, the newlyweds stayed at the Palmer House, a hotel reflecting the city's growing wealth. Built for a cool $3,500,000, this "palace hotel of the world" featured a gaudy French-styled façade, staircases made of Carrara marble, and an enormous Egyptian chandelier. In typical Chicago fashion, Potter Palmer pronounced his creation to be "the final result of a perfect plan worked out to full completion."[5]

Charles did not let the lack of a home interfere with his grand plans. Not long after his arrival in the city, he paid the $5,000 initiation fee and joined the Chicago Board of Trade, then housed in a building on Washington and LaSalle streets. Ever since 1848 Board members had bought and sold grain and other agricultural commodities, in the process helping fix the prices of these crucial foodstuffs. Many a fortune had been won and lost on the Board where, according to Frank Norris, "the rush of millions of dollars, and the tramping and the wild shouting of thousands of men filled all the air with the noise of battle!"

Early in 1882 the financier opened a branch office of his Philadelphia brokerage in a building one block south of the Board of Trade. In keeping with his new environment, Charles now specialized in grain and commodity speculation. He knew this line of business well, having started his career in a commission house—James P. Perot and Brother. In Chicago, Charles usually traded on behalf of customers, but sometimes he could not conquer the old urge to take the plunge himself. Apparently this urge became increasingly difficult to resist. By 1886 he was employing a "small army of clerks to keep track of his trades," at least some of which were successful. That year the broker reportedly cleared $200,000 on a wheat deal.[6]

As a new member of Chicago's business elite, Charles needed a suitable home for himself and his wife. They could have settled in any one of the city's three divisions: the North, West, or South side. Charles and Mary, however, had no problem deciding where to live. The choice was clear for wealthy Chicago residents: the near-South Side, with its abundant trees, spacious lawns, opulent mansions, and high status. The merchant prince Marshall Field, the meat packer Philip Armour, and the railroad car builder George Pullman all lived there.

Field, Armour, and Pullman resided on the same South Side street: Prairie Avenue, the "very Mecca of Mammon, the Olympus of the great gods of Chicago," in William Stead's words. The British journalist suspected that this thoroughfare contained "as many million dollars to the square inch" as were "to be found in any equal area on the world's surface." Marshall Field was the first millionaire to set up camp on Prairie Avenue. In 1873 he built a mansion on what was then "little more than a cowpath running through sand dunes," and soon Chicago's wealthiest citizens followed their Moses into the wilderness. "Presently there sprang up a double line of brick or stone dwellings," a Prairie Avenue resident related, "some built in blocks, others—the grander ones—standing proudly aloof behind iron picket fences in their own grounds, with stables in the rear and often a bulging glass conservatory as well."[7] In a brief period Prairie Avenue had become the center of the Chicago social set.

During the 1880s the city's social leaders abandoned their formerly democratic ways and, under the leadership of Mrs. Potter Palmer, began to imitate the haughty style of New York society. Upper-crust Chicagoans drew a line in the Prairie Avenue sand barring the "unworthy" from their ranks. As in Philadelphia, a person's address indicated one's place on the social sphere. Chicago highbrows even looked down on those who lived too far south on Prairie Avenue itself, and did not consider these unfortunates as real residents of "the Sunny Street that held the Sifted Few."

Charles and Mary purchased an unpretentious brownstone at 1726 South Michigan Avenue—only a block west of Prairie. Michigan Avenue was a broad, tree-draped street lined with beautiful, imposing homes, yet it was "out of bounds" for Chicago socialites. The financier quickly discovered that the city's social climate would not be a hospitable one.

Early in 1882 he managed to win election to the Union League Club, a local branch of the elite Republican organization his father had joined during the Civil War, and a citadel of the city's most powerful. Club members soon began to hear stories about Charles's past. They were shocked to discover that the broker had served time in prison, and were outraged to learn that he had divorced his first wife to marry a beautiful young woman half his age—a woman some believed to be an "ex-chorus girl." A credit reporter summed up the opinion prevailing in "respectable" circles when he declared that Charles "does not stand well morally." Determined to rid their club of this "immoral" man, Union League executives entrusted a special committee with the delicate task of securing the financier's resignation. The committee never carried out its duty, but Charles nonetheless heard of the secret proceedings. He never again set foot in the Union League Club's headquarters. A few years later the financier was refused admission to the Union Club, a "crack organization among the upper ten who dwell in the palatial mansions along Dearborn avenue, Cass street and the lake shore drive."[8]

Charles's past continued to haunt him during his early days in Chicago. In March 1883 his seventy-four-year-old father died in Philadelphia of what one newspaper called "paralysis of the brain." The last years had been hard for Charles, Sr. Following his son's business failure, he was forced to resign as the president of the Kensington National Bank. The elder Yerkes lost not only his standing in the community, a product of a lifetime of labor, but also most of his fortune, having assumed a good portion of Charles's debt. He painfully endured the agony of his son's trial and subsequent imprisonment. History repeated itself two years later when Henry and Joseph, his two other sons, plunged into bankruptcy and ruin during the Panic of 1873. Charles's divorce and remarriage added to the sting of scandal and only increased the father's misery. Capping all this tragedy, his second wife Margaret died in 1882. Charles, Sr., barely outlived his spouse. Once the proud owner of a stately mansion staffed by several servants, the former bank chief lived out his final years in a modest home with Henry's family, and worked as an assistant cashier at the Third National Bank.

Charles returned to Philadelphia to help settle what was left of his father's estate. But his old family ties were unraveling. He had grown apart from his stepbrothers, and would not even attend the funeral of Henry years later. His ex-wife Susanna still lived in Philadelphia with their son Charles Edward and daughter Elizabeth. Charles does not seem to have been on particularly good terms with Susanna and Elizabeth. He, however, had a better relationship with his son. The financier handed down to Charles Edward his Philadelphia Stock Exchange seat when the youth turned twenty-one. A chip off the old block, Charles Edward quickly gained a reputation as a "very lively member of the Exchange," the *New York Times* reported, a member especially popular among "the frisky bulls and bears who act . . . like a lot of schoolboys at recess time."

Charles's future was now in Chicago, and it looked bright. In his mid-forties, the financier enjoyed a moderately high income from his commodities brokerage business, and in 1885 could afford to move his firm to "one of the most expensive offices" in the Board of Trade's new gleaming 312-foot-tall tower, located at the foot of LaSalle Street. A cynical reporter visited Charles's new office and described what he saw with a pen dipped in vinegar. "The interior of the room is fitted up with all the paraphernalia of a regular bucket-shop—a big black-board for quotations, two tickers for grain and stock reports, chairs for the lambs to be shorn, and a well-guarded place for the cashier who takes in the margins," the journalist wrote. "On the transom over the door was in gilt letters the legend: 'C. T. Yerkes & Co.' It is one of the several dozen places in the city where people leave their money in the fond hope of fat returns."[9]

Charles's returns had already become fat enough to enable him to purchase more comfortable living quarters. In 1884 he and Mary settled into a spacious, new home at 3201 South Michigan Avenue—about fifteen blocks south of their old residence. Designed by the prominent local architectural firm Burling and Whitehouse, the $60,000 Gothic mansion measured forty-three by sixty-five feet, stood two stories high, and featured a tower on one corner. The interior was finished entirely in hardwoods, and boasted ornate furnishings. A conservatory adjoined the house; here Charles spent many hours a week, indulging his "passion for horticulture."

Domestic bliss reigned within the beautiful new home. During their first years in Chicago Charles and Mary got along extremely well, and, according to one friend, behaved "like a pair of lovers." This observer recalled that the businessman "always carried her photograph in his pocket and he had another on his desk." On balmy summer nights the couple would relax on their mansion's front porch, drawing snickers from neighbors. Chicago highbrows did not believe that the "best" people should sit outside in open view as if on display. The Yerkeses, after all, were not living in "a red brick Philadelphia cottage with white marble steps."[10] In those early years this criticism merely served to tighten the bond between Mary and her "Petty"—her favorite term of endearment for Charles. They drew upon each other's strength to ward off these attacks.

In a little over a decade, Charles had staged an amazing comeback. He had regained most, if not all, of his former wealth, and was worth perhaps $400,000 in the mid-1880s. He had a moderately successful business, a beautiful wife, and a fine home. Yet all of this was not enough for the supremely self-confident Charles. He measured himself against the business giants of his generation, such men as John D. Rockefeller and J. P. Morgan. These latter figures were transforming the nation with their activities, and making millions in the process. Even Kemble, Widener, and Elkins, his former associates, were doing big things in Philadelphia, modernizing and unifying that city's antiquated transportation system. Charles also wanted to do something big. "I hope when I leave the world I shall leave an impress on it, something accomplished, something lasting done," he once said. "Dollars and cents are well enough; we are all anxious to get them, but if I thought I would not leave some other mark I would not want to live."[11] He would soon get his chance to make a mark.

10 *Mass Transit*

On a sultry summer night in 1880, tens of thousands of Chicagoans flocked to the downtown lakefront in order to view what was expected to be a spectacular fireworks display. Jammed into a "dense, seething mass" on Michigan Avenue, the members of the crowd patiently waited for the show to begin. At 11:07 P.M. a witness reported observing "a red light and the tips of several rockets" and the "extreme ends of several stars." That was it. Most spectators left the "display" having seen little more than the moon playing peek-a-boo with the clouds. But greater disappointment lay ahead. As the disgusted Chicago residents began filtering home, they discovered that the city's three horsecar lines could not handle so many passengers. A few fortunate persons managed to squeeze into cars already "packed to overflowing," while everybody else either trudged wearily home or rustled up lodging in the downtown area. At one point during the long night a group of irate commuters vented their fury by overturning a horsecar. Like a man wearing a boy's shirt, big and brawny Chicago had a transportation network several sizes too small.

In that pre-automobile era the city resident possessed relatively few options for urban travel. Only the wealthiest persons owned horses and carriages, or could easily afford the high-priced fares of the hack drivers. The rest of the population got around Chicago either on foot or by horsecar. The last-named mode of transit did not offer much of an improvement over walking. Even under the best of circumstances, a ride on a horsecar tested a passenger's endurance. "When the poor animals start they jerk very frequently," one commuter complained, "and you feel as though your spinal column had been wrenched." The ride only grew worse after

99

this bone-jarring beginning. Horses could only travel four to six miles an hour, and quickly became weary under the strain of pulling. As a result, the jolting journey often took an unbearably long time. "When you jumped on board one of the rickety, trunk-shaped boxes at the corner of Washington and Clark streets bound for Chicago avenue, or Division street, or North avenue (a distance of between 1½ and 2 miles), you practically entered into an agreement with the company which meant either time or eternity," an observer quipped.[1]

Newspaper editors blamed the managers of Chicago's three major horsecar companies for the city's transportation woes. "The curse of Chicago for a quarter of a century has been its local transit," the *Daily News* complained in 1886. "Progressive and wide awake in everything else, in the matter of street railroading, Chicago, the third city in the United States, is on the level of a pioneer town. It is at the mercy of three monstrous corporations—grasping, selfish, and powerful—which threaten never to relax the hold they have upon her throat." These three firms—the South Side's Chicago City Railway Company, the North Chicago City Railway Company, and the Chicago West Division Railway Company— had divided the city up among themselves, and operated independently in their respective section of the metropolis. The different owners of these companies acted as if the other divisions of the city did not exist. As one consequence of this blinkered vision, Chicago possessed a badly fragmented transportation network. Persons journeying from one section of the city to another (from, for example, the West Side to the North Side) were forced to pay at least two fares to two different companies.

Even movement *within* a division posed problems. By the early 1880s the three horsecar companies had laid down only about 200 miles of track in a city that sprawled for thirty-seven square miles. Some parts of Chicago were simply not accessible by streetcar. For example, none of the West Side company's routes extended all the way to beautiful tree-shaded Garfield Park, a favorite destination for Sunday picnickers. After reaching the end of the nearest line, the unfortunate passenger then had to make "a delightful pedestrian trip across the virgin prairie" to get to the park. Making matters even worse, transfers were not commonly issued in those days. As a result, a person who traveled on two different routes operated by the *same* company had to purchase two fares.

By far the biggest headaches for commuters occurred during the morning and evening rush hours, when thousands of downtown workers jammed into the "old fashioned and filthy" streetcars. The average Chicago horsecar could comfortably seat perhaps two or three dozen occupants, yet during the peak hours (6:30 A.M.–9:00 A.M. and 5:00 P.M.–7:00 P.M.) sixty, seventy, and sometimes even eighty people were "packed like dressed beef" into the vehicles.[2] Critics argued that the companies could have prevented this overcrowding by running more cars.

For North and West Side residents, the already torturously slow daily commute often lengthened to epic proportions because of the so-called bridge nuisance. Their horsecars could enter and exit the downtown area only by means of the hand-driven swing bridges spanning the Chicago River. But ship traffic on the river all too often forced the raising of these bridges, cutting off the city center from the periphery. "The bridge nuisance is an incubus on all our movements," a West Side man declared in 1885. "For three hours each day there is a regular blockade, and traffic of every kind is greatly hindered and delayed." A clanging bell was employed to alert Chicagoans of an imminent bridge-raising. Alerted by this ringing, pedestrians often made a furious dash to get to the other side of the bridge before their way was blocked. A story became current that "you could always tell a Chicagoan in New York by the way he started to run at the first clang of a bell."

A local civic group studied the bridge problem and found that each day roughly 17,000 vehicles were stalled for an average of six minutes because of the opened bridges. One out of every five of these vehicles was a horsecar. North and West Side citizens soon began leaving for work minutes and even hours earlier than usual in order to compensate for the time lost at the bridge bottleneck. They had no choice. "The 'bridged' excuse became a byword and was no longer accepted as sufficient by employers," a witness explained. "If the employees lost a quarter, a half, or a full hour by reason of the delay of the horse cars, by being 'bridged,' or from other causes, he or she was 'docked,' and a discharge frequently resulted." Thousands reportedly fled to the South Side to escape the "bridge nuisance" and thereby salvage their jobs.[3]

At least some of these migrants may have headed south to enjoy the benefits of a new form of "rapid transit" adopted by the Chicago City Railway Company in 1882: cable traction. Nine years earlier San Francisco became the first city in the United States to make extensive use of this new mode of transportation. Andrew Hallidie, a London-born inventor, hit upon the idea of cable railways while watching in horror as an omnibus driver mercilessly whipped a team of horses struggling up a wet cobblestone street. He devised a scheme to propel a sturdy steel cable by means of a stationary steam engine. Specially built cars outfitted with a grappling device (appropriately known as a "grip") latched onto the moving cable and were carried along by it on a slotted track. This system worked well in hilly, mild San Francisco, and by 1880 the city boasted 11.2 miles of cable lines.

That year Charles B. Holmes, the ambitious and progressive president of the Chicago City Railway, visited San Francisco to inspect the city's new streetcar network. Though the South Side company did a fine business and earned fat dividends, Holmes was not happy with the horsecars. Horses were expensive (each one cost between $125 and $200), inefficient (they could travel only so far before tiring out), and highly susceptible to disease. In 1872 an influenza outbreak known as the Great Epizootic wiped out 2,250 horses in Philadelphia and killed or injured 18,000 more in New York City. Cold weather and even moderate snow also took a heavy toll on horses, and often brought service to a standstill. Perhaps most important, each horse posed a serious health hazard, dropping over ten pounds of manure on the streets each day. This manure served as a breeding ground for flies and diseases like dysentery and typhoid. Holmes believed that there had to be a better way to move people. During his San Francisco trip he became convinced cable traction offered that better way. The streetcar chief boldly resolved to bring the cable to Chicago.

Before proceeding with his plans, Holmes consulted Chicago Mayor Carter Harrison. The city's jovial chief executive patiently listened to the enthusiastic railway manager as the latter outlined his daring plans for nearly half an hour. Harrison then rendered his verdict. "Go ahead, Mr. Holmes, it will be a success," the mayor announced. Encouraged, Holmes soon set the wheels in motion that would revolutionize Chicago transit, devoting $2,000,000 of his stockholders' money to the cause. Laboring through "rain and snow, through heat and cold, when fingers and faces were frost-bitten," 1,500 workers took only four months to turn 8,000,000 pounds of iron, 300,000 feet of lumber, and 225,000 bricks into a nine-mile-long cable line on State Street.[4]

Chicago residents were initially quite captivated and even amazed by the new invention. While visiting the city in the 1880s, the young Norwegian author Knut Hamsun penned a letter to a friend that well expressed this early amazement:

> Let me tell you about it: they have trams here that go through the streets by themselves—no horses, no engines—you just see a row of carriages coming towards you, and you can't see what it is that drives them along. In fact, there's a kind of thingammujig under the ground that propels the carriages along, a cable several English miles long, and all along the route there is a slit in the road about half an inch, where an arm [the grip] connecting the carriages to the cables runs.

Eventually the enthusiasm for the South Side cable faded, especially after a series of breakdowns and accidents. Local newspapers reflected this change in sentiment. "The cable cars make good time for about twenty feet, but then there is what is known in punctuation as a full stop," the *Daily News* lamented in 1886. "This is followed by a sudden spurt forward, followed by a succession of half stops, which in turn is followed by a twenty-foot slide again. To people of strong constitutions this may not be so hard to stand, but to the man with the average Chicago liver such progression can only be likened to that made by the trip of a toboggan over a rocky mountain slide." Even Hamsun turned against the wondrous "trams." He later wrote a short story in which a man's head is sliced off by a cable.

Despite its drawbacks, the cablecar represented a great improvement over its predecessor. The cable-powered vehicles traveled twice as fast as the horsecars, yet cost less than one-half as much to operate per mile. Horses, after all, could only travel so far each day and therefore had to be frequently replaced. There were also other advantages. "A cable road does not eat anything when it is tied up," Holmes explained. "A car has no will of its own to thwart the will and efforts of its faithful driver."[5]

William Kemble, Peter A. B. Widener, and William L. Elkins, Charles's old associates, carefully monitored the progress of Chicago's cable railway. In the early 1880s they were busy forging a unified transportation network in Philadelphia, and hoped the cable was the answer to their need for greater speed and lower operating costs. These canny businessmen, however, always moved cautiously and deliberately. After viewing the partly finished State Street cable line in 1881, an unidentified member of this trio (probably Kemble) assured a Philadelphia reporter of one thing: "Nothing will be done here till after the system has been thoroughly tested in Chicago." Nothing in fact was done in Philadelphia until 1883, when Kemble and his partners finally decided that the cable had passed their test. They then began construction of only the third cable line in a major U.S. city.

Charles undoubtedly watched his former partners' activities with a tinge of envy—and regret. They were reshaping the face of an entire city and making millions while he remained little more than a glorified gambler, buying and selling stocks, bonds, and commodities. As the former secretary and treasurer of Kemble's Continental Passenger Railway, the financier had once been an active participant in the Philadelphians' schemes and might have remained so but for the 1880 dispute over the leasing agreement. He desperately wanted to reenter the street railway field. Charles later told a reporter that he thoroughly understood only "two branches of business—banking and the stock exchange and the street railway business." By the mid-1880s he had developed a strong disgust for the former line of work, with its ever-present uncertainty and risk. "I had seen dozens and dozens of acquaintances end with nothing [after speculating in the stock market]," Charles asserted, with his two stepbrothers Henry and Joseph probably uppermost in mind. "I have had them come to me again and again with the stories of how their loved ones at home needed shoes and even food. I had seen many suffer."[6] The streetcar business, on the other hand, promised far more reliable returns than the stock exchange and offered in addition a certain psychic satisfaction, a sense of doing something worthwhile.

But Charles could not easily enter Chicago's street railway scene. Three companies already monopolized the field. Sustained by healthy quarterly dividends, these firms' mostly elderly investors held on to their stocks for dear life. Even if Charles could persuade some stockholders to sell, he simply did not possess enough capital or credit to pull off such an expensive transaction.

Locked out of the local streetcar arena, Charles still found a way to become a force in transportation matters. Late in 1883, while dining at the Grand Pacific Hotel, he happened to meet an agent for an English carriage and cab factory. This Ohio man told Charles that there would be "millions" in a hansom cab venture he proposed starting. Intrigued, the financier helped his new acquaintance obtain monetary backing from some important Chicago businessmen, most notably Albert Pullman, the brother of the Palace Car prince. Satisfied with the progress of the scheme, the gullible agent then returned to his Ohio home for three months. While this man was away, Charles stole a march on him. Not at all eager to share in any potential profits, the wily broker organized his own company with a capital stock of $100,000 and purchased fifty hansom cabs. These vehicles—light, two-wheeled covered carriages—were then very popular in London among the fashionable classes, and Charles hoped that they would catch on in blue-collar Chicago.

The city then lay at the mercy of a gang of private hackmen, who "squeezed big money" out of innocent customers. "Only strangers who did not know any better, or sporting people, and men to whom for the moment, and especially in a methodical effort to vermilionize the town, money was no object, would patronize the hack for anything but funeral service," an observer claimed. Charles attempted to compete with the hackmen by offering a "high character of equipment," a "uniform low tariff," and an "excellent quality of horseflesh." The cabbies, though, outwitted the financier. They acquired imitation hansom cabs that "looked sufficiently like the genuine article to take in the unwary," and continued to rake in "big money." Charles struck back. In 1885 he guided through the Chicago City Council a measure regulating the hackmen's rates.

But Charles's efforts were all of no avail. His Chicago Hansom Cab Company slid slowly yet inevitably toward bankruptcy. Only the wealthiest of people could regularly afford the cab's twenty-five-cent fares. (The streetcars charged only five cents for a ride.) The company's service also did not please certain outspoken customers. Writing to the *Chicago Tribune* in 1884, a man identified only as XYZ assailed the firm. "The rates of fare of this company are of such an elastic character to permit the drivers to charge one almost anything they like," XYZ complained. This *Tribune* reader also arraigned the cab drivers for their "utter unreliability." They were always late, he claimed, and sometimes failed to show up at all.[7]

As he struggled to keep his hansom cab company afloat, Charles kept his eyes open for bigger opportunities. The chance of a lifetime soon presented itself. Late in 1885 the financier learned that a large block of the North Chicago City Railway's stock was up for sale. Voluntine Turner, the owner of this stock and the North Chicago City's president, suddenly required a whole lot of cash and in a hurry. The sixty-two-year-old widower had fallen in love and needed the money to finance a mansion on Lake Shore Drive for his soon-to-be bride. One of the original organizers of the North Chicago City in 1859, Turner had served as the company's president since shortly after the Civil War. A frugal man, he managed his railway in a frugal fashion, rarely building additional lines and almost never adopting new innovations. A critic said that Turner "was more apt to be behind public demand than in advance of or even with it." His company's roughly 20,000,000 annual passengers shivered during the winter in unheated cars, and all year round endured spartan accommodations, including seats without cushions. The North Chicago City's stockholders, though, had no reason to complain. They earned colossal returns on their investment. For them, Turner was a "good and safe" president.

Now the North Chicago City's chief wanted to retire and enjoy life with his new love. He gave an option on his 1,786 shares to a group of investors headed by Ferdinand Peck, a prominent Chicagoan most famous as the founder of the architecturally renowned Auditorium Building. Peck, a black-haired and black-mustached thirty-eight-year-old with a "thoughtful face, and at times a dreamy expression," owed his vast fortune to the "far-sighted and judicious" real estate investments of his Chicago pioneer father. Despite his wealth and upper-class upbringing the young man professed to be an "outspoken believer in the reign of the

common people," and preferred to be called Ferd instead of Ferdinand—
the latter being a "high-sounding appellation, suggestive of aristocrats
and titled royalty."[8]

Peck and his fellow investors agreed to pay a staggering $600 per share
for Turner's stock, an amount only partly in cash. Turner, though, did not
like Peck's choice to head the North Chicago City and the talks collapsed.
Miffed, Ferd decided not to exercise the option on the December 12 deadline date, but soon realized he had made a mistake. He again approached
Turner in the hope of securing another option. The North Chicago City's
president now took a hard line, demanding payment *entirely* in cash.
Though a millionaire many times over, Peck could not easily raise such a
sum since most of his money was tied up in real estate.

Like a lion eyeing his prey, Charles closely followed the negotiations
between Turner and Peck. When the deal fell through, he realized that his
time had finally come and what he called "the long-coveted opportunity"
had at last arrived. Charles was now at a crossroads. One path led straight
ahead to a future of continued modest prosperity and moderate achievement while the other beckoned with the promise of untold riches and
fabulous accomplishment. Choosing the last path, the businessman resolved to make a bid for Turner's stock. He scrambled to round up the
$1,000,000 in cash necessary to secure these shares. Charles at first sought
financial backing from Chicago "moneyed men" but came up short in his
efforts. "He was a newcomer and impressed few people here," a local broker later explained. "There were men who declined to enter into his
scheme because they doubted his ability to carry it out." Probably as a last
resort, Charles turned for assistance to his deep-pocketed old associates
Kemble, Widener, and Elkins. He strongly distrusted these three men and
in fact very possibly despised them. They had double-crossed him in the
past and might do so again. Yet Charles wanted more than anything else
in the world to head a great street railway enterprise. So, swallowing his
pride, he extended an olive branch to the Philadelphians and proposed
that they form a syndicate to take over the North Chicago City.

The proposal intrigued Kemble and his confederates. By this time
they had begun to look for new cities to conquer. They had reaped a fortune out of their Philadelphia streetcar operations, and were now eager
to invest some of this surplus money in other profitable enterprises.[9]
During his 1881 visit to examine C. B. Holmes's cable line, Kemble and
his partners had noticed how rapidly the city was growing and foresaw a
great future for the local street railway business. Five years later, the
Philadelphians returned to Chicago, upon Charles's invitation, and inspected the North Chicago City's property. "When I am making plans for

a new enterprise I do not ask myself, 'What am I going to make?' but 'Can I lose?'" Charles once remarked. Seeking an answer to this all-important question, Widener and Elkins stationed themselves on a busy downtown street corner and counted the people who could not get seats or even standing room in the North Side company's cars. Observing a large number of such persons, the two men concluded that they indeed could not lose and that it would pay handsomely to acquire and modernize the North Chicago City.

Accepting the pair's assessment, Kemble gave the go-ahead for the purchase of the streetcar line. He, however, did not want Charles to have a role in the firm if and when it was acquired. All three Philadelphia men had been furious at Charles when he had opposed their wishes and voted against the Continental Passenger Railway's lease. Widener and Elkins apparently forgave the financier for this "disloyal" act but Kemble never did. Like many Gilded Age politicians, the onetime state treasurer believed that disloyalty to a friend was the greatest sin. Kemble may have been especially aggrieved because of the long history he and Charles shared. Somehow the political boss was "in a measure quieted," and the broker rejoined the fold.[10] He was now within reach of realizing his dreams.

In March 1886 Charles made an offer for Turner's 1,786 shares. The North Chicago City's president still demanded $600 per share and expected the entire amount to be paid in cash. With the vast financial resources of the Philadelphians behind him, Charles could readily accept these conditions and did so. His task was not yet complete, however. The North Chicago City Railway had 5,000 shares of stock outstanding; majority control could only be obtained with 2,501 shares. The financier turned to Jacob Rehm, the railway's vice-president, for the remaining stock he needed.

"Jake" Rehm was one of Chicago's most notorious citizens. A former police superintendent and onetime member of the infamous Whiskey Ring, "a colossal scheme for the enrichment of organized bands of thieves," Rehm was more than willing to sell his 729 shares of North Chicago City Railway stock.[11] But, like Turner, he expected to be paid in cash. "No checks for me!" the ex-policeman supposedly exclaimed. "I want the cash—gold." The demands of Turner and Rehm did not intimidate Kemble, Widener, and Elkins. They sought help from Anthony Drexel, the mighty Philadelphia banker. Sixty years old in 1886, Drexel had reached the pinnacle of the financial world. He was widely recognized in the business community as a "man of great reserve power" who "always had money to lend." According to one knowledgeable observer, nobody "ever found the last of Drexel's money."

Drexel tapped the forty-something John Lowber Welsh, a trusted confidant, to handle the details of the North Chicago City Railway purchase. Welsh supposedly never lied to his clients and enjoyed a reputation as a cautious man who methodically mapped out every move before acting. Yet in his dealings with Kemble, Widener, and Elkins he seemingly threw caution to the winds. Kemble asked Welsh to visit Chicago and inspect the North Side line before advancing the money. But Drexel's aide refused to make the trip because it would "upset the routine of his daily life and interfere with his plans." A creature of habit, Welsh had in fact never been farther west than Pittsburgh. So without ever seeing the property he and Drexel were financing, the banker handed over $1,500,000 to Kemble's group. The Philadelphians relayed this money to Voluntine Turner and Jacob Rehm, and secured majority control of the North Chicago City Railway. "Jake Rehm, some years ago Chief of Police in Chicago, has just sold his stock in the North Division Railway Company of that city for $475,000," a Washington newspaper reported. "It pays to be Chief of Police—in Chicago."[12]

On March 24, 1886, Charles officially returned to the street railway field. Now forty-eight years old, the financier had finally completed what he called his "apprenticeship," and was ready to move on to a new phase of his career. "Young men are in their apprenticeship till the age of forty," he once explained. "At that age they begin to see the mistakes they have made, and the next ten years form the critical period of a man's life." When Voluntine Turner resigned as the North Chicago City's chief, Charles stepped in to take his place. He was now *the president* of the firm. Widener and Elkins then filled the seats vacated by Rehm and another director. An entirely new team had, almost overnight, assumed control of a forty-five-mile-long street railway network. Chicagoans wondered what the Philadelphia group would do next.

They did not have long to wait for an answer. On May 24, 1886, Charles and his associates leased the North Chicago City's property to a new firm they had created—the North Chicago Street Railroad Company. The streetcar magnates then issued $1,500,000 of the latter company's bonds and used the proceeds to pay back the money they owed Drexel and Welsh. Thanks to this "extremely clever piece of financiering," Charles and the Philadelphians gained control of the North Side railway *without having paid a penny*.

Now fully in possession of the company, Charles quickly made clear his future plans. He proposed to meet the "growing demand . . . for more rapid transit" by cabling three of the North Chicago City's major lines.

The financier also promised to solve the North Side "bridge nuisance" by laying his cable through an old tunnel underneath the Chicago River. But first Charles had to deal with the notorious City Council and an outraged press. Back in 1872, he had expressed a wish to never again be "called before the public notice."[13] That hope was about to be rudely shattered.

11 *Tunnel Vision*

A social earthquake struck Chicago just as Charles stepped
into the public spotlight. On the night of May 4, 1886, a small crowd
assembled at Haymarket Square to hear several anarchists protest a
recent incident of police brutality. As a light rain fell, a column of 180
armed policemen slowly advanced toward the gathering in an attempt to
disperse it. At that moment, an unknown person hurled a bomb into the
police ranks, instantly killing one officer and injuring dozens more. "The
city went insane," the labor organizer Mother Jones recalled, "and the
newspapers did everything to keep it like a madhouse." The hysteria
reached a climax when the police pinned the crime on eight innocent
men. A few of the accused were not even present at Haymarket Square
that terrible night.

Charles would later unfairly accuse Chicago newspapermen of having inspired the tragedy. By then, he had become embittered with the
press after suffering years of bad publicity. His public relations problems
began at the very outset of his career as a Chicago street magnate. In late
March 1886, the *Chicago Tribune* published a dispatch from Philadelphia
reporting the sale of the North Chicago City Railway. The article briefly
alluded to the financier's past. "Mr. Yerkes used to be a stock-broker in
this city, and was not in good repute," the piece cryptically stated. "He did
not escape criminal charges while here."[1] The businessman's secret history had been suggested. Chicago residents now had reason to be suspicious of the new president of the North Side road. How could anyone have
confidence in a railway run by someone "not in good repute"—whatever
that meant? Charles quickly moved to silence potential critics.

He turned for help to the very newspaper that had published the incendiary article—the *Chicago Tribune*. The 60,000-circulation *Tribune* may have had less readers than the *Daily News* but, editorially, it was every bit as influential as its great rival. A critic claimed that the *Tribune* "used everything short of gutter language in assailing its enemies and stopped at nothing when it advocated a cause." The newspaper's relentless style reflected the mood of Joseph Medill, its sixty-three-year-old publisher. Medill ran the *Tribune* as his own personal organ and he didn't care whom he offended. The bushy-bearded and fierce-looking journalist resembled an Old Testament prophet. "He was tall and he stooped a bit, his face was narrow and his eyes deep, his beard had turned from gray to white," Colonel Robert McCormick said of his grandfather. "He wore always a frock coat, string tie and black fedora hat." Using his newspaper's editorial page as a pulpit, Medill daily thundered against monopolists, anarchists, and immigrants.[2]

By 1886, power at the *Chicago Tribune* had begun to gravitate away from Medill and toward his son-in-law Robert W. Patterson, Jr., the paper's managing editor. Supposedly the only member of the *Tribune* staff courageous enough to stand up to the fearsome publisher, the thirty-six-year-old Patterson slowly guided the newspaper away from its long role as the mouthpiece of one man. The son of a Presbyterian minister, the well-educated editor seemed more suited to a classroom than a newsroom. Cold and aloof, he did not get along well with his employees, who retaliated by ridiculing the "managing-editor-in-law" behind his back. Patterson's vanity did not help his office reputation. During editorial meetings he often took out a pocket mirror and meticulously groomed his beard.

Charles appealed to the *Tribune*'s managers to publish a favorable autobiographical sketch he had prepared. The financier argued that the newspaper's allusion to his criminal record was "cruel, inasmuch as he had lived an honorable life . . . ever since the fire, and had endeavored to retrieve his reputation as a business-man." He claimed further that his crime had been merely "a technical violation of the laws in Philadelphia." Besides, Charles maintained, the jury had strongly recommended mercy and he was pardoned after only seven months in prison. Persuaded by these arguments (and perhaps by a cash payment), Patterson agreed to print the financier's life story written by a "friendly hand."[3]

Immodestly headlined "A SUCCESSFUL CAREER," the article portrayed Charles as a bold, risk-taking entrepreneur who, enduring adversity, triumphed in the end. His misdeed is glossed over in a few discreet sentences. The article never actually refers to the businessman's imprisonment and understandably fails to mention his own undercover maneuvering to obtain a pardon. While admitting his divorce, the sketch makes Charles's Fargo stay appear to be simply the result of chance.[4] The financier had revised his past in order to make it fit for public consumption. His version of events, though, would soon be challenged.

———————

Hopeful that he had adequately repaired his public image, Charles could safely return to street railway matters—or so he thought. He planned to convert the North Side road's most important lines to cable. The businessman, however, could not simply go ahead and make this change. He first had to secure the approval of the Chicago City Council, a body even then notorious for its corruption. In 1886 Mayor Carter Harrison estimated that "five-sixths of the [36] aldermen" were "dishonest." These Council members earned far more than the few dollars they were paid at each weekly meeting. When professional aldermen began building ornate houses and taking expensive trips, people started to wonder: "Where did they get it?" The answer was clear. The aldermen wrested much of this loot from corporations that needed to use the city's streets. Profit-laden horsecar lines, gas utilities, and steam railroads were their favorite targets. For a price the councilmen would pass ordinances granting these firms the right to operate on certain streets over a specified period of time. These so-called franchises could be as short as ten years or · as long as ninety-nine. Aldermen even routinely used blackmail to line their pockets. In so-called sand-bagging operations, the politicians gave valuable franchises to companies they themselves organized. Fearing competition, the owners of existing businesses frequently averted this threat by purchasing the Council-created corporations, often at a hefty price.

In the mid-1880s four men dominated the affairs of the Chicago City Council: William "Billy" Whelan, John Colvin, James Hildreth, and "Foxy Ed" Cullerton. Whelan, a tenor-voiced saloonkeeper, enjoyed a reputation as a man who always kept his word. He was so trustworthy in fact that his colleagues later tapped him to handle and distribute the Council's bribe and blackmail money. John Colvin possessed a respectable Civil War record but he labored in the shadow of his more famous father Harvey, a former Chicago mayor tainted by the Whiskey Ring scandal. James Hildreth had been a member of the Ring so he knew all about the scandal. He also had a close knowledge of whiskey. An unfriendly critic once claimed that Hildreth was "well-nigh habitually drunk." Though only in his mid-forties, Edward Cullerton could have been called the dean of the Chicago City Council. He won his first election to that august body in

1871, and would eventually serve forty-one years there. Even his greatest detractors admitted that "Foxy Ed" fully deserved his nickname. A *Daily News* editor went so far as to call Cullerton "one of the brainiest, most courageous, most politic men in this city." The so-called Big Four put in a total of sixty-six years of "service" in the City Council. "What these years cost the city, in money diverted from the public coffers to aldermanic pockets, would be an interesting study," a political insider noted.[5]

"King" Mike McDonald was one of the few persons in the city who could have answered this question. Many local journalists believed that McDonald was Chicago's top political boss, a man who "ruled the city with an iron hand." Some people even suspected that "King" Mike controlled Mayor Harrison himself. "He named the men who were to be candidates for election, he elected them, and after they were in office they were merely his puppets," the Chicago *Herald* alleged of McDonald. "He ran saloons and gambling houses, protected bunko steerers and confidence men and brace games of all kinds without hindrance." The *Herald* probably exaggerated "King" Mike's power. Individual aldermen ran each of the city's eighteen wards, and not even the mighty McDonald could rule in such a fragmented kingdom.[6]

Mike certainly had nothing to fear from Carter Harrison, now in his fifth two-year term as mayor. Harrison believed that it was a futile exercise to attempt to enforce antigambling laws. "You can't make people moral by ordinances and it is no use trying," he once declared. "This is a free town. I interpose no objection if the puritans go to church and stay there all day and wear themselves to the bone on bare planks praying for the regeneration of the wickedest city of the world, and that extremely wicked old man, Mayor Harrison." A former Kentucky planter and a onetime slave holder, the sixty-one-year-old burly and bearded Harrison cut a dashing and distinctive figure. He wore a signature black felt hat, tilted at a rakish angle, and roamed the city on a white steed.[7]

For Charles, Harrison was the wild card in Chicago's political deck. The aldermen and McDonald could be swayed by a liberal use of money to support his streetcar measures, but the mayor, with a reputation to preserve, tended to respond to the prevailing public mind. Hoping to influence that opinion, the financier shrewdly selected William Manierre, a "respectable" reform alderman, to introduce in the City Council an ordinance permitting the North Side road to operate cable lines. Manierre agreed to sponsor this ordinance because his constituents were clamoring for rapid transit. The alderman, however, warned Charles that he would withdraw his support for the measure if illegal "inducements" were used to secure its passage.

At the May 31, 1886, meeting of the City Council, Manierre submitted the cable ordinance, along with a diplomatically worded petition written by Charles, now president of the North Side street railway:

> It is the desire of this company to give to our citizens that service which the continued growth of the city requires, and with an improved motor enable us to accommodate more people and with greater dispatch. It is our wish to relieve the streets in a great measure of the horses and eventually to take from the bridges a large proportion of our cars.[8]

With this last statement, Charles signaled a desire to push his cable line through a dilapidated tunnel underneath the Chicago River.

The cable ordinance came up for a Council vote only one week after its introduction, on June 7. Aldermen John Colvin and "Foxy Ed" Cullerton skillfully guided the floor debate toward the inevitable outcome. Led by Samuel Kerr and Arthur Dixon, a small band of reformers grappled with the Big Four, and unsuccessfully attempted to amend the ordinance. Unable to make even the most modest of changes in the cable measure, the "respectable" aldermen began to suspect that the game was rigged, that money had been expended to secure a favorable vote. Manierre came to share these suspicions, and finally refused to support the very ordinance he had introduced. Late in the session, as Dixon doggedly strove to postpone the inevitable, a weary James Hildreth, a member of the Big Four, suddenly exclaimed: "Don't you know you might as well stop?" "That is a dying kick," Colvin was then heard to say. The Council meeting ended around 2:00 A.M. with the passage of the cable ordinance in a 24–11 vote.[9]

Two days after the stormy Council session, the *Chicago Times* charged that $127,000 had been spent to obtain passage of the cable ordinance. "The aggregate amount of the 'boodle' is larger than any that has ever been offered for a single franchise" in the city, the *Times* maintained. An anonymous informant claimed that the bribed aldermen had been divided into three grades: "those who received not less than $8,000 or $10,000 each, those who were given a few thousands less, and those who were glad to take about $1500 each." Supposedly some Council members in the last grade felt cheated, believing in retrospect that they were "suckers" who "sold themselves 'cheap.'"[10] The *Times* article may have been in part a fantasy. That said, Charles and his associates almost certainly did use money to secure the approval of the cable measure. In the Chicago City Council, bribery was a practice as common as voting.

Melville Stone, the thirty-eight-year-old publisher of the mighty *Chicago Daily News*, now trained his editorial guns on Charles. Stone had followed the "onslaught" of the "accomplished craftsmen from Philadelphia" with great interest. "When the bribery of officials became an open and unblushing business, I opened fire," the publisher later remembered. The balding, bespectacled, wiry Stone looked more like an accountant than the hard-bitten editor he was. A "transom-and-keyhole-peeper," he specialized in "detective journalism," and especially enjoyed hunting down criminals on the lam. "Mr. Stone had the natural or culti-vated air of a chief inquisitor," a colleague noted. "He missed becoming the world's greatest detective when he diverted his talents to founding a daring, alert and truly independent newspaper."

Stone first met Charles on a train speeding between Philadelphia and Chicago early in 1886. Accepting the invitation of a friend, the straight-laced publisher agreed to join a "crowd of good fellows" partying in a pri-vate Pullman car. Stone immediately regretted this decision. "I found myself in the company of a band of as jolly a lot of 'highbinders' one might care to see," he recalled years later. "Among them was 'Charley' Yerkes. They were going to Chicago to make a raid on our traction lines. There was no secret about their purpose. How they expected to do up the guile-less Chicagoans was made plain. There was much drinking, much Bac-chanalian singing, some dancing, and little or no sleep throughout the night." Stone never forgot his first fateful encounter with Charles. As a self-appointed public guardian, the journalist would use the power of the press to defend Chicago from this "invasion of corruptionists."

Charles and his Philadelphia partners deserved a gold medal for stu-pidity. Their behavior in front of a Chicago newspaper publisher betrayed either astounding arrogance or inconceivable ignorance. They antago-nized the one person who could have best helped ensure the success of their transportation schemes. Each day over 100,000 Chicagoans pur-chased Stone's evening newspaper while another 30,000 read his new morning sheet.

Not long after learning of Charles's acquisition of the North Chicago City Railway, Melville Stone assigned a young and tenacious reporter to hunt down the financier's past. For two weeks, Charles Faye shuttled between New York City and Philadelphia in quest of the financier's secret history. Using primarily old newspapers as his sources, Faye "did up Yerkes for about twenty columns of nonpareil."

On June 9, 1886, Stone splashed across his morning newspaper's front page the final result of Faye's research. Boldly headlined "EX-CONVICT YERKES," the article detailed, sometimes inaccurately, the events sur-rounding Charles's imprisonment. Faye (and Stone) sketched an unspar-ing portrait of the financier and his crime. "Charles T. Yerkes, now posing as a street-railroad magnate in Chicago, was once a prominent resident of Philadelphia, as he was also a prominent convict in the eastern penitentiary," the article began. "Yerkes left here suddenly in 1872 and behind him lives a record that for audacity, heartlessness, and peculiar 'financial' methods has never been equaled in this city." Faye then gleefully launched into that record, all the while making sure to accentuate the negative. The resourceful reporter closed his article with the (accurate) suggestion that Charles secured his pardon only by promising to lie about certain affidavits. "Whether or not the conscience of Yerkes sustained a single or compound fracture or no fracture at all this writer has no official means of determining at present," Faye concluded.[11]

Stone followed up this explosive story with yet another one the next day. In this second article Faye recorded his impressions of the Eastern State Penitentiary, where Charles had been incarcerated. Escorted by Warden Edward Cassidy, the journalist toured the jail and even visited Charles's old cell. Along the way Faye threw in some gratuitous comments. Of the penitentiary's bathroom, he remarked that it was not "such a bath-room as the president of a street railroad in Chicago may find at the Palmer house." The journalist then indulged in a bit of tasteless speculation about Charles's bathing experiences. "The application of coarse brown soap to his tender flesh must be still among the most vivid reminiscences of his life at the Eastern penitentiary fourteen or fifteen years ago," Faye sneered.

Stone apparently considered presenting yet another installment in the Yerkes saga, one detailing his divorce and remarriage to a woman nearly twenty years his junior. Faye's first article slyly alluded to these events: "In love, as in finances, Yerkes was also lucky, thus knocking out the Dumas proverb that a man who is lucky in love will be unlucky in fast financiering." Somehow learning that Stone intended to drag his wife into print, an enraged Charles confronted the newspaper publisher. "He threatened to kill me," Stone recalled, "but I went on." The editor, however, never did use the story on Mary Adelaide Yerkes.[12]

Charles would carry shrapnel from Faye's journalistic bombshell for the remainder of his tumultuous Chicago career. The articles stung him deeply. "The *Daily News* can publish anything it pleases about me until it goes too far, as it is likely to do one of these days," he warned a reporter who badgered him as he relaxed on his mansion's porch, attempting to fan away the heat. "Then we will see what we will do about it." In truth, Charles could do little about it, except issue meaningless threats. The financier was forever branded in the eyes of Chicagoans as an "ex-convict from a Philadelphia prison." Whenever "anybody wants to throw some mud at me they have always got it ready made," Charles once fumed. This statement revealed the inner fury that always boiled just beneath the financier's usually placid surface. No matter how hard he tried, he simply could not escape his past. Charles grew increasingly bitter at his inability to redeem his name.

Mayor Harrison must have sympathized with Charles. After all, the local newspapers treated him savagely as well. Lunching at a popular local restaurant on June 9, the two men discussed the cable ordinance and other matters. They hit it off well, perhaps instinctively sensing in the other a kindred spirit. The pair shared many characteristics. They were both charismatic, attractive men who derived a great deal of their immense confidence from their success with women. Harrison in fact supposedly defied nature, growing more handsome as he aged. Women were their greatest passion. "I cannot realize that any man is good enough to be the possessor of a perfectly. beautiful woman," Harrison remarked at one time. "I do not want her; but I do not want any one else to have her." Most important, both men rejected the Victorian era's moral codes and followed their own Inner Lights. "Yerkes never talked about morals," and, according to a friend, even insisted he "*was not living* for posterity."[13]

Charles convinced Harrison to approve the cable ordinance by agreeing to make certain concessions. Following his conference with the mayor, the businessman journeyed to Philadelphia to map out future plans with Kemble, Widener, and Elkins. The LaSalle Street tunnel was at the center of this strategy. This tunnel and another one at Washington Street had been built to ease traffic congestion at the bridges. Completed in June 1871 at a cost of $566,276, the 1,890-foot-long LaSalle Street tunnel quickly demonstrated its usefulness. On October 8, 1871, as the Great Fire raged above ground, thousands scrambled to safety through this structure and its Washington Street counterpart. Only ten years later, the tunnels had fallen into disrepair and disuse. An 1881 survey showed that out of 54,612 people who commuted from the business district to the North and West Sides on a particular day, only 1,349 traveled through the tunnels. The *Chicago Tribune* attributed this neglect to the "fancied or real dangers of plunging into a dark hole."

Charles reawakened interest in what one newspaper playfully called Chicago's "Big Bores." He realized early on that a cable line laid through the LaSalle Street tunnel might help solve the "bridge nuisance." The businessman later vividly recalled his fascination with the tunnel:

> When I conceived the cable idea the LaSalle street tunnel was, of course, an important factor in my calculations. I used then to think of the time when I could overhaul that tunnel. Its walls oozed slime, its roof dripped

with dirty water. It was paved with cedar blocks, which had rotted and gave off foul smells and germs of disease. It was lighted with gas and the jets had become clogged or broken and gave off a feeble, uncertain light. Frequently the place was flooded, and, as the pumps were usually out of order, fire engines were sent for to clean out the place. It was infested by tramps, who made it a convenience, and altogether was a plague hole, unsafe and practically useless. I thought of the time when I could clean those walls and keep them always freshly whitewashed, when I could mend the leaking roof, replace the cedar blocks with granite, and light the place with splendid electric lamps. I thought how I could always keep it dry and sweet with good pumps, and how it could be made to facilitate the goings and comings of thousands of people every day. I thought of all these things and I believed Chicago would be grateful. Well, the only reward I got was the accusation that I was stealing the tunnel.[14]

On the night of the cable ordinance vote, Alderman Manierre introduced in the Council a measure giving Charles's North Side road the right to use the tunnel free of charge. Led by Stone's *Daily News,* most Chicago papers assailed this "tunnel grab." "The request is monstrous in its audacity," the *News* editorialized. "As well might a railway company, after condemning a right of way through a man's farm, ask him to tunnel a hill thereon which happened to lie in the route of its rails." Mayor Harrison also expressed serious reservations concerning the tunnel ordinance. "I am certainly not in favor of giving away the tunnel," the mayor told a reporter.[15]

Charles and the mayor had in fact already discussed the matter of compensation. Following Harrison's suggestion, the financier agreed to accept an amended ordinance requiring the North Side railway to erect a new bridge at Clark Street. On June 14 the City Council's Committee on Railroads approved this new measure in a 3–2 vote. Appearing before the committee, Charles feigned disapproval of the bridge proposal. "I don't know what the company will do, but I'm not satisfied," he declared. "I would rather withdraw all propositions and submit the matter to three business men."

As the new tunnel ordinance glided through the Council, the *Daily News* continued to take potshots at the financier, even publicizing his Fargo exploits. Of the city's major newspapers, only the *Tribune* and the *Daily Inter Ocean* provided restrained coverage of the tunnel controversy. Managed by William Penn Nixon, "a dear old gentleman" who wore "smoked eyeglasses and Ballyhooly whiskers," the low-circulation *Inter Ocean* boasted that it was "Republican in everything, Independent in nothing." Finding the newspaper's pages open to him for a price, Charles used this forum to rebut his critics. "There is something very stupid in the attempt to defeat an enterprise by raking up the past personal record of its projector and charging fraud and trickery against him," he argued. The North Siders wanted the cable, and he proposed to furnish it. That was all that mattered, Charles asserted.

Though less friendly to the businessman than the *Inter Ocean*, the *Chicago Tribune* urged other newspapers to "BE JUST TO YERKES." "We cannot discover in all of Yerkes' Chicago career an action or suggestion that has been unworthy of a man of honor," the *Tribune* stated. The paper did, however, insist that Charles pay compensation for the use of the tunnel. The *Daily News* ripped into its great rival, claiming that the *Tribune* "has blown hot and cold" in its attitude toward the financier. The *News* slyly suggested that a *Tribune* cashier, who happened to own stock in Charles's North Side road, had influenced the editorial policy of Medill's paper.[16]

While the newspapers warred on him and each other, Charles kept his eyes on the tunnel prize. Reformers in the City Council were not happy with the bridge proposal and insisted that the North Side railway pay an annual rental for the use of the tunnel. The financier apparently bowed to these demands. An amended ordinance stipulated that the streetcar company hand over $20,000 yearly to the city, but there was a big catch. The firm could deduct from this annual rental a sum equal to the amount of money spent each year in tunnel renovation and maintenance. At the June 14 committee hearing, Charles had said that it would cost $19,235 yearly to keep the tunnel in good condition. So, the city would have in fact received less than $1,000 a year in compensation under the newly drawn ordinance.

On the humid evening of July 6, 1886, thirty-five aldermen (Manierre was conveniently absent) assembled to decide the future of Chicago and of Charles Tyson Yerkes. Victory on the financier's terms would mean the alienation of a powerful potential source of support—the *Chicago Tribune*. On June 30, the newspaper, impartial toward Charles so far, foreshadowed an abrupt change in its editorial policy. "The crucial test as to Yerkes' Chicago career will be made when the Council acts upon the LaSalle Street tunnel ordinance," the *Tribune* stated. "If the tunnel shall be given to his company for nothing or for a fraction of its true value, we shall say without a moment's hesitation that Yerkes has corrupted the Council."

Lounging in a wicker chair on the Council floor, "King" Mike McDonald made sure the aldermen voted "right" that night of Charles's "crucial test." As before, Aldermen Kerr and Dixon spearheaded the fight against the ordinance, but once again met defeat. Dixon, however, did manage at one point during the lengthy debate to rouse a snoozing Mayor Harrison with a particularly florid burst of rhetoric. The meeting dragged on until after midnight, when the tunnel ordinance was approved in a 23–11 vote.

By winning the tunnel on his own terms, without providing real compensation to the city, Charles had failed the *Tribune*'s test. The financier could no longer count on that newspaper's assistance, and, in fact, the *Tribune* would become one of his greatest opponents. He later offered an explanation for this editorial about-face. Charles said that he approached Robert Patterson, Jr., the *Tribune*'s managing editor, for help in securing passage of the tunnel ordinance. "What is there in all this for me?" Patterson supposedly responded. Charles failed to give a satisfactory answer, causing Patterson to feel "snubbed and humiliated." Following that encounter, the managing editor long nursed a grudge against the financier, or so Charles alleged. A witness at the meeting, however, later claimed that Patterson had merely made the comment in jest.[17]

Mayor Harrison surprised many observers when he vetoed the tunnel ordinance, calling it "objectionable in law, in form, and in substance." Recognizing that the city would receive meager compensation under the terms of the amended measure, the mayor proposed that Charles's firm pay a $25,000 annual rental with no deductions allowed. This yearly fee would be reduced to $10,000 once the North Side company gave the city enough money to build a new bridge at Clark Street, and would be eliminated altogether when funds were furnished for another bridge at Wells Street. In effect, Harrison proposed to swap the LaSalle Street tunnel for two bridges. Charles did not like this new proposal. "I considered it a very unfair transaction on the part of Mr. Harrison," he would say. The businessman was so disgusted he even considered giving up "the whole business" and letting someone else "utilize the LaSalle Street tunnel." Having already arranged to sell stock in his North Side road, Charles, however, had no choice but to accept the mayor's idea. The financier did not grin but he bore it.

After a bruising fight, Charles had secured the LaSalle Street tunnel. The new ordinance also permitted his streetcars to penetrate deep into the lucrative central business district—as far south as the Board of Trade building on Jackson Street.[18] Charles was now in a position to build a cable system rivaling that of the South Side's Chicago City Railway Company. But his victory had come at a great price. He had created many powerful enemies, men who would battle him every step of the way.

12 Getting a Grip

Charles and his Philadelphia partners employed frenzied financiering while constructing the North Side cable system. To give their methods an air of legitimacy—and legality—they formed the noble-sounding United States Construction Company to handle the building of the eighteen miles of cable road (sixteen miles on Clark Street, Wells Street, and Lincoln Avenue, and two miles in the central business district). The construction company received as payment for its work over $6,000,000 in stocks, bonds, and cash, yet an expert accountant later found that the lines could not have cost more than $3,141,741.32 to build. Charles and his associates had in fact divided up the extra $3,000,000 among themselves.[1]

The great expense of the North Side cable lines may have been *in part* due to the numerous obstacles encountered during construction. The Board of Education President Allan Story, a slightly shady lawyer, threw up one of these roadblocks. Ever since 1870, when he had attempted to revoke the South Side company's charter, Story had made a career out of attacking the street railways. In June 1886 he learned that Charles's North Chicago Street Railroad Company planned to lay a cable alongside his valuable Clark Street property. Fearful of declining property values, Story vowed to fight Charles and his firm. "A cable shall not go by my eighty feet until the Supreme Court says it is all right," the attorney declared. "My neighbors and myself will fight every inch." It was not an idle threat. Conducting an eight-month-long guerrilla war against the North Side cable, Story stubbornly refused to accept defeat. Rebuffed in one court, he simply jumped to another. Story employed some rather novel arguments to support his case. "Why, your honor," the lawyer told federal Judge Walter Q. Gresham at one point, "the soil over there [on the North Side] is largely quicksand, and the trains running there every two minutes will jar down the buildings." An unconvinced Gresham put an end to Story's quixotic battle.[2]

The attorney's legal assault represented only one of the many challenges Charles confronted while building the cable. The financier had to oversee what he called "one of the most intricate and difficult pieces of engineering in the railroad construction of the world." Some 56,000 feet of cable had to be laid underground in specially built steel tubes (known as conduits) that were themselves anchored in place by massive 400-pound iron yokes and encased in a bed of concrete. An intricate network of pulleys and wheels had to be installed in order to link the separate cable lines and "make the road continuous." Finally, power plants had to be constructed and equipped with immense steam engines and boilers. The planning of such a system demanded great precision. "Everything must be exactly fitted in the first place, and so constructed as not to be liable to get out of order," an expert asserted. "The entire structure, in fact, must be like clockwork."

The gears almost failed to mesh in the central business district where the two-mile-long cable loop was laid. A gas main, a water main, and a sewer blocked the line's intended route at one corner. The gas main and the sewer were easily relocated, but the water main posed a bigger problem. The city engineer Samuel Artingstall told Charles that to move the main would require the shutting down of Chicago's water works for an entire day, "a feat that could not be safely tried." This critical main happened to connect the North and West Side pumping stations. "But it must be done," Charles said to Artingstall. "If it isn't done, then all my work up to the present time goes for naught." For three weeks the city engineer pondered the puzzle, but could not come up with a solution. The financier, however, did devise one. He employed an entire foundry to manufacture a large number of curved metal bars. These curves were then rigged up in a way that diverted the water main out of the cable's path. The foundry workers received a princely sum for their efforts. "I had to have those curves," Charles later explained, "and expense was a consideration that did not enter into my mind."[3]

On March 26, 1888, after one-and-a-half years of hard labor and frustrating delay, the North Chicago Street Railroad Company opened its cable lines for service. A large number of prominent people gathered inside the newly renovated powerhouse on the corner of Clark and Elm to witness the beginning of a transportation revolution. "Aldermen and county officials elbowed corporation lawyers and preachers," a reporter noted of the crowd. Johnny Hand's band "doled out popular airs" near the four gleaming Corliss engines looming silently in the background. American flags, tropical plants, and brilliant flowers added a bit of color to what would otherwise have been a drab scene.

At 11:15 A.M. Charles entered the building, accompanied by a train of dignitaries, including Mayor John Roche, Carter Harrison's successor. The financier's appearance earned him a rare "burst of applause. Standing behind a table decorated with lilies and roses, Roche, William Hale Thompson, the father of a future mayor, and Charles B. Holmes, the South Side cablecar king, all delivered short speeches. Holmes recalled the "agony and sweat" he had also endured while building his cable line, and expressed the hope that Charles's difficulties were now behind him. "Just as sunlight comes after the storm, so may success come to our friends who have completed this great work which you see around you," Holmes stated.

Dressed in a tight-fitting frock coat, Charles then stepped up to address the crowd. "It is now in order for me to say something," he began, "but after the speeches which you have heard I find that there is nothing left for me to say. The previous speakers got hold of my notes and I am practically left out." The businessman thanked his employees, the North Siders for their "patience," the city officials for their aid, and, in a sarcastic jibe, the press for their "uniform kindness." "They have always been on our side," he joked bitterly.

Following an orchestral interlude, Charles rapped a gong two times, and Andrew Whitton, the road's chief engineer, then turned a valve connected to the boilers. With a whoosh of steam, the enormous engines' "great wheels and polished pistons" started to move. The audience members cheered, and swarmed outside to see if the cablecars had sprung into life. "They rushed and crushed onto the sidewalk and then into the street," a journalist reported. The cablecars, however, were nowhere in evidence. They were then located about two miles north at the streetcar company's so-called limits barn and required twenty minutes to reach the 2,000 or so people lined up along Elm Street on that raw, windy day. Once the first car arrived, every one of these shivering spectators, it appeared, made a mad dash to board it. "It seemed to be a positive mania with many of the people present to ride on the first car," an amused observer noted, "and they fought and struggled for the chance in a way that would have done credit to a prize fighter in training."

The first cablecar—Number 402—and the nine more behind it filled up with passengers so quickly that even Charles could not obtain a seat.

When Number 402 returned from its trip through the business center, the financier finally got a chance to ride on his new loop cable system. Proudly poised on the car's front platform, he beamed at the throngs clustered along the streets. The vehicle traveled south on Clark Street for a few blocks before switching onto LaSalle, where it immediately began to descend into the tunnel. As Charles had promised, the tunnel had been completely renovated and now sparkled under the brilliant glare of electric arc lights. The businessman's fellow passengers may not have noticed the changes. "The plunge into the tunnel caused many to shudder," a reporter noted, "and when the light of day from the south end made its appearance the crowd heaved a sigh of relief."[4]

As car 402 exited the tunnel, Chicago's financial district emerged into spectacular view, punctuated by the "black, grave, monolithic" Board of Trade building at the foot of LaSalle Street. Charles must have noticed how dramatically the cityscape had been transformed since his 1881 arrival. Isolated five- and six-story edifices had given way to concrete canyons, "solid rows of ten-story powerhouses, blocklike, not towerlike, in appearance." Turning onto Monroe Street, the cablecar passed the Montauk Block, the building that launched the era of the skyscraper. The celebrated architects Daniel Hudson Burnham and John Wellborn Root erected this structure on a revolutionary "floating raft" foundation—an innovation that made it possible to construct tall edifices even on Chicago's sandy, shifting soil.

Heading onto bustling Dearborn Street, the car slowly threaded through a maze of pedestrians and horse-drawn wagons. "The city is fearfully busy at all of its downtown corners," a tourist complained. "New Yorkers shudder at Thirty-fourth street and Broadway. Inside the Chicago loop are several dozen Thirty-fourth streets and Broadways."[5] While riding along Dearborn, Charles may have noticed the headquarters of the *Chicago Tribune* and the *Daily Inter Ocean*. One day he would own the latter newspaper.

Car 402 rounded the corner onto Randolph and then returned to LaSalle for a final trip through the tunnel. The entire circuit of the downtown area had taken only about seventeen minutes, but the trip could have been even quicker. The cables crossed each other several times just north of the tunnel. At this bottleneck, the car driver had to release the grip in order to avoid snagging an intersecting cable. Once past the obstruction, he had to again take hold of the cable. Unfortunately, only one out of every four cars successfully performed this "jump" over the crossing cable. The rest had to be pulled past the obstacle by a team of horses. On the line's inaugural day, a horse hitched to a still-moving cablecar panicked and stampeded into the crowd, knocking six men into the mud and slush.

This opening day mishap foreshadowed future disaster. Attempting to keep costs down, Kemble, Widener, and Elkins opted to use a grip they had already employed without success in Philadelphia. The appropriately named Low and Grim grip did not easily release the cable and in fact was, according to one expert, "as unyielding as a vise."[6] Charles's Philadelphia partners also tried to get by with a cheap cable. Even a quality cable would have had a tough time surviving on the Chicago loop system. The many sharp curves, the steep tunnel approaches, the Low and Grim grip, and the heavy traffic all wreaked havoc on the cable. "The destruction of the tunnel cable is something startling," a newspaper stated. "In the loop is 12,500 feet of cable. Taking thirty days as the average life of the cable, this means the grinding up of over four hundred feet each day."

The cable frequently ended its short life in dramatic fashion, fraying severely during rush hour and thereby forcing the temporary shutdown of the entire loop system. Delays on the North Side road became such a common occurrence that Henry Fuller referred to them in his 1893 novel *The Cliff-Dwellers.* "Something was the matter with the cable and they kept us in the tunnel nearly twenty minutes," a character complains in the book. "As I tell Ann, you can always count on that sort of thing when you've got anything of real importance on hand and not much time for it."

Even worse than the delays were the numerous accidents. As the cable frayed during heavy use, the strands sometimes wound around the grip, making it impossible for the driver to stop the car: "Instead of the grip having hold of the cable the cable now has hold of the grip." On July 1, 1888, a vehicle impaired in this manner plowed into another cablecar, injuring two women.[7] Many other accidents happened because of the drivers' inexperience in operating the cars. Passengers in a hurry also contributed to the problem by boarding and exiting moving vehicles. "A ride on one of Yerkes' street-car systems that is not interrupted by a fatality, an accident or a delay constitutes an event," the newspaper columnist Eugene Field quipped.

Charles deserved a good deal of the blame for his cable system's faults. He had conceived the network in its broad outlines. "I had the whole cable system mapped out in my mind before ever a stroke of work was done on it," the financier once boasted. Charles was a big idea man, and he left the details to his subordinates. But the financier's cable plan was badly flawed, requiring numerous sharp curves. "Curves are the bane of cable construction," a popular streetcar manual later warned. "Their first cost is enormous; they consume power, materially shorten the life of the rope, and are a source of endless care and anxiety to the management." The magnate had never laid out a cable line before and it showed.

Possessed of an indomitable will, the businessman never gave up on his cable scheme. "People made fun of him and thought the cable was all a myth, but he made it work," a North Sider said of Charles in 1927. The financier put in overtime to make the system work. "You might see his dog-cart bowling down Michigan avenue before clerks were out of bed, and see it returning often late at night," a local broker noted.

Charles installed a thicker, more durable cable, and adopted a modified switching arrangement north of the tunnel. He set up a network of electric signals that enabled the conductor of a car to communicate instantly with the powerhouse engineer miles away. If a strand wrapped around the grip, for example, the conductor could now order the engineer to stop the cable and thus avert a potential accident. Charles outfitted the cars with improved brakes as another precaution.

Some of these modifications did not work in quite the way intended. "In remedying one trouble . . . it often occurred that another was created," Charles remembered.[8] When the press and public demanded that the cars be heated in the winter, the magnate responded by equipping the vehicles with "double back action car warmers." These devices, though, had a nasty tendency to explode. The *Daily News* began referring to Charles as a "Jonah." "As everybody knows, a Jonah is a well-meaning person who brings bad luck trailing along after [him] and sheds misfortune on everybody and everything as a cat sheds hairs," the *News* explained. "Let one of these persons walk into a room and instantly everything breakable wakens up and is all alive and eager for the chance to smash itself."[9]

———————

The building of the cable lines marked only the first step in a full-scale campaign to develop the surrounding territory. The cable routes extended for miles north of Chicago into the adjoining Lake View Township, a sparsely populated area "given over to cemeteries and celery farms." Hoping to encourage Lake View's growth, Charles teamed up with Samuel Eberly Gross, a prominent local real estate developer. Gross would later gain his fifteen minutes of international fame when he sued Edmond Rostand, charging that the French author's popular play *Cyrano de Bergerac* was a plagiarized version of his own work *The Merchant Prince of Cornville*. Though no Edmond Rostand, the Chicago real estate man did have a flair for words, and he employed this talent with great effect in his advertising circulars. He specialized in the construction of affordable suburban homes for the working class—a group largely ignored by local realtors. Gross believed that suburban home ownership would foster in industrial workers "independence, self respect, better citizenship and stronger manhood."

Charles fully shared Gross's views. Having spent most of his career in Philadelphia, a city in which the majority of the population owned houses, the financier instinctively favored home ownership. He also championed suburban living as an antidote to urban congestion and crime. "In a crowded city the most desirable thing for the poorer classes is encouragement and opportunity to get out into the suburbs," Charles once asserted. The street railways provided this opportunity to escape from the city, and, as a result, they were one of the greatest promoters of suburban growth, "the advance agents to the spreading of the community." A newspaper explained how the streetcar gave birth to the suburb:

> First appear the street car lines, running out into the farming land on the outskirts of the residence district. Close behind are the city surveyors. Next the small board shanties of the real estate boomers and their agents spring up. Sidewalks, an occasional house or two, and some new streets laid out on the prairie grass appear. Then comes a saloon at each street intersection, and more houses. Afterward a drug store in every mile or two testifies to the growing population, and, if the houses become thick enough, grocery shops and meat markets also take up their locations along the car tracks. Then the lots beyond begin to sell fast and the homes spring up like magic all around, until both sides of the street in which the car tracks lie are lined with residences and places of business, and the city is there.[10]

A similar, if not quite identical, pattern unfolded in Lake View's Hamlin Park after Samuel Gross and Charles developed the area. Early in 1887 the financier purchased several dozen lots in the area and hired Gross to outfit the properties with streets, alleys, sidewalks, water pipes, and sewer pipes. Meanwhile, Charles obtained from the Lake View Board an ordinance permitting the North Side road to extend its horsecar lines past his new subdivision. According to a Hamlin Park resident, this streetcar extension initially "was not used for regular service, but merely to boom the realtors' subdivision." The ploy worked. At one point Gross reported selling thirty lots in only three weeks. Building suburbs gave Charles more than moral satisfaction. He reaped over $100,000 out of this real estate deal, and it was just one among many. Streetcars raised suburbs *and*, of course, property values. "Only let me know six weeks in advance where the City Railway intends building a cable line," a Chicago entrepreneur once remarked, "and I will make an independent fortune every time."[11]

Charles and his Philadelphia partners did not intend to limit their activities to the North Side. Their eventual goal was to buy up *all* of Chicago's streetcar lines and combine them into a united system. As early as the summer of 1886, Charles unsuccessfully attempted to secure control of the Chicago West Division Railway Company and its 100 miles of horsecar track. The largest, most populous, and poorest section of Chicago, the West Side also endured the worst transportation service in the city. The streetcar company's directors raked in immense profits and were not eager to change a system that worked—for them. "All they wanted was their dividends," a financial observer said of the Chicago West Division Railway directors, "and they didn't want to do anything to improve their lines because it would cost money, which they didn't want to pay out."

A reporter described the five directors as forming an "aggregation of gray heads and feeble bodies."[12] At age sixty-three, Joseph Russell Jones, the company's president, was the "youngster" in the group. When first approached by the financier in the summer of 1886, Jones refused to accept even $500 a share for his stock. Like Oliver Twist, he wanted more. "Mr. Jones and his associates in the directory of the road know when they have a good thing," a financial writer remarked, "and they are not anxious to relinquish it without extraordinary compensation."

One year after his first failed attempt Charles again went fishing for control of the West Side firm, now prepared to pay $650 for each of the 6,250 shares he needed. This time Jones was ready to make a deal. The negotiations, though, dragged on over a period of months, prolonged by Jones's insistence that the $4,000,000 be paid entirely in cash and in one lump sum. Charles's Philadelphia backers could not easily assemble such a huge amount at the time. They were then overextended financially, having expended millions of Anthony Drexel's money in the formation of the so-called Chicago Gas Trust and in other ventures. Making matters worse, Wall Street was then "in the midst of a scare that amounts almost to a panic." All too aware of these facts, Charles proposed to Jones that the $4,000,000 payment be made in four installments stretching over two years. To sweeten the deal, the financier promised to pay 35 percent yearly dividends on the one-half of stock remaining outside his control. Swayed by this remunerative offer, Jones and his fellow directors finally agreed to surrender control of their streetcar property.[13]

To carry out the terms of this transaction, Charles sought financial help from various moneyed Chicagoans. He and his Philadelphia associates had decided that "it would be politic to have a good-sized local party in the road to prevent hostility on the score of non-residence." The financier, however, found many influential local businessmen unwilling to render assistance. The banker Charles Hutchinson, for one, believed that the Philadelphians had paid far too much for the West Side company's stock.

Charles persisted in his efforts and finally landed the aid of four powerful local figures: the soap manufacturer Nathaniel K. Fairbank, George Pullman, Marshall Field, and Levi Leiter, Field's former partner. The streetcar magnate won over these men by appealing to their greed. He dangled before them the promise of free stock for every bond they purchased in the newly formed West Chicago Street Railroad Company. Seduced by this tantalizing offer, each member of the quartet bought $400,000 worth of bonds and received as a free bonus $400,000 of stock in the new company. Two of these fortunate fellows later sold the stock when it topped $200 per share and cleared $800,000 on "an investment of nothing."

Businessmen who had once doubted Charles's financial ability now reversed course. "They take off their hats to Mr. Yerkes now," a local broker asserted. But Field and Leiter would come to regret their decision to assist Charles at this "critical moment." "He is not a safe man," the ultracautious merchant prince would one day say of the financier, while Leiter would become perhaps Charles's fiercest business opponent.[14]

Joseph Russell Jones was at least happy with the deal's outcome. He sold for $4,000,000 the control of a road that had cost him only $300,000 in 1863. Jones personally netted $1,800,000 out of this transaction, and could now afford to take it easy. "I hope to be able to go fishing, as I have not had a nibble in twenty-four years," he told a reporter. "The fact is, I want rest, and will try to get it."

While Jones's career had come to an end, the fifty-year-old Charles was just getting started. His greatest achievements lay ahead of him. He immediately began work to modernize the West Side street railway, following a plan nearly identical to the one employed on the North Side. A cable line was again laid through a renovated tunnel (the Washington Street tunnel), and the Philadelphians again practiced their financial magic. The profits were even greater this time. Charles and his partners issued $6,000,000 of stock to cover both the road's purchase price and the cost of constructing the seventeen-mile-long cable line, reserving an additional $4,000,000 of stock for their personal benefit. The people of the West Side did not come up empty-handed either. They received the benefits of rapid transit, and could now travel by cable on two of their major thoroughfares—Madison Street and Milwaukee Avenue. "The starting of the cable was an event in the history of the West Side," a *Chicago Tribune* reporter declared on July 16, 1890, the day of the Madison Street line's debut.

By 1888 Charles had moved significantly closer to his ultimate goal of a unified Chicago transportation network. "I have felt that in the future, when Chicago was built up, and when we get to be a great metropolis, and not a scattering, big country town, as it were, it will be necessary for all the street railroads to be combined under one head," he later confessed.[15] The magnate now controlled the North and West Side streetcar lines—a network of over 150 miles of track, and nearly 1,000 employees. Many of these employees, however, were less than satisfied with their working conditions and they soon intended to rectify the situation—one way or another.

13 *Strike!*

In 1886 the young Norwegian writer Knut Hamsun roamed Chicago's streets for two weeks in search of employment, finally joining a crew of 500 railroad laborers. It was "punishing work," Hamsun told a friend: "Three men to carry an iron rail weighing 1200 pounds; one man to carry a barrel of cement weighing 400 pounds; likewise a barrel of screws, 450 pounds; the cement is the worst—it gets in my eyes. And the heat! It's been up to 100 degrees F in the shade. We work half-naked." Hamsun's misery soon came to an end. He was promised a position as a cablecar conductor on the South Side's Chicago City Railway. "This is a job with a future," Hamsun wrote excitedly. "It's a question of keeping in with the right man. I hope I can do it. There are hundreds of people after jobs like this, but I have the Superintendent's own word for it that I will get the job—he's made a note of my name—whoopee!"

Hamsun quickly discovered that cablecar work did not offer quite the "brilliant future" he had expected. Like other newly hired conductors and drivers, he started out as a "reserve" taking the place of absent or sick "regular" employees. In one month Hamsun received a promotion, gaining a place on a so-called set car. These cars operated only during the early morning and late evening hours—a staggered schedule that seriously disrupted an employee's daily routine. "This is the hardest part of the work," an observer noted, "and it is said but few men can stand it long, owing to the broken rest and the irregular meal times." Rising up in the ranks, Hamsun rapidly attained a spot on a much-coveted "day car"—a "car which comes out in the morning and does its regular number of trips one after the other." The Norwegian soon grew bored collecting fares from passengers, and he escaped to Minneapolis, having persuaded Philip Armour to finance his journey.

Hamsun's place would have been immediately filled by some other eager job-seeker. Thousands vied for work on a streetcar line, even though the pay was not that good. "Every car barn is surrounded by men anxious to take a car out on one trip a day and earn enough to keep them alive and from freezing to death," the *Chicago Tribune* reported. Hamsun had initially hoped to push his salary above $100 a month, but in the end could not even afford warm clothing. While it was not the road to riches, employment on a cablecar did at least offer a certain amount of status. President Charles B. Holmes of the Chicago City Railway called his cablecar conductors "superior men" clothed "with a sort of official dignity and importance."[1]

They deserved Holmes's praise. Work on a cablecar was not easy. The drivers and conductors *never* received a day off, and they constantly endured the elements, perspiring in the summer and shivering in the winter. The last season was by far the worst time of year for the cablecar employees, who devised different strategies to combat Chicago's ferocious cold. "One man pins his faith on home-knitted stockings," a reporter asserted, "another believes in the heaviest of felt-lined articles, while a third declares that nothing keeps his warm like tissue paper wrapped round his feet and ankles." In the winter months Knut Hamsun wore a layer of newspaper next to his skin. "His fellow-workers thought this was highly amusing," Hamsun's biographer wrote, "and enjoyed making him crackle by poking him with their fingers." Most cablecar drivers opted to wear heavy fur coats that "made them look about twice normal size."

Bad weather was not the only hardship confronted by the cablecar workers. They also had to abide by a bewildering array of company regulations. In what was the most feared rule, an employee had to report for work *exactly* on time or face demotion. If a man arrived even one minute late, he would immediately lose his favored position as a "regular" and would be thrown down into the pool of "reserve" laborers. Needless to say, the workers dreaded this regulation and spared no effort to obey it. "I have seen the boys running to the barns in the morning half-dressed," a cablecar worker related. "Once I saw a driver in the winter rushing through the snow in his bare feet, his boots in his hands; yet, poor fellow, he was two minutes late after all." The exhausted driver collapsed onto the ground in tears. One man hurried to the car barn despite the entreaties of his ailing wife, and later returned home to find her dead. According to another perhaps apocryphal story, a cablecar driver was about to utter "I will" during a marriage ceremony when his eyes rested upon a clock—the time indicating he would be late for work. Donning his cap and coat and leaving his bride at the altar, the groom raced to the cable powerhouse; once there he remembered having secured a one-week leave of absence![2]

In 1888 the men on Charles's North Side cable system had even more reason for complaint than usual. Launched in March of that year, the cable service was from the beginning plagued by breakdowns and accidents. Between the opening day and September 1888 over fifty mishaps occurred on the cable lines, including several fatalities. The drivers, known as gripmen, unwillingly contributed to the problem as they struggled to adjust to the new technology. They had to learn through trial and error when to latch onto the moving cable and when to let go of it using the "grip." Their task was made more difficult—and hazardous—by the numerous sharp curves and cable crossings. "Yes," a driver confessed to a reporter, "the line is a dangerous one, and I never kiss my wife good-by in the morning without feeling that it may be the last time. The cable is a cheap one and the curves are badly arranged by the engineers so that we are always looking out for trouble." The flawed cable posed a financial as well as a physical threat to the North Side men. The drivers and conductors were paid for every *trip* they completed, but because of the frequent delays they were now making far fewer trips each day than when the horsecars ran. Stirred into discontent by the malfunctioning cable, Charles's North Side employees began to openly contemplate the idea of a strike.

The 530 men of the North Chicago Street Railroad Company could never have considered such a possibility had they not belonged to the Knights of Labor. Founded nineteen years before as a secret organization, the Knights sought to better the lot of workers through education, beneficial legislation, and cooperatives. After staging a successful strike against the notorious railroad tycoon Jay Gould in 1885, the union mushroomed in size, growing from around 100,000 members to over 700,000. The Knights united in a "great brotherhood" an astonishingly diverse group of laborers—African Americans, Anglo-Americans, and immigrants —in what was "an historical moment of mutual recognition," according to one scholar. Alarmed by the growing power of the organization, employers counterattacked with lockouts, blacklists, yellow-dog (antiunion) contracts, and Pinkerton detectives.

As the Knights of Labor withered under this fierce onslaught, Terence Powderly, the group's national head, urged his members to tread carefully.[3] Powderly believed that strikes were futile and wasteful exercises. George Schilling, a Chicago leader of the Knights, vehemently disagreed.

"Is it not probable that should our order serve notice on the public that it has abandoned strikes every industrial baron and monopolistic tyrant will immediately 'put on the screws,'" the Chicagoan asked Powderly, "and if this comes to pass will it not force our members to join some other organization for their own protection?"

A cooper (barrel-maker) by trade, the German-born Schilling struggled his entire life to solve "the labor question." In his view, this problem first came to the forefront in America during the bloody strikes of 1877, when railroad workers fought federal troops. Schilling saw this event as marking a watershed in U.S. history. Before 1877 "the large mass of our people contented themselves with the belief that in this great and free Republic there was no room for real complaint," Schilling maintained. But in the wake of the great strikes Americans could no longer "thank God—with our former vanity—that we were not like other nations." Like Europe, the United States was splintering along class lines, and nowhere was this growing division more evident than in Chicago. "If revolution comes in this country Chicago will be its starting point," an Indianapolis editor wrote. "The extremes of wealth and poverty which are to be seen in Chicago are startling . . . It's but a step from Michigan boulevard to South Clark street, but what a gulf yawns between them."

Schilling hoped to avert the "cyclone of revolution" by organizing and educating workers. Described as a "faddist" by a rival labor leader, he termed himself at various points in his long career a "philosophical anarchist," an "individual socialist," and a "syndicalist." But at bottom he was simply a free-trade Democrat. A "man with a heart big enough for all Chicago," Schilling bravely battled to save the lives of the seven men unjustly convicted in the Haymarket trial. When three of the prisoners were executed on November 11, 1887, he did not give up his efforts in behalf of the surviving men.[4] Schilling never lost his faith in the political process and its capacity to deliver change. He realized, however, that workers sometimes had to take matters into their own hands. Believing that such a time had arrived, Schilling encouraged Charles's North Side employees to strike if their grievances were not met.

On July 21, 1888, a committee of streetcar men approached the magnate with requests for higher wages and an hourly rate of pay. Perhaps most important, the workers also demanded an end to the hated "set-car" system. "Gentlemen," Charles coolly answered his employees, "Rome was not built in a day, and it takes time to perfect a cable system. I am willing to admit that our road is not perfect. I am aware that its present defects are working to your disadvantage. But, gentlemen, think of the strain that is placed upon me, held, as I am, responsible by the stockholders, cursed by my patrons, and hounded by the newspapers. I suggest that this is not the proper time for you to ask for an increase of wages." The magnate went on to say that he could even consider making any "concessions" until the Lincoln Avenue cable line was completed, which he believed would be in two months. Only then would he be willing to discuss changing the time-table to "make the work as easy as possible." The committee withdrew, resolved to return in September.[5]

Giving the financier a "few days' grace," the union men met Charles again on September 23 and presented him with a series of specific demands. With wages then averaging nineteen cent cents an hour, "the most miserly of any road," cablecar drivers and conductors sought an increase to 27 cents an hour while horsecar drivers and conductors asked for twenty-one cents an hour. Again insisting on an hourly rate of pay and an end to the "set-car" schedule, the committee members also called for a seniority system, maximum hours, and nondiscriminatory treatment of union members.

Charles responded by reiterating his earlier position, telling the men that "the matter could not be taken up" until the "road is in proper running order." Not budging on the crucial question of wages, he said that the workers had signed contracts clearly specifying the rate of pay; they had, in effect, agreed to this rate and could not therefore expect an increase. Obtaining no concessions, this committee was followed by others equally unsuccessful. A member of one of these committees described Charles's slippery method of diplomacy:

> Mr. Yerkes would talk as nice as could be. He would say a thing one minute and we would be sure that we were coming out all right. Then he would talk all around it, and end by saying that the company could not for a moment entertain any such proposition. Some one of the committee would bristle up, and Mr. Yerkes would make a slight concession, then take it back again.[6]

A strike was inevitable. Charles never intended to meet his men's demands. He expected total obedience from his employees, and could not stomach "disloyalty" of any sort. Perhaps more important, the magnate did not like unions and wanted nothing to do with them. "Sooner than allow my company to be dictated to by a crowd of men under the leadership of Socialists and Anarchists I will discharge every one on the road," he would say. "I will not tolerate any union among the men, and every one who joins any labor association will be minus his job." Charles hated unions in part because their inherent collectivism offended his individualistic instincts. "After a man has once joined the organization he loses all freedom of either thought or speech," he claimed, "and is only allowed to do and say what his leaders dictate." But Charles especially loathed unions because they posed a strong challenge to his authority.

On October 3, 1888, the North Side streetcar men threw down the gauntlet. Meeting in a cramped hall, the 500 union members debated until 4:00 A.M. before unanimously resolving to strike immediately. George Schilling, however, advised the men to go slow—counsel that was greeted with shouts of "No more time!" and "Let us strike now!" The Knights leader continued to speak, arguing that the men were required by contract to give the streetcar company three days' notice before leaving work. His voice rising with passion, Schilling begged his hearers to postpone the strike until October 6, until the three days had elapsed. This delay, he declared, would show the public that the streetcar men were "wholly and absolutely in the right" and would provide "evidence that the strike was the fruit of a mature and honest purpose, diligently and carefully considered in advance." Schilling's stirring speech convinced the union to put off striking until October 6.

Schilling recognized that public sentiment had to be taken into account in a strike such as this—one that could tie up for weeks a mode of transit used daily by tens of thousands. The strike, in fact, probably could not be won without public support. But Schilling's call for delay also helped Charles, who was given extra time to organize against his men. Determined to break the union, the magnate imported drivers from Kansas City and Philadelphia, attracting them with the promise of a free ride to Chicago, high wages, and room and board. He also hired Mooney and Boland Company detectives to guard his North Side firm's property.[7] Charles was girding for battle.

At 6:00 A.M. on Saturday, October 6, the conflict began. The North Side streetcar men shut down a transit system of 1,800 horses, 400 cars, and nearly seventy miles of track. Beautiful and balmy, the first day of the strike passed quietly. Striking employees played baseball under the lengthening shadows of the autumn sun. Apparently enjoying the novelty of the event, North Side commuters meanwhile traveled on foot or in various makeshift vehicles pressed into service by horse-owning entrepreneurs: "little wagons and big wagons, long wagons and short wagons, high wagons and low wagons, aristocratic phaetons, high-strung cabs, plebeian buses, and ramshackle express wagons."

A majority of the public initially sided with the strikers in their fight. Partly influenced by the anti-Yerkes press, the North Side people blamed the financier for the cable mishaps and were eager to lash out against him in any way. At a rally speakers vented their fury, with one participant even likening Charles to a feudal lord. "In olden times there existed on the banks of the Rhine a race of petty tyrants termed barons," this person declared. "Their creed was robbery, their instinct was greed, and their acts were the acts of mean, despicable, overbearing tyrants. On the northern banks of the Chicago River we have a similar set of barons. They hail from Philadelphia, and instead of each one of them plundering on his own hook they have pooled their issues, and call themselves a syndicate under the leadership of the great, the only Baron Yerkes." Even conservative property owners joined the mass protest, but not out of any sympathy for the cause of labor. "The long suffering of the people at the hands of a grasping and soulless corporation is the cause of this feeling," the *Real Estate and Building Journal* maintained.

Children also got into the act. Young artists "decorated" the North Side car barns with crude caricatures of Charles drawn in chalk. Not knowing how the financier really looked, the youths depicted him in various unflattering guises. "Gigantic donkeys' heads, pigs' heads, and bulls' heads were sketched in strokes both bold and free and all bore inscriptions under them," a reporter noted. A few of the legends read: "Yerkes & Co., importers of scabs," "Yerkes the Philadelphia Snipe," and "He wants the earth." One somewhat sinister drawing depicted a stick figure labeled "Yerks" hanging from a scaffold.[8]

These attacks cut Charles deeply. Before the strike the magnate had believed the public discontent was simply the creation of a scandal-mongering press. He now knew better. The bad cable service had robbed him of community backing—a fact underlined by the widespread support for the strikers. Charles feigned unconcern for his deteriorating public image. "The multitude does not know me," he once said. "My friends do know me and I do know my friends. Therefore, the good opinion of my friends seems to be the thing best worthwhile." But, being an intensely proud man, he did in fact desire the praise of the "multitude."

Charles also liked to win, and he was determined to defeat his employees. On Monday, October 8, the magnate declared war on the strikers, sending out horsecars on two North Side lines. Protected by half of the Chicago police force, the cars slowly threaded through surging throngs crying "Scab!" and "Tramp!" "The new drivers were nervous and frightened," a journalist observed. "Every small boy yelled some taunt at them. Though a policeman stood on each side of them and an officer sat in the outer end of each seat the excited crowds made the job something of a terror." Charles sent out the cars merely to show his resolve; few commuters had the desire—or the nerve—to board the vehicles.

At one point a policeman took the place of a frightened driver who deserted his car. Schilling and his fellow Knights thought this officer was going far beyond the call of duty, and they made their feelings known to Republican Mayor John Roche. The forty-four-year-old walrus-mustached Roche had squeaked into the mayor's office one year before, thanks to a division in the local Democratic Party. A mechanically minded man, the Massachusetts native sold steam engines before entering politics, and even received a patent for designing an improved band saw. Possessing the objectivity of an engineer, Roche looked at problems with a cold and rational eye. After listening to Schilling's complaint, the mayor issued an order barring policemen from running the cars. In response to another union grievance, Roche persuaded Charles to dismiss the 150 Mooney and Boland detectives, who, "with blue and brass livery and insolent mien," posed a threat to the peace.[9] The mayor conceived of himself as an impartial representative of the broad public interest. Peace, above all, was his goal.

Acting as a mediator, Roche presided over a late evening conference between Charles and a union committee on October 8 in the mayor's office. Finally conceding an hourly wage, the magnate also agreed to increase the men's pay to twenty cents an hour on the horsecars and to twenty-two and three-quarters cents an hour on the cablecars. The committee submitted Charles's proposals to George Schilling, who sat in an adjoining room. The labor leader advised the men to demand a minimum of twenty-five cents an hour for cablecar work. Charles would not accept this wage increase, and the conference broke up at 1:00 A.M. with nothing resolved.

Learning of this failed meeting, the 1,300 employees of Charles's West Chicago Street Railroad Company voted to widen the strike. They had pledged their support for the North Side men in July. The West Siders were not acting entirely out of a sense of altruism. They went on strike in order to head off expected wage cuts. "The manner of Yerkes in dealing with the North-Siders left no option for the West Side men but to go out," Luke Coyne, the leader of the West Side streetcar union, explained. "It was apparent that he would not continue to pay his West Side men more wages than he was paying on the North Side, and that when the West Side system was changed to cables the men would be paid the same as the North Side men, which was 10 cents per hour less than the South Side grip men are paid."[10]

At 3:00 A.M. on October 9 a carriage thundered down Michigan Avenue, coming to an abrupt stop at Charles's South Side mansion. Out stepped a West Side streetcar man bearing an ultimatum from his union. A detective standing on the mansion's porch relayed the message to a man inside, who passed it on to the weary magnate.

"I'll answer it when I get downtown," was the response that filtered back from the financier's bedroom.

"Tell him he must answer it by 4 o'clock," the West Side union man instructed the detective.

"Not much," Charles bluntly responded.

"Then we'll strike," the visitor warned.

"Let 'em strike!" the magnate growled. And so they did.

Enormous in extent, the West Side streetcar system contained 4,200 horses, 1,000 cars, and 100 miles of track. The strikers brought that system to a crashing halt. On the first day of the West Side strike only three horsecars managed to complete a round-trip on Madison Street despite being escorted by police patrol wagons. Hurling stones, large raucous crowds swarmed around the horsecars and blocked their movement. The situation appeared to be getting out of control, especially when a company superintendent aboard one of the cars whipped out a revolver. Just as the superintendent began menacing the crowd with his weapon, a police lieutenant grabbed him by the throat. "Put up that gun," the officer shouted. "You damn fool, what do you mean?" "I mean to defend myself," the superintendent roared in response. "I've been hit with enough rocks for one day. This thing has gone far enough and I ain't going to stand it any longer."[11]

Violence escalated on the second day of the West Side strike. "Madison street as far down as Oakley avenue was then fairly packed by an excitable throng, with mouths full of curses and epithets and hands loaded with all kinds of missiles," a reporter asserted. One "flying brick" hit a police captain in the head, causing blood to stream down his face. "If this crowd wants to fight the Chicago police I want it to say so and begin," another officer subsequently warned the bystanders. "If it doesn't want to fight it had better behave itself or somebody will get a broken head." Also that day, enraged strikers surrounded two union members who had operated cars the previous morning. Taking out guns, the besieged pair fired into the crowd without injuring anyone.

Though calling the disturbances "trivial affairs," Schilling worried about their effect on public opinion. "I am perfectly satisfied that we will win the strike if nothing occurs that will shock the public conscience," the labor organizer wrote the *Daily News*. "Our great danger lies in scenes of violence. I am informed that Mr. Yerkes has been expecting and secretly wishing for it so that he might be justified in calling out the state militia and, if need be, the United States army." Determined to avert trouble, Schilling instructed the North Side union's leaders to "bend every energy to hold your men in line and avoid scenes of violence."[12]

Desperate to force Charles's hand, Schilling considered expanding the war to other fronts. He contemplated an extension of the strike to Pittsburgh, Philadelphia, and New York—places where Kemble, Widener, and Elkins also controlled cable lines. Traveling to Pittsburgh, Schilling met James Magee, a Knights of Labor official who had organized the streetcar workers in all three cities. The latter figure promised the support of his men. "All we needed then to do was to give the word," Magee recalled. "It would have been a labor movement of vast magnitude—opened with spirit and reached with determination." But the movement was never launched. Charles struck first.

The magnate had already attempted to make Schilling the issue in the strike. "From what I have lately discovered I am satisfied that George Schilling is at the bottom of all this trouble," Charles told a reporter on October 7. "I need not tell the people of Chicago who George Schilling is. He has been mixed up in every labor trouble in this city for a number of years. He has been mixed up in all the Stock-Yards strikes, in the West Side strike, in the brewers' strike, and he had to sail close to the wind to keep clear of implication in the Anarchist troubles." The financier intended to portray Schilling in a sinister light, as an "avowed Anarchist" leading the streetcar men astray.[13]

Edmund Furthmann, one of Charles's many attorneys, most likely suggested this strategy. Furthmann had played a major role in the Haymarket case, serving as the assistant prosecutor. Said to be "more of a detective than a lawyer," he worked closely with police Captain Michael Schaack in rounding up suspects, using methods "that would put to shame the most zealous Russian blood-hound." Furthmann and Schaack were fanatical foes of what they believed was a worldwide anarchist conspiracy. "Nothing but the uprooting of the very foundations and groundwork of our civilization will satisfy these enemies of order," Schaack wrote in his sensational 1889 book *Anarchy and Anarchists*. "Their fight is to the death. They will neither take nor give quarter. Are we prepared, or are we preparing for the shock?"

The North Side streetcar men were not prepared for the shock that occurred on October 11. That day the police arrested a union man for placing railroad torpedoes on a streetcar rail. Emitting a loud noise when struck by a train's wheels, torpedoes were used to signal the engineer and were harmless. Captain Schaack, however, claimed that the torpedoes were nothing less than dynamite. The police officer fancied himself an expert on the subject, having once conducted tests of explosives discovered in the home of Louis Lingg, a Haymarket defendant. "Lingg's bomb, which did all the mischief at the Haymarket riot was not more powerful than these four torpedoes," Schaack alleged. "There was enough to have blown the car to splinters."

The press gullibly swallowed Schaack's story, even though the police captain was known to be in open collaboration with Furthmann. "DYNA-MITE FOUND," the *Chicago Mail* screamed, hysteria that was echoed in other newspapers.[14] The miraculous transformation of four innocuous railroad torpedoes into bombs adversely affected public perception of the strike, lending credibility to Charles's assertion that anarchists were influencing his employees. The financier had shrewdly played the Haymarket card.

With their efforts literally torpedoed, the strikers began to lose support. Taking a more active stance in behalf of Yerkes, Police Chief Hubbard ordered all vehicles off Madison Street, except for the horsecars. Even the heretofore impartial Mayor Roche now openly condemned what he called the "nonsense and unreasonable demands" of the union men. As the strike crumbled, a group of influential West Side citizens intervened, meeting with Charles and the strikers' committees in the mayor's office. The magnate immediately made it known that he did not welcome this outside interference. "Well, really, I shouldn't like to settle difficulties with my men before a town meeting," he said to the leader of the citizens' group. This conference, though, helped end the four-day-old West Side strike. Luke Coyne's men managed to extract from Charles a guarantee not to reduce wages for five years.[15]

Despite diminishing odds of success, the North Side streetcar workers continued their fight. Service in that division of the city was gradually returning to normal, Charles having hired 201 men to replace the strikers. The Chicago police force greatly aided the magnate in his strike-breaking tactics. The financier grew accustomed to this assistance—perhaps too accustomed. When at one point he found an "inadequate" number of policemen guarding his cars, Charles loudly complained to the mayor. Weary of the magnate's incessant demands, Mayor Roche responded angrily:

> I am in receipt of yours of this date, and regret to say that I do not like your attitude in reference to the police force. The newspapers are constantly stating, as coming from you, in interviews, that you are not receiving police protection. I deny this most emphatically. If you are unable to run cars for want of conductors it is not the fault of the city or the police department. You certainly have had an opportunity for the past two days to run a much larger number of cars than you have put on.

In a postscript to this letter, Roche hastened to add: "The chief of police reports that he ordered a sufficient force for all the cars you desired to protect on the North Side. If any were withdrawn it was only temporarily, because of a misunderstanding. They are there now." Charles obviously intimidated the mayor. A participant at one strikers' conference recalled Roche hanging his head "as if afraid of his life" when the magnate entered the room.[16]

The mayor was more afraid of the strike's possible effects on his political career. On October 14—a crisp and sunny day—Roche dragged the warring parties back to the bargaining table. Meeting in Charles's office at 444 North Clark Street, the union men found themselves at a distinct disadvantage. They were on the magnate's home turf, and, more important, they did not have the assistance of George Schilling. Charles had refused to negotiate in Schilling's presence. But Mayor Roche promised to aid the men. "I assure you that Mr. Yerkes shall not have the slightest advantage on account of his superior knowledge," he told the committee members.

The conference got off to a bad start. In addition to demanding a wage hike, the union men wanted Charles to pledge to take back his old employees. The magnate, though, refused to fire the 201 replacement workers he had hired. As the talks appeared on the verge of collapse, Mayor Roche, fatigued from a lack of sleep, lost control of his temper. Pounding his fist on Charles's desk, he chastised the men for their unwillingness to accept the new hires. "You know as well as I do that when operations are resumed that the sifting-out process will begin, and that the old rule, 'the survival of the fittest,' will control you all," Roche declared to the streetcar workers. "The city of Chicago has some rights that neither railway employees nor railway corporations can ignore." The important question of the new hires was resolved unsatisfactorily, with Charles apparently agreeing to do the impossible: to employ both the old and new workers.

Roche next addressed the matter of wages. He pressed hard on the financier to increase his employees' pay. Charles thought he had already conceded enough. "I have agreed to take these men back, men for whom I have no use, men who have been a disturbing element in the company for years and who have cost the company thousands of dollars," he snarled. "I have agreed to revolutionize our methods and rules, and I ask if I ought to do more." Undeterred by Charles's objections, Roche kept up the pressure.

"I never yet saw a bargain that could be made with less than two," the mayor joked. "Now, men, you offer 8 per cent [increase in wages], and Mr. Yerkes meets you half-way. It is your turn to go half-way. Will you take 6 per cent?"

"I didn't say I'd give it," Charles muttered.

"Yes, we'll meet him half-way, and accept 6 per cent," the chairman of the strikers' committee answered.

"Then I'll meet you half-way and make it 5," the magnate said with a smile.

"Let me decide that for you," Roche countered.

"I know what your decision will be," Charles said. "I have raised to 5 per cent because it is a round number. If it wasn't, I wouldn't have raised."

"Make it 6 percent," the mayor begged, and then whispered something into the financier's left ear. At this critical juncture Roche received support from Frederick Winston, an attorney of Charles. Winston recommended that his client accept a 6 percent wage hike. The magnate reluctantly bowed to the advice of his lawyer.

"He gives 6 per cent, boys," the mayor announced jubilantly. Roche would not be so happy the following April when he lost the election—in part because he was seen as a "tool" of Yerkes.[17]

The strike was over. After eight days of bitter struggle, the North Side streetcar men had won most of their major demands: an hourly rate of pay, abolition of the "set-car" system, and higher wages. But it was a Pyrrhic victory. New workers had taken the place of nearly one-half of the 530 old employees. Charles was elated over his coup. "The men do not know not even now what the true agreement is," he crowed. "They do not know what they are doing. They are led by their leaders like a flock of sheep." Schilling, one of these leaders, berated the members of the strikers' committee for failing to follow orders. "I told those men not to be tricked into signing any agreement in Yerkes' or any other office," he explained. "I told them they should not conclude any agreement until they reported back to us and we had examined it. I was afraid Yerkes would fool the men; that he was too sharp for them. He tricked them and they are now to blame for the unfortunate conclusion of the strike."

Charles had broken the North Side streetcar union. The new men had signed yellow-dog contracts prohibiting union membership. The magnate subsequently undermined the West Side Driver's and Conductors' Association. Ten years after the strike, a City Council committee found no unions extant among Chicago's three major streetcar companies. Charles had succeeded in creating a docile workforce.

On October 27, 1888, a group of North Side residents approached the financier bearing advice and a petition. The men suggested among other things that an arbitration committee be set up to handle disputes between Charles and his employees. "Why, gentlemen, you are too modest," the magnate sarcastically answered his visitors. "There are some things you omitted to demand of me or to command me to do. One is to turn over the control of the North Side lines to your management. Do you expect me to pay any attention to such a ridiculous document?"[18] Ever since his prison experience, Charles had been obsessed by a need for control. In Chicago he attempted to create a safe environment completely under his command—an impregnable corporate fortress. But a worsening public profile threatened to thwart his ambitions. Charles would soon appeal to the heavens to help remake his image.

14 Reaching for the Stars

By 1892, Charles was one of the most powerful men in Chicago. Mayors, aldermen, judges, and ordinary Chicagoans alike all felt his influence. Outwardly symbolizing the magnate's might, his transit lines extended outward from the Loop in a dense web of iron rails fanning toward the north and west. Yet his vast empire was in peril. Recent newspaper stories exposed Charles's role in questionable real estate and stock transactions. These revelations threatened to deprive him of the financial means necessary to maintain his power. Charles had to do something dramatic to signal to the business world that he was someone who could be trusted with large sums of money. In short, he needed to demonstrate that he was a respectable figure and not an outlaw financier.

John D. Rockefeller had recently made a dramatic gesture of his own. Widely feared and hated because of his Standard Oil monopoly, Rockefeller had decided in 1889 to devote some of his millions to a worthy cause. He proposed to resurrect the defunct University of Chicago—which had closed three years earlier—with a $600,000 donation. But there was a big catch: He would only provide the money *if* the school's backers managed to raise an additional $400,000. This last sum was eventually secured, and Rockefeller, now firmly committed to the project, tossed in another million. He hoped that a big endowment would entice William Rainey Harper to head the university.

Short, bulky, and bespectacled, the thirty-four-year-old Harper did not look like "a man of force," but he was. A precocious child, he received his bachelor's degree at age fourteen, and his doctorate four years later. He taught Hebrew studies at Yale for five years before accepting the University of Chicago post. A driven man, Harper was in a hurry to build a world-class research institution in Chicago. "It seems a great pity to wait for growth when we might be born full-fledged," he wrote to Rockefeller in 1890. As part of his grand school-building strategy, Harper aggressively pursued renowned academics, wooing them with the promise of high salaries and low teaching loads. In one of his greatest coups, he captured almost half of Clark University's faculty, including Albert Michelson—the physicist who first accurately measured the speed of light.

Harper did not rely on Rockefeller's money alone to finance his ambitions. An expert salesman, the school president also persuaded many tight-fisted Chicago millionaires to cough up cash for the university.[1] Early in 1892 he targeted Sidney Kent and Charles as potential donors, possibly suspecting that the two businessmen were about to realize a fortune from a pending gas utility venture. Kent eventually succumbed, and agreed to fund a chemical laboratory for nearly $250,000. Kent's generous donation set a price standard for the university's buildings.

Compared to Charles, Kent was an easy conquest for the "captain of education." When Harper suggested that he bankroll a biology lab, the financier hemmed and hawed. At a New York meeting the persistent university chief lobbied a decidedly reluctant Charles. Stepping up his campaign, Harper enlisted the aid of Herman Kohlsaat, a newspaper publisher friend of Charles. Even Kohlsaat, though, could not wring from the financier a definite yes.[2] Another proposal, soon made by a young astronomer, would prove far more intriguing to Charles.

———

George Ellery Hale—the astronomer—dreamed of an observatory adequately equipped to study the sun, the center of his universe. "His sensitive mind, like a delicate musical instrument of many strings, responded to every contact with nature or the touch of poetry or music or art," a colleague said of Hale. For most of his twenty-four years the Chicago native had been responding to nature. At the age of five he began his scientific explorations, using a microscope to investigate the realm of the very small. "These were real adventures, as exciting as those I have had so often in later years," Hale recalled. "For I had made the discovery that simple instruments suffice to reveal new and wonderful worlds, hidden from the unaided eye." This "discovery" soon led to an interest in astronomy—the realm of the very large—and in telescopes. Hale, however, would never be content with what he termed "simple instruments." For the rest of his life he demanded ever-greater optical power to better disclose the wonders of the universe.

Even as a boy, Hale exhibited an eagerness to succeed. He may have been influenced by the example of his father William, who had built up in Chicago a profitable elevator-manufacturing business. According to the architect Louis Sullivan, William Hale was one of the two men "responsible for the modern office building." The elder Hale's elevators had made it possible for people to get around in the new skyscrapers. This man who helped lift the city skyline subsidized the future of the scientist who—more than any other—boosted the size of telescopes. William almost always reacted favorably to his son's frequent requests for scientific equipment.[3]

George Hale established himself as a figure of international note in 1889 when he invented the spectroheliograph. For years Hale had been a devotee of the so-called New Astronomy—the study of the physical nature of the sun, moon, and stars. The primary tool of this "new branch of astronomy" was the spectroscope, which for the first time showed the true chemical composition of the sun and stars. In the early 1880s Hale began studying the solar atmosphere with a spectroscope, and he was "completely carried off" his feet by the new device's power. Much to the intensely curious youth's dismay, however, certain important features of the sun could not be easily investigated: the solar prominences—bright filaments of gas visible only during total eclipses on the sun's limb. While riding in a South Side cablecar one summer day in 1889, Hale dreamt up a device for photographing the sun in a single wavelength of light—a device that permitted him to record the spectra of the mysterious prominences. This idea of the spectroheliograph, he remembered, "seemed to come straight from the blue."[4]

William Rainey Harper certainly respected Hale's achievements as an astronomer, but he also realized who the power was behind the dome. In 1891 William Hale had purchased for his son an observatory, complete with a powerful twelve-inch telescope (an instrument with a lens twelve inches in diameter). Greedily eyeing this Kenwood Observatory, Harper hoped to "annex" it to the University of Chicago. The school president offered Hale a teaching position in exchange for the observatory. This was too much for the proud scientist. "If I am not competent to obtain a place on my own merits at present, it will probably be best for me to wait until I shall have gained experience by future study," Hale indignantly wrote to Harper. A year later the astronomer and his father reconsidered their position. They agreed to accept Harper's proposal, but with one very long string attached. The University of Chicago had to build a new observatory costing not less than $250,000.[5] Hale wanted a bigger telescope for his solar studies, and he was willing to sacrifice his private observatory in order to realize that desire.

Not long after delivering his ultimatum to Harper, the astronomer learned that two forty-inch glass disks were gathering dust in the master optician Alvan G. Clark's Massachusetts workshop. Here was the chance of a lifetime! Clark specialized in the building of big telescopes. Most recently, he had ground the lenses for the great thirty-six-inch instrument at Lick Observatory—then the world's largest refractor. Intending to "lick the Lick," University of Southern California officials had ordered Clark to fashion the forty-inch disks into lenses. Unfortunately for them, the Californians ran short of funds before the optician even began to work on the glass blanks. When he heard this story, Hale inwardly rejoiced. Secretly deciding to capitalize on the California school's misfortune, he resolved to secure the disks for the University of Chicago.

Hale of course needed money—and lots of it—to seize the prize. The astronomer, "working like a slave," pounded the pavement for days, "begging" Chicago's rich men for funds. Discouraged by his lack of success, he finally sought the advice of the University Trustee Charles Hutchinson. "Why don't you try Mr. Yerkes?" Hutchinson suggested. "He has talked of the possibility of making some gift to the University, and might be attracted by the scheme." With Harper's approval, Hale sent the streetcar magnate a letter outlining the telescope project. The idea interested Charles, who arranged a meeting with the two academics. "The days of dreaming are passed," Harper wrote at about this time, "and now real action begins."[6]

On October 4, 1892—three days after the University of Chicago officially opened its doors—Harper and Hale met Charles in his "very unpretentious" office at 444 North Clark Street. Similar scenes had been enacted throughout history. Impoverished scholars have often sought the patronage of wealthy aristocrats. No less a figure than Galileo required the financial support of Cosimo II de' Medici, the grand duke of Tuscany. Only in this instance the scholars weren't so poor and the prospective patron wasn't an aristocrat. An inhabitant of the "modern Florence," Charles nonetheless conceived of himself as a latter-day Medici and tried to live like one. At that moment he was building in New York City a million-dollar mansion that, when complete, boasted a marble staircase, a conservatory, and a gallery full of European art treasures.

Harper and Hale shrewdly appealed to Charles's considerable ego in order to obtain his financial support for their project. This would not be just any telescope, the scholars argued; it would be the *world's largest telescope*. For a man who always desired the biggest and best of everything, this proposal naturally held allure. Hale suggested the outlines of his sales pitch in a letter that he sent to Harper the previous September:

The installation of such an instrument in the Observatory of the University of Chicago would immediately give it the first rank among the observatories of the world, and allow it to make most substantial contributions to the progress of astronomical science. It would become the Mecca of thousands of science-loving pilgrims, as the Lick Observatory, even in its isolated position, is to-day. And the donor could have no more enduring instrument. It is certain that Mr. Lick's name would not have been nearly so widely known were it not for the famous observatory established as the result of his munificence.

As an added incentive, Hale slyly hinted that the telescope mounting could be displayed at the upcoming Columbian Exposition, where it would attract a great deal of attention.[7]

Charles was swayed by these arguments. The financier realized that an observatory with his name on it would be one of the best advertisements in the world. He hoped the telescope would regain for him the respect of his fellow businessmen and help restore his credit. Charles also wanted to achieve notice in New York City—where his wife had transferred her social ambitions. And he certainly must have been tantalized by the possibility of achieving lasting fame. But why did he choose to fund an observatory and not a biology lab, for instance? Charles himself provided a possible answer to this question. During their October 4 conference, the magnate confessed to Hale that "he had dreamed since boyhood of the possibility of surpassing all existing telescopes." Hale had unknowingly tapped into Charles's memories of his Central High School days—memories closely associated with the inspirational astronomy teacher Ezra Otis Kendall.

The very delicate question of cost came up in the course of the meeting, and threatened to spoil Charles's reveries. Hale estimated that the telescope's lens and mounting could be had for $60,000, but he seems not to have mentioned the little matter of the observatory building—an item that would substantially increase the magnate's bill. Perhaps the astronomer simply assumed Charles would also bankroll the building. Or, more likely, he feared that the financier's knowledge of the total cost might doom the project. In any case, Charles indicated a willingness to go ahead with the telescope. Once safely outside the magnate's office, Harper gave vent to his true feelings. "I'd like to go on top of a hill and yell!" he exclaimed.

Before completely committing himself, Charles wanted to know whether Alvan G. Clark's firm could manage the painstaking task of grinding the forty-inch disks. Conferring with the optician on October 7, the magnate found Clark eager to accept the commission. Assured of

Clark's "genius," Charles agreed to fund the refractor. "Gentlemen, go ahead and build the finest telescope on earth and let it be equipped with everything that is needed to make it the best," he reportedly told the university officials. "When you have it all finished send the bill to me and I will pay it. Never mind the question of cost."[8]

Writing to a friend a few days later, Harper had nothing but praise for Charles. "The enterprise will cost Mr. Yerkes certainly half a million dollars," the school president asserted, apparently in the belief he'd been given a blank check. "He is red hot and does not hesitate on any particular. It is a great pleasure to do business with such a man." But when he discovered the true cost of the project, Charles did hesitate. While certainly prepared to pay for a telescope, he had never planned on funding an entire observatory building as well.

Unfortunately for the magnate (and fortunately for science), Harper's exaggerated notions soon found their way into the newspapers. Benefiting from a "little leak," the *Chicago Evening Post*'s New York correspondent first broke the story of the telescope on October 11, and a day later readers around the globe learned of Charles's "Princely Donation." Interviewed by a local journalist, Harper expressed regret that the news had been revealed prematurely, but was more than happy to report that "Mr. Yerkes has given us unlimited funds to draw upon." "It will be a grand affair, the finest observatory in the world," the captain of education declared. Hale, too, was outspoken in the presence of the press, telling a reporter that the entire project—observatory included—would cost something like $500,000. Thanks to comments like these, Charles was trapped into financing a complete observatory.

On December 5 the magnate informed Harper of his intentions concerning the telescope project:

> It was with much satisfaction I learned from you, that a lens for a large telescope could be purchased immediately; and I informed you that I would purchase the lens and have it finished; that I would also pay for the frame and mountings of the telescope, so that the two together would make a perfect telescope, to be the largest in the world . . . I have concluded to add to my gift, an observatory necessary to contain the instrument.

Reluctantly bowing to the inevitable, the financier finally agreed to give the telescope a "home."[9] Immortality did not come cheap.

Charles must have been delighted by the initial response to his "gift." The friendly *Daily Inter Ocean* outdid the other newspapers in its praise of Charles (and Sidney Kent). "What Lorenzo the Magnificent did for art in Florence, Kent and Yerkes, each in his own way, are doing for science in Chicago," the *Inter Ocean* puffed. News of the donation also may have temporarily bolstered the magnate's business standing, as he had hoped it would. According to Edwin Frost, a future director of the Yerkes Observatory, Charles suddenly "found that his credit was greatly strengthened, and that he could borrow all the money he needed for his business enterprises."[10]

The public response, however, was by no means unanimous. The *Chicago Times,* owned by the politically ambitious ex-Mayor Carter Harrison, refused to join in the chorus of praise. "The astronomical beneficence of Mr. Yerkes does not excuse his street railway's shortcomings any more than the educational liberality of Mr. Rockefeller justifies the methods of the Standard Oil Company," the *Times* roared. "It begins to look as if President Harper's success as a money raiser was due to his having shrewdly represented the Chicago university to divers men of wealth as a sort of conscience fund."

The criticism that hurt Charles the most came from his own wife. Having enormous sympathy for the underprivileged, Mary had wanted her husband to finance a great public hospital "where rich and poor, regardless of race or color, could be treated free of charge if without funds." "When he gave the big telescope and observatory to the University of Chicago I was disappointed that it was not a hospital," she would later recall, "and he promised me then that some time I should have my wish." Mary would not let the magnate forget his vow.

Charles reveled in his new reputation as a patron of science for only a short time. He believed that the University of Chicago scholars were out to rob him, and he soon saw in Hale's actions a confirmation of his suspicions. The astronomer had ordered the Pittsburgh optician John Brashear to construct three spectroscopes for the observatory—without bothering to inform Charles of the instruments' cost. Hale behaved so rashly because he was an impatient and impetuous man. "George always wanted things yesterday," William Hale once said of his son. Charles, though, did not see it that way. During a conference with Harper the magnate erupted in an outburst of anger, telling the university chief that he was "entirely out of patience" with Hale, who seemed "ready to ride a free horse to death." It took Harper almost two hours to calm the furious businessman.

The optician John Brashear unsuccessfully tried to explain to Charles the importance of spectroscopes for the modern science of astronomy. A discouraged Brashear later told Hale that "if you or some good spectroscopist like you does not have something to do with this work, I confess that I have no heart to make it for such a man as Yerkes, because he has absolutely no interest in its scientific value." Money was, of course, a

great deal more important to the financier than the abstractions of astronomy. Rejecting Brashear's price, Charles offered the optician $10,000 for
all three spectroscopes, only to be met with a firm rebuff. The magnate,
however, eventually managed to secure one of these instruments for
$3,000.[11]

The dispute between Charles and Hale went far deeper than the matter of money. They spoke a different language. Hale was "slight in figure,
agile in movement, of high-strung nervous temperament, overflowing
with formulae, technical facts and figures, theoretical speculations,
almost ad infinitum," a journalist noted. "His mind seems made of some
stellar substance which radiates astronomical information as a stove
sheds heat." Charles, on the other hand, understood astronomy merely on
a layman's level. For him, the science had little real value because of its
"uncommercial" nature. ("There is nothing of moneyed value to be
gained by the devotee to astronomy; there is nothing that he can sell," the
businessman once declared.) Residents of very different worlds, the passionate, pleasure-loving Charles and the reserved, bookish Hale also had
clashing personalities.[12]

Charles was becoming increasingly disenchanted with the telescope
scheme—and not just because of Hale. The financier wanted a site for the
observatory to be selected as soon as possible and in his view university
officials were not moving fast enough in the matter. He had a good reason
for this urgency. The telescope mounting could not be built until a location was found and the observatory's latitude determined. Charles hoped
that the mounting would be ready in time to be displayed at the Columbian Exposition, which was only six months away, so he demanded that a
site be chosen quickly.

Following the magnate's instructions, the University of Chicago's
board of trustees appointed a site selection committee on December 27,
1892. Harper and board President Martin Ryerson, the committee's only
members, were inundated with land offers. Civic boosters from as far away
as Pasadena, California, and as near as Morgan Park had seized this opportunity to put their towns on the map. Charles did not realize the magnitude of Harper's and Ryerson's task, and was clamoring for a decision.[13]

Worcester Warner and Ambrose Swasey were also impatient for a site
to be selected. The Cleveland iron founders had been hired to build the
mounting for the big telescope. They were, however, required by contract
to finish the job in time for the Exposition. In late March, with the Exposition only a little more than a month away, a worried Warner and Swasey
sent a note to Harper warning him that no further work on the mounting
could be done until the observatory's location was known. The Cleveland

men stressed the obvious point that Charles would be greatly disappointed if the mounting could not be exhibited at the Exposition. This argument was very persuasive to Harper, who already knew too well how unpleasant an angry Yerkes could be. On March 28 the observatory committee recommended a site in southern Wisconsin.

John Johnston, a LaSalle Street attorney, had offered the university fifty-three acres on the northwest shore of beautiful deep-blue Lake Geneva—a favorite summer haunt of Chicago's wealthy. Sherburne Burnham, the astronomer who had helped locate Lick Observatory, reported to Hale that this "site at Lake Geneva was quite as good as any to be found within one hundred miles of Chicago." According to Hale, Burnham's opinion tipped the balance in favor of the Lake Geneva location.[14] It is not known whether the arguments of Johnston, the land donor, had any weight in the final decision. He pointed out to Harper that legislation could be obtained for less money in Wisconsin than in Illinois. As a Chicago lawyer, Johnston knew all about purchasing legislation.

Charles had wanted the telescope to be located in a quiet place not too far from Chicago. Lake Geneva did not quite live up to the financier's wishes; it was located about eighty miles north of Chicago—a two-hours' ride by fast train. But at least the site decision allowed Warner and Swasey to finish the telescope mounting before the Columbian Exposition closed its gates. On the afternoon of August 23, 1893, a crowd of 200 scientists gathered to witness the unveiling of Warner and Swasey's work. Looming in the main aisle of the Exposition's vast Manufactures Building, the enormous telescope amazed the assemblage. The instrument's sixty-two-foot-long tube rested solidly on a massive forty-three-foot-high pier. The mounting stood near an exhibit of elevators—fittingly enough.[15] It was an elevator manufacturer, after all, who had launched the career of George Hale, the principal guiding force behind what would become the Yerkes Observatory.

15 Crashing the Party

Chicago put on a show that dazzled the world in 1893. The city's great Columbian Exposition of that year presented fairgoers with an intoxicating dream of an ordered and unified society. Wide-eyed visitors wandered amid a fairy tale setting of enchanted, colonnaded castles, serpentine canals, and cascading fountains. Daniel Burnham, the Exposition's chief architect, attributed the Fair's beauty to "the magnificent consensus of wills and aims" shared by the capitalists and artists involved in the grand project. In fact, the builders of the Fair did not agree on much of anything, and constantly fought among themselves. Charles, a member of the Exposition's managing board, often provoked these conflicts. The combative financier did not believe in consensus.

In 1882 a Chicago dentist had suggested that the city hold a fair to commemorate the 400th anniversary of Columbus's 1492 voyage to the New World. The idea languished until 1889, when it was learned that a group of influential New Yorkers planned to capture the Fair for their city. Alarmed by the prospect of a New York exposition, the powerful publisher Joseph Medill fired off a volley of editorials in an attempt to rouse Chicago from its slumber. "Chicagoans must not expect that such a fat morsel as the World's Fair will come to the city without an effort," Medill thundered in the *Tribune*. "Such a golden apple will not fall into their laps unless they shake the tree. They must work for the prize, and must understand that it will cost money to get it."

Quickly moving into action, Mayor DeWitt Cregier organized a committee of prominent citizens to "shake the tree," and persuade Congress to select Chicago as the Fair site. The "trees" requiring the most shaking were the city's millionaires, who alone possessed the capital necessary to fund the massive undertaking. "It takes too many little drops of water to make a financial ocean, too many ten dollar subscriptions to raise a million," Medill argued. After suggesting that one Chicago millionaire "break the ice today with a hundred thousand dollar subscription," the publisher issued a challenge: "Who will speak first?"[1]

Charles was not the first millionaire to speak—that honor belonged to George Pullman—but he ended up speaking the loudest. The financier pledged to buy $150,000 worth of stock in the "World's Columbian Exposition of 1892," a corporation formed to run the Fair. No other Chicago businessman ever topped that subscription. Exhibiting characteristic bravado, the magnate told Lyman Gage, a banker and Fair official, to call on him for the $150,000 in "cash" whenever he wanted it.

Backed by millions of dollars in pledges, a horde of Chicagoans descended upon the U.S. House of Representatives. Charles did not join this lobbying campaign, but he enthusiastically championed its aims. For him, Chicago was the *only* suitable place to hold the Exposition. Calling New York City "the most unqualified city in the United States," the financier maintained that the citizens there would give the Fair "less support than any place that could be mentioned." He also offered another, more intriguing reason for his advocacy of Chicago. "Why, New Yorkers themselves never come West, and they know little of the country," he asserted. "They think the whole world revolves around that city. When we consider the fact that the last President of the United States (Grover Cleveland) was never west of Buffalo before he was elected President, we can readily see how necessary it is that Chicago should be selected so as to induce some of our Eastern friends to see what their country is made of."[2]

Charles, of course, was not really acting out of a desire to educate "our Eastern friends" in the ways of the West. He realized that a World's Fair would bring to Chicago a vast number of visitors—visitors who would likely make use of his streetcars. The financier had the experience of the Centennial Exposition of 1876 as a revealing guide. During that six-month-long event, most of Philadelphia's horsecar companies carried record numbers of passengers, and enjoyed as a result hefty increases in revenue. "The International Exhibition of 1876 did more to develop the street railway business of Philadelphia than anything that ever occurred before," a newspaper reported. Charles subscribed for *so much* stock in the World's Fair corporation not merely to outdo his business rivals. He knew that a substantial subscription would guarantee him a seat on the Exposition's board of directors. As a director, he would have a voice in deciding such important matters as the Fair's location within the city.

Some of Chicago's most powerful men did not want Charles on the Exposition's board. That fact became evident at a meeting held on April 4, 1890, to elect the Fair's directors. (By this point the House of Representatives had already designated Chicago as the Exposition's host city, and the Senate was expected to follow suit shortly.) On that spring morning about 3,000 of the Exposition's 28,000 stockholders gathered in the cavernous Battery D to determine who would manage the Fair. Arriving at the hall early, Charles quickly learned that there was trouble ahead. The financier was, according to a reporter, "just coming down the (Battery D) hallway like a grip car emerging from the tunnel, with $150,000 worth of stock in his overcoat pocket," when Carter Harrison stopped him in his tracks. Harrison showed Charles the ticket of forty directors Mayor Cregier's committee had endorsed—a "ready-made, cut-and-dried" ticket submitted for the stockholders' approval. Both the magnate and Harrison were not on the list. Even worse from their perspective, the ticket contained the names of mostly *South Side* men. As conspiracy-minded as ever, an outraged Charles declared it to be "a scheme of the South Side Street railway company" to locate the Fair in its section of the city. Washington Hesing, a local German politician, agreed. "I charge it openly to the world that it is an arrangement of the South Side Railroad Company and the First National Bank," Hesing roared. "You have here forty names, twenty-six from the South side, four from the West Side and ten from the North Side. The West Side alone has over two-fifths of the population of Chicago. In nationalities the list has two Germans, not one single representative of the Polish and Bohemian population, or the other different elements."[3]

The Battery D assembly split into two hostile groups: a proticket contingent headed by Chicagoans of the "wealthier class," and an antiticket party demanding a "people's fair." Leading the latter faction, Washington Hesing and Carter Harrison attempted to increase the number of Exposition directors to a more representative seventy-five. This effort failed, and the Fair board ultimately gained only five additional members thanks to a proposal made by *Daily News* publisher Victor Lawson. The debate grew heated at times, and exposed the city's sharp class divisions. Thomas Bryan, a local lawyer, finally calmed tempers with a speech appealing for unity. "Let us have peace!" he exclaimed.

Charles, however, was not in a peaceful mood that day. When nominated as a Fair director, the financier arose from his seat and curtly announced that he "could take care of himself." He wasn't kidding. The final vote tally revealed Charles to be at the very top of the list of Exposition directors, with 488,244 votes cast for him. He had been elected by "nearly double the vote given the lowest successful candidate." This outcome did not mean that Charles was a popular man. A strong believer in the value of overwhelming force, he had simply used his 15,000 shares of World's Fair stock to elect himself.

The Exposition board chosen that April afternoon certainly did not represent the people whom Carter Harrison called the "small potatoes in the hill."[4] The banker Lyman Gage, the board's first president, claimed the forty-five directors were "fairly representative of the best business life of Chicago." He should have said the *wealthiest* "business life of Chicago" since over one-third of the directors were millionaires. Some of the most celebrated figures in Chicago's commercial realm sat on the Exposition board, including the hotel magnate Potter Palmer, the meat packer Samuel Allerton, and the reaper king Cyrus McCormick. The newspaper publishers Joseph Medill, Herman Kohlsaat, and Victor Lawson also occupied seats in this Chicago version of Mount Olympus. Lawson would later excoriate what he termed the "conscienceless greed of a money-grabbing and money-mad local board of directors." Others had a far higher opinion of the Fair managers. "They are not only competent to run the world's fair," an alderman said of the directors, "but are able to manage the affairs of the nation, were it necessary."[5]

Many of the business titans on the Exposition board did not welcome Charles's presence—to put it mildly. The verbally challenged Allerton, the South Side street railway's second vice-president, was at that very moment locked in a bitter contest with Charles over State Street. Lawson and Medill had long fought the financier in their newspapers. And then there was the boyish-faced, dreamy-eyed Ferdinand Peck, the founder of the architecturally inspired Auditorium Building. In 1885 "Ferd" had tried to gain control of the North Chicago City Railway, and he apparently never forgave Charles for wresting this valuable prize away from him. For his part, the financier did not enjoy the company of most of his fellow directors. He would later label Lawson and Medill "blackmailers," once derided Allerton as "a fussy, old fellow," and even supposedly called Cyrus McCormick "an insufferable prick."

The colossal egos on the Fair board clashed over many matters, but none created a greater disturbance than the question of site selection. Charles naturally held strong views on the subject. During his first trip to Europe he had visited the great Paris Exposition of 1889, and had come away with a firm conviction. "I believe the greatest element in the success of the Paris show is its location," he told a reporter. "It is in the heart of the city. It is a step there, and so everybody goes." The magnate consequently wanted the Chicago Fair to be situated near the city center, preferably along the lakefront where "a grand avenue with fountains the whole length" of it could be laid out.[6] As a second choice, he favored spots on either the North or West Side—either site being one that would capture for his firms a lion's share of the Fair-generated streetcar business.

Most of the Fair directors initially embraced the idea of a lakefront location, realizing the convenience of such a spot. But dissenting property owners and objecting Illinois Central Railroad officials—the line's tracks ran along the lake—helped sour this pro-lakefront sentiment. At the June 28, 1890, meeting of the Exposition board, James Ellsworth, a prominent local coal dealer, proposed another site for the Fair: Jackson Park. Situated nine miles south of the Loop on swampy ground, Jackson Park seemed to Charles a ridiculous locale for a fair. "I think the North and West Sides can rest without fear that the Exposition will not be taken to so remote a part of the city!" the financier bravely asserted.[7] Charles knew better. All along he had suspected that the South Siders were plotting to locate the Fair in their section of the city, and now his fears had been confirmed. The magnate resolved to defeat this "scheme."

His chance to strike back came during the July 1, 1890, Fair board meeting. A cool breeze wafted through the open windows of the board's Dearborn Street office on that brilliant day, offering little relief to the "fevered brows" of the twenty-five directors inside. Charles Schwab, a South Side man, dramatically increased the room temperature when he suggested that the Fair be held in two places: the lakefront *and* Jackson Park. Frederick S. Winston, a director and an attorney of Charles, countered with a proposal that Garfield Park on the West Side be used as the second site instead of Jackson Park. Charles certainly supported this idea —one calculated to increase ridership on his West Chicago Street Railroad Company's lines. The financier stoutly defended Winston's motion, maintaining that Garfield Park was only two miles from the Loop and not "away out on the prairie" as critics contended. Despite Charles's persuasive powers, the Garfield Park measure failed to pass, receiving only two votes. In the end the directors approved the dual lakefront–Jackson Park location. Charles, however, was not ready to give up the fight. During the war of words Winston had hinted suggestively that the West Side members of the Illinois legislature were all opposed to the Jackson Park site, and "would vote against the sanction of its use."[8] The battle now shifted to Springfield.

The Fair directors badly needed the support of the legislature. The City of Chicago had agreed to sell $5,000,000 worth of municipal bonds to meet the Exposition's ever expanding financial requirements. But the city had already reached its debt limit, and could not market any more bonds until it received an okay from the legislature. Under the Fair board's prodding Governor Joseph Fifer convened a special summer session of the General Assembly to consider raising Chicago's borrowing authority. Undoubtedly with Charles's encouragement, Frederick Winston instructed the West Side legislators to weigh down this needed legislation with burdensome amendments. These obstructions, it was widely understood, would be removed only after Garfield Park was designated the second site in place of Jackson Park. This blackmail plan misfired terribly, however, and the debt limit bill passed safely through the legislature.[9] Following this episode, some Exposition directors began to wonder whether Charles was willing to sacrifice the Fair to gain his own ends.

Charles's opposition to Jackson Park received a boost from an unexpected quarter in August 1890. After inspecting the various proposed Fair sites, the renowned landscape architect Frederick Law Olmsted delivered a report decidedly unfriendly to the South Side location. Calling Jackson Park "a morass, divided by a few low, narrow sand dunes," Olmsted expressed a clear preference for a 300-acre parcel of land situated on the North Side. Charles must have been elated by the architect's findings. Reflecting his state of mind, his North Side street railway's stock shot up eleven points in three days as news of the Olmsted report leaked out.

But, as Carter Harrison had noted, "the cards had been stacked, and a jack was turned at every deal—for Jackson Park." At a February 1891 board meeting, the directors decided to abandon the lakefront entirely, leaving Jackson Park as the sole site for the World's Fair. Significantly, Charles was not present during this pivotal vote. When he learned of the decision, the financier erupted in fury. "The present board has been false in its pledges both to the legislature and City Council," he declared. Banding together with a group of disgruntled railroad executives, Charles launched a campaign to purge the Fair board of some of its pro–Jackson Park members. Appointed to a nominating committee charged with drawing up a new ticket for the board, he made an especially strong stand against James Ellsworth—the original proponent of the Jackson Park site. "I have been annoyed more than I can tell you by the fact that it became necessary in order to agree upon any report of the Nominating Committee (which had five vexatious sittings), to temporarily drop your name," Ferdinand Peck, a committee member, informed Ellsworth in April 1891. "This is, as I explained to you, owing to Mr. Yerkes' determined opposition, which I regard as a compliment to you."[10] Though not placed on the ticket, Ellsworth was ultimately elected to fill the seat of a retiring Fair director.

Charles also targeted Lyman Gage. As the Fair board's president, Gage had used his considerable influence to swing the balance of the directors decisively against the lakefront location. For this reason, Charles hoped to knock Gage off the board. The esteemed vice-president of the First National Bank managed to survive this coup attempt, but the effort left an impression on him.

Charles must have watched with considerable irritation as the magical White City rose above the Jackson Park marsh in absolute defiance of his wishes. Yet he did not let his personal bitterness interfere with his obligations as a Fair director. Serving on the Fine Arts Committee, he helped procure European masterpieces for the Exposition, and even offered to exhibit works from his own private collection. In the summer of 1891 Charles was named an honorary commissioner to Europe, and was sent overseas to spread word about the Exposition. The financier was delighted with the response he received. "The people in France are very enthusiastic, as indeed they are all over Europe wherever I went," he reported. "I was agreeably surprised to find Chicago spoken of in the most enthusiastic terms. There is great anticipation for the success of the Fair."[11]

As a member of the Committee on Ceremonies, Charles also had a hand in planning the program for the Fair's October 1892 dedication day. Well aware of this fact, Harriet Monroe approached the magnate in the spring of 1891 with a proposal to write a poem for the dedication. She never forgot the "gallant courage" of Charles's reply. "I don't know what the other members of the committee may think about it," he said, "but I will make the motion. I hope we can give you the commission, because we shall want a poem that will live."

Monroe was in the vast audience that sparkling October morning to hear her "Columbian Ode" read by the "statuesque and beautiful" actress Sarah Cowell LeMoyne. Charles also witnessed the events of that day. As a lover of the grandiose, he had to have been pleased with the final results of his committee's work. The Exposition's chief architect Daniel Burnham had wanted the Fair's inaugural day to be "the greatest ceremonial of all time." While not quite measuring up to Burnham's expectations, the dedication still furnished an amazing spectacle. Roughly 140,000 people attended the ceremony, packing from wall to wall the Exposition's gargantuan Manufactures Building—an arched edifice nearly one-third of a mile long with an interior resembling "the inside of an umbrella." "Words failed one on entering the structure, on seeing the sky-like roof, the horizon-like walls, and the masses of humanity like heaps of insects," a *Chicago Tribune* reporter gasped. Peering through opera glasses, another journalist could barely glimpse on the other side of the hall the 5,000-member orchestra, which looked to him like a "whole cemetery with pinkish human faces rising in place of the thousands of gravestones."[12] Few in the great assemblage could even make out the words of the dignitaries on the speakers' platform, but no one seemed to care. The wondrous setting provided enough satisfaction for most.

From her vantage point in the crowd Harriet Monroe was able to hear the speeches. In her judgment, not one of the orators "had made the day his own forever, as Lincoln did at Gettysburg, by shaping the world's hope into a few sentences too beautiful to be forgotten." Monroe left the ceremony half-persuaded that she had fulfilled Charles's command to "write a poem that would live," almost certain that her ode "had a chance of longer life" than any other words she had heard that day. Her hopes were quickly dashed. Unable to sell copies of her "Columbian Ode," she used the pamphlets as fuel to heat her study during the subsequent harsh winter.

The severity of that season slowed the final months of construction, but the Columbian Exposition still managed to open on May 1, 1893, as scheduled—thanks largely to Daniel Burnham's firm guidance. Critics as different as Henry Adams, the patrician Easterner, and Theodore Dreiser, the plebeian Midwesterner, praised the Chicago Fair. Adams felt that as "a scenic display, Paris (the Exposition of 1889) had never approached it," while Dreiser, wandering amid "the Ionic facades, porticoes, roofs, domes, lagoons," found the Fair to possess "a brooding spirit of beauty." "Here all at once, as it were, out of nothing, in this dingy city of six or seven hundred thousand . . . was now this vast and harmonious collection of perfectly constructed and snowy buildings, containing in their delightful interiors . . . the artistic, mechanical, and scientific achievements of the world to date," Dreiser marveled. At night tens of thousands of electric lights bathed this "Fairy Venice" in an ethereal glow. "Turn your eyes to whatever building you please, you see hosts of suns, moons, and satellites illuminating this model of an earthly heaven," an Indian observer wrote. The overwhelming beauty of the White City at night moved one Dakota farm couple "to tears of joy . . . almost as poignant as pain."[13]

The Exposition attracted over 27,000,000 visitors during its six-month length, and actually showed a small profit—a rare thing for a World's Fair. The event proved to be a boon for local businesses as well. The South Side street railway especially benefited, having carried the bulk of the fairgoers. Charles, however, also had no reason to complain. "We have had our share," he assured his stockholders. His North and West Side streetcar lines enjoyed huge increases in ridership because of the Exposition—increases that translated into large profits. The North Chicago Street Railroad Company transported 60,311,673 passengers in 1893, almost 10,000,000 more than in the previous year, and earned $1,602,133. The West Chicago Street Railroad Company hauled 107,053,461 people in 1893, and netted $2,342,651. Both firms' profits were about $400,000 higher than the 1892 figures. This advance in revenue occurred despite a substantial rise in operating costs. Charles had nearly doubled the number of cars on his lines in anticipation of the Fair's traffic demands.

The World's Fair had provided a solution—albeit a temporary one—to one of the greatest problems plaguing Chicago's streetcar managers: the unequal distribution of traffic throughout the day. Most commuters used mass transit primarily during the rush hour periods, from 7 A.M. to 10 A.M. and from 5 P.M. to 7 P.M. As a result, for much of the day, streetcars had comparatively few passengers. Yet, the vehicles still had to be operated and the employees paid. How then could one fill up the streetcar seats during these so-called off-peak hours? Charles put his faith—and money—in spectacle. In 1888 he donated a lion to Lincoln Park—the North Side's great pleasure ground, conveniently located astride the Clark Street cable line. Two years later, he gave the park something even more spectacular—an electric fountain, possibly the first such fountain in the United States. Thousands, including Theodore Dreiser, traveled to the park (via streetcar) to watch the weekly summer show—a water and light show choreographed like a fireworks display. Arc lights shining through colored filters illuminated dozens of dancing geysers of water, some over 100 feet tall. "It is truly a grand sight," one observer remarked of the show. "There were all the colors of the rainbow, sometimes all turned on together."

Encouraged by the success of the Lincoln Park electric fountain, Charles began to plan even greater spectacles to draw people out of their homes and into his streetcars during the off-peak hours. The World's Fair—especially its thrill-packed Midway—served as a blueprint for the magnate's schemes. In 1895, he and several associates opened an amusement park—Electric Park—at Belmont and California avenues, adjacent, of course, to several important streetcar lines. The venture never proved profitable, and "after three years of a more or less uncertain career it burned and was never rebuilt."

Also in 1895, Charles worked with the engineer George Washington Gale Ferris to resurrect the latter's celebrated wheel. The "landmark of the Fair," the 250-foot-diameter Ferris Wheel, towering 140 feet above the Midway, was to Chicago what the Eiffel Tower was to the Paris Exposition in 1889. Roughly 1,400,000 customers had paid fifty cents each to take "the World's Greatest Ride," one revolution of the wheel lasting twenty minutes. Following the close of the Fair, the great wheel was dismantled and its parts stored in dozens of freight cars on a South Side railroad siding. With Charles's backing, Ferris rebuilt the wheel on a stretch of Clark Street not far from Lincoln Park. People, however, failed to patronize the relocated wheel—in no small part because of the hefty fifty-cent admission price, and the structure was ultimately sold for scrap iron. George Ferris did not live to see the ignominious fate of his great invention. He died in 1896 of tuberculosis.

The World's Fair closed its gates on October 31, 1893, shrouded in a pall of gloom. Three days before, an embittered, mentally unbalanced office-seeker had killed Carter Harrison. Early in 1893 Harrison had won his fifth term as Chicago mayor, the city choosing him to be "the symbol of its expansive spirit in the hour of its greatest glory." Nearly all of the city's newspapers had opposed "Our Carter's" election—all except the *Chicago Times,* which Harrison had purchased to promote his mayoral ambitions. Realizing the positive political effect of such a feud, Harrison had used the *Times* to pick an editorial fight with his friend Charles. At first mildly irritated by the newspaper's criticisms, the financier grew increasingly angry as the *Times* attacks continued. Charles was especially irate because he had just contributed $45,000 in support of Harrison's unsuccessful 1891 mayoral bid. Finally, the magnate reached the limits of his patience. Storming into Harrison's newspaper office, Charles exclaimed: "Carter, I always did know that you were an ingrate, but I never knew before that you were a scoundrel." Before a flabbergasted Harrison could respond, the financier swept out of the room with a curt "Good day, sir."

The two men had repaired their friendship since that unpleasant 1891 encounter. The news of Harrison's death devastated Charles. The magnate revealed the depth of his feelings for the mayor in a condolence letter that he sent to Harrison's oldest son. "It is with the most painful emotions I have heard of the horrible misfortune that has befallen your family and words fail in expressing my grief at the event and my sympathy," he wrote. "Being so near to Mr. Harrison and seeing so much of him in trying times, I had learned to think much more of him than an ordinary friend. It was an affection which I have for but few. It does not seem possible he has been taken from us, and it is only when I sit down calmly to consider the fact that I can realize that we are to have him with us no more. . . . If there is anything I can do in any way I hope you will do me the favor to let me know. Mrs. Yerkes is almost prostrated, as she was extremely fond of Mayor Harrison."[14]

On the Fair's last day, the maverick English journalist William Stead came to Chicago. He was "the queerest guest our city ever sheltered," a local newspaperman asserted. That was saying something! The son of a Congregationalist minister, Stead brought a religious fervor to his journalism. As the editor of London's *Pall Mall Gazette* in the 1880s, he championed a whole host of causes in a zealous effort to reform society. "You are too strenuous, too uniformly strenuous," the prince of Wales, an avid *Gazette* reader, chided Stead. Many believed that the crusading editor went too far when he purchased a teen-aged girl for five pounds to dramatize how easily children could be sold into prostitution. Stead went to prison for this action, but he had made his point. As a direct result of his antivice campaign, Parliament passed a law raising the age of consent for young women. Following his release from jail, the unrepentant journalist continued to assail the forces of reaction in the *Gazette* and later in the *Review of Reviews*, the magazine he founded in 1890.

When Stead arrived in Chicago on October 31, 1893, he found a city overcome with despair. Mayor Carter Harrison had just been assassinated, and the effects of the financial Panic of 1893 were finally beginning to be felt. The enormous amount of economic activity generated by the Fair had delayed the depression's onset in Chicago. "The bright banners, the music, and the tinsel of the World's Fair, gorgeous as they were, soon faded," the reporter Ray Stannard Baker recalled. "They were followed with dizzying haste by another pageant, sombre and threatening, that of the depression and panic of 1893–94, nowhere else so severe as in Chicago. It was marked by unprecedented extremes of poverty, unemployment, unrest."[15]

Stead was horrified by what he saw in Chicago: the swelling army of the jobless, the wide-open prostitution and gambling, the yawning gulf between the rich and the poor. He may have been horrified, but he was not at all surprised. "He had been told . . . that of all places on earth, Chicago was undeniably the wickedest," Melville Stone noted of Stead, "and therefore it was obviously the fittest spot for an evangelist's missionary effort." True to form, Stead embarked upon a crusade to "save" Chicago. He was well equipped for the task. Both his appearance and the power of his words impressed observers. "He was a fiery orator, with strong religious convictions, a virile sturdy man with a bushy red beard, and unusually large blue eyes, set widely apart," Ray Stannard Baker wrote.

At a "remarkable" November meeting held in the Central Music Hall Stead asked his audience "to consider whether if Christ visited Chicago he would find anything he would wish to have altered." Speaking for Christ, the editor went on to list some of the city's sins: prostitution, intemperance, municipal corruption, and public apathy. He then boldly suggested a plan to "drive the devil out of Chicago." "You have got to organize for the kingdom of God," he asserted, "as energetically, as persistently, and as steadily as the political rings organize for the triumph of their own candidates."[16] Taking the hint, a five-member committee formed a group dedicated to eliminating "all the elements of evil" in Chicago. This so-called Civic Federation would soon identify Charles as one of the community's primary forces for "evil."

Melville Stone, the former *Chicago Daily News* publisher, made sure Stead was aware of Charles. Stone never stopped hating the financier—a man who had after all once threatened to kill him. A recent event had only magnified the newspaperman's bitter feelings. In 1891 Charles, as a Fair board director, had helped thwart Stone's ambition to become the Exposition's chief of the department of foreign affairs. "I did not imagine that so many men on the board were under Yerkes' influence," Stone said at the time. "And yet I might have guessed that one so thoroughly used to the ways and power of discipline would not have neglected an opportunity to again demonstrate its value. I have a profound contempt for him and his following, however, and a corresponding gratitude toward those of the directors whom I am proud to number among my friends and who stood by me."

In a series of meetings, Stone told Stead the story of Chicago, a city marked by "an inordinate devotion to dollars." The former publisher also incidentally provided the British journalist with the details of Charles's career. Stead came away from these conferences fully sharing Stone's "profound contempt" for the streetcar magnate. Convinced that Charles posed a threat to the public welfare, the Englishman resolved to "go for Yerkes among others" in a speech he planned to deliver on January 16, 1894. "I have come to the conclusion that on Tuesday night it will be necessary for me to speak out about Yerkes," Stead informed Stone four days before the lecture. "I shall not go into his personal antecedents and shall assume that he is an angel of light. I shall only point out that he is a bandit of the worst type and that society would be justified in extracting his eye teeth as the Normans did those of the Jews in the middle ages."[17] Exercising rare restraint, Stead appears not to have specifically mentioned Charles in his January 16 speech. He did, however, allude to the "predatory rich" who bribed aldermen to obtain valuable franchises.

Stead did name names in his *If Christ Came to Chicago*—a muck-raking expose of the city published shortly after he left the Midwestern metropolis. Charles had a starring role in the book, and was even show-cased on the cover. There, in a reproduction of Hofmann's famous paint-ing of Christ driving the money-changers from the temple, an alert reader could spot the financier's unmistakable features in the face of the most prominent trader—the one "hastily raking his scattered gold" into a trea-sure chest shaped like a streetcar. The other moneychangers were drawn to resemble "some of the richest and most notable business and political leaders of Chicago." "These are the people who have polluted the temple, by which I mean the city government," Stead explained to Ray Stannard Baker, "and they should be driven out one and all."[18]

The Englishman singled out Charles for his most virulent attacks. "Of the predatory rich in Chicago there are plenty and to spare, but there is one man who stands out conspicuous among all the rest," Stead de-clared in his book. "He may not be a greater sinner than the rest of his neighbors, but he has succeeded in doing with supreme success what a great number of his fellow citizens have done or tried to do and failed. I refer to Mr. Charles T. Yerkes." In a sly allusion to Charles's "period of seclusion" Stead openly wondered why the "City Council showered such lavish generosity (in the form of streetcar franchises) upon this immigrant from a Philadelphia penitentiary." "It could hardly be for love of his beau-tiful eyes," the journalist joked, "nor can we suppose that Mr. Yerkes exercised any hypnotic powers or fascination over the city fathers in the City Council." Answering his own question, Stead boldly suggested that Charles secured these franchises through bribery.

Not even the magnate's generous gift to the University of Chicago elicited a kind word from Stead. "By way of diverting the attention of inquisitive eyes which would keep squinting into his franchises he gave $250,000 for the construction of the largest telescope in the world," the British editor charged. "It is much better for people like Mr. Yerkes that the scrutinizing gaze of the public should be turned to the heavens than to the scandalous manner in which he neglects his obligations to the people."[19]

Stead left Chicago with far more than an indelible portrait of Charles as an unscrupulous "freebooter" whose absolute disregard for law en-dangered the community. He had given Chicagoans a means to "drive the devil" out of their city. His Civic Federation and its energetic offshoot, the Municipal Voters League, would provide a rallying point for those peo-ple opposed to the streetcar magnate. Charles may have considered Stead to be little more than an English crackpot, but the journalist managed to awaken a slumbering citizenry and galvanize a strong anti-Yerkes movement. This Victorian Savonarola had transformed the "modern Florence."

Stead went down with the *Titanic* in 1912. He selflessly assisted women and children aboard lifeboats on that terrible April night. One survivor recalled looking back at the sinking ship and seeing Stead standing "alone at the edge of the deck in silence and what seemed . . . a prayerful attitude of profound meditation."[20] The evangelist of reform remained true to his ideals until the very end.

16   Current Events

The Chicago World's Fair first demonstrated the potential of electricity to bring good things to life. A visitor to the Fair could ride in an electrical gondola, sail in an electrical buoy, or stroll at night under the electrical lights. For many, electricity seemed to be an almost mystical force. No less an observer than Henry Adams was bewitched by the electric dynamo, which he likened to an "occult mechanism." Charles too would fall under the power of this "occult" force.

For decades inventors had labored in vain to build a practical electrically powered streetcar. Such a vehicle became a possibility only after 1870 with the development of the first really reliable dynamo—a machine that generates electricity. Nine years later Werner Siemens, a prominent German engineer, devised a semi-successful electric streetcar system featuring a third rail that carried an electrical current from a central powerhouse to a motor fastened underneath the car. This set-up, however, posed no small danger to the unwary pedestrian who happened to step on the electrified rail.

Charles Van Depoele, a Belgian native who immigrated to the United States in 1869, reduced the danger of electric railways by moving the current off the ground. Under Van Depoele's "trolley" scheme the streetcar and its motor were connected to overhead electric wires by means of a wheel-driven pole mounted on the vehicle's roof. Van Depoele's invention quickly caught on, and by the end of 1887 his firm had installed a dozen electric street railways and over sixty miles of track.

Though initially quite popular, Van Depoele's system was far from perfect. According to one authority, the electric railway lines of the era "all had one thing in common—a maddening unwillingness to work right for any length of time."[1] The brilliant engineer Frank J. Sprague was the first person to get electric streetcars to work right in a consistent fashion. Only thirty years old in 1887, Sprague—an intense, driven man with an intelligent face and a spare build—had already compiled an impressive list of accomplishments. He was an honors graduate of the U.S. Naval Academy, and in 1882 had served as the secretary of the scientific jury at London's Crystal Palace Exhibition. A ride in the smoke-clouded London underground—then operated with steam locomotives—had convinced Sprague of the need for railway electrification, and set the wheels of his mind in motion toward the idea of a trolley. Shortly after returning to America, the engineer obtained a job in the construction department at Thomas Edison's Menlo Park laboratory. The two egotistical geniuses did not get along well, and within a year Sprague had resigned his position. According to Sprague, Edison was "jealous of any man who finds in the whole realm of electric science a corner . . . not occupied by himself."

In 1884 Sprague set off on his own in a search for corners not yet taken up by the "wizard" of Menlo Park. Shortly after forming a company that manufactured high-quality motors, he began to work on his trolley idea. Before long he had designed an electric railway system that was far superior to any then in operation. Sprague mounted the streetcar motor "between the axle and a spring, wheelbarrow fashion, and secured a sure mesh by having his motor engage with a cogwheel on the axle." Van Depoele and the other electric railway pioneers, in contrast, had fastened their motors "either on the axle, where it suffered from shocks and jarring, or in some other fashion, so that gears or belts presented problems of a proper mesh."[2]

Sprague's big break came in 1887 when a syndicate of Richmond, Virginia, businessmen hired him to build a twelve-mile-long trolley line and to furnish it with forty cars and eighty motors. "This was nearly as many motors as there were in use on all the cars throughout the rest of the world," he later recalled. Given only ninety days to complete the job, Sprague welcomed "the thought of this new adventure." He, however, soon became discouraged by the sheer magnitude of the project, with the looming hills of Richmond posing perhaps the most formidable obstacle to success. Sprague doubted whether the electric cars could manage the heavy grades. The matter was put to a test on an election night in November 1887. Sprague himself manned the controls of the car on that initial run and all went well until the foot of the steepest hill was reached. "We won't make it," the nervous engineer told an associate on board. The latter coolly remarked that they "could climb the side of a house if the wheels would hold." The wheels did hold, and the car rode up the hill and into history. A "witch's cauldron of troubles" beset Sprague in the months succeeding this memorable trip, but he eventually managed to get the Richmond trolley system into working operation. By the summer of 1888, the line was an established success, and streetcar magnates from across the nation began visiting Richmond to view Sprague's creation.

Henry Whitney, the president of Boston's West End Railroad, made the pilgrimage and was impressed with what he saw. Whitney proceeded to adopt the trolley on his streetcar lines. The swift new vehicles that suddenly appeared on the winding boulevards of Boston and Cambridge amazed the octogenarian Oliver Wendell Holmes. "Look here!" Holmes exclaimed. "There are crowds of people whirled through our streets on these new-fashioned cars, with their witch-broomsticks overhead . . . and not more than one in a dozen of these fish-eyed bipeds thinks or cares a nickel's worth about the miracle which is wrought for their convenience. They know that without hands or feet, without horses, without steam, so far as they can see, they are transported from place to place, and there is nothing to account for it except the witch-broomsticks and iron or copper cobweb which they see stretched above them. . . . We ought to go down on our knees when one of these mighty caravans, car after car, spins by us, under the mystic impulse which seems to know not whether its train is loaded or empty."[3]

Whitney's endorsement of the "broomstick train" sent a strong signal to the nation's streetcar managers, and by 1890 the United States boasted 126 companies operating 1,261 miles of electric railroad. The Cicero and Proviso Street Railway was one of the first trolley roads to run in the Chicago area, beginning service in February 1891. Edmund Cummings, a real estate developer, had promoted the eight-mile line's construction, hoping to use it to "boom" his west suburban properties. Cummings discovered that operating a trolley road was not easy in that pioneering era. "In the first place . . . we put on double truck cars, when they didn't have any motors in those days that were strong enough to run them," Cummings remembered in 1906, "and when we got a little bit of snow we were stalled all over. There were no electric sweepers, no devices to shovel up the snow. We had to hire men in the town to haul the cars. Sometimes they [the trolley cars] had to stay out all night with passengers in them, and trolley overhead construction was very poor . . . and it was continually making trouble." Nature as well seemed to conspire against Cummings and his road. Once, during a heavy rainstorm, the Desplaines River overflowed its banks and washed away the block pavement between the streetcar tracks. Cummings had to order his employees to build "little booms down the different points to catch the blocks as they came down the streets." Beset by all manner of misfortune, the Cicero and Proviso line struggled for years to gain a firm financial footing.[4]

Charles closely watched the progress of this suburban electric railway. He was eager to find a substitute for the antiquated horsecars that still ran on over 200 miles of track on the North and West sides. Only forty-seven miles of his companies' lines had been converted to cable and the magnate was dead-set against building any more cable facilities. The reason for his stubbornness on this issue was simple. He had grown disenchanted with the cable method of transportation, plagued as it was by frequent breakdowns. The construction and maintenance of cable lines also cost a lot of money—money that could not be recouped on any but the most heavily traveled routes. And in Chicago cables already covered the busiest streets.

Charles certainly appreciated the benefits of Sprague's trolley system. For one thing, overhead wires could be installed relatively cheaply. Cable lines cost about $150,000 per mile to build while trolley railways could be put in for less than $10,000 per mile. Equally important, trolleys could be operated far more cheaply than cablecars, were twice as fast, and provided what the economic historian George Hilton called "greater flexibility." Hilton explained: "An electric car could back up; a cable car could not. An electric car could switch itself at the car barn, and it could go into or out of a powered siding. . . . An electric car could make up lost time; a cable car could not. . . . No single failure . . . could tie up an entire electric system."[5]

Though aware of the advantages of the trolley, Charles knew as well that Sprague's system still had many flaws—a fact borne out by the troubled operations of the Cicero and Proviso road. The magnate also realized that large segments of the public were wary of the "deadly" trolley. The electrically charged overhead wires and the fast-moving vehicles were considered to be potential hazards. "The people want no trolley system in the heart of the city or its limits," the *Chicago Tribune* declared, in a fit of alarm. "They know that the system is unsafe, that while it would move them more rapidly it would kill them more swiftly." Charles had additional reservations about the trolley—aesthetic ones. He believed that the overhead wires were unsightly. "I saw the telephone and telegraph wires come down with pride," he told a Chicago City Council committee in 1899, "and was anxious when it appeared that electricity was the coming motive power that something else than the over-head trolley should be used in the business district."[6]

Charles did try hard to find a practical alternative to the trolley. Early in the 1890s he pinned his hopes on an underground electric system of transportation. During the previous decade the engineers Edward Bentley and Walter Knight had developed a streetcar that could be powered by means of an electric wire situated in an underground conduit. The invention proved to be "technically unsatisfactory and too costly," but that did not prevent others from attempting to improve upon it, including John E. Love—a Philadelphia man who had enjoyed "a varied career as railway builder, miner, promoter, and inventor." Love dreamt up what he believed was an improved underground conduit system, and persuaded Charles to try out his contraption on a one-and three-quarter-mile section of track belonging to the North Chicago Street Railroad. Satisfied with the invention's initial performance, the financier put the Love underground line into regular operation in April 1892.

The Love road, though, was "a child born without friends," and among its many enemies were Peter Widener and William Elkins. Charles's business partners favored Sprague's system, and were just then trying to introduce the trolley in Philadelphia against enormous opposition. They urged Charles to abandon his experiments with Love's invention. The financier, however, held his ground, telling the "Traction Twins" that he could run his business "without their help." Charles and the Philadelphians were already on bad terms thanks to a recent gas utility dispute, but the rift between them now threatened to become a chasm.

Ironically, the magnate did ultimately give up on the Love system. During heavy rains the underground conduit frequently filled up with water, causing the imperfectly insulated electric wire within to short out. In winter the conduit often closed up, blocking the electrical contact between the streetcar and the wire. "While the weather was good it worked first rate," Charles later said of Love's invention. "Then came bad weather and it was a failure. We changed the insulation and worked at it a year and a half, but could not make a success of it. I then made up my mind the underground system could not be made to work in Chicago, and think so still." The greatest drawback of Love's scheme was the cost of its construction—two-thirds more than the expense of building a trolley line.[7]

Charles did not confine his experiments to Love's underground conduit system. He in fact tried out all sorts of motors—compressed air motors, battery-powered motors, and even steam motors. He came to favor the Connelly gas engine, a device created by two New Jersey brothers. First tested with some success on Chicago's streets in 1890, the Connelly gas motor cars began running regularly three years later. Almost immediately the noise and smell of the motors generated public complaints. Echoing this widespread dissatisfaction, a newspaper reporter listed some of the "advantages" of the engines. "First, a man who has the misfortune to be blind and deaf can always tell when a gas motor is coming—by the smell," this journalist joked. "Second, it will scare all the horses off the street, thus securing quiet and repose. Third, gas motors have a pleasant habit of blowing up occasionally. This will furnish diversion for the entire locality and make business good for surgeons." The Connelly motors were, in truth, explosion-prone. Several blew up before city officials banned their use late in 1893.[8]

By this point, Charles had overcome his initial aversion to Sprague's trolley. DeLancey Louderback was largely responsible for the magnate's change of mind. A brilliant manager of men and material, the dynamic, diminutive Louderback undoubtedly would have been a successful general had he chosen an Army career. With his erect bearing, walrus mustache, and penchant for wearing high-cut military coats, he indeed resembled a soldier. He even possessed what appeared to be a war wound: His left eye had been damaged during a hunting expedition in 1876 when a charge exploded in his face, propelling fourteen bullet fragments into his brain and skull. Born too late to fight in the Civil War, the Iowa native found more than enough action on the battlefield of business. At the age of twenty, he took on the powerful Western Union Company, his onetime employer, opening up a string of telegraph offices stretching from New York to Chicago. Essentially a promoter of new technologies, Louderback later had a hand in the organization of several telephone and electric firms, including the Chicago Edison Company. In 1888 he entered the fledgling trolley field, and within a few years had established himself as a streetcar magnate of the first magnitude.[9]

By 1891, Louderback's reputation had grown so great that he was able to enlist the financial support of "most every large capitalist in Chicago," including Marshall Field and Philip Armour, for an electric road he planned to construct linking the northern suburb of Evanston with Chicago. The ambitious scheme, however, ran afoul of Charles, who did not relish having a potential competitor so near to his own streetcar lines. Louderback needed downtown access for his Chicago North Shore Railway, and he hoped that Charles would permit a connection between the Evanston trolleys and the Clark Street cable. After months of negotiation the magnate apparently agreed to this traffic arrangement. Shortly afterward, when Charles was safely away in Europe, Louderback started to build the seven-and-a-half-mile-long North Shore road, completing it in only eighty-seven days.

Charles returned from Europe and was shocked to find Louderback's railway nearly finished. The businessman began to have second thoughts about the traffic arrangement he had already signed off on, especially after the North Shore road proved to be a "phenomenal" financial success. During a conference regarding the cable connection Charles attempted to size up his opponent, at one point requesting a list of the North Shore's stockholders. "When Mr. Yerkes saw this list he asked me what my intention was in regard to the company," Louderback recalled. "I told him that I had no disposition whatever to extend the company's lines beyond the cable, but that we were prepared, if we could not go down to the cable, to condemn a right of way through private property or to build an elevated railroad to make connection with our surface road." Even more ominously for Charles, Louderback indicated that the North Shore was only the first of several suburban electric roads he and his powerful backers intended to construct.[10] Impressed by his rival's resolve, Charles decided to cancel the proposed traffic arrangement, not wanting to give aid and comfort to a possible enemy.

In the weeks following this conference, the financier pondered what Louderback had said. "It set me thinking," Charles related in 1895, "and I saw there might be danger in making such contracts with companies that might not always be friendly. I saw that these outlying roads must be built and I made up my mind that it would be a good thing for me . . . to build them and a good thing for the cable companies to have them built and managed by friendly hands."

Shortly after making this momentous decision, Charles formed an alliance with Louderback and secured control of the North Shore road. This purchase marked the beginning of a colossal spending spree that would dramatically enlarge (and complicate) the magnate's street railway empire. Between 1894 and 1897 Charles acquired no less than eight suburban electric railways ringing the city's northern and western rim: the North Chicago Electric Railway, the Chicago Electric Transit Company, the North Side Electric Street Railway, the Evanston Electric Railway, the Chicago and Jefferson Urban Transit Company, the Cicero and Proviso Street Railway, the Ogden Street Railway, and the Suburban Electric Railway. Some of these roads (like the Chicago Electric Transit Company and the North Side Electric Street Railway) had only existed on paper when Charles bought them, having been organized by "a lot of blackmailing politicians." Other lines were already in operation, like Edmund Cummings's Cicero and Proviso Street Railway. Louderback himself had formed only one of these eight companies—the North Chicago Electric Railway.[11]

Charles intended to use these new roads as "feeders" diverting suburban passengers to his cable railways. This system of mass transit, with its branch and trunk lines, had probably been inspired by the example of

William Kemble, Charles's late mentor; Kemble had forged a similarly structured streetcar network in Philadelphia before his 1891 death. Though Charles claimed to advocate "the harmonious development of the whole system," he preserved separate corporate identities for the eight suburban roads. The financier did this for a very good reason. He hoped to escape the provisions of a City Council ordinance requiring that streetcar companies charge passengers a single five-cent fare, no matter how long the ride. "There was a limit . . . to the distance that passengers could be carried with profit for 5 cents," the financial journalist Frank Vanderlip explained, "and while it was desirable to occupy the outlying territory, it was not desirable to bring passengers from that territory to the heart of the city for one fare. Mr. Yerkes therefore organized a number of auxiliary companies." As Charles himself put it, "you can carry a passenger about so far for five cents and no farther."

The formation of so many companies also served another purpose, giving Charles an opportunity to issue a vast amount of securities for his own personal enrichment. He reserved for himself *almost all* of the stock in these eight firms.[12] In the businessman's view, he was fully entitled to this windfall. Charles believed that great risks deserved great rewards, and he saw himself as taking an immense gamble by extending trolley lines into areas of low population density—a gamble, of course, predicated on the hope that the roads would help build up the adjacent territories.

The energetic Louderback wasted no time in constructing the suburban trolley lines. It took him, for example, only four months to get the Chicago Electric Transit Company's road into operation. "The Chicago Electric Transit Company has broken all records for speed in building an electric power house," a reporter asserted. "Aug. 11, 1894, the neighborhood about Roscoe boulevard and the north branch of the Chicago River was an ideal spot for a picnic. A handsome grove of trees and unbroken fields were all that was visible on the west bank of the river. Dec. 22 of the same year cars were being operated from the great electrical power plant built at that point." By 1897, thanks to Louderback's Herculean efforts, Charles had added over fifty miles of track to his streetcar domain. These outlying railways encircled the magnate's cable lines, forming a sort of defensive perimeter—and a profitable one at that. "In controlling these outside lines we have built up a defense for ourselves," Charles informed his West Chicago stockholders in 1897. "We make a great deal of money out of the passengers turned over to us. . . . There is now no outside line in our territory [the West Side] or in the territory of the North Chicago Road."[13]

The magnate had by now become a firm believer in the trolley. In some ways, Charles was fortunate that he had waited so long to adopt the overhead wire system. Trolley motors and other electrical equipment had been greatly improved since the early days of the invention, and their costs had appreciably decreased, in some cases by as much as one-half. New safety devices had also been devised that materially reduced the dangers inherent in running trolleys.

Charles never did things by halves. Once he became convinced of the trolley's practicality and efficiency, he resolved to change nearly all of his North and West Side horsecar lines to electricity. In May 1894, Charles hired the ace electrical engineer James R. Chapman to undertake this immense task. Chapman was up to the challenge, having spent much of his career roaming the West as a first-class railway builder. Leading a semi-nomadic existence, the shy and reclusive engineer worked in a few short years for a succession of railroads, including the Denver and Rio Grande. In 1891, he changed scenes and switched gears, moving to Grand Rapids, Michigan, to take charge of that city's streetcar company. Chapman converted the firm's forty miles of horse and cable roads to electricity, and in the process established himself as a force to be reckoned with in the emerging trolley field.

Chapman swept into Chicago with his customary energy. Setting up shop in a former residence across the street from Charles's North Side office, the engineer and an army of expert assistants prosecuted their work in zealous fashion. Within five years of his hiring, Chapman had overseen the construction of over 400 miles of electric lines—lines once traversed by the plodding horsecar. By then, the newspapers had stopped referring to the trolley as "deadly." As Chapman pointed out in 1900, "the personal injury account growing out of 47 miles of cable slot exceeds that of 451 miles of overhead trolley."[14]

The trolley dramatically transformed Chicago. Locales once considered remote were suddenly brought into easy contact with the Loop, and entire new communities became possible. The change wrought by the trolley sometimes occurred astoundingly fast. Early in 1895 an electric line was opened on Elston Avenue in a sparsely populated section of northwest Chicago, and within a matter of weeks people started flocking to the area. "The number of new roofs that are now to be seen from an Elston avenue car window are to be counted by the hundreds," one observer reported in May 1895. "There are places along the line where the country is white with new pine lumber." The trolley hastened the growth of the city and its suburbs, in the process paving the way for the commuter culture of the twentieth century.

With his eager embrace of technology, Charles showed that he was a proponent of what the economist Joseph Schumpeter would later call "creative destruction." According to Schumpeter, the structure of capitalism was constantly being destroyed and recreated by "the gale of creative destruction"—the process of innovation. In this economist's view, only a very few businessmen were true innovators, willing to overthrow the old order of things with new technologies. Charles certainly belonged to this select group.

Not long after the financier purchased the *Daily Inter Ocean*, a remarkable editorial appeared in that newspaper. "The truth is that destruction goes before construction," this editorial declared. "The world owes much to the besom of devastation." Charles, the creative destroyer, undoubtedly shared this sentiment. In his New York home's entrance hall, he proudly displayed a bust of Nero—the emperor who, according to legend, burned down Rome in order to build a new city.[15]

17 An Elevating Prospect

Charles's alliance with DeLancey Louderback proved to be a turning point in his Chicago career. Louderback brought Charles into close contact with a clique of powerful businessmen centered on John Mitchell, president of the Illinois Trust and Savings Bank, and in the process rehabilitated the magnate's credit. The so-called Mitchell crowd included such luminaries as Marshall Field, Philip Armour, and Levi Leiter. Charles's marriage of convenience with these eminent Chicagoans would be a brief and stormy one—in part because of irreconcilable differences over an elevated railroad.

Only a few cities ever possessed elevated railroads, the first and foremost of which was New York. Originating in the late 1860s and greatly extended over the years, Gotham's elevated railway system led the nation in terms of mileage and by 1892 a staggering 500,000 passengers were riding daily on its antiquated steam locomotives. Brooklyn, Boston, Kansas City, and even little Sioux City, Iowa, would follow New York's lead and adopt "transit on stilts."[1]

There were good reasons why elevated railroads never caught on as a popular mode of urban transportation. Most important, they were extremely expensive to build—even more expensive than cable railways—requiring an outlay of between $500,000 and $1,000,000 per mile. Many persons also judged the elevated's iron skeleton structure to be an eyesore that subtracted too much light and added too much noise to a locale. Property owners in particular objected to elevated roads for this reason, fearing a consequent depreciation in the value of their real estate.

Elevated railways, though, had their ardent defenders. People like the newspaper publisher Victor Lawson championed 'Ls'—the popular Chicago term for them—in the belief that they offered a long-suffering public "genuine rapid transit"—transit unimpeded by the surface traffic of the streets. In 1892, the street railway expert C. B. Fairchild attempted to address the criticisms of those opposed to elevated roads, but in a not entirely convincing fashion. "Many objections are urged against elevated structures because they are unsightly, noisy, and affect the value of abutting property," Fairchild wrote, "but, the road once in successful operation, its appearance is seldom noticed, the noise (which is not a necessary adjunct) ceases to disturb, the increase in the value of suburban property more than balances the supposed damage to property along the line, while the increased facilities and comforts outnumber the discomforts."[2] Fairchild damned with faint praise.

Hoping to boom their suburban properties, Chicago real estate developers were more than willing to overlook the supposed disadvantages of elevated roads. Beginning in 1887, they inundated the city with one elevated railway scheme after another. The promoters, however, quickly discovered that it was a long way from a paper company to a fully operational elevated road. "There is," the *Chicago Tribune* maintained, "a combination of three requirements necessary to build an elevated railroad—the consent of the property-owners on every mile of the route, a satisfactory ordinance, and money."[3] Putting together this winning combination proved to be an extraordinarily difficult task.

The first obstacle to 'L' construction had been erected by the Illinois legislature in 1883. That year the legislature had enacted the Adams Law, requiring the sponsors of elevated roads to secure the written consent of a majority of the abutting property owners located within each mile of the intended route. Armed with this statute, many property owners zealously defended their real estate holdings against the threatened 'L' invasion and refused to sign the consent forms. The more opportunistic among them routinely demanded money for their consent signatures. If the 'L' promoters somehow managed to satisfy the stringent requirements of the Adams Law, they then had to apply to the City Council for an ordinance authorizing the building of the road. Here many an elevated project perished. "It seems that in the case of elevated railroad schemes, real estate men propose and existing circumstances and the city Council dispose," a commentator noted.[4] Finally, the would-be 'L' magnate needed money—and lots of it. Investors, though, tended to steer clear of such risky and potentially profitless ventures as elevated roads.

Between 1887 and 1893, only three Chicago 'L' schemes managed to surmount these formidable hurdles and reach the construction phase. The first 'L' out of the gate was that belonging to the Chicago and South Side Rapid Transit Railroad Company. Organized by a group of New Yorkers, this railway was constructed largely over alleys in order to escape the objections—and exactions—of property owners, and, as a result, gained an endearing nickname—the Alley 'L.' The initial three-and-six-tenths-mile leg of the road was completed by June 1892. By then, the line had fallen under the sway of the mighty Chicago City Railway. The directors of the South Side streetcar company had concluded that it was bad policy to permit a potential rival to remain outside of their firm's ever-widening orbit.[5]

Chicago's second 'L,' on the other hand, threatened Charles's West Side streetcar properties. The Lake Street Elevated Railway had as its driving force none other than "King" Mike McDonald, the political boss and gambler. "Mike's Upstairs Railroad" was in fact not McDonald's first foray into the transportation field. In the early 1880s, he had formed the Chicago Passenger Railway as a competitor to the West Division horsecar company. As he had hoped, the latter firm ultimately paid him a pretty price for his interests in the Passenger Railway. Charles suspected that McDonald was now trying to work a similar "sandbagging" job on him—this time with the Lake Street Elevated as the club.

The politically powerful and less than scrupulous McDonald had little difficulty in procuring an 'L' ordinance from the City Council. Obtaining money to finance the venture was another matter entirely. For one thing, investors did not at all like the Lake Street Elevated's proposed mode of propulsion. Morris Alberger, president of the Lake Street 'L,' had persuaded the company's directors to adopt the so-called Meigs system of transit. In this innovative system developed by Joe V. Meigs, a steampowered, streamlined, futuristic-looking train glided along a single rail. Backers of this monorail touted the fact that the railway required only a single truss supported by a row of columns.[6]

The Meigs system, unfortunately, had largely been untested except for a short experimental line in East Cambridge, outside of Boston. Most experts who examined this model road concluded that the Meigs monorail would be impractical to operate on a large scale—an opinion shared by the mechanically minded Chicago Mayor John Roche, who visited East Cambridge in 1888. Unable to market bonds to investors skeptical of the scheme, the Lake Street Elevated's directors ultimately gave up on the Meigs system. The former Union General Benjamin "the Beast" Butler expressed dismay at the actions of McDonald and his associates. "The whole performance of those people who are attempting to build an elevated railroad on Lake Street is as disgraceful as they are dishonest," Butler declared to a Chicago acquaintance.[7] The Bostonian's unhappiness was understandable: He, after all, was an attorney for the Meigs company.

"King" Mike had no intention of becoming an elevated railway magnate, and so late in 1891 he offered control of the Lake Street road to a party of New York financiers. At first, the latter group had trouble taking McDonald seriously. "His reputation as a mere boss gambler had preceded him," a source explained. "This was all the worse for him, because he and his crowd wanted to get out. They were tired and sick of the difficulties they had encountered and, besides, 'action' was too slow in comparison with their previous experience." McDonald's "magnetism" eventually won out, and a syndicate headed by the baking powder baron William Ziegler acquired control of the Lake Street Elevated. The company's new ownership and its president—ex-Mayor John Roche—vigorously prosecuted construction work on the partially completed road.[8] In October 1893, the Lake Street Elevated finally commenced regular passenger service along most of its six-mile-long route.

Charles had done his best to prevent this outcome. He did not like the idea of a competitor penetrating deep into his West Side territory. Despite the claims of some 'L' promoters to the contrary, there was no doubt that elevated roads seriously cut into the traffic of adjacent streetcar lines. New York provided an instructive case study on this subject. The city's Third Avenue horsecar road had carried 30,500,000 passengers in 1878. That year an elevated railway opened on Third Avenue, and almost immediately robbed the horsecar line of over 7,000,000 customers. In subsequent years, ridership on the elevated continued to increase at the expense of the surface road. "In 1890 the elevated road carried 73,000,000," an expert noted, "while the surface road carried only 30,000,000, having not yet quite regained the position that it lost twelve years before."[9]

If Charles had gotten his way, there would never have been any elevated railroads in Chicago. In an early attempt to realize this objective, he entered into a pact with certain West Side property owners who had organized to combat the elevated roads. The businessman's association with the "Lake Street Protective League" was hardly a secret: LeGrand W. Perce, an attorney on the payroll of Charles's West Side company, happened to be a prominent member of the group. Taking full advantage of the Adams Law, the financier harassed the Lake Street Elevated with a string of lawsuits questioning the validity of the railway's frontage consents. Charles was even suspected of being the force behind a legal effort to revoke the road's charter on the eve of its opening. This story contained more than a shred of credibility: States-Attorney Jacob Kern, the sponsor of this quo warranto proceeding, had been secretly observed conferring with the magnate.[10] Despite Charles's plotting, the Lake Street Elevated and another road, the Metropolitan West Side Elevated, managed to secure footholds in the heart of his territory.

Charles could have followed the example of the Chicago City Railway and bought out his elevated rivals, but for the longest time he resisted making this move. He had trouble believing that the Chicago 'Ls' would ever be profitable ventures, and not without reason. Charles's mentor William Kemble, the Philadelphia streetcar titan, had carefully investigated the matter of elevated railways in the late 1880s. "Two questions presented themselves on the threshold," Kemble later explained. "What would it cost to lay the railway and what amount of business could be transacted on it." He discovered that elevated road construction soaked up roughly $500,000 per mile—an amount requiring "a business much greater than can be furnished on any street in Philadelphia." As for Chicago, Kemble estimated that an 'L' would need to make three times the earnings of the West Side streetcar company in order to merely pay its interest and operating expenses.

As late as 1893, Charles was an avowed skeptic regarding elevated railways. "The city is not ready for elevated roads," he announced in May of that year. "The city is gridironed with cable roads, which are always fatal to the success of elevated traffic. If there was anything in the elevated road business I would have been in it long ago."[11]

Yet, only a few months later, the magnate entered the elevated railroad field—albeit reluctantly. It was no coincidence that Charles reversed course shortly after tying his fortunes to those of DeLancey Louderback. Louderback and members of the Mitchell crowd had long contemplated building an elevated road on the North Side and the financier decided to go along with this plan. As a North Side 'L' seemed inevitable anyway, Charles calculated that it would be "much better for the North Chicago Street railroad company to have the competing line in friendly hands."[12] Besides, he couldn't afford to alienate his new allies in the Mitchell crowd who wanted the 'L'—weighty men like Marshall Field and Levi Leiter. The businessman needed the financial support of these men in those horrific economic times as he was no longer able to count on Peter Widener and William Elkins for aid and comfort. The roster of the Northwestern's investors read like a who's who of Chicago high society: Field, Leiter, Philip Armour, Charles Hutchinson, McCormick, and on and on.

Charles's Northwestern Elevated Railroad Company enjoyed the distinction of being "the first elevated railway . . . ever designed exclusively for electricity," in the words of the engineer Bion Arnold—the first, that is, except for the Columbian Intramural Railway. The thirty-two-year-old Arnold—a Michigan native possessed of "rare mechanical skill"—was one of the principal masterminds behind the construction of this roughly three-mile-long 'L' line that snaked along the grounds of the World's Columbian Exposition. The Intramural Railway had been designed as an "experiment on a large scale, tending to prove or disprove the claims of electricians regarding the merits of electricity for the propulsion of heavy trains." The experiment was outfitted with "the first example of third-rail construction" in the United States, and proved to be a tremendous success both mechanically *and* financially. Some 5,800,000 people used the railway during the six months of the Exposition without a single death having occurred. Elevated railroad managers took notice, and began to adopt electricity on their roads—a trend inaugurated by Chicago's Metropolitan 'L.'[13]

Some experts seized upon electricity as a panacea for the ills of elevated roads. Electrically powered engines were faster and less noisy than steam locomotives, and they did not belch smoke plumes into the air. They were also a great deal cheaper to operate than their predecessors. A municipal statute had mandated that the steam locomotives burn anthracite coal. In an electrified operation—where the coal was burned at a stationary powerhouse—the cheaper soft coal could be used. This switch alone meant a substantial reduction in costs, with anthracite coal averaging $5 per ton and soft coal only between $2 and $3 per ton. Electricity also reduced labor expenses. Two men were required to run a steam locomotive while only one was needed to operate an electric train. These cost savings added up. "The Metropolitan road will be run by electricity at a saving estimated from $200,000 to $300,000 per annum as against steam power," one expert concluded.[14]

The potential benefits of electricity helped propel Charles into the elevated road arena. His Northwestern Elevated was a direct offspring of the Columbian Intramural Railway—a fact attested to by the presence of Bion Arnold as an incorporator of the road. Charles bravely insisted that the new 'L' would have little impact on his North Side cable lines. "My experience with elevated roads is that they interfere with cable traffic little if any," he stated. "They create some new business for themselves, but the cable cars do as much as ever." Just the same, he made certain that the Northwestern's route ran well west of his Lincoln Avenue and Clark Street cable lines for most of its length.[15]

Charles's sponsorship of the Northwestern threatened to derail growing plans for an elevated loop. Rapid transit promoters had long recognized the need for such a structure—a loop of track situated in the central business district serving as a common terminal for the city's 'L' roads. As the situation stood in early 1894, Chicago's elevated roads possessed terminals on the outskirts of the business district or entirely outside of it. 'L' managers increasingly believed that the success of their roads hinged on gaining entry into the city's heart, where the department stores and skyscrapers were located. "The public demand was for transportation to points far east or north of the present termini of the 'L' roads now running," an observer explained. "It was seen that women who desired to shop on State street or Wabash avenue would rather take twenty minutes longer by coming down in the surface cars than walk several blocks from the present 'L' road stations. The same fact was true of thousands of persons who are employed east of LaSalle street and north of Harrison."[16]

Separate downtown loops for each elevated road were out of the question—thanks to the stubborn opposition of big property owners like Levi Leiter. "I am not in favor of many elevated tracks down-town," Leiter declared in 1894. "The streets are crowded now and the traffic congested."[17] In Chicago's central business district, Leiter's word was law—or nearly so.

The backers of the Lake Street Elevated spearheaded the early efforts in behalf of a common terminal loop. In September 1892, Frank Underwood and Willard Green, of the Lake Street 'L,' formed the Elevated Terminal Railway Company to build a downtown loop linking the lines of the Lake Street road, the Alley 'L,' and the Metropolitan 'L.' This particular plan never went past the paper company stage, but the elevated loop dream did not die. By June 1894, the officials of the three elevated railroads had held several meetings and were apparently close to reaching an agreement on a terminal loop—an agreement, however, that did not include Charles's Northwestern 'L.'[18]

The magnate swiftly moved to remedy this oversight. He approved a route for his Northwestern 'L' that sliced through the heart of the city—and through buildings—in a forty-foot swath. Not coincidentally, the Northwestern's path was slated to cross the northern leg of the planned loop. DeLancey Louderback, Charles's partner, made it abundantly clear that he was in a hurry to build the Northwestern's downtown link. "I know there has been talk of our using the proposed down-town loop in connection with the operation of the road," Louderback told a reporter. "The loop is not there, though, and we cannot afford to wait for it." Charles's 'L' road rivals got the hint. "If a way is not found to stop it," one such rival warned, "the Northwestern 'L' will balk the building of any down-town loop, except on its own terms."[19]

The officials of the Lake Street Elevated concocted an audacious plan to checkmate the Northwestern and thereby save the loop. On the night of June 7, two platoons of seventy-five men armed with picks and shovels and a fleet of wagons loaded with sand, stone, cement, and iron converged upon a pair of alleys in the business district. After tearing up the alley pavement, the men began digging holes in preparation for the erection of the loop's first link. "We shall build all night and get up all we can," the Lake Street Elevated's Willard Green vowed. "And we shall keep on building. There will be no nights or Sundays from now until we get this loop finished. We shall build it just as soon as we can." By the crack of dawn, the workers had succeeded in placing "enough iron in position to be called a structure." The Northwestern had been checkmated: A wall of iron now stood in its way. "Trains on the proposed Northwestern Elevated Railroad," a journalist quipped, "will need wings or long experience as hurdle racers when they leave the north side, the river, and South Water street behind and start on their across-lots-and-through-blocks run to Madison street."[20]

An injunction put a temporary stop to the loop construction, and shortly thereafter Charles decisively ended it in his inimitable fashion: He seized control of the Lake Street Elevated Company. Acting in behalf of the magnate, the banker John Mitchell acquired 52,000 of the 100,000 shares of Lake Street stock. On July 3, William Ziegler sold to Mitchell his 4,127 shares of stock at $18 per share, in the process surrendering control of the road to Charles. Ziegler subsequently agreed to join in a "combine" with the new directors of the road, having been persuaded by Mitchell that "a new impetus would be given to said railroad company, its lines of traffic extended, its down town facilities completed and improved, and the value of its stock enhanced."[21]

Removing any "lingering doubts" as to who was in charge of the Lake Street Elevated, Charles in late July tapped two of his own men—Warren Furbeck and John B. Parsons—to serve on the company's board. A few months later, Louderback replaced John Roche as president of the railroad and Robert Laughlin assumed the treasurership. A business reporter guessed that Laughlin was a representative of "large financial interests in Philadelphia." He, in fact, was an old broker friend of Charles who had been a source of comfort during the financier's darkest days. Twenty-three years later, the time had arrived for Charles to repay the favor, Laughlin having "struck the toboggan to bankruptcy." As the Lake Street Elevated's new treasurer, the former Philadelphia man earned a good living, but soon his luck ran out again. He got into "an entanglement with a woman" and the news ultimately reached Charles's ears. A conference between the two men ensued. Laughlin admitted the truth of the rumors and Charles fired him. Laughlin was "a broken man" when he shortly thereafter left Chicago. According to the attorney Clarence Knight, a close associate of Charles, the financier "loved his friends and when a person once gained his confidence he trusted him in every respect, but his confidence once lost was lost for all time."[22]

The Lake Street Elevated offered Charles far greater problems than Robert Laughlin's "entanglement." The road turned out to be in far worse financial shape than the magnate had expected. McDonald and his successors had issued securities "far in excess of any legitimate expenditures." Louderback estimated that the six-mile-long line should have cost roughly $3,317,500 to build and equip, and yet the liabilities of the railway exceeded $17,000,000! Charles was thus saddled with an overburdened road that "ran to no place from nowhere"—except possibly the poorhouse. "Mr. Yerkes has made the first big mistake of his life in Chicago transportation affairs," a commentator declared.[23]

The businessman executed a wild maneuver to repair the Lake Street Elevated's sorry financial state. He devised a plan to trim the road's bond debt by roughly $2,000,000—to $5,625,000. In this so-called scaling arrangement, a majority of the Lake Street bondholders were "seductively induced" to endure a 40 percent reduction in their initial investment. A few loud voices, however, roared in protest against this unusual scheme, with the loudest voice belonging to William Ziegler. In April 1895, the baking powder baron filed suit in federal court against the Lake Street Elevated's new owners, charging them with attempting to wreck the road. A man "not handicapped with a college education or ethical theories," according to the muckraker Lincoln Steffens, Ziegler seemed to thrive on battle. He had spent much of his career fighting rival baking powder manufacturers who used alum as an ingredient instead of the cream of tartar he so favored.[24] Behaving true to form, Ziegler duked it out in the courts with Charles for over five years before the Lake Street matter was finally settled.

Charles's recipe for elevated railway success involved more than debt reduction. "There are two ways out of the trouble," he once explained. "One is for the roads to cut down their debt, and the other is to build up their business so that they can pay their interest." The magnate realized that a terminal loop would help the Lake Street Elevated achieve the latter goal. He consequently pushed ahead with long-existing plans to extend the road all the way to Wabash Avenue in the commercial district. "If the extension is built it will be the first step toward getting a downtown loop," Louderback predicted.[25]

Louderback neglected to mention the fact that Charles's downtown loop was not necessarily open to every one of the city's elevated roads. The

financier did not intend to promote the interests of the rival Metrop
West Side Elevated, then nearing completion. "There is not a bigger
in the country than the Metropolitan Elevated railroad," he infor
reporter in September 1894. "It was organized, just as the Alley Elevated
railroad was, to sell securities." Charles wasn't being fair to his competitor. Determined to build the finest 'L' system in existence, the New York
owners of the "Polly 'L'" had spared no expense in construction—a fact
borne out by the road's selected route. According to a journalist, "in laying out the line the engineers did not swerve for apartment buildings or
for any other class of improvement"—a course of action necessitating
roughly $5,000,000 in payments to property owners. Charles would show
no mercy on the Polly 'L,' taking "good care" to plant trolley roads on
either side of the Metropolitan's sixteen-and-a-half-mile-long right of
way. A broker likened the Polly 'L' to "a beautiful fly caught in a spider's
web woven by Mr. Yerkes out of trolley lines."[26]

Interceding in behalf of the Metropolitan 'L,' a group of influential
downtown property owners appealed to Charles to include all four elevated roads in his loop project. Back in 1893, these men—among whom
numbered Marshall Field and William Hale, father of the astronomer—
had organized the Central Elevated Railroad Company to furnish a terminal loop for the city's 'L' roads. This plan had miscarried, and now they
rested their hopes on Charles. After "mature deliberation," he agreed to
unite Chicago's quartet of 'Ls' in a common loop—a decision marked by
the November 1894 incorporation of the aptly named Union Elevated
Railroad Company. "The Gordian knot has been cut," the *Chicago Tribune* proclaimed on November 23. "The question of an elevated railroad
terminal is settled. There is to be one terminal loop and that will be used
by all the companies."[27] The new company would be the owner of the
loop structure, with the four 'L' roads paying a toll to operate on it.

Not everyone believed that the Union Elevated would prevail where
so many similar schemes had failed.[28] The project would put the magnate's skills to the test.

The Adams frontage law (requiring the written consent of abutting
property owners) posed the greatest challenge to the Loop. There was no
small irony in this fact, Charles having long employed this very same law
to combat the elevated roads. Now he was himself an elevated railway
magnate and the tables had been turned. Anti-'L' property owners—his
former allies—had become his enemies, stubbornly refusing to sign the
necessary frontage consents for the Loop.

Early in 1895, representatives of Chicago's four elevated railways had
tentatively agreed that the Loop would be a rectangle of track bounded on

the north by Lake Street, on the west by Fifth Avenue, on the east by Wabash Avenue, and on the south by Harrison Street. The north leg was already nearly a done deal, an ordinance having been secured for it by the Lake Street Elevated company in 1894. Fifth Avenue turned out to be the next link in the Loop. A majority of property holders there showed a kindly disposition toward the Loop—but only after receiving from the Northwestern Elevated $50 for every foot of frontage they owned.[29]

Stiff opposition to the Loop developed on Wabash Avenue—bastion of such wealthy property owners as the hotelier Potter Palmer and the mining magnate Erskine Phelps. Members of the newly organized Wabash Avenue Protective Association objected to the 'L' structure out of an expressed fear that it would ruin the street and depreciate property values. Charles was not at all surprised to learn that some of the Wabash Avenue landlords harbored far more mercenary motives: They wanted money for their frontage consents—and lots of it. "You may talk about sandbagging Aldermen and other sandbaggers at the City Hall," the magnate angrily reflected, "but they are not to be compared with some of the gentry who frequent the best parlors and drawing-rooms in the city. That is the place to look for the more accomplished 'hold-up' with a nice silken sandbag concealed under the tails of his clawhammer coat." Charles had earlier bluntly compared some of the leaders of the Wabash Avenue Protective Association to "wolves who follow a caravan and grab what they can."

The Wabash Avenue "wolves" did much better in the end than their counterparts on Fifth Avenue, obtaining an average of $100 for every foot of frontage they owned. Money ultimately carried the day—as it usually did in Chicago—and Charles captured the thoroughfare. On October 14, the City Council capped the businessman's triumph, passing an ordinance allowing the Union Elevated company to use Wabash Avenue.[30]

Only one leg of the Loop remained: the southern. Here the struggle would be most severe. Shortly after the passage of the Wabash Avenue ordinance, Union Elevated officials decided to build the Loop's final link on Van Buren Street instead of on the originally planned Harrison, two blocks to the south. The managers of the Metropolitan Elevated had urged this change, preferring that their line connect with the Loop closer to the commercial district. Charles endorsed the revised Loop route. "Loops should always be as small as possible," he argued.[31] Levi Leiter, however, refused to accept this new plan. And the hot-tempered Leiter was used to getting his way.

A native of Leitersburg, Maryland, the stocky, bearded Leiter was one of Chicago's "foundation builders." He had helped guide the early fortunes of five of the city's major institutions: the Chicago Art Institute, the

Chicago Relief and Aid Society, the Chicago Historical Society, the Commercial Club, and the Illinois Trust and Savings Bank. For twenty-five years, he had been a partner in Marshall Field's wholesale and retail business. By all accounts, the two men did not get along very well—thanks to their contrasting temperaments. "Field was suave with customers; Leiter, sharp," an historian has written. "Field gloried in the retail division; Leiter, in the wholesale." In 1881, Leiter dissolved his partnership with Field, and before long he and his wife had relocated to Washington, D.C., where they opened "one of the great social campaigns in American history." The Leiter name gained international notice in the spring of 1895 when Levi's daughter Mary wedded the English nobleman George Nathaniel Curzon, a future viceroy of India.

An adoring Mary Leiter called her father "an example of conscientiousness, integrity, firmness and reserve." He was *also* a model of shrewdness. After the Chicago Fire, he purchased, for a song, sites in the devastated city center, and in this manner amassed a downtown real estate empire of immense value.[32] Leiter primarily opposed the Loop link on Van Buren Street in order to protect what was widely deemed to be the most desirable of his holdings: the lot on the corner of State and Van Buren streets, home to the Siegel Cooper department store. Though he had gone on record in favor of an elevated loop, he didn't want the ugly structure right next to his most valuable property. Leiter had a second motive for favoring an 'L' on Harrison instead of Van Buren: He believed a loop would help extend the business district that far south and thereby elevate land values in that neglected area, his son Joseph having property near Harrison. Leiter's faith was shared by many. "The general belief now is that property that is within the boundaries of the loop will constitute the business district," a local newspaper asserted.[33]

In late October 1895, Leiter declared war on the Loop, issuing a metaphorical call to arms to Van Buren street property owners. "It would be the height of folly, in my opinion, to put an elevated structure along Van Buren street and congest this thoroughfare," Leiter later told a reporter. He argued that Van Buren was simply too narrow an avenue to accommodate an elevated road. Many of his fellow Van Buren street landlords also did not want a "rumbling railroad up over their heads," and Leiter had no problem rallying them to his side.[34]

Charles seems to have been taken aback by Leiter's opposition. Leiter, after all, had long been a key supporter of the magnate's transit projects, even aiding in the overthrow of the Chicago City Railway's Charles Holmes. Careful not to alienate a man who was still potentially his ally, the financier initially behaved in a temperate (for him) fashion, simply criticizing what he termed Leiter's "selfish course." "We have to give and take occasionally," he added, offering advice that he himself never heeded. The controversy, however, quickly and perhaps inevitably degenerated into a contest of egos, with Leiter and Charles ultimately trading shots in the newspapers. The magnate supposedly declared that "if Harrison is the only street open for the southern line of the loop the loop will forever remain unbuilt." Leiter was just as adamant on his side, vowing that the "loop will never run through Van Buren street." The gloves were now off, and Charles felt free to indulge his penchant for sarcasm. At one point he described a circular issued by Leiter as "twaddle." "It is silly," he asserted in an interview, his eyes sparkling and his cheeks full of color. "It sounds like the talk of a lot of old women." A Leiter supporter had the last word, characterizing Charles's "utterances" as the product of a "man who is not angry, but mad, and very much so."[35]

By early 1896, Leiter appeared to have won the Loop war. The stretch of Van Buren Street between Wabash Avenue and the Chicago River extended for some 4,200 feet. Property owners representing 3,800 feet of Van Buren frontage had joined Leiter's protective association. Consequently, there was no apparent way Charles could fulfill the terms of the Adams Law, which required majority consent for an 'L' road to be built. Instead, well over a majority of the landlords on East Van Buren had registered their disapproval of an elevated railway.[36]

The businessman, however, was not ready to admit defeat just yet. He and his associates hatched a brilliant plot to thwart Leiter. The plan involved securing, as one newspaper explained, "a sufficient number of consents west of the river to overcome the opposition east of the river." To accomplish the goal, the Union Consolidated Elevated Railway was formed in March 1896 and empowered to construct an 'L' structure on Van Buren from Wabash west to a point near Halsted Street—a distance of one mile. Charles never intended to build the portion of the road west of the Chicago River, but he of course didn't tell that to the property owners there. "I don't want to rejoice prematurely, because I never count the poultry before it is hatched," he informed a journalist the day his "ruse" was revealed. "I have every reason to believe, however, that a majority of the signatures of Van Buren street property owners west to Halsted street will be secured." Leiter, on the contrary, expressed confidence that the property owners there were "practically unanimous in their opposition to Mr. Yerkes' plan." Leiter, it turned out, was very wrong, and by mid-April, Charles had procured the necessary frontage consents for the final Loop link.[37]

The Loop opened for business on Sunday morning, October 3, 1897, amid little fanfare. At 7:00 A.M., a Lake Street Elevated train rumbled around the two-mile-long Loop. Fittingly, the only passengers, besides the motorman and conductor, were five or six construction workers who had helped make this day possible. They went along for the ride in order to be recorded as the first regular passengers to use the Loop, but, in a cruel twist of fate, no reporter bothered to list their names. According to a witness, the trip was accomplished with "as little friction as a clock runs around the hours." The event was a historic one, marking "a new era in the history of the great west side." "There were hosanna and hymns of praise and thanksgiving," a journalist remarked, with no little exaggeration, "and at one swift pull, the Cicero prairies were connected directly with State street." On October 11, the Polly 'L' began operating on the Loop, followed one week later by the Alley 'L.'[38]

Charles's financially plagued Northwestern Elevated would not join the Union Loop for over two years. The road's troubles began in December 1895, when Widener and Elkins failed to take up $1,300,000 in Columbia Construction Company stock that had been set aside for them. (This construction company was building the elevated railway.) After inspecting the Northwestern's route, the "Traction Twins" had concluded that the 'L' road would inflict too much damage on their North Side streetcar interests. Charles was left holding the $1,300,000 bag. He had no end of trouble in disposing of these securities, even after offering to prospective investors a bonus of 40 percent Union Elevated stock.

The Northwestern Elevated was in part a casualty of the Loop war. Unhappy with Charles's course of action during the conflict, some of Levi Leiter's associates in the Mitchell crowd refused to invest any more money in the Northwestern. These men were displeased with the financier for another reason as well: Charles had reserved for himself much of the stock in the Union Loop construction company, thereby denying them any share in the enterprise's potential profits. Widener and Elkins were also not let in on "the ground floor" of the Union Loop venture, and this was another grievance they had against the magnate.

A big stockholder in the Northwestern Elevated, Levi Leiter himself spearheaded the minority faction of owners opposing "the rule of Charles T. Yerkes." Leiter actively worked to undermine Charles's hold on the road. He began playing "the part of the bull in a china shop" at the Columbia Construction Company's stockholders' meetings. In a September 1896 gathering, he engaged in a heated exchange with Charles. The former threatened to forgo paying the assessment on his stock, prompting the magnate to respond that he "would not stoop to such actions as Mr. Leiter had been guilty of." Leiter parried this thrust with one of his own, remarking that "Mr. Yerkes had stooped to much lower actions on numerous occasions."[39] Debates such as this certainly did not improve Charles's standing in the Chicago financial community. DeLancey Louderback, not Charles, would ultimately raise the money to complete the Northwestern Elevated.

Louderback also deserved a good deal of the credit—or blame—for the construction of the Loop. "I built it [the Loop], got the funds and did the whole business," he later testified. The Union Loop was Charles's—and Louderback's—greatest legacy to Chicago. It would even give its name to the city's business district—the Loop. From the very beginning, however, it was a subject of controversy. In 1897, a *Times-Herald* reporter praised the Loop, calling it "a unique solution" to the mass transit problem. The *Chicago Tribune*, on the other hand, promptly judged the Loop to be "one of the greatest nuisances in the city." The *Tribune* editorialist believed that the structure's support columns—many of which were placed directly in the street—seriously interfered with horse and wagon traffic. Other people deemed the iron rectangle to be an eyesore that plunged the streets into a perpetual gloom.[40]

And then there was the not so little matter of noise. In May 1898, *Chicago Daily News* editor Charles Faye warned his boss Victor Lawson to steer clear of the Loop when he returned to the city. Having taken a long vacation overseas, Lawson had yet to be exposed to a fully operational Loop. "The noise made by the three elevated road trains on this loop is not only stunning, but it is fiendish," Faye wrote Lawson, "and add to the elevated trains the tremendous noise and clanging of bells of the cable cars and the trolley cars beneath the loop structure and you have as near pandemonium as we are apt to find in this world."[41]

Postcard view of Yerkes Observatory, ca. 1905. Yerkes initially balked at funding an entire observatory building. (John Franch Collection)

Gradually adopted by Yerkes, the trolley rapidly transformed Chicago. In this photo, a new settlement has sprung up alongside a trolley line extending into the lonely North Side countryside. (*Yerkes System of Street Railways*, 1897)

C. A. Graham painted this image of the great Yerkes telescope (minus lens), then on display in the Manufactures Building at the World's Columbian Exposition of 1893. Yerkes hoped the telescope would repair his battered public profile. (*Chicago Tribune Art Supplement*, 1893)

Trolley cars thread their way through dense traffic near the corner of Dearborn and Randolph streets in 1909. In Chicago, rapid transit often was more an ideal than a reality. (John Franch Collection)

If Yerkes could have gotten his way, Chicago would never have had any elevated railroads at all. Circumstances, however, forced his hand and he became the reluctant father of Chicago's Loop Elevated—his most famous legacy to a city he had grown to detest. The Van Buren Street and Wabash Avenue corner of the Loop Elevated (ca. 1905) is shown on this postcard. (John Franch Collection)

DeLancey Louderback, Yerkes's dynamic right-hand man, deserves much of the credit for the building of the Loop Elevated. Not visible in this photo, Louderback's left eye was damaged during a hunting expedition in 1876 when a charge exploded in his face, sending fourteen bullet fragments into his brain and skull. (*Yerkes System of Street Railways*, 1897)

Illinois Governor John Peter Altgeld (1847–1902) had "a smile like a suffering Christ." Altgeld was one of the few politicians Yerkes couldn't purchase. (University of Illinois Archives)

The interior of Yerkes's New York mansion, 864 Fifth Avenue, as seen from the entrance. Yerkes spared no expense in the furnishing and design of his mansion. (*Chronicle of the Yerkes Family*)

Yerkes stands in his New York palace's Italian garden, almost lost amid the green-ery, ca. 1902. (*Chronicle of the Yerkes Family*)

Emilie Grigsby was the great passion of Yerkes's life. He would build a mansion for her on Park Avenue, only blocks from his own home. (Library of Congress)

Charles Tyson Yerkes in London, painted by Benjamin Constant, ca. 1901. The Thames can be seen outside the office window. Yerkes hoped that the London Underground would be a monument to his memory. (*Yerkes Collection*, vol. 2, 1904)

18 Business and Pleasure

Long before the Loop was completed, Charles had decided that Chicago wasn't his kind of town. "I am in Chicago to make money," he once confided to an associate, "and if it were not for what I expect to make out of it I would take the first train to New York and never set eyes on the beastly place again."

The magnate had begun a gradual withdrawal from the city. In 1893, he started to erect a palatial mansion on New York City's Fifth Avenue. He had opened a business office on Wall Street, and had even purchased a mausoleum in Brooklyn's Greenwood Cemetery for himself and his wife. New York City was becoming Charles's home, with Chicago being merely his place of work.

In a very real sense, Charles occupied two worlds. He drew a sharp line between his business and home lives. "I can not impress upon you too much the difference between the home and the office life of a business man," he once told a reporter. "For example, I love pictures, but when a man comes here [to his business headquarters] to show me a picture it provokes me. If he insists upon seeing me I usually find some reason for not taking what he has to offer. But if the same man comes to my house I will sit up and talk pictures with him until 2 o'clock in the morning. I always throw aside business cares the moment I am away from business." Charles was decidedly not the kind of businessman who brought home the "severities" of the office.[1]

He usually began his day around 5:00 A.M. with a vigorous exercise session. Dumbbells were his workout tools of choice until 1895, when he became a self-confessed "bicycle crank." "I formerly spent hours daily in such exercises as are found in the gymnasium," he announced that year, "but I have given all that up. The wheel is the thing and I am positive of it." Fashionably clad in knickerbockers and a tight-fitting sweater that showcased his still-athletic form, Charles pedaled each day along the South Side boulevards, sometimes traveling as far as twelve miles.

Following his morning workout, Charles would bathe and then eat breakfast. At 8:00 A.M. sharp he left for work, frequently taking a Chicago City Railway streetcar to reach his downtown destination. He appreciated the irony of the situation: Chicago's foremost traction titan had no choice but to often ride on the lines of a rival firm. "Living on the south side, as I do, I am of course obliged to contribute 10 cents daily to Mr. Wheeler's company," he once wryly remarked. Charles spent the first half of his workday at 444 North Clark Street, the headquarters of his North Side transit system. Around 2:00 P.M. he shifted scenes, setting up shop in an office on the corner of Jefferson and Washington streets—where his West Side streetcar operations were centered.[2]

Charles worked long hours and he demanded that his subordinates do the same. "There was no limit to Mr. Yerkes' capacity for work and there was none to that he expected of his employees while on duty," Warren Furbeck, the financier's private secretary, asserted. "Eighteen hours a day were not uncommon." Another worker put the matter more succinctly: "While in the office he was a veritable slave driver to his men." At least some of Charles's employees did not mind toiling hard for their boss. They found the magnate to be an inspirational leader. "He was a remarkable man to work for and kept you keyed up to your work constantly," a one-time office boy at 444 North Clark Street related in 1928. "He had a remarkable mind and always had every detail of his business at his finger tips, and he expected everyone working for him to keep in as intimate touch with each detail as he did. At one time when he owned nineteen street railways on the north and west sides he could tell you the number of cars running on each line, their time schedule and earnings."[3]

Though he knew every facet of his firms' operations, Charles did not let himself get bogged down with what he called "detail work"—the setting of streetcar time schedules, the payment of wages, and the like. "I never do any detail work," he stated in 1895. "I plan; others see that my plans are carried out. I make all of the contracts for construction, maintenance and material. The vast interests under my control have been so systematized that they run like clock work."

The businessman absolutely relied on his lieutenants to keep his corporate machine running smoothly. Expert engineers like DeLancey Louderback and James Chapman handled the mechanical end of operations, closely supervising the design and construction of the streetcar lines. Charles desperately needed the assistance of such men because his own engineering knowledge was sorely lacking. The financier had demonstrated his woeful ignorance of mechanical matters early in 1889, when he officially opened the Lincoln Avenue cable route. While addressing a crowd gathered within the line's powerhouse, he referred to the huge drum supporting the cable as "an engine." "That isn't the engine," a wise guy in the assembly yelled. A red-faced Charles then asked his chief engineer A. D. Whitton "to arbitrate the question." Whitton ruled against the magnate—much to the latter's embarrassment.[4]

Charles depended upon lawyers as much as engineers to sustain his empire. Almost every day his various firms were in the courts, waging legal war on rival corporations or fending off personal injury and property damage suits. The businessman also required attorneys to draw up legislation and contracts, and, perhaps most important, to lobby politicians in his behalf. According to DeLancey Louderback, Charles usually had about fifteen lawyers on his staff, but would employ many more when he needed "their influence in reaching other people." He chose as his legal emissaries primarily those men who wielded a great deal of clout in Chicago's political realm, individuals like the ex-Judge Egbert Jamieson and the veteran attorney William Goudy. A friend once described the wily Goudy's method of procedure: "The course that Mr. Goudy pursued for the attainment of an object reminded me of an Indian, who in hunting elk never goes straight toward the game, but pursues an indirect course to the leeward, taking advantage of wind, weather and position."

The financier was himself devious, even when dealing with business allies. Sometime ally George Henry Wheeler, president of the Chicago City Railway, was once the victim of Charles's double-dealing. Wheeler didn't try to hide his disgust at being swindled. "Henry [Wheeler] says that Yerkes has lied to him and that he is sick of the whole job," Joseph Leiter, a Chicago City stockholder, gleefully reported. "I laughed at him and asked him what he expected.... It is lamentable but funny to see the 'ship without a rudder' look that Henry has now that he has discovered that his prophet and erstwhile guide is animated by the sinister motives of his own gain and not by a noble feeling of interest for him and his."

Charles was often an enigma to his own employees as well. He rarely gave his men explicit instructions. "Mr. Yerkes was a very reticent man," the attorney LeGrand W. Perce recalled, "and when he wanted anything done, he did not say, 'I want such and such a thing, and I want such and such a thing.'" DeLancey Louderback also found his boss to be rather tight-lipped. "My relations with Mr. Yerkes were not consultations,"

Louderback asserted in 1906. "All our business was done in monosyl-lables. . . . I don't suppose Mr. Yerkes and I had five minutes' conversation in all our eight years' experience."[5] This silence served a purpose, obscur-ing Charles's role in the corporate chain of command. As a result, he could always claim to have been "out of the loop" when a controversial business decision was made.

Charles expected unswerving loyalty from his lieutenants. "He was born a leader, imperious, autocratic, demanding—and obtaining—implicit obedience from his followers," a magazine writer said of the magnate. He required faithful managers for a very good reason. "The Yerkes crowd make their money out of their construction companies," an informed observer explained. "That makes it desirable for them to have about them in the responsible places their own henchmen. There is a juggling between the Philadelphians as stockholders in the street car company and the Philadel-phians as owners of the construction company that must be kept a secret all the while."[6]

Careful to protect his companies' secrets, Charles stocked his firms' boards with trustworthy men who would rubberstamp his every deci-sion—men like Warren Furbeck, the broker John Charles Moore, and the lawyer Frederick Winston. The magnate carefully orchestrated each board meeting: Directors were told beforehand what resolutions they should offer. Charles even stage-managed the annual stockholders' meet-ings. After giving his investors an invariably optimistic report of the year's business, he would submit a familiar slate of directors for election. Satisfied with their fat dividends, the stockholders always voted for the men Charles endorsed. The meetings were "all cut and dried and run through by Yerkes," the stockholder Azariah Galt reported. "I never knew anybody to oppose him at any meeting. It was always a unanimous thing and always went through."

This well-oiled system, though, sometimes broke drown. People were unpredictable and sometimes resisted being controlled. While serving as a director of the North Chicago Street Railroad Company, the manufacturer Hugh McBirney once objected to a proposition that came before the firm's board. McBirney took his case to Charles. "I don't know what is going on here," the elderly director complained. Charles's response revealed a great deal about his management style. "Do you expect to run the road by a Board of Directors?" the magnate chided McBirney. A few months later, the dissatisfied McBirney resigned from the North Chicago board.

Charles also could not prevent the occasional intrepid reporter from pulling back the curtain. For instance, Frank Vanderlip, an ace *Chicago*

Tribune journalist, once purchased a share of stock in each of Charles's streetcar firms—"a legal ticket of admission to the annual meeting of the company's stock-holders." While attending one of these yearly gatherings, the journalist—an expert stenographer—recorded one of Charles's most controversial utterances. "The short hauls and the people who hang on the straps are the ones we make our money out of," the magnate informed his stockholders, much to Vanderlip's delight. A modified version of this legendary quote eventually entered the history books: "It is the straphangers who pay the dividends." The statement may have been unwise, but it was quite true. Straphangers usually did not ride very far on the streetcars, and therefore consumed less of a line's operating expenses than the so-called long hauls—those journeying to the end of the road, or close to it.

Cold, austere, and unapproachable during business hours, Charles exhibited a more open personality when not at work. He in fact liked to think of himself as two persons: "the man circumstances have made him, and the man he is through his own choice." In his view "circumstances" had forced him to take a ruthless course as a businessman. Outside of work, however, he reverted to his "true self"—"a sensitive, reserved, quiet gentleman of the most refined tastes, absorbed in the beauty he has gathered about him."

In the early 1890s the magnate began to carve out separate spheres for the two sides of his nature. Chicago continued to serve as the arena for the gladiator of business while New York City became the home for the pleasure-seeking gentleman of leisure.[7] In 1891 Charles purchased as a home site a large parcel of ground on one of the "most desirable corners" of Fifth Avenue, overlooking Central Park. "It is at the crest of a hill that slopes down toward 59th street in one direction and toward Harlem in the other," a journalist noted of the location, "and in that neighborhood are some of the finest residences in the world." Dubbed "Millionaires' Row," this section of Fifth Avenue was populated by a healthy assortment of America's wealthiest men, including John Jacob Astor, George Gould, and William Whitney. Charles had undoubtedly chosen this exclusive locale with his wife's social ambitions in mind.

Working over a three-year period and expending roughly $2,000,000 of Charles's money, the celebrated architect Robert H. Robertson erected on the Fifth Avenue site a magnificent brownstone mansion. "It was such a house as an Athenian of the Golden Age might have built had he lived in New York in the twentieth century," the writer Edwin Lefevre raved. Critics praised the palatial home's restrained Italianate exterior, which, they felt, possessed "greater dignity" and "better taste" than the gaudier facades of neighboring residences.[8]

Inside the mansion presented "a vision of magnificence rarely equaled in a private home." Entering the main hall through a pair of heavy iron doors, the visitor was confronted with a splendid scene. "At first one is conscious only of the beauty and polish of the white marble, which greets the eye on all sides and reaches the broad circular balcony of the second story," one such visitor reported. Italian marble was used *everywhere* in the museum-like house. The broad "Grand Staircase"—and even Charles's bathtub—had been fashioned out of the expensive stone.

The four-story mansion contained a maze of elaborately furnished rooms, each with a different theme. In the India room (on the second floor) a luxurious divan, "massed high with gorgeously perfumed cushions," was suspended from the ceiling by four chains. "Here Mr. Yerkes may lie, and swing and dream, and believe that there is nothing prosaic in the world," a writer remarked. The conservatory, which occupied two floors, may have been the most impressive room in the house. The journalist Viola Rodgers likened the conservatory to the hanging gardens of ancient Babylon. "Here against a background of marble are wonderful palms, trees, ferns, flowers," Rodgers gushed. "Fountains throw graceful streams of water in the air. . . . The scent of orange blossoms and of lilies of the valley fill one's nostrils, and the sun shines through the glass covered roof as naturally as if there were no glass between." Rare tropical birds flew through the air and brilliantly hued goldfish swam in the waters of this fantasy world.[9]

Charles's favorite room was the wood-paneled art gallery, located on two floors in the rear of the mansion. Art had always appealed to the businessman, but ultra-expensive masterpieces remained out of his price range until he discovered the gold mine that was Chicago. Beginning in 1889, he embarked upon annual pilgrimages to Europe in search of fine art. Making up for lost time, Charles purchased over 140 paintings in four years. The businessman scored one of his greatest collecting triumphs during the summer of 1890, when he managed to secure Millet's famed *The Pig-Killers* from a French aristocratic family in "rather sore need for cash." In this and other transactions the magnate demonstrated a willingness to spend fabulous sums for art. When it came to his great passions, money was no object.

Charles quickly became adept at separating owners from their prized art possessions. The businessman once described in detail how he operated as a collector:

Well, when you go abroad and see a picture you think you would like to buy, the process of getting it takes a long time. You first send your card to the owners of the picture and he calls on you at your hotel. Then he invites you to make a call at his home and become acquainted with his family. They are all there and you make a long call and refreshments are passed. The next day you will go there, and at this visit, if you are rash, you will casually ask the man if he wants to sell the picture which you have seen and admired. The man will look grieved, and as you leave he will tell you to call again. On the occasion of your next visit the man may have communicated your wish to the other members of his family and you will be received a little differently. Each one in the family will have something to say about the picture and there may be a little weeping on the part of some of them. You won't think, while on the call, of mentioning a price for the picture, but perhaps when you make your next call you may suggest the value of it to you. Finally, if you are patient, you will secure the picture.[10]

Employing this strategy, the financier amassed in a relatively short time a noteworthy collection of paintings. In the end, the collection contained over 200 works, with old and modern masters about equally represented. Paintings by Rembrandt and Berchem—of the Dutch school, Rubens and Van Dyck—of the Flemish school, Boucher—of the French school, and Raphael—of the Roman school, all could be found hanging in the magnate's gallery. Charles claimed that the subject of a picture was not as important to him as "the technical treatment of the work." Yet he does seem to have favored landscapes, especially pastoral scenes.

When it came to paintings, Charles was a traditionalist. He gravitated toward artists like Detaille and Daubigny who depicted the world in a "realistic" manner. Like many other Gilded Age art patrons, he steered clear of the impressionists, seeing in their work little more than "blotches of ill-assorted colors." Indeed, only "traditional" painters were eligible to win his annual "Yerkes prize"—an award that he established in 1892 honoring Chicago's most talented artists.

Among contemporary painters, Charles particularly enjoyed the work of the "Belgian dandy" Jan Van Beers. Working in a Paris studio "filled with women's clothes and Japanese fetishes," Van Beers cranked out portraits that were nearly photographic in appearance. Some unkind critics in fact suspected that the eccentric artist achieved this amazing effect by simply painting over photographs. "Whatever may be the process by which Van Beers produces his portraits they look like colored photographs and their artistic value cannot be much greater," an art writer sniffed. "They tickle the fancy of the Philistine with their well-licked smoothness and the filigrane details, but have no truly fine qualities as paintings." Charles, though, greatly admired Van Beer's work, and, in absolute defiance of the critics, filled his galleries with the Belgian's paintings. The businessman even commissioned Van Beers to paint his portrait and that of his wife. Mary Yerkes seems to have been—if possible—a greater fan of the playboy artist than was her husband. The handsome and debonair Van Beers exuded an oily charm, after all, and he had a way with words—and women. "A beautiful sitter is like a rare gem—each time you look at her you discover a new beauty," he liked to say of his wealthy women patrons.[11] As she approached middle age, the appearance-obsessed Mary became increasingly susceptible to such talk.

A good number of art experts applauded Charles's aesthetic sensibility, viewing his fondness for Van Beers as a pardonable lapse in judgment. An Austrian art specialist who visited Chicago during the World's Fair was particularly effusive in his praise of the financier. "Of the private collections of old masters in Chicago the most complete and valuable is that owned by Mr. Yerkes," Eugene Fischhof raved in a newspaper interview. "I consider this one of the most important private collections in the world. It contains about sixty works of the highest quality by the most famous masters of all schools." The poet Harriet Monroe also admired Charles's artistic taste, finding it to be more "adventurous" than that exhibited by the Chicago coal dealer James Ellsworth.

The acclaim was by no means universal. The eminent art connoisseur Bernard Berenson judged Charles's collection of paintings to be only "so, so," and he uncovered two "certain forgeries" in it, including "a pallid and wooden copy" of a Botticelli painting in London's National Gallery. Berenson did not consider the magnate to be a "serious" collector, but rather an "over-rich" amateur who bought pictures "without first making sure that they were what they were given out to be." Charles does seem to have been an easy mark for the unscrupulous art dealer. Reportedly, the "polished and insinuating" Van Beers once teamed up with the Paris dealer Stephen Bourgeois to foist on the magnate a bogus Rembrandt. Van Beers is said to have received a large commission for his efforts.

Berenson, however, did think highly of Charles's "unrivalled" collection of rugs.[12] In the 1890s the businessman began to scour the globe for the finest Asian carpets, in the process becoming one of the first Americans to collect this form of art. By 1905—the year of his death—Charles had brought together "the most remarkable group of sixteenth- and seventeenth-century Oriental rugs that has ever been assembled," according to the writer John Kimberly Mumford.

The magnate was also a pioneer when it came to collecting sculpture. He enjoyed the distinction of being the first American to own a work by the great French sculptor Auguste Rodin. The frank sexuality of Rodin's figures shocked many Gilded Age people, but not the iconoclastic Charles. He purchased several Rodin sculptures, including *Cupid and Psyche,* which daringly depicted two nudes entwined in an embrace. Other Americans soon followed the financier's example; the historian Henry Adams, for one, bought a Rodin in 1895. "They [Rodin's sculptures] are mostly so sensually suggestive that I shall have to lock them up when any girls are about, which is awkward," Adams confessed to a woman friend, "but Rodin is the only degenerate artist I know of, whose work is original."[13]

Why did Charles collect art so obsessively? There is no one answer to this question. The pursuit of art may have been for him in part a competitive game, one that he engaged in with avid collectors like his business associate Peter Widener. Like Henry Frick, the financier also probably hoped that his collection would bolster his social status. On a deeper level, he may have been trying to recapture his youth through art. Many of the images hanging in his galleries must have evoked memories of his Philadelphia childhood. Paintings of tree-dotted landscapes traversed by winding rivers and portraits of strong-faced middle-class gentlemen transported the fifty-something-year-old tycoon back to the semi-rural Northern Liberties of the 1830s and 1840s.

On the deepest level of all, the businessman may have discovered in art, in a love of the beautiful, a substitute for religion. Ever since his father's expulsion from the Society of Friends, Charles had lived in a world without religion. His cultivation of the beautiful may have helped fill a spiritual void. "It was not the love of the beautiful that is pagan," a shrewd observer noted, "nor the love of the beautiful that is competition, display; it was to him what religion is, a prayer of the heart. In building his home on Fifth avenue he built himself a chapel, an altar, where he could shut out the world and live in this religion—uplift his soul from the corduroy road of his financial life. There was not a nook or corner in his palatial home that was not sacred to him, something that was not sacred to this worship of his for the beautiful, sacred to his idea of the beautiful. There was not a painting, or a bit of statuary, or bit of architecture, or plant, or flower, or tapestry that did not mean something to him personally, something that answered the prayer of the soul of which the outside world knew nothing."[14] Art gave meaning to the businessman's life.

Charles loved women even more than he did art. A visitor to the millionaire's New York palace could hardly have failed to grasp this fact.

Representations of women in various states of undress were scattered throughout the home. Two sculptures featuring nude females flanked the "Grand Staircase." One of these figures happened to be Frederic Mac-Monnies's *Bacchante*, a work that had been literally banned in Boston. In the theater on his mansion's top floor Charles proudly displayed William Adolphe Bouguereau's *Invading Cupid's Realm*, a wildly erotic painting that, according to one critic, "would have been better situated in a brothel." In the Louis XV room a fabulously ornate bed (rumored to cost $80,000) boasted a foot-board with the likeness of a voluptuous nymph, nude and provocatively posed. Not surprisingly, the financier had suggested this design to the bed's manufacturer.

Women still found Charles attractive even though he was well past middle age. His hair had turned snowy white and his girth had increased, but he remained a strikingly handsome figure. He was successful with women, however, not simply or even primarily because of his looks. The businessman possessed a charismatic personality, "a subtle magnetism," that few could resist. Men as well as women felt the force of his nature. There was in Charles's presence something "invisible, even inexplicable, that makes him stand out not merely physically but mentally and imaginatively from all the others by whom he is surrounded," according to the Irish journalist T. P. O'Connor. "Wherever he sits, whoever is around—strong men, pretty women—you can't keep your eyes off that pale-faced, dark-eyed, white-moustached, immutably serene man who is sitting there in their midst, and yet, apparently, not altogether of them," O'Connor wrote.[15]

Women were particularly vulnerable to Charles's peculiar charm. Harriet Monroe frequently visited the magnate's Chicago home to view his constantly expanding art collection, and as a result she came to know him quite well. She found him to be "a strange combination of guile and glamour, thrilling with power like a steel spring, loving beauty as a Mazda lamp loves the switch that lights it." Even the prim and proper wife of the astronomer George Hale fell under the financier's spell. Evelina Hale judged Charles to be the most charming man she had ever encountered.

The suave and self-confident businessman knew how to speak to women. A brilliant conversationalist, he was also an expert in the fine art of flattery. Charles fully demonstrated his verbal dexterity in a revealing December 1891 letter to the actress Ada Rehan, who he had met in Europe the previous summer. "Today I sent you per Adams Express a case of sweet champagne as promised you in London," he wrote. "I remember well your remark that it 'helped the voice' and therefore sincerely hope you will find this just what you desire. Not that I think it needs any assistance for that is *one* of your great charms—your voice—but at the same time if it is a comfort to you then I am happy in sending it."[16]

According to legend, Charles had a small army of mistresses scattered throughout the United States and Europe. "He himself was a Louis XIV in the number of mistresses and in his financial generosity toward them," a magazine writer claimed. The legend contained more than a few grains of truth. Indeed, many Chicagoans seem to have known of the magnate's extracurricular activities. The author Ernest Poole remembered his parents' "dark talk about Yerkes as a bold bad man, who had married an ex-chorus girl and had 'fancy women' friends." Charles's behavior, however, may not have been that unusual for the period. Many of his contemporaries—and not just the wealthy—appear to have defied Victorian-era moral strictures and sought satisfaction outside of marriage.[17]

The names of all of the businessman's Chicago mistresses have been lost to history—all, that is, but one: Clara Louise Hyllested. The former Clara Floto was born in 1865 in Brooklyn, the daughter of German immigrant parents. Clara's husband August was a Swedish-born musician of some note. After being educated in Copenhagen and Berlin, young August had "roamed over Europe and Great Britain, one of the brilliant pianists of his day." He came to Chicago in 1885 when only in his twenties and obtained a teaching position at an area musical college. A serious and studious man, Hyllested seems to have paid more attention to his craft than to his beautiful "pleasure-loving" wife Clara, who "liked company and had a weakness for late hours."

Charles met August and his wife sometime in the early 1890s, perhaps at a piano recital. (The businessman was also a devotee of music.) Clara was a remarkable woman, independent, intelligent, and extremely passionate. "The weak and colorless personalities that fade in the background of this world do not understand and scarcely credit the passions of a few strong and scintillating personalities," she once declared. Clara's "vivacity, physical charms and animal spirits" strongly appealed to the magnate, and the two began a lengthy affair. The indiscretion seems to have gone on for three years, possibly in the 1894–97 period—when August was on an extended European concert tour. The pianist learned of his wife's unfaithfulness and he eventually left her. Charles's ardor for Clara eventually cooled, but he continued to maintain her for years in a "luxurious" Superior Street apartment. The magnate may have had difficulty ending his relationship with her. "When I find a personality that interests me . . . I am not easily driven from the battlefield," Clara would warn a future lover, "*and I refuse to be cast off as a soiled and broken toy.*" His ideals "shattered," August Hyllested left the United States in 1903 for

Scotland, where he lived until his death at the age of ninety.[18] As for Clara, she would officially divorce August in 1908 and embark upon a career as a globe-trotting "promiscuous woman of adventure," in the words of one source.

Some women demanded a high price for their silence. The magnate was "frequently annoyed legally, and otherwise by discarded women, who wanted to hang on, and extort money from him," DeLancey Louderback, Charles's right-hand man, claimed. "He generally broke with them in a nice way and continued to have their kind regard," Louderback continued. "When he found one otherwise, he managed to have someone else ingratiate themselves in with them, at his expense, and when exposed, he would brow beat them, and threaten to show them up, as blackmailers, and always got the best of them, in the end. Money was no object in such matters, either to defeat an enemy or secure what he desired." The gentleman of leisure could be as ruthless as the business gladiator.

Charles's womanizing took a heavy toll on his marriage, beginning about 1890. Mary Yerkes had always prided herself on her beauty, and she could not understand why her husband felt a need to stray. Her natural insecurity grew as she learned of Charles's numerous infidelities. The formerly close couple became increasingly quarrelsome. Charles somewhat illogically blamed the worsening domestic discord on his wife's temper. For her part, Mary began to seek validation outside of her marriage. She concentrated her energies on winning for herself and her husband the acceptance of New York City's social elite—the fabled Four Hundred. Charles demonstrated a willingness to advance his wife's ambitions, well realizing that social recognition might help repair his bruised business reputation. Probably under the magnate's influence, *Town Topics*—a scandal sheet devoured by the New York elite—published in 1893 a series of glowing notices regarding Mary. "When the fine house Mr. Yerkes is building on Fifth avenue is completed, and the family takes up permanent residence here," one such notice puffed, "Mrs. Yerkes will have much in the way of personal charms to commend her for enrolment in the 400." Other *Town Topics* items referred to Mary's beauty and to a $100,000 diamond she owned, "a jewel worth the ransom of a prince."

Mary's campaign for social status ultimately failed. Like their Chicago counterparts, the members of New York City's elect never opened their doors to the second Mrs. Yerkes. Disappointed in her marriage and in her dreams, Mary would eventually turn to alcohol to console herself. "Wealth has not brought me happiness," she would later lament amid the splendor of her Fifth Avenue mansion. "I have longed for it—always."[19]

19 The Temptation of Governor Altgeld

By 1895, Charles had given up entirely on Chicago. He decided to sell his streetcar properties, and completely escape the ungrateful metropolis. Getting out, however, was anything but easy. Before he could leave the Windy City, he had to attend to some unfinished business. Most important, he hoped to secure an extension of his companies' franchises—many of which were set to expire in 1903.[1]

The road to escape passed through Springfield, the home of the Illinois legislature. Only the legislature could amend the Horse and Buggy Act of 1874, which limited the life of franchises to twenty years. On February 6, 1895, Senator Charles Crawford, a loyal ally of Charles, introduced two bills intended to implement the magnate's plans. Senate Bill 138—the more important of the two measures—repealed the Horse and Buggy Act, and permitted city councils to grant railroad franchises of up to ninety-nine years' duration.[2] Charles absolutely needed a bill like this. Investors, after all, were not likely to purchase streetcar firms resting on an unstable franchise foundation. As Charles himself admitted to ex-Judge Samuel McConnell, the "chief value of a street railway company was in its franchises and not in the rail, ties, cars, and barns."

Senate Bill 137—the other measure introduced by Crawford—was designed to eliminate the possibility of further competition among Chicago's elevated railroads. Charles's struggling Lake Street Elevated road had recently acquired from the Council the right to extend its line as far east as Wabash Avenue in the city's center while his Northwestern

Elevated was also attempting to invade the business district. Charles planned to use these two elevated road extensions as the northern and western segments of the Union Loop. Not coincidentally, a key provision of Senate Bill 137 prohibited elevated roads from crossing each other at grade, a regulation that would have transformed the Union Loop into an iron barrier to competition in the city's heart.

Charles's two bills glided through the Illinois Senate as if guided by some divine force. But there was nothing sacred about the Illinois Senate in the year 1895. A *Chicago Times-Herald* reporter explained how this "illustrious" body worked:

> The senate is small and compact. It is built as ingeniously yet as simply as one of the watches turned out by the Elgin Watch Company, whose interests are protected in the Senate by Henry H. Evans, of Aurora. Unless it is wound just so often with a golden key it runs down, adjourns from day to day or ticks spasmodically. Its actions are occult to the casual observer. It meets in various places—in a corporation lawyer's office in Chicago, in the rooms of "Jim" Campbell at the Leland Hotel, or in the barrooms of this town frequented by "Hank" Evans or "Charley" Crawford.[3]

Despite "Charley" Crawford's skillful guidance, Senate Bill 137 hit a snag in late February, failing to gain enough votes for passage. Crawford, however, practiced a little bit of political voodoo and resurrected the dead bill with a motion to reconsider. Within two weeks of this "miracle," both traction measures received the Senate's imprimatur.

In the House the bills passed into the capable hands of Speaker John Meyer, Republican, and Clayton Crafts, Democrat. A "rugged character," the balding, handlebar-mustached Meyer came of immigrant stock, having been born in Holland. Despite his foreign roots, he rose to a prominent position in the Cook County Republican Party, and served four terms in the General Assembly. Meyer had compiled a fairly impressive legislative record, even sponsoring some notable reform measures. In 1887, for example, he backed a bill that made the granting of streetcar franchises contingent upon the consent of property owners—a bill that had given Charles a great deal of trouble. But by 1895 Meyer had become an obedient tool of corporate interests. According to some critics, the Republican politician had sold out in order to secure the coveted (and lucrative) speakership.[4] The massive-jawed Clayton Crafts, a former speaker himself, dominated the Democratic side of the aisle. A reporter described Crafts as "a lawyer whose face was seldom if ever seen in the courts, a legislator whose name was never associated as proposer with any really important measure . . . a democrat whose closest friends were republicans."[5] These two able legislators muscled Charles's bills through the House, securing their passage on May 1. Only one more obstacle had to be overcome—John Peter Altgeld, the governor of Illinois.

The German-born Altgeld had triumphed over youthful poverty. His family had moved to rural Ohio only three months after his birth in 1847. Young Altgeld escaped the drudgery of farm work during the Civil War, enlisting in a 100-day regiment. He contracted a malarial-type infection during his tour of duty, and never fully recovered from the disease. Following stints as a railroad section hand, schoolteacher, and county prosecutor, Altgeld moved in 1875 to Chicago, where he eventually gained a name for himself as a lawyer and real estate developer. Active in Democratic politics, he was elected a judge of the Cook County Superior Court in 1886. Though becoming a wealthy man, Altgeld never lost his sympathy for "the common people of the land." He knew better than most the part that luck played in the attainment of material success. After all, it was the patronage of the influential Chicago lawyer William Goudy that made the difference in Altgeld's career.

Altgeld had publicly exhibited a strong humanitarian sense as early as 1884. That year he wrote *Our Penal Machinery and Its Victims*, a searing indictment of the U.S. criminal justice system that opened up the eyes of a young Clarence Darrow. But Altgeld's progressive instincts remained somewhat muted until he attained the Illinois governorship in 1892 after a hard-fought campaign. "I want power, to get hold of the handle that controls things," Altgeld had told his good friend George Schilling, the labor leader. "When I do, I will give it a twist."[6]

Altgeld was as good as his word. Only six months into his term, he unconditionally pardoned the three imprisoned Haymarket defendants. This decision unleashed upon the governor the fury and scorn of much of the world. With this courageous act, Altgeld made a decisive break with his past, forever discarding convention for conviction. Suddenly no targets were too big for the fearless governor to take on. Even the 300-pound president of the United States was fair game. When Grover Cleveland dispatched federal troops to Chicago during the 1894 Pullman Strike, Altgeld bitterly protested the president's decision as a usurpation of states' rights. Writing to Judge Lambert Tree, the governor, however, expressed doubts about the effectiveness of his attacks on the status quo:

> Don Quixote you remember attacked windmills—I have attacked a good many things and will probably fare as he did. Shooting all over the woods does not bring down any game but it stirs it up and gives others a chance to bring it down. The conditions in our country are such that there is no possibility of bringing down any game very soon so I have deliberately

concluded to stir some of it up and trust to other and better marksmen to bag it in the future.[7]

Notwithstanding his apparent pessimism, Altgeld was at that moment preparing a populist assault against the national Democratic Party establishment, then dominated by Eastern financial interests.

In ordinary times Charles could not have expected the progressive-minded Altgeld to even consider approving the traction bills. But 1895 was not an ordinary time for the governor. Financial woes threatened to overwhelm Altgeld. A few years before, he had used much of his capital to construct a sixteen-story skyscraper—the Unity Building. Asked why he was taking such a financial gamble, he replied, "Because I have no children I have to create something and so I am creating buildings." Altgeld foolishly chose John R. Walsh, president of the Chicago National Bank, to underwrite a $300,000 bond issue financing the building's construction. A former owner of the *Chicago Herald* and "a democrat whose democracy never [got] the better of his business judgment," the unscrupulous Walsh served as an intermediary between the city's political and business elites. His banks often held state and city funds, money that was loaned at very low interest (if any) to Walsh's associates. Having access to the enormous sums of the public treasuries, Walsh possessed great power, both financial and political. "Little, indeed, goes on in the politics of Chicago in which Walsh does not have or seek to have a hand, and always against the public interest," the reformer Walter Fisher charged. Fisher called Walsh one of the "most dangerous and demoralizing political influences in this community."

Altgeld had delivered himself into the hands of this dangerous influence. The governor found it increasingly difficult to keep up with the interest payments on the Unity Building bonds after the 1893 Depression smothered his rental income. True to form, Walsh mercilessly tightened the screws on his debtor.[8] Charles certainly knew about the governor's shaky financial condition, very probably through Walsh himself, a heavy investor in streetcar securities. Always probing for a weakness in his opponents, the magnate had discovered what he thought was Altgeld's Achilles' heel. Money, Charles calculated, might help persuade the governor to sign the traction bills. The financier had already amply demonstrated the effectiveness of large sums in overcoming opposition.

In early May, Charles visited Altgeld at the governor's office in the Unity Building. The businessman was acting as a representative of the Gas Trust as well as of his traction interests. Gas utility officials wanted Altgeld to approve two measures: the anticompetitive House Bill 618 and Senate Bill 362, which legalized the Trust's existence. Charles and the governor were a study in contrasts. The still handsome traction magnate, now fifty-eight years old, exuded self-confidence and control. Ten years younger, the homely, sad-faced Altgeld resembled the tortured painter Van Gogh. He kept his reddish brown hair closely cropped and concealed a harelip underneath a thick beard. "He was squat and disfigured, and he knew that," an admirer said of Altgeld. "The big scar on his upper lip gave him a look so diabolic that once, when she saw him in a crowd, my wife exclaimed: 'What a horrible man!' But I told her: 'Wait till you see him smile!' For he had a smile like a suffering Christ!" The sickly governor possessed a melancholic, brooding nature, a disposition reflected in his favorite form of architecture—Gothic. Charles and Altgeld differed in more than appearance. The governor's belief in Jeffersonian democracy— in the power of the people—seemed to have no place in the dawning corporate and consumerist era inaugurated by Charles and his kind.

Yet there were striking similarities between Charles and Altgeld. Both of these fiercely individualistic men were outcasts, one vilified for his prison record and brutal business methods, the other for his supposed radicalism. Indeed, the *Daily News* humorist Eugene Field reserved his cheapest shots for Charles and Altgeld, sometimes skewering them both in the same column. Both men, too, were loners and great haters; they never forgave their enemies. One observer suspected that Altgeld's bitterness stemmed from "the fact that he was a sick man all through his career, with some creeping spinal disease that made him limp and often even drag himself along." Finally, Charles and the governor were not squeamish about the means they employed to obtain their ends. Carter Harrison, Jr., believed that Altgeld had "a willingness to accept the backing and support of any political or economic unit that would help place in his hands the power to establish the business and governmental theories in which he believed with all the vigor of his profound intellect." Clarence Darrow, a close friend of the governor, was even more explicit. "He [Altgeld] would do whatever would serve his purpose when he was right," Darrow maintained. "He'd use all the tools of the other side—stop at nothing—but always with an end in view—to do good for the poor man. He was perfectly unscrupulous in getting ends, but absolutely *honest* in those ends."[9]

Altgeld and Charles had met before. In 1889 the magnate had filed suit against a man who owed him $5,500 in commission fees. As a judge of the Cook County Superior Court, Altgeld presided over the resulting trial. At one point during the proceedings the defendant's attorney attempted to impugn Charles's credibility by bringing up the latter figure's prison term. "Mr. Yerkes, have you ever been convicted of any crime —felony?" the attorney asked the witness. Judge Altgeld didn't think this was a relevant question. "This is a matter that has absolutely nothing to do with the issues in this case," he declared. But Charles *wanted* to answer the query. Acceding to this request, Altgeld gave the financier as much time as he needed to fully explain the circumstances leading to his conviction. Charles never forgot the kindness Altgeld had shown him on this occasion.

The two men then were not implacable opponents when they met in the governor's Unity Building office on that warm spring day. But Charles and Altgeld could never be friends; they believed in far different things. In *The Titan* Theodore Dreiser brilliantly captured the importance of their meeting. "Ideals were here at stake—the dreams of one man as opposed, perhaps, to the ultimate dreams of a city or state or nation—the grovelings and wallowings of a democracy slowly, blindly trying to stagger to its feet," Dreiser wrote. "In this conflict—taking place in an inland cottage-dotted state where men were clowns and churls, dancing fiddlers at country fairs—wcrc opposed, as the governor saw it, the ideals of one man and the ideals of men."[10]

Charles was frank with Altgeld as he explained the merits of the gas and railroad bills. The magnate maintained that these measures were necessary to protect corporations from "sand-bagging" aldermen engaged in the bartering of valuable franchises. He also claimed that the bills would increase the marketability of his streetcar securities and thereby allow him to finance additional trolley lines. The governor himself owned a streetcar line in Ohio, so he could appreciate the force of this argument. Altgeld believed that the great corporations were entitled to some protection, but, for him, the public interest was paramount. The governor asked Charles whether he would agree to a provision in the bills setting up a board of utility commissioners. Altgeld was thinking of a state board similar to one in Massachusetts that regulated gas charges. The governor later admitted that he "had reached a point . . . where I would have winked at monopoly provided I could have felt that there is a strong, powerful agency of the law standing between the public on the one hand and monopoly on the other." But Charles's response to the commission idea did not reassure Altgeld: The magnate said that he was already taking care of too many commissions.[11]

Charles did not merely rely on his verbal skills to persuade the governor. The businessman told Altgeld that certain prominent Chicago and New York capitalists were holding $25,000,000 of Gas Trust certificates in anticipation of the governor's approval of House Bill 618 and Senate Bill 362. The enactment into law of these measures was expected to spark a dramatic rise in the price of the trust certificates (then hovering near sixty on the New York Stock Exchange). Charles invited Altgeld to share in the anticipated windfall.

"The stock of these certificates will go to par [100] and beyond the moment these gas bills have been signed and approved by you," the magnate told Altgeld.

"Your approval of the measures will be a great favor to the gentlemen who hold these securities," Charles continued. "They will appreciate it and they are in a position to offer substantial evidence of their appreciation. I am not offering you a bribe, but am simply putting you in the way of making a legitimate profit from a legitimate business speculation."

The financier next estimated the immense profit that could be realized from this "legitimate business speculation."

"Figuring the advance in gas certificates alone which will follow the approval of these bills, and figuring on the most conservative basis, taking into account all the chances of the market and incidental, it is clear that a profit of at least $8,000,000 can be made out of the gas certificates held by our friends," Charles calculated. "They are all wealthy men, who will be satisfied with a reasonable profit. I am sure that a net profit of $5,000,000 on their gas certificates will satisfy them."

Charles now made Governor Altgeld a very generous offer.

"Our friends stand ready to set aside in your name enough gas certificates to insure, on the basis I have figured, a profit of at least $1,000,000, and more if necessary," the businessman assured Altgeld. "They will make the profit likely to accrue $2,000,000 if necessary."

"These certificates, sufficient to realize the amount I have mentioned, can be placed in escrow with any responsible Chicago person whom you may name, or they can be handled, if you choose, without the knowledge of any third party," Charles concluded his pitch. "My friends will undertake to place them on the market at the most favorable time. My friends will put up the margins and in all respects handle the securities so placed in escrow as a part of their own speculations. When the securities have risen to the desired figure—and there is no doubt of the rise—they will be sold and the profit on the transaction will be turned over to you. A fortune is in your own hands."[12]

A fortune indeed! The exact amount of this infamous bribe has long been disputed, the accepted figure usually being $500,000. But, according to Altgeld's own account, the actual sum was $1,000,000 or, if the governor so chose, a fabulous $2,000,000. Assuming that the value of the trust certificates would have risen forty points (from about sixty to 100) upon the approval of the gas bills, only 25,000 of the 250,000 outstanding certificates could have secured Altgeld a $1,000,000 windfall. With merely the sweep of a pen, the governor could have recouped his lost fortune, freed himself from a crushing debt, and retired in comfort.

Never content to attack on only one front, Charles dispatched the lawyer Samuel McConnell to Springfield. McConnell, an ex-judge, found Charles to be "a strange character, a rather likable man" but with "little conscience." Nevertheless, the attorney agreed to lobby his close friend Altgeld in behalf of one of the traction bills. Meeting on the sprawling lawn outside of the governor's mansion, McConnell tried to sell Altgeld on the measure's good points. The governor agreed that the bill had some merit, but said that he could not sign it into law since he had campaigned on an antimonopoly platform. Then, in a confidential tone, he told McConnell that he had been offered a bribe to approve the measure. "Now, as a friend, what would you advise?" Altgeld asked. "Why, I would veto the damn bill!" McConnell exclaimed.[13]

Of all his friends, the governor seems to have consulted only McConnell regarding the traction and gas bills. Left in the dark, Clarence Darrow and Altgeld's other confidants debated whether the governor would veto the measures. As the days passed, the suspense increased. "Altgeld sat silent and pensive, gazing out beyond the petty affairs of men," Darrow recalled of that tense period. Would their hero disappoint them?

On May 14 the answer came in loud and ringing tones. That day Altgeld vetoed Senate Bills 138 and 139, and House Bill 618. In a strongly worded veto message, the governor maintained that these three measures would have legalized monopoly without making adequate provision for the public's protection. He refused to "fasten a collar on the future and to levy tribute on generations yet to come, and all this simply to further enrich a few private individuals." It was "the business of the government to protect all interests alike, and if any interest is to receive special attention it should be the weaker against the most powerful," Altgeld declared. He recognized that monopoly was already a reality in Chicago, but argued "there is a great difference between enduring an evil which cannot be avoided and deliberately taking it into your arms." The governor suggested public ownership of streetcars and gas utilities as a possible solution to the problem of private monopoly. "I love Chicago," Altgeld concluded his message, "and am not willing to help forge a chain which would bind her people hand and foot for all time to the wheels of monopoly and leave them no chance of escape."[14]

The Chicago press welcomed the governor's triple veto, especially the *Chicago Times-Herald.* Owned by Herman Kohlsaat, a onetime friend of Yerkes, the *Times-Herald* had spearheaded the newspaper fight against the "eternal monopoly" bills, even sending lawyer John Ela to

Springfield to keep watch on the measures' progress. The stridently anti-Altgeld *Chicago Tribune* also commended the governor's action, but it had been conspicuously silent as the bills sailed through the assembly. The crusading *Peoria Journal* blamed the *Tribune*'s silence on its Springfield correspondent, John Corwin. According to the *Journal*, Corwin was "earning his 'rake off' by defending certain measures and practices of Speaker John Meyer and the other corporation attorneys, and abusing the only man who had the backbone to stand up for the people, Governor Altgeld."[15]

Somewhat surprisingly, Charles expressed little public concern over the veto. "I have no doubt that Governor Altgeld did what he thought was his duty in vetoing the street railway bills," the magnate told a reporter, "and I am not prepared to say that he acted unwisely in so doing." The bills, he suggested, had some provisions "the people sadly need" and others "they can just as well get along without." Privately, Charles was amazed that the governor had refused the bribe. For perhaps the first time in his career the businessman had encountered an incorruptible politician. "I do not believe in Mr. Altgeld's principles, so far as government are concerned," Charles would later say. "I think he is honest and believes what he says."[16] The magnate's expressed lack of concern over the veto may not have been entirely feigned, however. Charles had faith in the miraculous powers of his favorite Springfield legislators.

Speaker John Meyer was determined to override the governor's triple veto, "to shoot 'em over his head." Meyer had been stricken with liver disease, and his life was perceptibly ebbing away as the legislative session waned. He needed money not for himself—his time was nearly up—but for his thirty-eight-year-old wife and eleven-year-old daughter Daisy. And money could be obtained. Cooperative legislators were promised a cut of a so-called watermelon—a corruption fund—upon the passage of the traction and gas bills. Driven by the needs of his wife and daughter, Meyer was more than willing to bend and even break parliamentary rules to further the measures' progress. Yet he still had difficulty rounding up the 102 votes necessary to undo Altgeld's action. Despite the promise of financial reward, many lawmakers evinced a reluctance to support legislation almost universally condemned by the press. Meyer therefore stepped up the pressure. Upon his orders, bills desired by resistant legislators were locked away in committees until the speaker got his way.

As June 14—the last day of the legislative session—dawned, Speaker Meyer still had not obtained the number of votes needed for a veto override.[17] With much legislation still held hostage in committee, Meyer expected members to fall in line once convinced of the very real threat to their pet bills. In the Senate, Charles Crawford easily secured passage of the streetcar and elevated railroad bills, while the gas consolidation bill (Senate Bill 362) proved to be too much even for that body to swallow. The House having scuttled House Bill 618, Charles's traction measures became the sole focus of the great legislative struggle.

Gilded Age corruption was in full view in the House chamber that sweltering June afternoon. The author and reformer Brand Whitlock, then a clerk in the secretary of state's office, saw what occurred that day underneath the great golden dome of the Illinois State Capitol:

> The House was in its shirt sleeves; and there was the rude horse play of country bumpkins; and paper wads were flying; now and then some member sent hurtling through the hot air his file of printed legislative bills, and all the while there was that confusion of sound, laughter, and oaths and snatches of song, a sort of bedlam, in which laws were being enacted—laws that must be respected and even revered, because of their sacred origin.[18]

Wading through this chaos, Governor Altgeld's lieutenants scrambled to avert a veto override. At one point John Yantis, an Altgeld ally, learned that "a lot of cheap skates" were receiving far less than the $10,000 going rate for votes. Inspired by this information, the wily Yantis told one of these "cheap skates" (slated to receive only $200) about the enormous sums being received by others. Feeling "swindled," this proud legislator and some of his "cheap skate" friends changed sides, and withheld their support for Charles's bills.

Despite defections from their ranks, Charles's forces felt confident enough to bring the elevated railroad bill to a vote by mid-afternoon. The sickly Meyer was once again in the speaker's chair after having spent much of the day resting on a sofa. As the roll was called for the vote, lobbyists buttonholed wavering lawmakers. At this critical point Brand Whitlock witnessed what he called an event of "moral beauty." A lobbyist targeted a poverty-stricken legislator from southern Illinois, wooing him with "the argument that the bill concerned only Chicago, and that the folks down home would neither know nor care how he voted on it, and then—how much two thousand dollars would mean to him." The lawmaker paused a moment before answering. "I reckon you're right: I'm poor, and I've got a big family," he finally replied. "And you're right, too, when you say my people won't know nor care; they won't; they don't know nor care a damn; they won't send me back here, of course. And God knows what's to come of my wife and my children; I am going home to them to-morrow and Monday I'm going to hunt me a job in the harvest-field; I reckon I'll die in the poorhouse. Yes, I'm going home . . . but I'm going home an honest man."[19]

The roll call yielded too few votes to override the governor's veto. Yet Clayton Crafts, the Democratic leader in charge of the elevated bill, was wearing a wide grin. Crafts had reason for his confidence: He had kept several representatives in reserve for an emergency like this. The names of those not yet having voted were then called. A suspiciously long delay ensued as the final vote was tallied. 89–55. Thirteen votes short. Altgeld's veto stood. Or so it seemed. But Crafts refused to admit defeat. He motioned that another roll call be held at 8:30 P.M. Amid vehement protest, the powerful Democrat's motion carried by a wide margin. Crafts had bought time to piece together a winning vote.

In the succeeding hours, Speaker Meyer and his associates used the bottled-up bills to bludgeon representatives into supporting the traction bills. Yet, much to Meyer's disgust, an alarming number of lawmakers refused to keep their end of the bargain after their pet measures were passed. According to the *Times-Herald* correspondent, these legislators felt "no more bound to stick to the terms of the compact than is an honest citizen who agrees to the subsequent carrying out of stipulations with a highwayman who holds a pistol to his head."[20] Bridling under Meyer's dictatorial rule, representatives were only too eager to double-cross him. As the thirty-ninth session of the Illinois General Assembly neared its close, Charles's increasingly desperate forces turned the clock back two hours, but, even with this manufactured time, managed to collect only ninety-eight votes—four shy of the needed number. "Every means known to human ingenuity and legislative methods was used to bring about this result," the *Tribune*'s Corwin noted. "It simply wasn't in the pins."

Somehow fittingly, the legislature nearly adjourned in a riot after a janitor was forcibly dragged out of the chamber. The janitor, it seems, had been answering to the names of members not voting. The resulting commotion precipitated a miniature panic. "Lawmakers rushed pellmell, neck or nothing, over desks and chairs, as if their lives and the lives of the few remaining bills on the calendar depended on their seeing Scouten (the janitor) thrown out," a reporter observed. With shouts and screams piercing the air, visitors in the galleries headed for the already crowded exits. Five minutes elapsed before order was restored. One-half hour later—at 12:25 A.M. on June 15—the General Assembly adjourned. "May Illinois never witness another such law-making body," the *Peoria Journal* sighed.[21]

With the failure to override the governor's veto, Charles had suffered a temporary setback. Getting out of Chicago wasn't going to be as easy as he had hoped. The Illinois legislature would next meet in 1897, giving the magnate plenty of time to work for the election of a friendly governor. But Altgeld would not go down without a fight. Already the governor had begun reaching out to the Populists in an effort to reorient the Democratic Party along more progressive lines. Altgeld's efforts would pave the way for the emergence of William Jennings Bryan as the Party's 1896 standard bearer. Terrifying the nation's businessmen, the presidential campaign of the charismatic Bryan sent ripples through the money markets and in the process nearly overturned Charles's streetcar empire. For the second time in his life, the magnate's financial health would be threatened by a money panic emanating from Chicago.

20 On the Brink

Charles's latest round of difficulties began on July 9, 1896. That day a young, relatively unknown Nebraska politician addressed 16,000 Democrats gathered at the cavernous Chicago Coliseum for their Party's national convention. William Jennings Bryan had waited much of his life for an opportunity like this and he "seized it with the grip of a master." His arms wildly flailing over his tousled, raven-hued hair, Bryan delivered a spellbinding speech that simply overwhelmed the sweat-soaked convention delegates. Conjuring up the ghosts of Thomas Jefferson and Andrew Jackson, "the Boy Orator of the Platte" hurled defiance at the "few financial magnates who in a back room corner the money of the world." "What we need is an Andrew Jackson to stand as Jackson stood, against the encroachments of aggrandized wealth," Bryan declared. The speaker singled out the gold standard for special attack. The gold standard, he maintained, restricted the money supply and thereby limited economic opportunity for "the plain people of this country." "You shall not press down upon the brow of labor this crown of thorns," Bryan thundered in conclusion. "You shall not crucify mankind upon a cross of gold."

Bryan's speech received a thunderous ovation lasting fifteen minutes. It was the "yell of a mob stirred beyond any possibility of self control," a witness reported. "In all parts of the great, rambling, ugly hall, men were shouting, cursing, throwing into the air anything movable, embracing each other, fighting each other, weeping—yes, weeping real tears of honest emotion." The journalist Willis Abbot noticed two elderly Southern farmers hugging each other and "crying bitterly, great tears rolling from their eyes into their bearded cheeks." "No man, young, impressionable, sympathetic with the downtrodden of his kind, could have lived through that scene without a true spiritual exaltation," Abbot later remarked. Bryan had won over the convention by the sheer power of his oratory, and the following day he was nominated as the Democratic Party's presidential candidate.

Though John Peter Altgeld had championed the candidacy of Missouri's Richard Bland, the Illinois governor had reason to be happy with Bryan's nomination. The Nebraska congressman ran on a platform enshrining the "liberal philosophy that the Governor had consistently espoused." The platform enunciated "almost all of the principles that have motivated the Democratic party during the twentieth century," and among other things called for the reintroduction of silver as a form of money. "Bryan later during the campaign gave voice to Altgeld's thoughts and so became in the public mind either prophet or anarchist, all depending on the point of view," an astute political observer noted. "But he was little more than the silver-tongued mouthpiece of the thinker."[1]

Bryan and Altgeld spoke for a large segment of the American population—farmers, laborers, small businessmen, and others who had been victimized by the emerging corporate economy. During the recession-plagued 1890s, millions of these victimized Americans had joined the Populist movement—an uprising of Westerners and Southerners against the excesses of corporate capitalism. The Populists demanded an income tax, federal ownership of the railroads, and an increase in the money supply.[2] In 1896 the Populists fused with the Democratic Party, and threw their support behind William Jennings Bryan. Many rank-and-file Populists objected to fusion, seeing it as a betrayal of their movement.

Nonetheless, for the first time in decades, the two major political parties in the United States offered the public a real choice at the polls. The nation's wealthiest businessmen did not exult in this fact. For them, the "Popocrat" Bryan was nothing less than the devil incarnate whose victory would mean revolution and ruin. "Bryan's election would set our country back a century," the Standard Oil bigwig Henry H. Rogers announced, "and I believe it's the sacred duty of every honest American to do what he can to save his land from such a calamity."[3] To avert this "calamity," worried big businessmen flocked into the camp of William McKinley, the Civil War major marching under the banner of the Republican Party and the standard of gold. Like the combatants in a war, both parties believed that God was on their side.

Tumbling stock prices served as an accurate barometer of business fear. Charles was amazed by the severity of this "Bryan panic." "I have watched the New York Stock Exchange since 1857, and, with the exception of the breaking out of the war, I have never seen a situation like this," the streetcar magnate told a reporter. "Through all other depressions there have always been men of wealth who would go up and down Wall street looking for bargains. Now there are no bargain hunters. Low as prices have gone, nobody seems willing to take the risk of buying even at panic prices."[4]

Charles was vacationing in Europe when the Bryan panic hit the Chicago Stock Exchange. This "side-show of New York's big board" had come a long way since its sleepy early days, having been roused to life by Charles's North and West Chicago stocks. Housed since 1894 in a thirteen-story skyscraper designed by Louis Sullivan, the Chicago Stock Exchange now possessed a magnificent exterior that proclaimed its newfound respectability and maturity. Charles's streetcar stocks continued to be the most heavily traded securities on the Exchange—a fact the magnate did not especially like. After all, the Exchange no longer remained the exclusive preserve of the bull, as it had once been. "I think it is a great detriment to West and North Chicago securities that they are listed on the Chicago Stock Exchange," the financier frankly asserted in 1893. "It would be much better, in my opinion, if they were handled, as was the case formerly, over the counter by the banks and bond houses. As it is now, a lot of fellows get long or short a line of stock and then put out some cock-and-bull story calculated to scare or elate holders, thereby influencing the market in a way that will likely prove profitable to themselves, although detrimental to others."[5] The Stock Exchange left Charles at the not-so-tender mercy of the market.

The 1896 panic confirmed the magnate's distrust of the Chicago Stock Exchange. Shortly after Bryan's nomination, the prices of North and West Chicago stock began to plummet. North Chicago fell nearly forty points in a one-month period while West Chicago dropped precipitously from 108 to eighty-five. Peter A. B. Widener and William Elkins spearheaded this bear campaign, dumping thousands of streetcar shares on the market. The "Traction Twins" seem to have declared all-out war on their former business associate after not getting their way in a dispute involving the Northwestern Elevated. The fall in the North and West Chicago stock prices soon precipitated a wave of panic selling by outsiders. "Stockholders of the various companies seemed to think there was something wrong in the inside history of the corporations, and clamored for news and aided in the efforts to break the markets by selling right and left," a financial journalist reported. Thanks to the herd mentality of investors, the North and West Chicago stocks appeared to be "doomed to a greater decline."[6] The bottom was nowhere in sight.

The bear raid on his companies' stocks couldn't have come at a worse time for Charles. The magnate had borrowed from Chicago banks enormous amounts of money at high rates of interest in order to finance the construction of his electric and elevated lines. He used as collateral for these loans primarily the securities of his North and West Chicago firms. With the value of the streetcar stocks on the wane, the banks would inevitably demand more margins or even call in the loans. Exacerbating matters, Charles could no longer count on the support of a key group of Chicago investors associated with Levi Leiter—thanks to the Loop war. Once again Charles was overextended and standing on the brink of financial ruin. But there was one important difference from 1871: He now had the power to master his fate.

Learning of the crippling bear raid while in London, a stunned Charles immediately wired his brokers Alexander Dewar and M. M. Jamieson to buy as much North and West Chicago stock as they could get. On July 18 the magnate cut his vacation short, sailing from England on the *Liverpool*. He intended to be on the ground in Chicago, where he would personally conduct the buying operation and stop the bleeding of his stocks. Probably acting according to Charles's instructions, Jamieson took the unusual step of directly appealing to investors in a newspaper advertisement urging the purchase of North and West Chicago stock.[7]

Jamieson demonstrated a willingness to put his money where his mouth was. He bet a fellow broker $1,000 that West Chicago—then hovering near ninety-five—would sell at par (100) within seven days. Amazingly enough, the stock reached par only seven *minutes* later. A financial journalist correctly attributed West Chicago's almost miraculous ascent to "the strong right arm of Charles T. Yerkes." Arriving in Chicago on July 27, Charles took charge of his army of brokers and managed to restore most of his stocks' lost value. The businessman's titanic efforts sustained the entire Chicago stock market. But the achievement came at a tremendous price: Charles had purchased over $3,000,000 of his firms' securities.

The Illinois Trust and Savings Bank, captained by the affable John Mitchell, furnished the magnate with most of the "sinews of war" required for this bull campaign, including one critical $800,000 loan. Two other men desperately needed this sum at that very moment. The king-sized brothers William and James Moore were then engaged in a truly gargantuan speculation on the Chicago Stock Exchange. The ambitious promoters had pushed Diamond Match stock up over 100 points in less than a year. Having secured financial backing from some of Chicago's biggest businessmen, including Philip Armour and George Pullman, the ever-cheerful Moores must have been happier than usual as they blew up their speculative bubble to unmanageable proportions. But the Bryan panic disrupted the brothers' scheme, making it more and more difficult for them to raise money to support Diamond Match. Almost overnight the distended bubble burst. "At the moment when we supposed everything to be in good condition, we were pressed for heavy money for additional margins," James Moore explained. "This came unexpectedly from one or two brokers, who, in turn, may have been pressed by banks interested in their business. They called on us, and we did not have the money. That is all there is to it. We had to quit because we did not have the cash." In fact, that wasn't the whole story. James Moore later blamed Charles for the failure of Diamond Match, suggesting that if the "Yerkes party had not found it necessary to borrow a million to stop the operations of the bears in West and North Chicago stock there would have been no trouble."[8]

On August 3 the Moores abandoned their attempt to support Diamond Match stock. It appeared inevitable that the Chicago stock market would crash the following day, dragged downward by a free-falling Diamond Match. If that happened, the banks would be in deep trouble, having loaned millions to Charles and the Moores. Bank runs loomed as a very real possibility. Fearful of the financial consequences of a crash, Philip Armour summoned to his Prairie Avenue mansion Chicago's most powerful businessmen for an emergency conference. Lyman Gage, president of the First National Bank, John Mitchell, and numerous other heavyweights answered the urgent call. Indeed, most of Chicago's business titans (with the notable exception of Marshall Field, who was on vacation overseas) gathered in Armour's parlor that warm evening. "The aggregation of wealth at that meeting could pocket the loss of the capital stock of several companies like that of the Diamond Match without feeling inconvenience," a journalist remarked.[9]

Arriving at the conference somewhat late—"about the fiftieth in a procession of men in straw hats"—Charles breezily entered the parlor, and was greeted by somber stares and grim faces. "I never was at a funeral before where there were so many straw hats," he joked. The quip didn't generate much laughter. The "funeral" became even gloomier when James Moore informed the assemblage that he and his brother could no longer sustain the price of Diamond Match stock. They also could not—at that moment—pay back their loans. One of the gathered businessmen then turned to Charles, and asked him what he planned to do about *his* loans.

"You ask me what I am going to do," the financier coolly replied, according to one account. "Nothing, and I tell you this—if the Chicago Stock Exchange opens tomorrow there will be several banks that won't, that's a certainty. You're ruined, I'm ruined, and we're all ruined."[10] Charles was remarkably consistent. When asked a similar question in the aftermath of his 1871 failure, he also stated that he would do nothing.

Not at all happy with Charles's answer, a banker at the Armour conclave intimated that he and his colleagues might be forced to sell the magnate's collateral. Charles said "he wished they would—that he had been trying to sell for sometime and had been unable to do so, and he hoped they would have better luck." The financier's steely nerve absolutely astounded his fellow businessmen. It may have been on this occasion that Lyman Gage remarked of Charles: "That man has the heart of a Numidian lion!"

Charles's blunt arguments persuaded Armour and his associates: The Stock Exchange did not open the next day. The magnate had pulled off what was widely hailed as "the bluff of his life." He of course welcomed the decision. "The closing of the Stock Exchange has given holders time to reason," he informed a reporter, "and they must realize our securities are as good as before. . . . Otherwise, timid investors might have been frightened into surrendering their holdings, and brokers might have tried to bear stocks."[11] For the reformer Henry Demarest Lloyd—the man who had first exposed John D. Rockefeller's methods—Charles's "assassination of the Stock Exchange" was yet another example of business buccaneering. Lloyd told the private banker A. O. Slaughter that "you and the few men like you . . . ought to send Yerkes back to his penitentiary. We let the meanest men 'work us and our institutions' . . . until they get to be Caesars, and then we find that the only law they recognize is that of their own accursed greed or money and power."

Charles had simply bought time for himself. He was by no means out of trouble. He owed millions of dollars to a cash-hungry horde of brokers and bankers. In the days following the Stock Exchange's closing, Charles scrambled to raise funds. It wasn't an easy task. "At present it is doubtful if he could borrow a dollar in Chicago," one banker noted of Charles. Despite the shaky state of the magnate's finances, rumors circulated in commercial circles claiming Charles was "the largest individual holder of government bonds in the world."[12] The businessman could only smile at these rumors, and wish that they were true. As Charles begged money from the bankers, he must have been overwhelmed by a strong sense of déjà vu, with memories of his 1871 failure crowding his brain.

Charles's worst fears seemed to be confirmed when certain banks began calling in his loans. Other banks were just slightly more reasonable, agreeing to renew loans for only fifteen days at a time while charging interest rates at the "pawnshop price of 10 per cent a month." The Illinois Trust and Savings Bank—Charles's bulwark—also threatened to call in his loans. This move would have ruined Charles. Philip Armour and Marshall Field, heavy investors in the Illinois Trust and Savings Bank, discussed the situation with John Mitchell, the bank's president. The suggestion was made to "summarily stop all Yerkes' operations in the local banks and discredit his securities." Field patiently listened to this bold proposition and then spoke. "He [Charles] is not a safe man," Field declared. "Such action as is proposed will cause a panic. People will not understand it. Let Mr. Yerkes alone and he will come to his own end."[13]

John Mitchell did not call in Charles's loans, and in fact advanced the magnate a "reasonable amount." The Illinois Trust and Savings Bank chief knew that Field had been right, that to "embarrass Mr. Yerkes meant to break a whole lot of other people and possibly cause a run on the banks and a local panic." Charles reciprocated as best he could, furnishing the Illinois Trust additional collateral. "He [Charles] has given us $100,000 worth of securities since the trouble, and that is doing pretty well," Armour reported to his wife. "But he has got to a point where he is stiff legged and won't do anything more. I don't know that his securities are worth much more than cabbage leaves, but he has done pretty well to put up what he has for us. It has given us some trouble to get it, and I am not better impressed with Mr. Yerkes' ability or fairness the closer I get to him." In another letter—this one written to his nephew—Armour confessed that the Illinois Trust "will probably carry him [Charles] along on the balance for some time to come."[14]

Charles had to satisfy the brokers as well as the bankers. He promised to settle his stock trades—amounting to over $3,000,000—by November 30. In the meantime, he agreed to pay the brokers 7 percent interest. The plan was accepted only after Charles threatened to repudiate his trades.

The magnate hoped that by late November his borrowing power would be restored, thereby enabling him to take care of his creditors. His hopes hinged on a critical outcome: the defeat of William Jennings Bryan and, with it, the revival of business confidence. Like many other businessmen running scared of Bryan, Charles tried to influence how his employees voted. "There is no doubt whatever in my mind that the most severe financial panic that this country has ever seen would follow the election of Bryan," he stated in a letter to his workers. "After the wrecks of this panic would be cleared away the condition of the street railways would be such that it would be impossible for the employees or officers to think of drawing the wages and salaries which they are doing at the present time."[15] The message of this missive was clear: Vote for Bryan and you will have your wages cut.

As early as October 1, Charles confidently predicted a McKinley victory. "I am not a prophet nor am I the son of a prophet," he explained to a reporter, "but I simply voice the judgment of those whose prominence in the business world gives them ample opportunity to feel the political pulse." The prediction came true on November 3, when McKinley defeated Bryan by a little less than 600,000 votes. Though hardly a decisive triumph, euphoric businessmen did not quibble over the results. Charles was relieved by the outcome. He had viewed Bryan as a radical whose election would have meant a "complete revolution, not only in politics, but also in the social conditions of the United States."[16]

McKinley's victory boosted the markets, and bankers all but threw open their vaults to Charles. "With the election of the advance prosperity agent, no restriction was placed on the amount of money which Mr. Yerkes could have borrowed," one observer reported. The news was also good on the Chicago Stock Exchange, which reopened November 5. North and West Chicago stock moved upward instead of declining precipitously as many market watchers had expected. Within days of the exchange's reopening, West Chicago had reached 100 while North Chicago gained twenty points. "It looks as though the president of the West and North Chicago Street Railroad companies was again himself," a newspaper writer noted, "and that in place of the sellers of stock placing him in a tight box, he had turned the tables on them. Evidently he is still 'the baron.'"

With his credit temporarily restored, Charles succeeded in scrounging up enough money to satisfy his broker creditors before the November 30 deadline. He expended over $3,000,000 to settle his stock trades—a personal amount that was, according to one authority, "the heaviest on record in the history of the city."[17] Furious at what he believed was the Chicago bankers' unfair treatment of him, the magnate had turned to New York City for the money to get him out of this particular financial scrape.

Charles's next step was clear. His current troubles had been caused by his firms' enormous bank debt—a debt that rendered him extremely vulnerable to his many Chicago enemies. The businessman cooked up a clever scheme to fix the problem: He planned to have his West Chicago company issue $10,000,000 in bonds, the proceeds of which would be used to pay off the bank debt. The bonds would be sold primarily to eastern and foreign investors in order to prevent "the possibility of the local (Chicago) crowd which was 'after him' being able to make it at all uncomfortable for him again." In effect, Charles intended to shift the bulk of his corporate debt burden from Chicago to Boston, New York, and London.

The financier arranged with New York's Central Trust Company to take up a sizable portion of the $10,000,000 bond issue. He dispatched M. M. Jamieson and Alexander Dewar to London, where they attempted to market several blocks of these bonds. The Chicago brokers found the climate in the English capital rather uncongenial. A blistering column in the *Financial Times* that heralded their arrival certainly didn't help matters. The influential newspaper called into doubt the value of the securities being hawked by Jamieson and Dewar, and, even worse, questioned the character of their boss.

Despite this attack, Jamieson and Dewar somehow cobbled together a syndicate to purchase the bonds. Then disaster struck. Word reached London that the Chicago City Council had passed an ordinance reducing streetcar fares one cent—to four cents a ride. The London syndicate dissolved upon the receipt of this news, fearing the loss of corporate revenue occasioned by this ordinance. Charles had just completed the New York end of the bond negotiations, and was in Philadelphia when he received a telegram summoning him back to Gotham. "There is something wrong with the city council," the telegram matter-of-factly stated.[18]

From Charles's perspective, something was indeed very wrong with the Chicago City Council. Reform had come to the corrupt Council—thanks to the Municipal Voters' League. An outgrowth of William Stead's Civic Federation, the Municipal Voters' League had been formed to combat corruption in municipal politics. Headed by the diminutive dynamo George Cole—"a little sawed-off giant of reform"—the League set as its first aim the election of honest men to the City Council. Chicago reformers had long sought this elusive goal, but Cole and his associates actually devised a workable plan to realize this "iridescent dream." "We're going to publish the records of the thieves who want to get back at the trough," Cole announced. Employing the weapons of the politicians—newspapers, canvassers, bands, mass-meetings, parades—the League "let light into that den of thieves," and during the 1896 municipal election campaign succeeded in defeating twenty of the twenty-six "boodle aldermen" it had marked for slaughter. "We have broken down the two-thirds majority in the City Council," Cole proclaimed after the April vote.[19] Now an honest mayor could veto a bill without fear that the aldermen could muster a two-thirds majority to override.

The Municipal Voters' League gave Charles headaches almost from its inception. The League-reformed City Council passed the four-cent ordinance in December 1896 and wrecked the financier's bond negotiations. Mayor George Swift, however, vetoed the ordinance, enabling Charles to again attempt to market the bonds. The magnate's initial efforts met with little success, and, as a result, his companies' stock prices plummeted. Financial catastrophe once again seemed imminent. Brokers on the Chicago Stock Exchange began whispering that Charles was "'at the end of his rope,' that he was 'financially busted,' and that all the great properties with which he was connected 'would be in the hands of a receiver before the year '97 was many days old.'"

The predictions were premature. A desperate Charles did the unlikeliest thing imaginable, and turned for help to his old associates Widener and Elkins—the two schemers who had precipitated the trouble. The "Traction Twins" agreed to buy a large portion of the bonds but only after the financier had made the "most flattering terms to his old-time friends and more recent enemies." "It is another case of the lying down together of the lion and the lamb," the *Chicago Tribune* commented. "Some believe Mr. Yerkes is the lamb."[20] In time Charles would get his revenge, demonstrating to Widener and Elkins that *he* was in fact the lion.

21 The Franchise War

In 1895 Charles had resolved to escape Chicago, but within a year he was fighting simply to maintain his position in the city. His carefully constructed streetcar empire was crumbling. His firms' securities were nearly unmarketable, and his hold on the City Council had been broken. In 1897, the magnate again looked to Springfield for aid to shore up his empire. He had a better chance of success this time, Governor Altgeld having been defeated along with Bryan in the November elections.

The catastrophic events of 1896 had taught Charles a hard lesson on the need for franchise extensions. The financier had experienced so much difficulty selling the West Chicago bonds largely because of the franchise question. He maintained that "it was next to impossible to negotiate those securities because we stood on a such a rickety foundation"—a rickety franchise foundation. In 1903, the North and West Chicago companies' operating rights on some of Chicago's most important streets would expire, and it seemed more and more likely that a reformed City Council might refuse to grant reasonably long franchise extensions. Charles still wanted out of Chicago, but he needed these extensions if he hoped to obtain a good price for his companies. Investors showed an understandable reluctance to bankroll firms with such uncertain futures.

As crafty as ever, Charles decided to do an end-run around the City Council, and apply directly to the state legislature for franchise extensions. His attorney Egbert Jamieson drew up a bill that provided for an automatic forty-year extension of streetcar franchises beginning in September 1897. Adopting ex-Governor Altgeld's 1895 suggestion, Charles also backed a measure establishing a state commission to regulate street and elevated railroads. Composed of three persons appointed by the governor, the commission would have possessed powers once reserved to the city councils, including the right to determine whether new streetcar lines should be built. Charles realized that it would be far easier and cheaper to "take care of" the three men on a commission than the sixty-eight men in the City Council—especially a reformed City Council. In an effort to appease the public, he proposed a third measure requiring streetcar firms to pay 3 percent of their gross earnings to state and municipal authorities.[1]

Senator John Humphrey, a grizzled veteran of the legislature, introduced the three bills on February 17, and immediately the Chicago press raised an outcry. "For a mess of red pottage the people are asked in the Humphrey bill . . . to sell the magnificent heritage of their streets to the corporations now operating street car lines over them," the *Chicago Tribune* thundered, firing the first shot in the franchise war. Almost all of Chicago's newspapers opposed the Humphrey bills from the start, claiming that the measures offered inadequate compensation for the use of the streets. The bill setting up a state commission was singled out for especially bitter attack. "Literally, the measure takes from the council of Chicago, the mayor and the citizens all the control of the street and elevated railways . . . and places it in the hands of three men located at Springfield, and who are to be appointed by the governor," the *Times-Herald* huffed. In the view of many editorial writers, the commission bill threatened Chicago's home rule—its right to govern itself.

Chicago publishers rejected the Humphrey bills for another reason: because Charles wanted them. In a revealing January 1897 editorial, Joseph Medill—the venerable owner of the *Chicago Tribune*—explained why he and his newspaper colleagues so despised the "arrogant, reckless and vindictive" streetcar magnate:

> The press of Chicago has no favorable regard or respect for a fellow who treats Chicago as a milch cow, and who takes the butter and cream to New York to be consumed there; who grabs franchises in Chicago and uses their excessive profits with which to erect a palace in New York crammed with pictures, statuary, bric-a-brac, and luxuries of the most costly kind, paid for by the men and women who are allowed to hang on the straps; who debauches Councils, plunders the city, and charges wartime rates of transportation.[2]

Charles, however, was not alone in his desire for the Humphrey bills—far from it. For one of the few times in his Chicago career, he enjoyed the unalloyed backing of the city's biggest businessmen: Marshall Field, Philip Armour, George Pullman, and even Levi Z. Leiter—the man who put up such a determined fight against the Loop Elevated. These men were all heavy investors in the Chicago City Railway, and naturally desired for their company the stability that franchise extensions would bring. Calling a halt to all hostilities, Charles entered into an uneasy truce with the Chicago City and with the Chicago General Railway, the upstart Twenty-second Street trolley line.

It was therefore a unified contingent of street railway men that descended on Springfield in early March to plead their case. Charles's arrival in particular caused quite a stir at the state capital. Dozens of rural legislators congregated at the entrance to his hotel parlor, "anxious to see the multi-millionaire of Chicago, about whom so much has been written in the metropolitan papers." When the famous man and his companions strode into the hotel's dining room, almost every head in the place turned amid whispers of "Where is he, where is he?" and "There he goes."

The next day—March 10—Charles appeared before a large, buzzing crowd of lawmakers in the State Capitol's Hall of Representatives. Looking and acting every bit the sober man of business, the "modestly attired" financier "rattled off statistics like a lightning calculator adds up long columns of figures." He confessed to not being entirely happy with the Humphrey bills. "I make it a point in life to be satisfied with everything as it is," he told a legislator. "But if you mean to ask if these bills are just as we would have drawn them, then I will say no." This was a surprising statement since he and his attorneys *had* drawn up the measures. Predictably, Charles expressed the most displeasure with the gross earnings bill, saying that it was not "worth the paper it is written on." He was far more charitable toward the state commission measure. The lawyer Samuel McConnell offered perhaps the best defense of this bill. "I think it was very scandalously said . . . that if there was an attempt to put the Ten Commandments through the City Council of Chicago it would require money to get a vote of approbation," McConnell asserted, provoking a torrent of laughter. "That is the reason it is a good deal better that a commission should be empowered to grant those franchises instead of the City Council."[3]

Charles made it abundantly clear to the lawmakers that the gross earnings and state commission measures were of secondary importance, and that what he *really* desired was an extension of his streetcar franchises—the lengthier the better. When asked by a representative whether forty-year franchises would increase the value of his companies' stocks, he replied: "I do not know as it would enormously, but it would place them on a good, solid foundation, and that is what I would like to see. I have in the last eight months had a very severe object lesson in regard to that." Taking the hint, a committee of senators unveiled the following day, in addition to the commission bill, a new measure that extended streetcar franchises for *fifty* years, and that fixed the rate of fare at five cents. As a "sop to the public," the traction companies were required to pay to the state and city 3 percent of their gross earnings for the first fifteen years, 5 percent for the next twenty years, and 7 percent for the last fifteen years.[4] Charles could easily live with those terms. In all other respects, the bills were exactly what he wanted.

The financier's Springfield appearance generated screaming headlines, and stirred up the Chicago reform community. Declaring itself "unalterably opposed to the so-called Humphrey street railway bills," the Civic Federation sponsored a "monster" protest meeting on March 20. Learning of the planned gathering, Charles wrote to the Civic Federation president William T. Baker requesting that the streetcar men be given an opportunity to present their side of the question at the rally. Baker quickly rejected this request. "I am sorry this is your decision," a hurt Charles responded, "for the reason that it seems evident some of the members of the Civic Federation do not wish a fair expose of the subject which is to come before the meeting."

The 3,000 people who crowded into Battery D on the evening of March 20 did not come for a "fair expose of the subject," and in this they were not disappointed. "The speakers did not mince words and their utterances were cheered loudly," a *Chicago Tribune* reporter observed. The tall, muscular, bald-headed Alderman John Maynard Harlan dominated the proceedings both physically and verbally. The son of a Supreme Court justice, Harlan electrified the audience with a powerful speech that emitted "political lightning flashes of high voltage." "We do not want violence," he intoned, "but we want to make our protest felt at Springfield in thunder tones so stern, so full of warning that our representatives in the Legislature will not dare to show their faces in Chicago if they vote for that infamous bill."[5]

John Maynard Harlan was already a favorite of Chicago's most zealous reformers, including a young Harold Ickes. "He stood six feet tall, all bone and muscle," Ickes wrote of the thirty-something alderman. A former Princeton football center and an amateur boxer, Harlan pulled no punches when in the political arena. "John Harlan doesn't call a spade a spade; he calls it a dirty shovel," one observer remarked. Swept into the City Council with the reform class of 1896, Harlan quickly set off political fireworks. "Harlan's year in the council had been full of pyrotechnics," Carter Harrison, Jr., recalled. "He had eagerly poured vials of wrath on Yerkes and his ilk." The egotistical Harlan desired "more than anything else in the world to be Mayor of Chicago," according to Ickes, and in 1897 made his first of several runs for that post. He enjoyed the formidable support of William Kent, the *Chicago Daily News*'s Victor Lawson and the Municipal Voters' League. Harlan also attracted to his side a less traditional crowd—"an army of lusty young two-fisted chaps whose admiration was based more on his reputation as a scrapper than on the things for which he stood ready to fight."[6]

Running as an independent against the Republican Judge Nathaniel Sears and the Democrat Carter Harrison, Jr., Harlan attempted to make the Humphrey bills and Charles Yerkes the key issues of the mayoral campaign. While on the stump, the alderman charged that Charles had contributed money to both the Republican and Democratic candidates— a common tactic of the magnate. A courageous *Times-Herald* reporter visited Charles during the heat of the campaign and asked him what he thought about Harlan's allegations.

"Mr. Harlan is an ass," Charles frankly replied, his teeth bared in "an aggressive manner."

"You don't care to be quoted as saying that Mr. Harlan is an ass, do you, Mr. Yerkes?" the journalist countered.

"Yes, that is just what I wish to say. He is not only an ass, but he is a humbug as well."

"Have you read what Mr. Harlan said about you?" the reporter persisted.

"No. I really have not seen the newspapers."

"Here is one of the evening papers, Mr. Yerkes," the *Times-Herald* man offered.

"No, I don't care to read it," Charles answered with an air of indifference. "Life is too short to waste time on Mr. Harlan. He is an ass. I guess that covers the whole subject."[7]

Though he had given money to both the Republican and Democratic candidates, Charles undoubtedly favored the son of the martyred mayor he had admired so deeply. Thirty-six years old in 1897, Carter Harrison, Jr., had difficulty living up to his domineering father's expectations. After being educated at Yale, young Carter had struggled to find a suitable career for himself. He spent several unhappy years as a lawyer, and then drifted into journalism, assuming control of the *Chicago Times*—the newspaper the elder Carter had purchased to promote his political ambitions. With Harrison, Jr., in charge, the *Times* stoutly defended Eugene Debs and his American Railway Union during the Pullman strike, one of the only Chicago periodicals to do so. As the owner of a cash-strapped, circulation-starved newspaper, young Carter naturally identified with the "little fellows struggling for life against mighty corporations." Giving up the journalism game late in 1894, he made the inevitable move toward politics. Harrison, Jr., had a lot going for him politically. He of course possessed a magical name—the name of one of Chicago's most beloved mayors. He also had a background likely to appeal to a wide range of voters. "A Protestant by birth, educated in Germany, at Irish-Catholic St. Ignatius, and at Waspy Yale, he was nearly a balanced ticket all by himself," one historian wrote.[8] On the negative side, young Carter was inexperienced in politics, somewhat insecure, and a terrible speaker.

On the day of his mayoral nomination, Harrison appealed to Charles for assistance. "Perhaps I was too prone to meet with any Tom, Dick or Harry whose aid might prove profitable in my baptism of political fire," Carter would later confess. Charles had a mythical reputation as the man who ran Chicago, so he was a natural target for political aspirants. While riding in a carriage, the magnate and the would-be mayor discussed the campaign. Charles refused to make any promises, but agreed to consider supporting Harrison. During a subsequent meeting at the financier's Michigan Avenue mansion, the two men got down to serious business. Charles expressed his fear that the newspapers would "practically own" Carter in a short time, converting him into an enemy. Harrison responded that he had no use for the newspapers that had so hounded his father and preferred to have "their enmity than their good will." Persuaded, the businessman offered to do what he could to elect Carter. An embittered Charles later claimed that he had made this decision merely out of respect for Harrison's deceased father.

Only one of the mayoral candidates actually pledged to stand by Charles. Unfortunately for the magnate, this particular candidate was a fictional one—Peter Finley Dunne's Martin Dooley. "I'm f'r that gran' old man Yerkuss," Mr. Dooley declared. "I am aware bad things are said about him be people that ride on his sthreetcars, but ye must admit that he's done manny things f'r th' divilopmint iv this gr-reat an' growin' city. I believe in encouragin him f'r he carries th' prosperity iv Chicago on his shoulders, an' 'tis betther to give him more sthreets than to make him take them away fr'm us with an ax."

Carter Harrison, Jr., emerged as the victor of the mayoral race. By his own admission, Harrison had up to that point developed "no definite policy as to traction franchises." He had in fact waged a campaign on the traditional Democratic issue of personal liberty.[9] Events, however, forced him to develop a franchise policy very soon after his election early in April. The newspaper agitation against the Humphrey bills was then reaching a fever pitch as the measures neared their final Senate vote.

His Springfield debut having won rave reviews from the politicians, Charles decided to make a return visit to the state capital at this crucial juncture. According to the *Chicago Journal* reporter H. Gilson Gardner, the magnate's second coming created "a disturbance of the local waters which might be likened to the swell of an ocean liner, plowing its course through a fleet of fishing smacks." Gardner went on to describe Charles's Svengali-like effect on the Springfield lawmakers:

> Members of the legislature seem overawed in his presence. He seems to impress them in some powerful and mysterious way. It is as if he irradiated some wondrous influence similar to the fascination of the expert hypnotist. Men cringe in his presence. Representatives of the sovereign people trot about to do him favors. They mark his coming and going and talk of him in awed whispers behind their hands. They gather in groups in the hotel rotunda and discuss him.[10]

Facing off before a Senate committee, Charles mounted a vigorous defense of the Humphrey bills. "There was fire in his eyes," a reporter noted. "Every move he made was a signal of aggression." The financier asserted that these bills would give his streetcar properties "security against the raids that are continually made on them by certain people in Chicago and elsewhere," and he then glared fiercely at the reformer John Hamline, who was sitting near him. This time Charles's words did not go unchallenged. A "stern looking band of Chicagoans" was present at the hearing, prepared to assail the bills and Charles in no uncertain terms. John Hamline belonged to this group. After dramatically asking who had corrupted the Chicago City Council, Hamline pointed his right fore-finger "in the direction of the region where Mr. Yerkes sat." The latter figure gave no answer to this question, but his eyes flashed at Hamline "what seemed to be a message of hate."

Charles had until now comforted himself with the belief that his opponents were a bunch of "aristocrats" who did not even patronize the streetcars. He therefore must have been disturbed to see union men in the "stern looking band." The crusading journalist Henry Demarest Lloyd had enlisted the Chicago Federation of Labor in the fight against the Humphrey bills. P. F. Doyle, president of the Chicago Federation of Labor, proved to be the star of the Senate hearing, offering a blistering attack on Charles. "Here is Mr. Yerkes," Doyle declared. "He works the laboring man for his nickels. Then he goes to New York and builds a mansion, and then comes out in a public statement that popular government is a farce." While listening to these words, Charles leaned back in his chair and gave a "good imitation of a man trying to look happy while sitting on a red-hot stove." Doyle understandably could not forgive the financier for his heavy-handed conduct during the 1888 streetcar strike and for his subsequent union-busting tactics. The federation chief would later characterize Charles as "the man who has crushed the manhood out" of his employees. Doyle opposed the Humphrey bills because he believed that they would give the magnate "a tighter grip upon the throats of the workingman."[11] Charles's Chicago past was catching up with him.

Despite the vehemence of the opposition to the Humphrey bills, the measures passed the Senate in a 29–16 vote amid pervasive rumors of bribery. Outraged and stunned by the Senate's action, Chicago reformers staged a mass protest meeting on Easter Sunday. John Harlan once again stole the show. In an explosive speech Harlan warned "that proud and haughty bandit" Charles Yerkes to be careful or he might end his career by "decorating a lamp post." His courage bolstered by an impressive showing in the mayoral contest, the alderman also dared to take on the directors of the Chicago City Railway—some of the city's most powerful businessmen. "We have got to hold the right people responsible," Harlan cried. "We have got to name the directors of these companies, call them up." He then proceeded to "put on the stand" Erskine Phelps, Levi Leiter, Marshall Field, George H. Wheeler, and Samuel Allerton, accusing them of complicity in the Humphrey bills "steal." Harlan was especially rough on the millionaire meatpacker Allerton, a vocal defender of the measures. "My God, my God, is he not satisfied?" the alderman asked of Allerton. "Must he need rob us in order to load down his bank account?"

The frenzy over the Humphrey bills peaked on April 20 at a Battery D rally packed to the rafters. Ex-Governor Altgeld injected a rare dose of moderation into the proceedings, urging that the streetcar companies be given adequate protection. Though well received, Altgeld's speech was overshadowed by the "pitiless" resolutions reform Alderman William Kent offered to the assemblage. Drafted by Kent and Peter Finley Dunne, the resolutions branded the Cook County legislators who had voted for the Humphrey bills as Judases, as men doomed to "be followed by contumely, contempt and insult to their graves." "Let the awful curse of an outraged people be upon them forever," the resolutions concluded. "*That is perfectly terrible,*" an elderly man was heard to gasp after the reading of the resolutions. Most of the audience members, however, liked what they heard, and they greeted the resolutions with wild applause, "waving their arms, dancing on chairs and expressing intense and vehement emotion." Harold Ickes did not exaggerate when he said that Kent could "push a punishing pen."[12]

Assuming an attitude of unconcern, Charles labeled the speakers at the various rallies as "a lot of blatherskites." The increasing passion of his rhetoric, however, indicated that something was stirring beneath his placid surface. He blamed the press for the superheated state of public opinion. Every Chicago newspaper—except the *Daily Inter Ocean*—opposed the Humphrey bills. This fact prompted Charles to begin speaking of a "newspaper trust." "The newspaper trust has done its best to deceive the people and to prevent them from obtaining information in regard to the Humphrey bills," he told a *Times-Herald* reporter. "They have stultified themselves in a most disgraceful manner; they have imposed upon the public and have done everything which should bring upon them the contempt of the decent people of this city." Charles hoped that Mayor Harrison would sympathize with his viewpoint. "I have yet to find a single person in the city who is acquainted with their [the Humphrey bills] true purport and meaning," the magnate complained in a letter to the mayor. "The mass meetings . . . have tended to mislead the people rather than enlighten them."[13] Charles had sought sympathy from the wrong person, Harrison having already decided that the Humphrey bills should be defeated.

William Rainey Harper was seeking something other than sympathy when he wrote Charles on April 19. The school president requested more money for the nearly completed Yerkes Observatory, maintaining that it still needed, among other things, a set of eyepieces, an astronomical clock, and a comet-seeking telescope. The letter could not have been more ill timed. It arrived at Charles's office on a day when Harper's name was featured prominently in the newspapers. During a meeting of the Civic Federation on the previous evening, Harper had urged that resolutions be drafted in honor of the group's retiring president, William T. Baker. Charles exploded when he came across this story in the news columns. It was bad enough that Harper belonged to the Civic Federation—the organization spearheading the fight against the Humphrey bills. But Harper's implicit praise of William Baker's conduct as the leader of the Civic Federation really infuriated the magnate. Baker, after all, had absolutely refused to allow the street railway men to speak at the first Battery D meeting.

Around most people Charles tended to wear a mask that concealed his true feelings. But, for some reason, he often discarded this mask when dealing with the genial Harper. The financier did so again, dashing off a venomous response to the university president. In this remarkable message, Charles vented the fury that had accumulated within him since his imprisonment—fury at his status as an eternal outsider:

> On the same date that I received your letter, I also read of a meeting of the Civic Federation, at which you were present and whereat the retiring president, Mr. Baker, was lauded to the skies. It was a notable gathering

of the great and good few who represent the great and good part of our city, and I see by the names that these people are the ones who uphold all the charities of our city, who are always fairly throwing away their wealth so that others may be benefited thereby, who are building up the great institutions of this city in a most reckless and daring manner, which such people as myself, according to the theory of your friends, are doing their best to pull it to pieces and destroy what little honor and integrity and worth is left in our community.

Charles closed his reply with the sarcastic suggestion that Harper apply to his Civic Federation friends for funds.[14]

Though strenuously opposed by the Civic Federation and other reform groups, the Humphrey bills did not simply die in some out-of-the way legislative committee. Charles and his associates were determined to ram the measures through an increasingly unfriendly House, using any means necessary—including bribery on a massive scale. Most political observers suspected that money was being exchanged for votes, but they had no proof. "It is not necessary to see the money pass from hand to hand to discover the evidences of corruption," the *Chicago Journal*'s H. Gilson Gardner wrote. "To the eye that is experienced in observing legislation, it is as clear as the noonday sun. The petty subterfuges, the gauzy pretense of virtue, the diaphanous show of fairness and logical consideration, simply brings out in clearer relief their labels of corruption." Gardner's accusations of bribery apparently hit too close to home for Gus Nohe, a Cook County legislator and an ardent supporter of the Humphrey bills. In early May, Nohe pounced on Gardner from behind and struck the muckraker in the mouth.

Gardner's suspicions received dramatic confirmation on May 7. That morning A. L. Hamilton, editor of the *West Chicago Journal*, happened to be lounging in the seat of a Representative Flannigan whom he resembled "in a general way." An elderly, near-sighted state senator approached Hamilton, tapped him on the shoulder, and said: "I would like to see you a moment." The senator led Hamilton to the rotunda of the Capitol building where W. C. Garrard, secretary of the state board of agriculture, waited. "Mr. Flannigan, I want to fix it with you on those Humphrey bills," Garrard bluntly stated. "We have 77 votes, but want 90. The fact that the bills went to second reading without opposition shows our strength. . . . If you will give us your vote I will fix it so that you can have a present of $20,000 the moment the bills are signed."[15] Hamilton's account of his meeting with Garrard inspired a bribery investigation that was ultimately suppressed by a local district attorney.

Charles and his fellow streetcar men also employed what Edward Price Bell called "moral terrorism" to persuade recalcitrant legislators.

Bell, a reporter for the *Chicago Record*, was told about these undercover tactics during an 1899 investigation of the legislature. According to Bell, "professional vamps, both beautiful and clever," were hired to work their magic on stubborn lawmakers:

> They diligently flirted with the men whose votes were needed by the street railway interests. They went about it slowly. They gave themselves time to "fall in love." They gave their attractions time to take effect on their victims, generally married men with families. And finally a resolute agent of the "system" came upon the scene. He imparted the news that he knew everything. The case was bad from the point of view of the men who "skidded." Their reputation for respectability was an asset they could not play with, could not afford to have clouded in the slightest way. Their families must not be forgotten. Constituencies in America were almost morbidly resentful of illicit love-making on the part of their public men. Such was the agent's argument, and the erring solons wilted under it.

Even "moral terrorism," however, could not save the Humphrey bills. The ill-starred measures came to a final House vote on May 12. A large and enthusiastic crowd had gathered in the galleries to witness the event, almost as if it were a baseball game. Mayor Harrison and a small contingent of Chicago reformers stationed themselves in strategic places on the House floor as the lawmakers decided the fate of the franchise extension bill. Ironically, the clock struck noon during the vote; to one observer, "it seemed to be tolling the funeral knell of the measures which have caused such an agitation throughout the state." Upon the announcement of the bills' defeat in a resounding 123–29 decision, "a shout of applause went up from the floor and was echoed by the galleries." "Ladies waved their handkerchiefs, members clapped their hands, and even the pages whistled and yelled," a reporter noted. The state streetcar commission died about fifty minutes later, provoking a similar response from those present. "The atmosphere in the state of Illinois is about 25 per cent clearer than it was half an hour ago," the reformer John Hamline was heard to remark.

Charles predictably did not take the House's verdict very well. "In the defeat of the Humphrey bills," he fumed in an interview, "I congratulate the socialistic element of this city, and also the anarchistic element, which is now working from the top, instead of from the bottom, as it did eight years ago." The furious magnate sputtered on for a while longer, labeling the Civic Federation leaders a bunch of "frauds" and castigating the newspapers for printing "brazen and glaring untruths" about the Humphrey bills.[16]

Charles had suffered a temporary setback, but he wasn't going to give up the fight. The financier had not yet marketed the entire West Chicago bond issue, and he had little chance of doing so without franchise extensions for his firms. The streetcar companies' financial future—and his—hinged on a franchise extension. Streetcar securities, after all, constituted the bulk of his private wealth. The events of the last year—when he faced business ruin for the second time in his life—had taught him a bitter lesson. Besides all that, Charles simply liked to win, having been reared on the gospel of success. And winning became increasingly important to him as the reformers' rhetoric grew more violent. For Charles, the struggle had turned into nothing less than a contest of wills.

On May 14, Adams Goodrich—Charles's chief lobbyist—returned to Springfield to renew the franchise war. "There's no use in being beaten," Goodrich informed a reporter. "We are here now to see if we can not get something which will be satisfactory to both the people and the street car companies." Trying to appease the critics, Goodrich drafted a new bill that did not violate home rule. Introduced by Senator Charles Allen—a legislator from a rural town that did not even have a single streetcar—the new measure gave *City Councils* the right to grant fifty-year franchise extensions. In addition, the so-called Allen bill allowed noncompeting streetcar companies to consolidate their lines and it fixed a five-cent fare for twenty years.

Joining Goodrich in Springfield on May 18, Charles assumed personal command of the lobbying effort. The businessman's demeanor had changed markedly since his previous visit to the state capital when he "wore a look of smiling self-confidence." He now appeared sadder and more subdued, but "nevertheless there was dogged determination in his face, as if he would accomplish his object." Charles set up his headquarters in the Leland Hotel and began mingling with the politicians that congregated there. "The street car baron is like the head of a comet and his tail is a procession of tagging solons," H. Gilson Gardner wrote. Charles put aside his characteristic "mantle of reserve," and began treating legislators familiarly, slapping them on the back and treating them (and even reporters) to cigars. A brilliant conversationalist, the magnate kept the lawmakers entertained with his "verbal thrusts" at the Chicago newspapers. According to Gardner, Charles's comments were tinged with an intense bitterness. "His disappointment at his first notable failure to dictate legislation has changed to vindictiveness," the *Journal* man asserted, "and some of his expressions might almost be designated as anarchistic."[17]

Charles's mental state at this time is reflected in a letter that he sent to William Rainey Harper on May 24. The financier expressed a fear that his enemies might try to sabotage the great telescope now in place at the Yerkes Observatory:

> A thought has come to my mind in regard to the great care that should be taken to guard the instrument against either accident or malicious acts of anyone who might feel disposed to injure it. It is a sad fact which forces itself upon my mind, and I thoroughly believe that there are many persons—some of them high in the social scale—who would even be pleased to see an accident happen to the telescope.

In an amazing coincidence, only five days later, the moveable floor of the observatory dome collapsed.[18] Though the floor's manufacturer was responsible for the mishap, the increasingly paranoid Charles probably believed that his enemies had indeed struck.

Those enemies—the Chicago reformers—were caught off guard by the Allen bill. The measure seemed fairly innocuous, and even appeared to protect the public interest: It contained a provision requiring a citywide referendum for the approval of any franchise extensions. One of the most vocal opponents of the Humphrey bills, in fact, decided to endorse the new piece of legislation. Herman Kohlsaat, publisher of the *Times-Herald* and *Evening Post*, editorialized in favor of the Allen bill, calling it, somewhat illogically, "the ultimatum offered by the people to the street railway companies." Kohlsaat's "inexplicable change of front" astonished Victor Lawson, owner of the Chicago *Daily News* and *Record*. A leader in the battle against the Humphrey bills and a longtime opponent of Charles, Lawson did not want to see *any* franchise measures passed that year—no matter how harmless. Desperately attempting to repair the damage done to the reform cause, the *Record* publisher dispatched telegrams to twenty lawmakers, including Speaker of the House Edward C. Curtis. "Chicago looks to you for help in this emergency to the full extent of your powers properly exercised," Lawson wrote Curtis. "Kohlsaat's remarkable attitude must not be taken as representing any change of sentiment among the good citizens of Chicago. There is no earthly reason for street car legislation of any sort this session. . . . No surrender."[19]

Lawson's frantic message came too late. Speaker Curtis had already surrendered, exhibiting a change of front as inexplicable as Kohlsaat's. On May 26 Curtis—a staunch foe of the Humphrey bills—had yielded the speaker's post to Representative Charles Selby, a well-known adherent of the "railroad gang." Curtis claimed that he couldn't fulfill his duties that day because of an "excruciating pain" in his jaw. Once in the speaker's seat, Selby took full advantage of his position. The Allen bill was then mired in an apparently hopeless situation, there being over 200 measures ahead of it on the calendar and the legislative session nearing its end. Selby was well aware of these unpleasant facts, so he proposed to push the streetcar bill to the front of the calendar by making it a special order of business. (Special orders have precedence over other pieces of legislation.) Acting Speaker Selby declared the Allen bill to be a special order after a 67–66 vote, even though such an action required the assent of *two-thirds* of the House. Selby's outrageous ruling provoked a storm of futile protest from the reformers. As for Speaker Curtis, one wag joked that "Dentist Yerkes" had "extracted his nerve and put in a gold filling." The statement may have been truer than the jokester realized. A reporter later told Theodore Dreiser that Curtis had been promised $20,000 in bonds for his support of the Allen bill.[20]

Selby had cleared the way for the Allen bill, which passed the House on May 28 in an 85–60 vote. The reformers now feared that the Senate would severely amend the measure, transforming it into another Humphrey bill. Warned that the Allen bill was merely a "Yerkes stalking horse for senatorial amendments," Herman Kohlsaat began to rethink his support for the measure. Speaking to a representative of Charles via telephone, Kohlsaat demanded that certain provisions be added to the Allen bill—provisions that he believed would protect the public. The newspaper publisher wanted a clause inserted in the bill instructing the City Council to grant extended franchises only "upon such terms and conditions as may be deemed best for the public." Charles agreed to this suggestion, but Kohlsaat was not finished. He also insisted that a line be added to the measure requiring the streetcar companies to give thirty days' notice in the newspapers before applying for a franchise extension—thus denying Charles the element of surprise. The magnate couldn't swallow this proposition, considering it "a scheme to sell newspapers," and he ordered the negotiations with Kohlsaat to be broken off. In a rapid response, the publisher promptly trained his editorial guns on the Allen bill, denouncing it as "a sham and a cheat."[21] Kohlsaat apparently wasn't too worried about consistency.

The Senate amended the Allen bill by dropping out the referendum clause, and the measure returned to the House for consideration. On June 4—the day of the final vote on the Allen bill—Charles positioned himself in a "huge armchair" located just outside the House chamber and underneath a painting of George Rogers Clark—the conqueror of the Northwest Territory. The seated magnate calmly issued orders to his lieutenants and listened to their latest reports from the legislative battle-field, "seeming for all the world a commanding general directing his troops." In the midst of the fight, Mayor Harrison—now a leader of the reform forces—dared approach the financier as he reclined on his "throne." "Are you accomplishing much, Mr. Mayor?" Charles asked in a conde-scending tone. "Maybe not here," Harrison angrily responded. "But in Chicago, yes! We are arousing the public. The part of wisdom for you, Mr. Yerkes, would be the abandoning of Springfield and making your approach direct to Chicago. You will secure a better trade today than you will ever make later!"[22]

Charles had no intention of abandoning Springfield. He had lined up more than enough votes to carry the Allen bill through the house. Just to make sure, Representative Lawrence Sherman had been rustled out of his sickbed and transported via buggy to the House, where he was laid out on a lounge in the Speaker's room. When the Allen bill came before the House, two of Sherman's friends hustled him onto the floor and held him up as he voted. While the roll was being called, Charles took out a penknife, quartered an apple, and began to eat it. He had just finished the fruit when it was announced that the Allen bill had passed the House in an 81–71 vote. Without betraying a flicker of emotion, the magnate wiped off his penknife, pocketed it, and went uptown, "where he drank two glasses of cold milk." "He showed no more feeling over this bill than the average member would over the triumph incident to the passage of a dog and sheep law," a *Chicago Tribune* reporter remarked.[23]

The Allen bill passed into the hands of John Riley Tanner, the twenty-first governor of Illinois. Tanner possessed the dubious distinction of hav-ing been the only Illinois governor who was ever tried for manslaughter. A veteran of Sherman's army, Tanner had come out of the war "a wild and reckless young man, who delighted in carousal, drank his whiskey straight, and loved fighting as a pastime." Shortly after the war, he shot to death a man in a dispute over money. The man had threatened Tanner with an axe, but some observers thought that the latter figure was a little too quick on the draw. Convicted of manslaughter, Tanner was acquitted in a second trial after persuading the jury that he had acted in self-defense. He recovered well from this bad beginning, gradually working his way up in the Illinois Republican hierarchy. Tanner gained a reputation as a shrewd, if rather unscrupulous, political manager. Illinois reformers were suspicious of the new governor from the start. Victor Lawson, for one, called him a "common bar-room loafer." Whatever his defects, Tanner was certainly courageous. The Republican governor would later shock his major business backers, including Charles, and openly espouse the side of labor during a brutal miners' strike.[24]

In this instance, Tanner surprised no one. He signed the Allen bill, even in the face of a threat from Joseph Medill. The *Chicago Tribune* publisher had urged the governor to reject the measure or else "part from the confidence of your friends and of the people of Chicago . . . during the rest of your life."[25] As it turned out, Medill's warning was not an idle one. Tanner had in fact signed his political death warrant.

22 The Battle of His Life

Charles experienced another great personal triumph several months after his victory in Springfield. On October 21, 1897, he witnessed the culmination of his boyhood dream with the dedication of the Yerkes Observatory. After five years of "incessant labor" and the expenditure of $285,500, the world's largest refracting telescope was at last ready to pierce the heavens. "Charles T. Yerkes has written his name in the book of the immortals—builded a monument for himself that will endure as long as the world lasts," a *Chicago Times-Herald* reporter gushed.

The road to immortality had been a rocky one. Convinced that the astronomer George Hale was taking advantage of him, Charles had since early 1894 absolutely refused to spend any more money to equip the observatory. At about the same time the magnate began to worry that one of the observatory's two smaller telescopes might be named after Hale. "Now, considering the fact that I am presenting this building, together with the telescope to the University of Chicago, I wish it clearly understood that no telescope whatever is to go in this building which has any name attached to it," Charles warned in a letter to William Rainey Harper. "While I do not ask to have them called the Yerkes telescope, yet, they must be neither the 'Hale' telescope, or any other." The businessman went on to explain why this apparently trivial matter so concerned him:

> As I understand it, in an institution of that kind, the discoveries are generally made with the smaller glasses, and these discoveries are verified and expanded with the large telescope. It would therefore seem almost ridiculous for me to expend the amount of money which is necessary to

do here, and have the credit for the discoveries which might be made go into another channel.[1]

Charles seemed unaware that the credit for an astronomical discovery goes to the discoverer—and not to the person whose name happens to be on the telescope.

Following the groundbreaking late in 1894, the Yerkes Observatory finally began to rise on the shores of Lake Geneva in Williams Bay, Wisconsin. The architect Henry Ives Cobb had specially designed the observatory to appeal to Charles's love of the grandiose—and to his vanity. Laid out in the form of a Greek cross, the building boasted opulent interiors and a fabulous Romanesque façade complete with shield-bearing gargoyles. In a nice touch, Cobb decorated the shields with a bold letter *Y* to let visitors know whose observatory it was.

Charles got his first look at *his* observatory on the evening before the dedication. He traveled alone to Lake Geneva on the 5:50 train. His wife did not accompany him, the two having become more and more estranged. Mary probably would not have gone in any case. She never liked the observatory idea, preferring that her husband establish a hospital instead. Upon his arrival at the Lake Geneva train station, Charles was welcomed by George Hale and driven directly to the observatory, where a contingent of visiting astronomers awaited. After dinner, the magnate inspected the facility, watched the great dome rotate, and even peered through the forty-inch refractor at the overcast Wisconsin sky. He gave his verdict on the observatory to a small crowd of reporters. "Everything is in excellent condition," he reported after his inspection tour. "I am satisfied with the entire plant, as I presume it might be called. The management, too, could not be improved upon." Charles then patted Hale, the observatory's director, on the back—as if to indicate there were no hard feelings between them. In a cheerful mood, the businessman could not resist cracking a joke. "Don't be surprised if a few comets and new stars are discovered through that big tunnel—O! I should say telescope," he quipped. Only those journalists who knew how important tunnels were to Charles's career would likely have laughed at this somewhat obscure reference. The magnate spent the rest of the night in the observatory's library attending an illustrated lecture by the celebrated astronomer Edward Emerson Barnard. According to Hale, the assembled scientists gave Charles a reception that delighted him.[2] For once, the businessman felt genuinely appreciated and accepted.

This feeling was magnified a thousand-fold the following morning. Dedication day dawned chilly and cloudy. Lake Geneva's usually placid waters were tossing wildly and churning into foam under the influence of a raw east wind and a steady drizzle. Eight hundred Chicagoans had descended on the sleepy town of Williams Bay for the ceremony, having been transported from the train station in steam launches or in "grotesque wagons drawn by more grotesque horses." The crowds converged on the floor of the observatory's great dome, gathering in the shadow of the enormous refractor. Around 11:30 A.M. a procession of orange- and scarlet-hooded academics in flowing gowns entered the dome, followed by Charles, who looked somewhat out of place with his drab frock coat. As he made his way to his place on the flower-bedecked stage, Charles kept his eyes fixed on the floor, glancing only once at "the master telescope of the world." When he finally reached his seat—unmistakable because it was draped with laurel wreaths—the entire assemblage arose and applauded wildly. "A great din arose all over the observatory and there was not a hand in the whole 800 pairs that did not join in ringing welcome to the donor of the world famous observatory," a reporter maintained. An embarrassed Charles stood up, and bowed several times in acknowledgment of the applause. The ovation lasted fully five minutes.

An even more impressive demonstration greeted Charles when he attempted to address the audience. According to one source, "round after round of applause filled the hall and made the vast dome ring." The blushing patron of science eventually was allowed to speak. After clearing his throat several times, a visibly nervous Charles delivered a short speech recounting the history of the observatory project and expressing his pleasure in making this gift to the University of Chicago. Following his address, he reached into his coat pocket, took out the papers of transfer, and handed them to Martin Ryerson, president of the University's Board of Trustees. Once again, the crowd applauded heartily. "It was a day of triumph from beginning to end," a *Times-Herald* writer declared. "A name which has long been a power in the world of finance was written among those who will be everlastingly remembered as having contributed to the intellectual achievements of the world. It is that of Charles T. Yerkes."[3]

One day after the observatory dedication, Charles entertained a group of scientists and university officials at an expensive Chicago restaurant. Some of the city's most eminent businessmen were present at this gathering, including the lumber baron Martin Ryerson, the banker Charles Hutchinson, and the developer Ferdinand Peck—all university trustees. Peck—no friend of Charles—brought everyone's thoughts down to earth, reminding the assemblage of the ongoing franchise war during a "roast" of the magnate. "I have heard it suggested that the aims of Mr. Yerkes are even beyond this earth in his desire to elevate and advance our institution of learning," Ferd said, with tongue firmly planted in cheek. "It is rumored he has conceived the idea that the luminaries of the heavens will be brought so near by means of the great lens . . . that cable and electric roads can be constructed to the great planets and stars. . . . It does not appear how the franchises for these roads are to be obtained, but it is said he anticipates friendly legislatures in these starry worlds, though hostile common councils may prevail there as well as here."[4]

Peck's barb must have stung Charles. It remained an open question, though, how hostile the Chicago City Council would really be to the idea of fifty-year franchises. The magnate had obtained only a partial victory with the passage of the Allen bill. That measure simply gave City Councils the power to grant franchises of twenty years' duration and longer. Consequently, the financier still had to apply to the Chicago City Council to get what he wanted. In former days, Charles had almost always been able to count on the Chicago aldermen to deliver—of course, after he had given them a little financial incentive. But the Municipal Voters' League had changed things dramatically. The Council now contained a sizable minority of reformers—a minority strong enough to uphold any mayoral veto. Faced with an unreliable Council and an antagonistic Mayor Harrison, the magnate decided to pitch his appeals directly to the public. He would use the *Daily Inter Ocean* as his bully pulpit. At the age of sixty, Charles had become a newspaper publisher.

Rumors of Charles's purchase of a large stake in the *Daily Inter Ocean* had circulated in local newspapers as early as October 22—the day when the Yerkes Observatory dedication dominated the headlines. The news received confirmation exactly one month later in the *Inter Ocean* itself.[5] The steel magnate John W. Gates and a clique of Republican politicians including Martin Madden had joined Charles in this buy-out.

Charles promptly shook up things at the stodgy *Inter Ocean,* a newspaper one critic called "the greatest repository of dullness in the United States." For his first move, he brought in a dynamic new editor to replace its current manager, the old-fashioned William Penn Nixon. George W. Hinman was the antithesis of Nixon—young, hard-driving, and "not bound by the rules which some of the older men have inflicted upon themselves."

With Charles's blessing, Hinman proceeded to prune the dead wood from the *Inter Ocean* staff, reversing the time-honored policy of his predecessor. The kindly Nixon had treated his employees as if they were members of a "great family," and rarely fired anyone. But Charles and

Hinman had little use for sentiment. Hoping to create a respectable—and profitable—newspaper, they began to break up Nixon's close-knit "family" in a rather ruthless fashion. "Mr. Yerkes, as a newspaper owner, as in the position of car-magnate, evidently believes in obliterating everything that smacks of slowness," one wag noted two years after Charles's purchase of the *Inter Ocean*. "The first to go was the old 'Dr.,' called familiarly 'Old Deaffy,' who for years did book reviews. The poor old man was so unworldly-wise that he could not always discriminate between realism and romance. 'Miss Mary,' the art critic, was next. William Penn Nixon himself has become a mere pensioner, and comes to the office occasionally in a heartbroken way and wanders about where once he controlled. Now his nephew, a big, good-natured incompetent, noted for his denseness and his antipathy to bathtubs and hairbrushes, is to lose his time-honored job of dramatic critic. Everybody will miss 'Charley'.... He has been known to show himself in a dress coat with a neglige shirt and bicycle cap, knee breeches and tan shoes. His dramatic criticisms were scarcely less funny than his costumes yet everyone liked poor old 'Charley' and the question is, What will become of him?"

Observers wondered what the *Inter Ocean* would become with Charles in control. The first edition under the new management provided a clear answer. The *Inter Ocean* would be nothing less than Charles's personal organ, his bully pulpit—with the stress on bully. The newspaper began to feature regular articles extolling the traction companies. On a typical day, readers could also find stories and editorials containing vigorous defenses of long streetcar franchises. With reason, critics started speaking of the *Inter Ocean* as the "Daily Yerkes." "He's a great journalist," Peter Finley Dunne's Mr. Dooley said of Charles. "All he needs is a bald head an' a few whiskers an' principles to be a second Horace Greeley."

As it turned out, the newspaper simply did not possess enough readers to materially influence public debate on the franchise question. Charles and Hinman therefore attempted to manufacture circulation. Cranking up the printing presses, the duo blanketed the city with copies of the *Inter Ocean* in an effort to get out the streetcar companies' message. Unfortunately, many people did not appreciate receiving a free gift of the "Daily Yerkes." "It [the *Inter Ocean*] confronts the workingman as he emerges from his home and the housemaid as she sweeps the steps in the morning," one observer complained. "It is thrown into hallways, vestibules and cellars. The writer one morning had eight copies of it left at his residence—four at the front door and four thrown into the basement."[6]

Charles could manufacture circulation but not consent. A public weary of crowded streetcars and slow service proved to be unremittingly hostile to the idea of long franchise extensions. Back in 1895, a regular patron of Charles's North Side cable lines had described the ordeal of a trip to work: "Men and women were packed together like herrings in a barrel, so that they breathed in each other's faces, sneezed in each other's ears, trod on each other's toes, fell helplessly on top of each other as they rounded the curves, and had to climb over each other to get out." This hapless commuter hoped one day to severely punish the man he held responsible for his daily plight. "O, for a pair of copper-toed boots and the legs of Sandow and an opportunity to kick a certain man over the entire route of his cable car lines," he wrote. "How I would enjoy kicking him up hill and down, kicking him around the curves, kicking him through the tunnels, kicking him until he fell, then kicking him until he got up, kicking him in the ribs, kicking him on the shin, kicking him in the stomach, and kicking him in the back. When I had kicked him to Diversey street, on the return trip, I would then like to finish up with one wild kick that would land him in the middle of Lake Michigan."

The *Inter Ocean* had also utterly failed to influence the editorial policy of rival newspapers. Hinman's mud-slinging campaign in fact strengthened the resolve of certain key journalists who were opposed to fifty-year franchises. For Charles Faye, the *Daily News* managing editor, the franchise war had become a personal crusade—thanks in no small part to Hinman's vitriolic attacks. Faye was hoping for "an aldermanic revolution" during the April 1898 elections, a revolution that would bring an honest majority to the City Council. "I want to see it because I want to have developed the possibilities of Mr. Harrison as a public officer under the most favorable conditions of honest help," Faye explained to Victor Lawson, "and I also wish it for the purpose of everlastingly bursting my old friend and companion in grief, Charles Tyson Yerkes. I believe that Yerkes is nearly at the end of his string, and unless he can extend his franchises, float increased bonded indebtedness, dump his holdings on the market and return to New York with a bag of millions, that this great misguided fellow will go down in the ruin of the sick structure he has built about himself."[7]

Such an outcome seemed far more likely after the April elections. Despite Charles's tireless efforts to influence the vote, a large number of reformers won seats in the new City Council. George Cole, the president of the Municipal Voters' League, estimated that there were now between thirty-eight and forty aldermen "who will be arrayed against the gang."

"This election marks the downfall of Charles T. Yerkes as the dominant force in the City Council," Cole confidently asserted.

Though later counts put the number of reform aldermen at only thirty, the election nonetheless was a tremendous setback for Charles. In the previous Council, the magnate could have depended on the votes of thirty-four aldermen, with eleven more up for grabs. According to Mayor Harrison, "it seemed certain all Yerkes had to do was to pay the price of an ordinance and over my veto it was cock-sure to go." Why didn't Charles act then, instead of waiting for a new Council to be elected? Harrison believed that the financier intended to provide a clear demonstration of his power by crushing at the polls "the very backbone of the honest minority"—such reform aldermen as Adolphus Maltby, Albert Beilfuss, and Charles Gunther.[8] Charles also may have wanted to secure a more comfortable majority in the City Council. He needed, after all, forty-six votes to override a certain mayoral veto. Whatever the reason for the delay, it was a fatal miscalculation.

Charles had already gauged Mayor Harrison's opinion on the franchise question. Shortly after the passage of the Allen bill, the magnate visited Harrison at the latter's modest West Side home. Fearful of a blackmail attempt, the mayor stationed his wife and brother on a staircase to listen—out of sight—to the conversation. After small talk, Charles asked Harrison how he planned to act on the franchise matter. The mayor stated that he was absolutely opposed to franchises longer than twenty years. He also said that he advocated the repeal of the Allen Law. Charles listened patiently. "All the while I talked Mr. Yerkes faced me, his steel-blue eyes never flickered from mine, a handsome man with a wonderful pair of eyes, searching eyes that seemed to read the very soul of the one on whom they were fixed," Harrison recalled nearly forty years after the event. When the mayor had finished speaking, Charles leaned toward his host and asked in an insinuating tone, "Tell me, Mr. Mayor, what do you want anyhow?" The question—and its implication—offended Harrison. "Mr. Yerkes," he responded indignantly, "you may not mean by that query what I think you mean. If I happen to misunderstand, if I misinterpret its significance, please pardon me and consider my words unspoken. If, however, I construe your query correctly, let me say, there is not enough money on God's footstool to induce me to vary my position in the slightest degree." Charles stared at Harrison for a moment, and then steered the discussion in a safer direction. After a short period of pleasant chatter, the financier took leave of Harrison. "It was the last talk I was to have with him," Harrison remembered. "My wife and brother had overheard every word. I felt safe."[9]

The April 1898 election results bolstered Mayor Harrison's confidence. "If Yerkes can pass an ordinance over my veto I'll eat that old brown fedora," the mayor declared, and pointed to a battered, floppy hat lying on his desk. While the odds were certainly stacked against him, Charles did not concede defeat in the franchise war. He very much wanted to see the mayor eat his words—and his hat.

The magnate fought Harrison with a bludgeon and a rapier. The *Inter Ocean* pounded the mayor day after day, accusing him of being a tool of the "newspaper trust" and questioning his sanity. Charles also backed a legislative investigation of corruption in the Chicago Police Department with the intent of embarrassing Harrison's administration. Finally, pulling an ace out of his sleeve, the businessman recruited his friend Richard Croker to lobby the mayor at the eleventh hour. Croker, the powerful boss of New York's Tammany Hall, carried a lot of weight in Democratic circles. His "pull" would be extremely useful to a possible presidential candidate like the ambitious Harrison. Meeting the mayor in Room 1166 of the Auditorium Annex, Croker bluntly argued that long franchises were necessary to protect the financial fortunes of Charles and other street railway investors. "I know that," Harrison answered, "but I am not interested in his private fortunes, but the public fortune of the city." Croker would later report to Charles that it "was absolutely useless trying to do business with Mayor Harrison."[10]

The long-awaited franchise ordinances were finally introduced in early December. According to rumor, Charles had planned to make his move the previous summer but delayed because of the "hoggishness of several Aldermen." "These city fathers . . . appraised the value of their votes altogether highly," an anonymous source claimed, "and Mr. Yerkes simply refused to be held up." The aldermen eventually lowered their fees—probably because of the imminent convening of the state legislature. The Illinois legislature was expected to repeal the Allen Law and thereby deprive the aldermen of the ability to grant franchises longer than twenty years.

Alderman William Lyman, of the South Side, had the dubious honor of introducing the franchise ordinances. Charles had tried unsuccessfully to line up a reform alderman to sponsor the measures but was finally forced to settle on "Angel Billy." When a visibly embarrassed Lyman rose to introduce the ordinances at the December 5 City Council meeting, murmurs of surprise spread across the chamber floor and up into the packed galleries. The alderman, after all, had pledged during the recent election campaign to support the mayor. Lyman's ordinances provided for a fifty-year extension of streetcar franchises and required the traction companies to pay up to 3 percent of their gross earnings to the city.[11] For the reformers, the measures were an outrage. According to the recent findings of a Council committee headed by John Harlan, the richest streetcar companies could have afforded to give the city up to 20 percent of their gross earnings.

Lyman's ordinances provoked a storm of protest in Chicago. Mayor Harrison condemned the measures as "black, damnable, vitriolic," and called for 150,000 citizens to gather at the City Hall. "Let the aldermen face a crowd like that and they will feel the weight of the responsibility that rests upon them," the mayor declared. Peter Finley Dunne, now a *Chicago Journal* editor, advised Harrison to use "Cromwellian methods" to vanquish the "shrewd, calculating, crafty" streetcar men. "It is no time for parleying and bandying words and listening to smooth promises and deceptive overtures," Dunne wrote. "It is no time for nice observance of the law, parliamentary or statute." The newspaperman was not alone in this sentiment. The following advertisement appeared in an afternoon paper:

> WANTED: 10,000 Strong-limbed and fearless men. Apply at the council chamber, with ropes, the night the aldermen attempt to pass the fifty-year franchise robbery. Come prepared to do business.[12]

Chicagoans began wearing buttons decorated with a hangman's noose, and the aldermen started becoming nervous. "I will not be surprised to see some hanging done in the streets of Chicago," Harrison remarked, only half-seriously.

Expressing shock at this "rope talk," the *Inter Ocean* castigated "the pitiable and unbalanced young man who in this crisis is the head of our municipal government." The newspaper was also sharply critical of its press competitors for inciting "the criminals and outcasts with their predictions of hangings and dynamite explosions." "At the present moment we have in this city a press as lawless as the Arbeiter Zeitung and the Alarm in the spring of 1886," an increasingly desperate *Inter Ocean* roared. "It is as defiant of law and order, as reckless of legal rights and as inflammable in its appeals to the dangerous classes as any Anarchist press that this city or any other city in the United States ever has seen."

The Chicago franchise war captured the nation's headlines. Joseph Pulitzer's crusading New York *World* took particular interest in the conflict. For the *World*'s editorialists, the issue at stake in the matter was nothing less than the fate of democratic institutions. "For if laws can be bought and the rights of communities bartered away through bribery, is not popular government something worse than a failure?" the newspaper pointedly asked. The franchise war provided "a test of the ability of the second largest city in the Union to govern itself and to protect the rights of its inhabitants."

Visiting the City Hall on December 7, Charles looked as serene as ever—the eye at the center of a political hurricane. "That rope talk doesn't seem to worry him very much," a very much worried alderman said of the magnate, "but I'll bet you he doesn't show up here the night we try to pass these ordinances over the mayor's veto, eh?" Charles stood by a window as a Council committee debated the franchise ordinances, watching the proceedings with "the calm, deliberate air of a man who is in a great battle and knows it, and feels that every word spoken and every move made means a great deal." The financier lost his cool only once that day. When Charles informed a throng of reporters that he was not familiar with the work of the aldermen, one cynical scribe remarked facetiously, "Oh, I don't know." His face darkening, the businessman glowered at the impudent journalist.

The following day Charles was scheduled to defend the franchise measures before the Council committee. "Will you give the aldermen what they want to know?" a reporter asked. "I shall give them everything they want," the magnate replied, and then realizing how that sounded, added with a smile, "in the line of information."[13]

One observer likened the financier's performance before the Council committee to that of a skillful actor. "Sometimes there was a smile on his persuasive lips which his gray dragoon mustache did not entirely conceal," a *Chicago Chronicle* writer noted. "Sometimes there were tenderer curves of pathos, sometimes the sharp lines of determination and sometimes a fanciful dash of hauteur. But whatever the expression that gamboled or rolled over his cold, gray countenance, every word that fell from his lips was heard as distinctly as if it was a silver dollar jingling on a paving block."

Looking like the defiant captain of a sinking ship, Charles stood on a raised platform in the crowded, smoke-filled Council chamber, his hands jammed into his trouser pockets. Enduring occasional hisses from a largely unsympathetic audience, the magnate spoke for two hours in a passionate defense of his position. He said that the streetcar firms needed fifty-year franchises to ensure their financial health—to enable them to market securities. He portrayed himself as a defender of the North and West Chicago traction companies and their 3,600 stockholders. "I am not the owner of these street railroads by any means," Charles maintained, "but I am the guardian of them, and so long as I have life in me I shall guard them to the best of my ability. It won't matter what I have to run up against. I am equal to the occasion, I think." He concluded the day with an appeal for a "fair deal" from the city. Charles's speech won rave reviews. "Well, boys, I guess he'll do," one alderman was heard to say. "The 'Baron' ain't no slouch, is he?" another remarked.[14]

Charles of course did not simply rely on words to woo the aldermen to his side. According to the New York *World*, the promoters of the Lyman ordinances had promised $1,200,000 to the aldermen upon passage of the measures. Supposedly, the politicians were already squabbling over the division of the spoils. The Council's leaders demanded three-fourths of this sum for themselves, leaving thirty or so aldermen to divvy up the remaining $275,000. "Now the small-fry thirty don't like this," the *World*'s correspondent reported. "They ask: 'Why should we get a paltry $9,000 or $10,000 while four or five gobble up $100,000 and nearly a dozen get $40,000 each? We won't stand it.' Here, then, from a boodler's point of view is a bad mess, and harmony far in the distance."

Bribery was only one of the methods that Charles used to round up Council votes. One alderman—a contractor—was suddenly given the opportunity to build an addition to Charles's office at 444 North Clark Street. Another Council member allegedly received a contract to furnish uniforms for the employees of the North and West Chicago streetcar companies. Charles personally lobbied other city fathers. Happening to run across ex-Alderman Isaac Horner at the Auditorium Hotel, the magnate treated him to cigars and champagne. "Ike says Yerkes did not know that he is no longer in the council," Mayor Harrison quipped, "and he would like to meet some other railway presidents on the same terms."[15]

On December 12, the Lyman ordinances faced a crucial test vote. Seven hundred persons poured into the galleries overlooking the Council chamber, ready to do battle against the hated measures. Just outside the chamber, some 3,000 Chicagoans, including 100 members of a German fife and drum corps, buzzed. Positioned in front of the fidgeting aldermen, with gavel in hand and cigar in mouth, a standing Mayor Harrison calmly waited for the proceedings to begin. He was without question the star of the show: Every other person in the galleries sported a badge inscribed with his image.

Certain unfortunate aldermen had been delegated to champion the Lyman ordinances. They quickly discovered how unpopular the measures were—thanks to the Greek chorus in the galleries. "We need all we can get from the traction companies," Alderman William Mangler, one of the unfortunates, said during the course of his remarks. "How much do you get for that speech?" a voice in the gallery suddenly yelled. "You don't dare come down here and talk that way to me," Mangler roared in response, a fist waving in the air.

Alderman Michael McInerney, another supporter of the ordinances, had an even rougher time of it. As McInerney tried to defend the measures, he was greeted with a chorus of hisses. "I came from a country where nothing but snakes hiss," the Irish-born alderman snapped. "There ain't no snakes in Ireland," a wag in the gallery countered. McInerney's trials did not end there. Shortly after resuming his speech, the German fife and drum corps outside began blaring and booming, drowning out McInerney's words. "Why don't you bring in your Salvation Army?" the irate alderman shouted at Mayor Harrison through the noise.

The key moment in the Council meeting came when Alderman Maltby rose to offer an important resolution. A leader of the reform aldermen, Maltby had rushed back to Chicago from his California ranch when he learned of the franchise ordinances' introduction. Maltby proposed that the Council suspend the rules and postpone all consideration of any franchise measures until the Allen Law was repealed. To the astonishment of many, the resolution received thirty-eight votes in its favor and only twenty-five against—just a few votes shy of the two-thirds needed for its passage. "As I look at it, we have made a distinct gain this evening," Mayor Harrison announced after the meeting. "A majority of the Council has gone on record as against the extension ordinance."[16]

A correspondent for the *Chicago Chronicle* informed Charles via telephone of the Council vote. Not accustomed to defeat—especially in the Council—the magnate was genuinely surprised to learn that a majority of the aldermen had registered their disapproval of the Lyman ordinances. He indicated to the reporter that a new policy would have to be formulated. And so, under Charles's direction, a Council committee spent the following few days fashioning a new ordinance calculated to mollify the public. The measure extended franchises for only twenty-five years and compelled the traction companies to pay to the city between 3 and 5 percent of their gross receipts. One provision in the ordinance even allowed for eventual city ownership of the streetcar lines. Compared to the Lyman ordinances, the new measures seemed positively "Utopian."[17]

But Charles's critics were not satisfied. They would not have been happy with the most Utopian of measures. They wanted nothing less and nothing more than Charles's total defeat. In a *Daily News* interview, George Cole, onetime chief of the Municipal Voters' League, expressed the viewpoint of many of the reformers. "Charles T. Yerkes knows only too well that his financial plans imperatively demand franchise extensions for at least thirty-five years," Cole asserted. "He is fighting to retain his footing in this city. If he fails, as he certainly will, in his efforts toward securing the passage of long-term ordinances, the result will probably be the driving of Yerkes from Chicago and her world of finance."[18] The reformers certainly hoped for such a result.

The franchise war came to a close on the rainy and foggy evening of December 19. The Council chamber's galleries were again thronged with boisterous citizens. At one point during the meeting, a spectator smacked a city official in the ear, and was promptly escorted out of the room by five blue-coated policemen. The real battle, though, occurred on the Council floor. Alderman S. S. Kimbell had been entrusted with the task of introducing the new franchise measure but he never got the chance. Mayor Harrison sprang his trap too quickly. Early in the meeting, Alderman William Mavor—a Harrison man—stood up and moved that all franchise ordinances be referred to the Committee on City Hall. Johnny Powers, the leader of the "gang" aldermen, had banished a group of reformers to this committee on "lonesome roads"—a committee that had never met before. "It was considered a great joke at the time," a *Chicago Tribune* reporter noted.[19] But the joke was now on Powers and his confederates.

After Mavor had presented his motion, an enraged Powers jumped out of his seat and roared an objection: "The ordinances are certainly matters pertaining to streets and alleys of this city under rule 44, and under that rule they must go to the Streets and Alleys committees of the various divisions and cannot go anywhere else."

"It does not refer exclusively to streets and alleys," a smiling Mayor Harrison answered.

"I would like to ask the chairman what are they pertaining to if not to the streets and alleys of the city," an increasingly desperate Powers countered.

"To a great deal more," Harrison said.

"I call the attention of the chair and ask him to refer this matter to the Council," the alderman pleaded.

"The only thing for the chair to do is to put the matter to a vote of the Council as to what committee the Council wants it to go," the mayor ruled. "The first motion is to send it to the Committee on City Hall. If that is voted down then the Alderman can make a motion for any other committee."[20]

Mavor's motion passed in a razor-thin 32–31 vote, and the galleries cheered, "long, loud, and deep." A triumphant Mayor Harrison glanced up at the celebrating spectators and beamed. Everyone knew that the mayor had prevailed in the franchise war. All franchise measures were now buried in the Committee on City Hall—a tomb from which they would never emerge. As one newspaper headline put it, the "council gang" had been hanged with its own rope.

Charles had suffered a terrific loss. He could not expect to secure franchise extensions from the Chicago City Council—on any terms. The magnate greeted the news of his defeat with sarcasm. "I am glad this question is intrusted to people of such intelligence," he fumed. "The Mayor has shown intelligence throughout. There is intelligence in the Council from the Mayor down. They are eminently fit to settle such a question."[21]

Ironically, two gang aldermen—"Bathhouse" John Coughlin and Michael "Hinky Dink" Kenna—had helped engineer Charles's "Waterloo." These two denizens of the notorious First Ward formed the oddest of odd couples. An enormous man, Bathhouse John dressed colorfully and spoke even more colorfully in fractured phrases. The diminutive "Hinky Dink," on the other hand, was a quiet man and a less obtrusive dresser. Even reformers liked Kenna. "The Dink is a real person," William Kent often said. "He keeps his word." Mayor Harrison claimed that Kenna never told him a lie—"a thing practically unique in my experience." Kenna and Coughlin had promised Harrison that they would vote against the franchise ordinances—and they remained true to their word. "I have recently joined the church," the Bath explained.[22]

Looking back on the franchise war, a *Chicago Journal* writer would pay his respects to Charles in an 1899 editorial. "He has been a splendid fighter, though not always a wise one," this anonymous journalist said of Charles. "He has struggled with odds that might have appalled any man. He has given battle to a whole city, and he has done so single-handed, for though he has been followed and encouraged by a number of wealthy men of this city. . . , he knew they were merely the jackals that followed the lion, that feared to fight as he fought and that would desert him at the first sign of defeat. Perhaps there was never before in this city the spectacle of one man defying all public opinion, violating every principle of justice and honor that it could be to his advantage to violate, and provoking a community to the verge of riot and violence, without other support than his own indomitable courage and almost unconquerable will. Leaving its moral aspects out of consideration, it has been magnificent."[23]

23   *End Game*

December had always been the cruelest of months for Charles. His mother had died during a long-ago December. He had been convicted of larceny in December. And, now, in yet another December, his hopes for franchise extensions were shattered. An embittered Charles never forgave the citizens of Chicago for what he considered to be their "ingratitude." The magnate revealed the full depth of his anger in a conversation with the attorney Adams A. Goodrich, a participant in the franchise war. Stopping by Charles's New York City office in May 1900, Goodrich and the financier began reminiscing about the "old fight." Touching an obviously sore spot, the lawyer kidded Charles, questioning "what good the Allen bill had done him, when he fell down in getting the franchise through the Council." Becoming visibly agitated by the memory of this event, still fresh in his mind, the magnate suddenly blurted out in fury, "I am through with Chicago, I have come to a city where a white man has got a chance."

Charles would never admit that the reformers might have had good reasons to oppose franchise extensions. He insisted that the campaign against him had been merely fueled by envy—"the most dominant passion of the human race." "It is part of human nature to push back every one who is struggling for great things," he would later reflect on his Chicago experience, "and any one who attempts to push back human nature has a large contract on his hands."[1]

In truth, the businessman had courted conflict while in Chicago. He had seemingly gone out of his way to make enemies. An associate believed that he had a "naturally belligerent disposition." According to another acquaintance, "Nothing was worth having to Yerkes unless he fought for it." Charles himself would claim that the newspapers had forced him to become belligerent. "I would not have been the man that I am today if they (the newspapers) had not put energy, and heart, and courage into me by giving me good reason to fight back," he declared. "A reasonable capacity for combativeness is one of the requisites for success."

The pint-sized reformer George Cole had predicted "the driving of Yerkes from Chicago and her world of finance" following his defeat in the franchise war. In fact, Charles had long planned to escape the untamable colossus that was Chicago. Before leaving, however, he had wanted, in his words, "to get the companies in such a position that my successor . . . would have nothing to do but to go on with the work laid out."[2] In other words, he had hoped to pass on to a future traction manager a unified streetcar system protected by long-term franchises.

Charles had recognized since his earliest days in Chicago that the transportation problem could only be solved by a consolidation of the city's streetcar firms. The original owners of Chicago's three major traction companies had planned their lines only with regard to their respective divisions. As a result, Chicago was a divided city, overlaid with three clashing streetcar grids and burdened with a complicated system of multiple fares. Hoping to rationalize this outmoded and inefficient system, Charles had embarked upon a furious twelve-year-long campaign to conquer the Chicago streetcar field. But the South Side's blue-chip Chicago City Railway had remained stubbornly outside of the magnate's grasp. A powerful contingent of stockholders led by Levi Leiter had blocked all of Charles's many efforts to secure a controlling interest in the firm.

Things changed in the summer of 1898. A consolidation of Chicago's big three streetcar companies finally became a real possibility. Levi Leiter —the owner of 7,000 shares of Chicago City stock—suddenly signaled a willingness to include the South Side streetcar firm in a merger of the city's traction lines. Leiter well knew that the participants in a consolidation often reaped fabulous profits. And, as it turned out, he desperately needed money, having lost a fortune in his son Joseph's recent disastrous wheat speculation.

The twenty-nine-year-old Joseph Leiter was "the jewel of the family," according to his sister Mary. A spoiled, arrogant young man, the beefy Joseph believed that he had a natural talent for making money. Events would prove him tragically wrong. In the spring of 1897, he spearheaded what the *Chicago Tribune* termed "probably the most gigantic and sensational attempted coup in the history of modern commerce." He had set for himself no less than the gargantuan task of buying up all the surplus wheat in America. Joseph hoped to "corner" wheat with the aid of his father's money and thereby dictate the price of that breadstuff. By the fall of 1897, he had purchased some 40,000,000 bushels of wheat on the Chicago Board of Trade and had engineered a thirty-cent rise in the price of the grain—to over $1.00 a bushel. Leiter's high-handed scheme began to go awry in December 1897 when Philip Armour flooded the market with an unexpected horde of wheat. The canny Armour had employed ice-breakers to clear the way through a frozen Lake Superior for a fleet laden with wheat. Joseph was ultimately forced to abandon his venture in June 1898. Following a government forecast for a bumper wheat crop, the price of the commodity plunged precipitously. The Leiters—father and son—were left with 50,000,000 bushels of wheat, and a loss estimated at $9,750,000. Such an enormous sum was too much for even the ultra-wealthy Levi to bear losing. In order to raise funds, he started selling off chunks of his Chicago real estate empire, including the valuable lot on the corner of State and Van Buren streets—the property that he had so zealously defended during the Loop war.[3]

Charles spied a grand opportunity in the Leiters' grave misfortune. He approached Joseph and pointed out to the failed speculator how his fortune could be regained by engineering—with his father's help—a merger of Chicago's street railways. Charles's proposition had the backing of the financial heavyweights Peter Widener, William Elkins, and the aptly named Thomas Fortune Ryan—a businessman notorious for his shrewdness and his silence. William Whitney once described Ryan as "the most adroit, suave, and noiseless man" he had ever known. Ryan and his Philadelphia associates had made millions when they consolidated most of New York City's streetcar lines into the Metropolitan Traction Company, and they were eager to stage a repeat performance in Chicago.

Joseph Leiter was swayed by the suave financier's arguments. Enlisting his father's aid, Joseph began lobbying skeptical Chicago City Railway stockholders in behalf of the consolidation scheme. "The eastern people, having made such a success of the Metropolitan Traction combination, are looking around to make others," Leiter explained to one influential Chicago City investor. "My only thought was that if the present rate of dividend of the City Railway could be guaranteed in such a way as to make it absolutely secure and the stockholders be given the right to participate to a certain extent in a consolidation, it might be of advantage."[4] In the end, the negotiations with the Chicago City investors collapsed. Widener, Elkins, and Ryan were only willing to guarantee a 10 percent dividend on Chicago City shares instead of the 12 percent desired by the stockholders.

Despite this setback, the Widener group still contemplated purchasing Charles's interest in the North and West Side lines. The buy-out talks dragged on for months—in part because Charles refused to deal directly with Widener and Elkins, men who had given him no end of trouble in the past. Acting as a go-between, the Chicago banker John Mitchell skillfully bargained with the magnate. It was a tedious, painstaking process, but by March 1899 Mitchell had made substantial progress. "I find that Mr. Mitchell has secured many details which he did not have when I last saw him," Joseph Leiter reported to Ryan that month, "and has also gotten a statement with regard to the price asked for the properties."[5]

Charles initially wanted more for his stock than Widener, Elkins, and Ryan were willing to pay. The negotiations were also hampered by the crucial franchise question: There seemed little point in buying traction lines that might soon lose the right to operate on the city's streets. Finally, following a series of grueling conferences with the lawyer Henry Crawford at 444 North Clark Street, a "meeting of minds" occurred in early May 1899. Charles agreed to accept $275 a share for his 20,000 shares of North Chicago Street Railroad stock and $130 a share for his 32,000 shares of West Chicago Street Railroad stock. He would thus receive a total of $9,360,000 for his holdings in the two roads. Widener, Elkins, and Ryan secured this huge sum by a clever stratagem. They organized a new firm—the Chicago Union Traction Company—to lease the North and West Side lines, and had it issue $12,000,000 of preferred stock. This stock was then sold and the proceeds used to purchase Charles's securities. As for the franchise issue, "eminent lawyers" assured Widener and his associates that the traction companies' original charters gave them a ninety-nine-year right to the use of the streets.[6]

Charles seemed to have been satisfied with the amount his streetcar holdings had realized—an amount equal in today's money to roughly $182,000,000. "I never saw him so happy in his life," an acquaintance remarked of Charles following the deal's close. "His face was beaming, and he was all ready to take up his residence in New York. I think he is delighted with the change."

But appearances were deceiving. Charles's smiling exterior cloaked an inner anger. The previous February, he had folded seven of his outlying suburban roads into a new firm—the grandly titled Chicago Consolidated Traction Company. He had made a pretty package of these "sloppy lines" but unfortunately one that failed to entice his former associates. Widener and Elkins suspected—rightly, as it turned out—that the Consolidated company's $15,000,000 capital was largely water, representing little real investment, and therefore they refused to meet Charles's price for these securities. Consequently, the enraged magnate was left with the "stub ends" of his once mighty streetcar empire—over 200 miles of mostly unprofitable trolley lines "creeping beyond the Chicago limits to drowsy suburbs."[7]

Characteristically, Charles decided to *force* his old partners to swallow the Consolidated system. Before he relinquished control of the North and West Side companies and before they were incorporated into Union Traction, he executed a remarkable agreement between these lines and his Consolidated firm. Approved by his dummy directors on May 25, 1899, this agreement gave the Consolidated Traction Company the right to run its cars into the city's heart via the tracks of the North and West Chicago lines.[8] Charles had thus transformed his struggling Consolidated Traction company into a potentially formidable competitor of the mighty Union Traction—a competitor, ironically, with operating rights on the latter firm's own tracks. The financier had pulled off quite possibly the most devious maneuver of a very devious career.

Shortly after taking charge of the Union Traction Company in early July 1899, the lumberman Jesse Spalding learned about this amazing agreement. He discovered many other disturbing things about the firms he had inherited. Arthur Young, an accountant hired by Spalding, had inspected the books of Charles's old companies and had found widespread evidence of financial chicanery. Young discovered that the North and West Side firms had largely financed the construction of the seven lines that made up the Consolidated Traction Company. For years, the cash balances of the North and West Chicago roads had been diverted to the use of the suburban roads. "During all these years this money of North and West Chicago while so diverted was earning no interest for its stockholders," Young reported. "This cash was being risked by the officials in enterprises unknown to the stockholders, who received no benefit in interest or otherwise." Indeed, Charles had reserved almost all of the Consolidated Traction stock for himself and his acquaintances. Young uncovered one other interesting item: Charles had occasionally dipped into the treasury of the North Chicago company, borrowing large sums "either for himself or for one or other of his outside enterprises."[9]

Young's report bolstered the position of the Union Traction men in their now "very active dispute" with the Consolidated company. According to one almost certainly apocryphal account, Charles was summoned before a meeting of the Union Traction directors, and—so the story goes—ordered to scrap the controversial Consolidated operating agreement. "Mr. Yerkes, you have been guilty of a criminal offense," a director is supposed to have said. "Make restitution, or you will be brought to justice.

Unless you cancel this outrageous contract I'll see to it that the penitentiary doors close behind you." Charles then, the account maintains, stood up, "fixed his wonderful eyes upon every man at the table," and calmly uttered the following words: "Gentlemen. Perhaps you may succeed in sending me to the penitentiary, but when I enter its doors, you and you and you"—pointing to certain particularly distinguished men of business arrayed around the polished table—"will one and all accompany me. I know many things about you, gentlemen, things it would not be nice for the world to know; I shall not hesitate in case of necessity to take the authorities and the public into my full confidence."[10] Though false, this story does reveal much about popular perception of the magnate.

Charles may not have employed personal blackmail but he did somehow persuade the Union Traction directors to buy out his interest in the Consolidated company—the goal he had sought all along. The Widener group probably decided to make this purchase for a very simple and logical reason: to eliminate the Consolidated as a serious competitive threat. The settlement was a very lucrative one for Charles. Under the agreement, completed in April 1900, the $15,000,000 of Consolidated stock was sold to Union Traction at $45 a share, and then exchanged for $6,750,000 worth of gold bonds bearing four-and-a-half percent interest. Bonds made a safer investment than stock: dividends weren't guaranteed but interest was. Charles received the lion's share of these bonds—an amount totaling $4,494,000. This was a very nice sum, especially considering the fact that he had paid nothing for the Consolidated stock.

The Union Traction directors were not only generous; they were also forgiving. They granted Charles a release of "all claims and demands of every name, nature or kind whatever" that the old North and West Chicago companies might have had against him.[11] The magnate had undoubtedly insisted on this release as part and parcel of the deal.

Union Traction was doomed from the start. Before acquiring the North and West Chicago companies that were folded into Union Traction, Widener and his associates had demanded to see balance sheets showing the performance of these firms for the last few years. Charles had complied with this order, even guaranteeing the accuracy of the data he submitted. The figures were indeed impressive: Between 1896 and 1899, the North Chicago company had apparently paid an annual dividend of 12 percent on its capital stock and the West Chicago firm had managed a smaller, though still respectable, 6 percent yearly dividend during that time. The figures, though, didn't reveal the fact that Charles had artificially maintained these dividend rates, using borrowed money and stock proceeds to pump them up. Widener, Elkins, and Ryan simply accepted the financier's assertion that the firms were "handsomely paying properties."

As it turned out, streetcar lines tended not to be big money-makers. In an unguarded moment, DeLancey Louderback had once admitted this fact, telling a University of Chicago professor that "the profit is not in operating the road so much as in selling its stocks and bonds." Of course, the elevated railways deserved some of the blame for the mediocre financial performance of Chicago's surface lines. Between 1895 and 1896 alone, the West Side streetcar roads lost some 6,000,000 riders—thanks largely to 'L' competition.

Widener, Elkins, and Ryan realized too late that Charles had unloaded a "gold brick" on them—underperforming firms burdened with a crushing $25,000,000 debt. Widener and his partners were not exactly innocents in this transaction. They made a bad situation worse by piling even more obligations on Union Traction, including having the new firm guarantee the interest payments on the $6,750,000 of Consolidated Traction bonds. They also reserved for themselves $14,000,000 of the Union Traction stock as a "promotion" fee—"an exhibition of gross greed that startled even the case-hardened veterans in Wall Street." According to a financial journalist, "Union Traction was practically insolvent from the day it was formed." In 1903, the inevitable occurred: Union Traction fell into receivership after failing to meet its heavy liabilities.

Charles would later deny that he had sold his former associates a "pig in a poke." "Well, it is not difficult to recall that those gentlemen drew that pig out and examined it very closely during a period of several weeks," he claimed several years after the sale. "I am surprised now to learn that after this careful and thorough examination they did not discover that the pig was unhealthy or, discovering that it was, went on with the trade."[12]

As his Chicago career neared its end, Charles began thinking about his legacy. Late in 1899, he described the unification of the North and West Side surface lines as the fulfillment of a long-held dream. "I have dreamed and dreamed," he stated, "and now I can see that my dreams are coming true—are taking on material form. And if I should pass away tomorrow I know that my plans—dreamed years ago—would be carried to consummation by others. It has given me a pleasure to know that I have marked the intramural system of Chicago. These markings have aided in determining the whole which will result." He then lapsed into a simile:

"It is just as the man who goes out on the prairie and marks it off and puts up his fences. The others who come after must follow the lines he has drawn or tear down his fences, and that wouldn't be lawful."[13]

The magnate had indeed marked Chicago but in more ways than one. "His entry was an epoch in the city's history," his sometime rival Lawrence McGann declared. "His very boldness in all his dealings marked the inauguration of a new man and new methods." Charles had given the metropolis one of the world's largest—and finest—streetcar systems. In 1886 and 1887, he had inherited two ramshackle horsecar companies, one on the North Side with only thirty-five miles of track and the other on the West Side with 100 miles of track. Within the space of thirteen tumultuous years, he had introduced the cable car and then the trolley, and in the process tripled the track mileage on the North Side and doubled that on the West Side. His other major accomplishments included the Northwestern Elevated, the Consolidated Traction network of suburban lines, and, last but certainly not least, the Union Loop. By the time he was done, he controlled a network of rails well over 500 miles in extent that carried roughly 250,000,000 passengers annually. Even his bitterest enemies acknowledged his accomplishments in the transportation field. Melville Stone, one particularly fierce enemy, would grudgingly confess in his autobiography that Charles "really did a great service in improving the transit facilities of the city."

The Yerkes transportation network, however, was far from perfect. In 1899, roughly forty-seven miles of obsolete cable line remained in operation on some of the city's most heavily traveled streets. Indeed, cablecars and horsecars still inched around the Loop—thanks in part to the City Council's partial ban on overhead trolleys in that district. The system also suffered from a faulty design, being too heavily oriented toward the central business district. Not enough cross-town lines had been built, making it difficult for the commuter to travel within a respective section of the city.

The greatest flaw of the network, though, was its fragmented nature. Bowing to legal, financial, and political pressures, Charles the great rationalizer had ironically operated his streetcar systems as if they were independent entities. Consequently, under the Yerkes regime, a Chicagoan could never commute between the North Side and the West Side or vice versa without having to transfer to a new streetcar and pay an extra fare. Of course, it had been the businessman's secret desire all along to effect a merger of the city's streetcar lines.[14] This hope, though, was never realized during Charles's tenure in Chicago, but he certainly had paved the way for such an outcome.

By dramatically expanding the region's transportation grid, the magnate had—for good or ill—directly contributed to the growth of Chicago and its suburbs. The city had nearly tripled in population since 1886—the year Charles acquired the North Chicago City Railway—to over 2,000,000 souls. It also had grown exponentially in size, with its built-up sections extending north to Evanston and west to Oak Park. This expansion, however, was by no means uniform. Tentacles of settlement stretched out from the central city, closely paralleling streetcar and elevated lines. Tens of thousands used the trolley to flee from the crime and congestion of the urban center, and some of these migrants settled in housing subdivisions financed by Charles himself. The businessman had deliberately encouraged the building of suburbs. As he once explained, "the very existence of many a suburb sprang from our policy of running lines far into the prairies when they were practically uninhabited." "We have made these prairies blossom with cottages and neat stores and all that goes to make up a pretty suburb," he boasted.

The financier would later go so far as to maintain that the streetcar had helped erase the "slum district" from the map of Chicago. "We extended our lines, and eventually we got them some 12 miles out on the prairie from the center of the city," he told the Royal Commission on London Traffic in 1904. "Immediately there was a great rush of the poor people and laboring people to the prairie, and instead of a man wasting his time in the corner saloon after he had got through his work, and living with his whole family in one room, he began to get into the cheap houses that were built by private enterprise out on the prairie. That built up towns, and now in Chicago there is no, what we call, slum district at all."[15]

Charles exaggerated enormously. The streetcar in fact did not bestow its benefits on everyone equally—far from it. Many Chicagoans simply could not afford to patronize rapid transit facilities on a regular basis: the five-cent fare was too high. On the West Side—the poorest division of the city—the average person rode a streetcar only ninety-five times in 1900; in contrast, the typical North Sider used a streetcar 167 times that year. Unable to escape to less populated areas, a large number of Chicagoans remained trapped in crowded inner-city districts. In the 1890s, nearly one-half of the city's population lived in dwellings with more than ten occupants. Writing in 1900, one expert estimated that "if all of Chicago were as densely populated as its average slums (270 persons per acre) the city would have 32,000,000 people; if it were as densely populated as its worst slums (900 persons per acre) the whole of the Western Hemisphere could have been housed in Chicago."[16]

Lewis Mumford would later condemn the streetcar for removing the natural limits to urban growth. For Mumford, mass transit systems were "man-sewers, in which the mass of plebeians could be daily drained back and forth between their dormitories and their factories." He pointed out, quite correctly, that streetcar lines often exacerbated urban crowding. "So far from relieving congestion," Mumford wrote, "these colossal pieces of engineering only made more of it possible: by pouring more feeder lines into the central district of New York, Boston, Chicago, or where you will, rapid transit increased housing congestion at one end and the business-congestion at the other."[17] It was no wonder, then, that Charles never solved the problem of overcrowded streetcars and erratic service. According to the engineer Bion Arnold, as late as 1902, "large numbers of people" still walked to their Loop workplaces primarily because they couldn't get a seat on the jam-packed streetcars.

Charles also played an important—though often overlooked—role in the city's cultural growth. He had financed the building of a fabulous fountain in Lincoln Park, donated animals to a local zoo, and loaned paintings and sculpture to the Art Institute. (He brought the first Rodins to Chicago.) He had served as a director on the World's Columbian Exposition Board, helping make the Fair an artistic and financial success. He had encouraged local artists with his annual Yerkes Prize. Perhaps most important, the magnate had materially advanced the science of astronomy—and the University of Chicago—by founding the Yerkes Observatory.

Charles's very real achievements, however, had a dark side. For Matthew Josephson, the rapacious Gilded Age millionaires were "Robber Barons"—a term meant to evoke thoughts of the bandit princes of the feudal era. Josephson argued that the American Robber Barons exploited the public, amassing their wealth primarily through financial manipulations and political corruption. More recently, some historians have stressed the critical role the Robber Barons played in the development of the American industrial economy and have accused Josephson of taking a simplistic view of a complex situation. The historian Maury Klein has gone so far as to claim that the bad historical image of the railroad financier Jay Gould—perhaps the most notorious of all the Robber Barons—was largely the manufactured product of a hostile press.

To be sure, the legend of Charles Tyson Yerkes was *in part* the creation of a crusading newspaper establishment. Reformers hoping to clean up Chicago's politics mobilized public opinion against an invented image of an evil traction baron. But many of the charges levied against Charles had a strong basis in fact. He had gained his ends often through very questionable means. "I believe he would stop at nothing," one critic said of him. "He would dare any means to carry a point that seemed to him essential." The financier's tactics during the franchise war revealed the truth of this assertion. He seemingly *would* do whatever it took to win.[18] Charles thus well deserves a place in the ranks of Josephson's Robber Barons—somewhere perhaps near Jay Gould. The columnist Eugene Field regularly referred to the magnate as "Baron Yerkes" not without reason.

Charles's Consolidated Traction operations demonstrated his fundamental unscrupulousness. The magnate certainly had bequeathed to the city a magnificent streetcar system—but one that groaned under the load of an insupportable and bewildering thicket of securities. It would take Chicagoans decades to unravel this traction tangle—in a poisonous political climate of distrust and hostility that was another one of Charles's legacies.

The young reporter Edward Price Bell obtained a frightening glimpse of the dark side of Charles's Chicago career. Though only twenty-nine years old in 1898, Bell was a veteran journalist, having worked on a string of Indiana newspapers. That year he migrated to Chicago and secured a position on Victor Lawson's celebrated *Record*. An idealist, Bell harbored lofty notions regarding his profession. "Journalism, after all," he once confided to his diary, "is only a tool—a tool wherewith the editor seeks to accomplish something—toward the master aim of history—to make man divine."[19]

Like less high-minded journalists, Bell also loved a good scoop, and when a big story came along he went after it with zeal. In December 1898 his opportunity arrived in the person of Russell Wing. An attorney specializing in personal injury suits, Wing imparted to Bell a sensational bit of news, if true: "Charles T. Yerkes's hirelings are bribing every jury in Cook County in the interests of the street railway lines." The lawyer pointed out the curious fact that the streetcar companies were suddenly winning more personal injury cases than they were losing, often thanks to hung juries. "You know quite well that juries don't love street-car barons or barons of any other kind," Wing explained. "Left to itself, any jury will find for the plaintiff, if at all possible, in such cases as these: cases of killed and mangled men, women, and children not spry enough to escape the wheels of street-cars." The attorney guessed that the streetcar firms were influencing jurors through bribery—but of course proof was needed.

Spurred on by Wing, Bell embarked upon an investigative odyssey that took him from brothels to opium dens in search of jurors with stories to tell. With the aid of an elite group of undercover police officers known as the "night-flying squad," the reporter uncovered evidence of a wide-ranging system of bribery linking "the aristocratic people who furnish the cash and the unprincipled jurors who accept it." Bailiffs, it was discovered, often served as the mediators in this corrupt system, consummating "the villainies planned by other and brainier men."

Drawing upon Bell's findings, a Cook County grand jury indicted ex-Bailiff James Lynch on bribery charges, and for a time even toyed with the idea of summoning to the witness stand Charles Yerkes himself. Lynch stood accused of bribing jurors in behalf of Charles's West Chicago Street Railroad Company. After being freed on bond, Lynch fled from Chicago. When he finally returned to the city in 1901, the ex-bailiff explained why he had taken it on the lam. "I was not alone in wrong-doing," Lynch maintained. "I served men who were far more powerful than myself. Some of these men were desperate. They knew that if I faced trial secrets which would involve them might come to the surface. This meant ruin to them. Had I staid here it would have meant death to me."[20]

Following his explosive expose of Cook County jury bribery, Bell turned to a study of corruption in the Illinois state capital—Springfield. The reporter learned that what an African American legislator had told him was indeed true, that representative government in Illinois was "as dead as Queen Anne." "Indubitably, government both in Chicago and in the state had been filched from the people," Bell asserted. "It was in the hands of a few men, financiers and corrupt politicians, a government by men of money and men to whom money made an all-powerful appeal." The journalist located at the apex of this political pyramid "the highly perfumed trio, Yerkes, Lorimer, and Tanner."[21]

The editors of the Chicago *Record* and Victor Lawson himself were very impressed with Bell's hard-hitting accounts. Early in 1900, they rewarded the youthful journalist with a plum assignment—the newspaper's London correspondent post. Ironically, Charles would arrive in London only a few months after Bell. Not long after his arrival in the British capital, the magnate extended an olive branch and invited the *Record* man to visit him. In the truly revealing interview that followed, Charles would furnish a confession of sorts as well as a defense of his Illinois career.

As he ascended in the elevator to the magnate's ornate apartment, Bell was understandably nervous. Worrisome questions crowded his brain: "What does the gentleman want?" "Will he use a gun or a club on me?" Bell could at least answer this last query in the negative. He knew that neither gun nor club had ever been a weapon of choice for the financier. All that Bell could be certain of was that Charles wanted something. "Lost motion is hereditarily abhorrent to him," the reporter recognized.

Ushered into the great man's presence, Bell found the "ruddy, plump, white-mustached, magisterial, loftily-contemptuous Yerkes" as handsome as ever. And, strange to say, the businessman seemed to be in a quite jolly mood.

Mr. Bell," Charles began, "you are the man who drove me out of the State of Illinois." The magnate said this without a trace of malice. He, however, was not exactly being sincere, merely telling Bell what the journalist wanted to hear.

"No, Mr. Yerkes," Bell responded. "The *Chicago Record* drove you out."

The financier shook his head firmly, and then spoke frankly: "Futility had marked everything *The Record* said and did concerning me prior to your work."

"Well, let us say then that the *facts* drove you out," the reporter countered.

"Yes," Charles replied, not wanting to argue, "and you got the facts." He then went on to offer a very different interpretation of those "facts."

"What I wish to say to you is that I am no more a depraved or dishonest person than you are or Mr. Lawson is. Mr. Lawson is a splendid man of immense ability. Kindly report to him briefly on what, I suppose, might be termed my *apologia* or pleading off. I was fighting the Devil in Illinois, and I fought him with fire. But for the fire, he would have destroyed the properties for which I was responsible to thousands of innocent people who had put their savings into street-railway securities."

"I bribed juries!" Charles exclaimed, his voice dripping with irony. "What sort of juries? Where did you find most of the men who inveighed against 'jury-hangers'? You found them in the lairs of Chicago, the barrelhouses and the opium dens, and worse. Some, I will concede, were honest men. But some were the tools of ambulance-chasing shysters and had been trained in schools for the subornation of perjury. I could cite many cases of organized attempts to bilk my companies on absolutely fictitious testimony. We had to fight some suits, formidably prepared, against lines which had not been built at the time when the injuries were alleged to have been inflicted! As for Springfield, the boodlers held the gap there. One could not pass, be one's bill good or bad, without uttering clearly the essential watchword. And you know what that word was."

"Tell Mr. Lawson I did what I think he would have done: the best I could in the circumstances," Charles concluded. "He and I were merely on opposite sides of the barricade."

Bell later reported to Lawson what Charles had said. "Possibly," the publisher replied, a smile on his face. "But it surely was a good thing we all were not on Mr. Yerkes's side of the barricade."[22]

24 London

On July 8, 1899, Charles said goodbye to the employees of his Chicago surface lines. Seated behind an enormous desk in his old office at 444 North Clark Street, the magnate thanked a select gathering of secretaries, clerks, conductors, and drivers for their dedicated service. "I wish to impress upon you the regard I have for you and the feeling of pride I have in you, and at this parting to wish you all godspeed," Charles concluded his short speech. He then rose from behind his desk and shook the hands of everyone in the room. The scene was an emotional one. "The half-dozen women in the group burst into tears and most of the men bit their lips as they shook his hand," a journalist reported.

Chicagoans wondered what the man they loved to hate would do next. Rumor had the businessman retiring to his New York mansion, sailing for Europe, or even purchasing a yacht and "devoting himself to pleasure." Having just turned sixty-two years old, Charles admitted to feeling a need for a "long rest."[1] But an intriguing opportunity was suddenly thrust before him—the opportunity, it seemed, of a lifetime.

Only a day or two before taking leave of his employees, Charles had met with two Englishmen at his new Chicago office in the Royal Insurance Building. The promoters Thomas Reeves and H. H. Montague Smith had journeyed to America in search of money for their Charing Cross, Euston and Hampstead Railway—a projected five-mile-long underground line connecting central London with its northern suburbs. Though told that their fishing expedition was a "forlorn hope," Reeves and Smith persisted in their efforts and they eventually attracted the notice of the New York broker Arthur Housman and his employee Henry C. Davis. Though

Housman had recently carried out stock transactions for Charles, it was Davis who guided the financier into the Englishmen's net. An expert railroad man, Davis firmly believed that the Charing Cross railway would be a "good thing" and he vigorously lobbied Charles in behalf of the project. Intrigued, the magnate agreed to confer with the two Englishmen.[2]

H. H. Montague Smith outlined the history of the Charing Cross, Euston and Hampstead Railway Company. In 1893, the road's promoters had navigated through Parliament an act incorporating the firm and authorizing it to construct an underground electric road between Charing Cross in central London and the growing northern suburb of Hampstead. English investors, however, had spurned the scheme—underground or "tube" roads not yet having demonstrated any strong profit potential. The railway's backers more than once rescued their pet project from oblivion, securing Parliament's assent to extensions of the construction deadline.[3]

Following Smith's history lesson, Thomas Reeves made Charles a tantalizing proposition. The English engineer offered to sell the Charing Cross Company's charter for a relatively measly $200,000. There was, of course, one large string attached: Charles would be required to honor the various contracts that the road's projectors had already made, including a construction contract with Reeves's own engineering firm. Reeves was optimistic about the railway's profit-making ability. "I had a good thing and it was for the man to whom it was offered to recognize whether it was a good thing or not," he had told Davis.

Charles sat quietly as the Englishmen talked. He explained that "he had come there simply to listen." At the close of the interview, the businessman expressed a willingness to give the matter some consideration.[4] In fact, the proposal strongly appealed to Charles. He had visited London almost annually since 1889 and knew that the English capital desperately needed improved mass transit facilities. When talking to reporters about his European trips, he would frequently refer to London's "backwardness" in transportation matters.

———————————

In 1900, London was the largest city in the world—a metropolis teeming with over 6,000,000 souls. More than that, it was the largest city the world had *ever* seen. Since 1875, it had added 2,500,000 to its population—the equivalent of two Berlins, a Paris, or a New York City. London's metropolitan area had grown enormously in size as well as in population during this period. Various critics had likened the city and its spreading suburbs to a "fungus-like growth," to a "great hungry sea, which flows on and on," and, most dramatically, to "a tumour, an elephantiasis sucking into its gorged system half the life and blood and bone of the rural districts." The sheer scale of the metropolis often overwhelmed visitors. A person would have had to walk between six and fifteen miles in order to reach the "rim" of London's outer suburban ring.[5]

The so-called heart of the empire—an empire encompassing more than one-quarter of the globe's land area and one-fifth of its population—suffered under the strain of clogged arteries. On a typical workday, over a 1,250,000 people migrated into and out of London's commercial and financial center—the City—a narrow maze of winding streets and alleys stretching for a square mile along the banks of the Thames. "An army greater than the host of Xerxes is mobilized daily over six hundred miles of territory in Middlesex, Surrey, Essex, Kent, Buckinghamshire, and Herts, poured into central London each morning, and moved back again before night," one observer asserted. "It is a stupendous phenomenon, this diurnal advance and retreat of a million human beings, and its magnitude is more likely to increase than diminish."[6]

This swirling sea of humanity threatened to swamp London's outmoded transportation facilities. The age-old horse remained the backbone of the metropolis's transit network. A force of roughly 250,000 horses were employed to pull trams, carts, cabs, and omnibuses. The antiquated omnibus—essentially a wooden box on wheels that could seat perhaps twenty-five people—dominated the city scene, strung out in long processions like elephants on parade. For Americans like William Dean Howells, these vehicles were almost "as gross an anachronism as the war-chariot or the sedan-chair"—the omnibus having disappeared long ago from most U.S. streets. According to one tally made at the beginning of the century, a staggering 690 omnibuses an hour passed the Bank of England during peak periods. Congestion on central London's busiest thoroughfares often stopped traffic for a total of five hours a day. A Royal Commission warned in 1905 that "the life and growth of the Metropolis will be slowly, but not the less surely strangled by the choking of the great arteries of traffic."[7]

The city's transportation woes most severely affected the working classes. Partly as a result of the lack of a cheap and adequate means of locomotion, London laborers were forced to live near their places of work in inner-city industrial districts. Housing was scarce and rents were high in these areas—a lethal combination leading to overcrowding. The 1901 census revealed that a staggering 700,000 persons lived in overcrowded conditions in the County of London. Reformers like Charles Booth and Samuel George Burgess seized upon a "rapid and cheap means of transit to the suburbs" as a partial answer to the housing problem.[8]

This new and improved means of transit was widely desired, but not easily achieved. Parliament had prohibited the horsecar and the newfangled electric trolley, with its unsightly and very possibly dangerous overhead wires, from the "charmed circle" of London's central district. In any case, these vehicles likely would have only added to the congestion of the city's streets. The real solution to the transportation crisis lay underneath the Londoners' very feet. "Under the County of London as we know it with all its life and stir and multiplicity of interests and conflicting forces," an English writer explained in 1900, "there is another County of London, an unknown land for the most part, a great void of silence and darkness in which there are absolutely no human interests to come into conflict and in which the only force is the *vis inertiae*. If we could drop these surface railways of the County . . . down into this void below, the land they occupy would be just so much gained for public purposes."[9]

In fact, some railway men *had* taken advantage of the 121 square miles of lateral space underneath the County of London by burrowing through the blue clay. As early as the 1860s, the Metropolitan and the Metropolitan District roads had constructed a shallow subway just under the city's streets on the edge of the "charmed circle." These lines were extremely expensive to build, having been obstructed seemingly every inch of the way by sewers, pipes, and, last but not least, grasping property owners. Once in operation, the roads offered less than satisfactory service. Passengers quickly discovered that steam engines and confined tunnels were a bad mix.

Technology, however, had greatly advanced since the days of the building of the Metropolitan and Metropolitan District subway. By 1900, it had become possible to construct high-speed railways dozens of feet below the surface—well clear of obstructions like pipes and sewers. In other words, Londoners could now have real rapid transit. Three inventions—the elevator, the electric motor, and the Greathead shield—helped inaugurate this transportation revolution. The elevator enabled a large number of people to easily move from the surface to the underground line and back in a short amount of time. "All consideration of physical exertion in getting up and down to the lines has been simply eliminated," the writer G. F. Millin noted. "Whether your railway is just below the surface, or 100 feet down, is a difference involving merely a few seconds of time." The electric motor permitted fast travel without the pollution of the steam locomotive. Finally, the Greathead shield (designed by the engineer James Greathead) offered "a comparatively safe, simple and easy method" of tunneling. The shield—an enormous iron tube with a sharp cutting edge—was pushed through solid earth by means of hydraulic jacks.[10]

Utilizing these new technologies, the world's first electric underground road—the City and South London Railway—opened in 1890 and ran for three miles between King William Street in central London and the southern suburb of Stockwell. The line was something of an engineering disaster, with its tunnels too small and its electrical operation marred by flaws. The City and South London was also a financial failure. It carried a large volume of passengers only during rush hour periods—*Punch* called it the "sardine box" railway—but at other times the cars were largely empty. In 1898, a second "tube" (as the English affectionately termed these deep-level underground lines) appeared on the London scene—the Waterloo and City, a modest one-and-a-half-mile-long venture popularly known as "The Drain." Two years later, the famed "Tuppenny Tube"—the Central London Railway—began operation, linking the City with the western suburb of Shepherd's Bush. Offering attractive stations, comfortable, well-lighted cars, rapid, reliable service, and a flat two-pence fare, the Central London quickly became "one of the principal sights of the metropolis," according to the journalist Edward Price Bell. That was saying a lot in a tourist Mecca like London. "Visitors nowadays," Bell maintained, "do not first inquire of one another: 'Have you been to the abbey?' or 'Have you seen the Crystal palace?' Their first question is: 'Have you ridden in the 'twopenny tube'?'"[11]

The Charing Cross, Euston and Hampstead Railway would have made a significant addition to London's growing underground system, bringing the benefits of rapid transit to the city's northern suburbs. Charles was strongly tempted by the English duo's proposition, but he didn't like the fact that Reeves and his partner John Price already held a contract to build the road. The magnate had made a career out of wringing money from construction contracts, and now these Englishmen threatened to cramp his style. He therefore asked that Price and Reeves cancel their contract. Though initially resistant to this idea, the pair eventually agreed to waive the contract—for the right price, of course.[12]

Charles still hesitated to take the plunge into London's blue clay. For one thing, pressing Chicago matters continued to claim his attention. He was busy overseeing the completion of his beleaguered Northwestern Elevated line. He was also entangled in complicated negotiations regarding the sale of his Consolidated Traction Company to Union Traction. But—most important—the financier simply felt that he did not know enough about the Charing Cross line and its potential for profit.

In February 1900, the picture became a little clearer for Charles. The railway expert Henry C. Davis had gone to London to scout out the Charing Cross road's prospects and found the signs to be very encouraging. "Underground best proposition ever saw," an enthusiastic Davis cabled to his boss Arthur Housman. "Certain that railroad will commend itself provided Yerkes will show interest in it. . . . Hope Louderback will come."[13]

DeLancey Louderback finally did come, arriving in London on March 31. Charles dispatched his right-hand man and an electrical engineer by the name of Jackson to confirm or deny Davis's impressions of the Charing Cross railway.[14] Louderback thoroughly investigated the traffic situation in the English capital and concluded that Londoners were "far behind in their city conveyance." He was especially struck by the curious fact that streetcars were not permitted in London's central district, an area "congested with cabs and omnibuses." It seemed then that the underground lines would have this profitable territory all to themselves, if one excluded the cabs and omnibuses. A British official emphasized this point in a discussion with Louderback. "I saw Sir William Preece who has charge of Govt. Telegraph Service and is also changing the Metropolitan District Railway Co. over to electricity," Louderback reported to Charles. "He says he thinks anyone who secures good underground franchises in London has a gold mine, as he does not believe they will ever allow the surface car to come down in the city as the congestion is getting worse and worse." Persuaded, Louderback secured from Price and Reeves an option on the "gold mine" that was the Charing Cross, Euston and Hampstead Railway's charter.[15]

On April 23, Louderback met Charles in a New York office and briefed him on the underground venture. He estimated that it would cost a little over $10,000,000 to build the road and figured its promoters would reap a tidy $1,545,000 profit in the process. He advised that the five-mile line be extended in order to make it "the best underground railroad in London." Louderback emphasized the fact that "the proposed road would at last provide the splendidly situated highest point of London [Hampstead Heath] with adequate traffic facilities."[16] In sum, he endorsed the project.

Yet, Charles held off from making a firm commitment. He wanted to see the tube's proposed route for himself. Having at last carried through the sale of his Consolidated Traction Company and witnessed the completion of the Northwestern Elevated, the businessman set sail for London in mid-July on the steamer *St. Paul.* Arriving at Southampton in the early morning hours of July 26, Charles hurried on to London via mail train and reached the sleeping metropolis shortly before 3:00 A.M. If the financier had hoped to sneak into the city without attracting undue attention, he was sadly mistaken. His debut on the international scene captured headlines across the globe. "Mr. Charles T. Yerkes, erstwhile King of Chicago's street railways, seeks a new crown," a *New York Herald* correspondent proclaimed. "He has come to London to attempt to consolidate the City's rapidly developing railways into a great electric system."[17] Charles was moving up in the world. A few years before, he had merely been a "Baron"; now he was a "King."

The *Herald* reporter asked Charles what his "mission" was in London. As secretive as ever, the magnate stated that he had simply come "at the invitation of capitalists here, who own the charter on the Underground Railway." He was careful to deny having any grand schemes in mind. "I have not come here with any plan to revolutionize the transportation system of the city," he maintained with a straight face. "I have not come at the head of any syndicate, nor with any project. I am past that stage in my career." Charles, however, did go so far as to admit that a revolution was in order. "London is certainly in crying need of modern traction facilities," he stated, facilities that would "give the laboring classes opportunity to get away from the densely populated parts into healthy, uncrowded localities."[18]

On August 3, Henry Davis escorted Charles and his private secretary Braxton Grigsby—ex-Rough Rider and brother of the magnate's favorite protégé—over the projected course of the Charing Cross, Euston and Hampstead Railway. The weather that day worked in Davis's favor, as he explained in a letter to Housman. "We started from Charing Cross in a driving rain storm and reached Hampstead Heath in brilliant sunshine," Davis wrote. "He [Charles] was not at all communicative until we reached the summit of the Heath and looked to the North, when he exclaimed: 'this settles it.'" From his 400-foot-high perch on the lush Hampstead Heath, Charles could look south and see the vast expanse of sprawling London, its spires and towers glistening in the strong sunlight. Yet it was the view to the north that seems to have captivated him: "a panorama of pastoral landscape, with here and there bits of forest and clustering villages."[19] The magnate saw more than beauty in this bucolic scene. He also spied opportunity —miles and miles of land waiting to be developed by a railway.

In truth, Charles had probably resolved to back the Charing Cross railway before he even reached Hampstead. During the cab ride through the crowded streets of central London and its northwestern suburbs, the magnate had peered out of his window in quiet amazement. The density of the population along the entire route astounded him. Even in a mammoth city like Chicago, the population began to thin out quite dramatically some two miles from the urban center. But that was not the case in London. The businessman later confessed that "he had never ridden through five miles of people before in his life."[20] Five miles of people translated into potentially astronomical passenger receipts. Here indeed was "a gold mine," or so it seemed.

Following this momentous ten-mile journey, Henry Davis took Charles to the office of Robert William Perks, the lawyer for the Charing Cross railway. Charles informed Perks of his fateful decision. "Mr. Yerkes made the statement," Davis reported, "that while he had been much interested in the proposition from the first time that it was submitted to him, and had been firmly convinced by Louderback's report and his conversations with Louderback, it was not until he had gone over the line that he was prepared to say that it was the best proposition that had ever been called to his attention." According to Davis, the financier "emphasized this statement by saying that he would personally subscribe for one-quarter of the capital required, and give his personal endorsement to the scheme."[21]

The meeting marked the beginning of a great friendship—or at least collaboration—between "Yerks and Perks," as *Punch* dubbed the duo. Twelve years younger than Charles, Robert William Perks occupied a position near the summit of London's commercial, political, and legal life. Political opponents delighted in caricaturing the humorless Perks as a "long-faced" Puritan. The grim-visaged, silver-haired, compactly built lawyer certainly fit the part. He was a pro-temperance man and a bitter foe of gambling. Like the stereotypical Puritan, he also seemed to lack any poetic sense. Once, he and Henry Jefferson, a former teacher, visited the site where Joan of Arc had been burned at the stake. Jefferson asked Perks to stand on the "historic slab" marking that terrible event, and the latter complied, albeit reluctantly. "How do you feel?" the teacher inquired, expecting an emotional response. "I feel, sir, exactly the same as I did when I stood on that other stone," Perks replied.[22]

Observers were struck by the oddness of the pairing of a moralizing English attorney with an amoral American financier. "But what puzzles us more than anything else is that Mr. Perks, of anti-gambling fame, is acting as solicitor for this notorious gambler," a British journalist wrote. "Perhaps Mr. Perks does not know."[23] The two men, however, did have points in common. Both Charles and Perks were strong individualists certain of their places in the world and both spoke the universal language of business. In any case, they needed each other. Charles served as a conduit to American sources of capital while Perks provided unparalleled access to the corridors of power in Parliament. The two made a powerful team.

Though embroiled in a tough election fight, Perks—a member of Parliament—rushed back from campaigning in Lincolnshire to be at Charles's side for the closing of the Charing Cross, Euston and Hampstead Railway deal. On September 28 at noon, the various parties to this deal assembled in Room A of the Charing Cross Hotel. According to Thomas Reeves, Charles functioned at the gathering as a sort of master of ceremonies, acting as "a host in himself." After examining the various agreements and other documents "in the most minute fashion," the magnate handed over to Price and Reeves a check for $200,000 and received in return the Charing Cross road's charter as well as 451 shares of stock that had been issued. As his first act as owner of the railway, Charles selected himself chairman of the company and appointed a new board of directors. "We will build the best road we know how," he declared after the meeting. "We expect to invest a total of $13,000,000 and have the line in operation in a couple of years."[24]

On October 6, Charles and his wife Mary traveled back to the United States on the *St. Paul*. The magnate planned to wrap up his Chicago affairs and thereby gain some additional capital that he could reinvest in London. He especially hoped to find a buyer for his long-suffering elevated roads. Charles had another important reason to return to the States. He wanted to vote in the November presidential election and help defeat the dreaded William Jennings Bryan, whom the Democrats had once again chosen to run against William McKinley. Charles, however, failed to reach Chicago in time to meet the voter registration deadline. Mary's father died on October 11 after a short bout of pneumonia, and the businessman had to attend his funeral in Philadelphia.[25]

Charles publicly expressed his disappointment at not being able to vote in the upcoming election. He, indeed, had a huge stake in the presidential contest. The financier had resolved to purchase a commanding interest in London's Metropolitan District Railway but only if Bryan was defeated and a likely financial panic was thereby averted. Control of the District road would carry Charles much closer to his ultimate goal—mastery over London's entire rapid transit system. He had already revealed this titanic ambition to an undoubtedly startled H. H. Montague Smith in 1899. "A little bit of cheese didn't satisfy him," Smith observed of Charles, "he wanted the whole meal."[26]

25   *Building a Monument*

The journalist Ralph Blumenfeld first learned of the extent of Charles's London designs during a ride in the magnate's private hansom cab. Charles told Blumenfeld that he intended to go ahead with the building of the Charing Cross road "in spite of the opposition which he meets at every turn." He predicted that in a generation London would be "completely transformed," thanks to the electric train. People will "think nothing of living twenty or more miles from town" and the horse omnibus will have disappeared from London's streets, Charles informed his astonished passenger. "Although he is a very shrewd man," Blumenfeld confided to his diary regarding the magnate, "I think he is a good deal of a dreamer." In this case, the dreamer's predictions proved to be remarkably accurate.

In February 1901, Charles sold his Chicago elevated railway holdings to a syndicate of capitalists headed by the New York banker Henry Blair. With Chicago now out of the way, the magnate turned his full attention to London. In order to realize his grand plans there, he first needed to gain a foothold in the metropolis's central district. The Metropolitan District Railway would have given him such an advantageous position. "The Metropolitan is to London what the Union Loop is to Chicago," DeLancey Louderback explained. "It belts that part of London known as the 'city,' or the business district. It is the termini for all the other lines." According to no less an authority than the American trolley pioneer Frank Sprague, the Metropolitan District and its sister road the Metropolitan held "the key to any immediate improvement in the rapid-transit situation in London."[1]

The Metropolitan and the Metropolitan District were the first underground railways to be built in the world. London's far-sighted City Solicitor

Charles Pearson had been the primary guiding spirit behind these early subways. "A poor man is chained to the spot; he has not the leisure to walk, and he has not the money to ride," Pearson asserted in 1846. The city solicitor put his faith in an underground line as a cheap and efficient means of enabling the poor to escape the congested and unhealthy urban center. Pearson did not live to witness the completion of the first stretch of the Metropolitan line. He died only four months before the January 1863 opening of the three-and-a-half-mile-long segment between Farringdon Street and the western suburb of Paddington. The subway had been built using the so-called cut and cover method: A shallow trench about 100 feet wide was excavated along the route of the line and then covered with a brick arch. The Metropolitan turned out to be a tremendous initial success. In its first year, it transported nearly 10,000,000 passengers, and paid 5 percent dividends on its capital stock.[2]

Encouraged by these promising early results, the backers of the Metropolitan resolved to extend the underground line at both ends to form a complete circle (or really oval), roughly thirteen miles around, encompassing London's central district. In July 1864 royal assent was given to the Metropolitan District Railway Act, which granted authority to construct the southern half of what ultimately became known as the "Inner Circle." Forced to navigate through a maze of gas mains and sewers and saddled with costly property purchases, the Metropolitan District managed only with difficulty to carry the underground road from Paddington south and east to Mansion House in the heart of the city. By 1871, the Inner Circle was nearly finished, with only a short stretch on its eastern end remaining. The managements of the Metropolitan and Metropolitan District, however, came into conflict, and not until 1884 was the circle finally closed. It had taken twenty-four years and $50,000,000 to bring this project to an end.[3] The managers of the Metropolitan and the Metropolitan District would carry their feud into the twentieth century.

The Inner Circle proved to be a financial disaster. The expected increase in passenger traffic never materialized. At least some people avoided traveling in the underground because of its notoriously unpleasant atmosphere. The subway's steam engines belched thick clouds of black smoke into the tunnel, fouling the air in that narrow and enclosed space. In 1889, the *Chicago Tribune* publisher Joseph Medill endured the "grimy mephitic atmosphere" of what he termed "that horrible subterranean hole." "My lungs did not fully recover from the injurious effect for several days, and they are by no means weak," Medill maintained. As a remedy for this problem, the Chicagoan suggested that compressed air motors be used in place of steam engines. In 1897, a committee appointed by the Board of Trade investigated the matter and concluded that the Inner Circle should be electrified.[4] By then, electricity had become the motive power of choice for transit managers.

Frank Sprague—the man most responsible for this transportation revolution—visited London in 1901, and, not surprisingly, agreed with the Board of Trade about the advisability of electrifying the Inner Circle. The American engineer had himself come full circle, as it were: An 1882 ride in the smoke-befouled London underground had set in motion a train of thought that ultimately led to his brilliant trolley idea. During his 1901 visit, Sprague concluded that a noxious atmosphere was only one of the Inner Circle's problems. The Inner Circle functioned as a "common trunk line," presenting what Sprague called "one of the strangest anomalies of railway operation" in the world. Circle trains were run on only one of the two tracks, while trains from mainline steam roads and from the Metropolitan's and Metropolitan District's own suburban lines were operated on both tracks. As a result, service was terrible. Averaging only eleven-and-a-half miles per hour, Circle trains ran at ten-minute intervals—an unacceptably long headway in Sprague's view. Divided management complicated matters still further, with the Metropolitan controlling the northern half of the Circle and the Metropolitan District the southern half. With good reason, Sprague condemned the operation of the Inner Circle as "a travesty on rapid transit."[5]

Charles intended to overhaul the Inner Circle, but first he had to obtain control of the Metropolitan District Railway—the more financially vulnerable (and therefore more easily obtainable) of the two circle roads. Following the defeat of Bryan and acting on the advice of Louderback, the magnate gave orders for the purchase of District stock through the London brokerage firm of Messel and Company. By February 1901, he had acquired $3,000,000 worth of District stock—an amount short of majority control. Charles eventually secured this control by forming alliances with other big shareholders. Robert Perks, a large District owner himself, cleared the way for his American associate.[6]

On the afternoon of June 6, 1901, Charles and Perks revealed that they were "masters of the situation" at a special shareholders' meeting of the District Railway. The District's proprietors overwhelmingly approved the pair's plan to electrify the road. There were, however, a few voices of dissent—voices questioning Charles's "philanthropic motives in coming to rescue London." One man objected to turning over the District to "unscrupulous Yankees," who, he charged, would endanger the stock holdings of the railway's "many widows and orphans." Charles said nothing during the meeting, but did talk to reporters after it was over. "The remodeled underground railway will be far superior to existing London 'tubes,'" he confidently asserted, referring to the Inner Circle. "The people who built that knew nothing except how to dig holes. Everything else is wrong." The businessman emphasized that he was bringing in *American* engineers to oversee the District electrification. "They know nothing about that sort of thing here," he explained.[7]

The financier quickly moved to implement his scheme. As required by British law, he submitted his electrification proposal before Parliament and testified in its behalf. His experience before the Parliamentary Committee merely confirmed his already low opinion of the state of British electrical knowledge. "The ignorance displayed by the Parliamentary Committee, and, in fact, by everyone that had anything to do with the matter, was really amusing," Charles declared. He clearly was not winning any points for diplomacy.

The attitude of the Metropolitan Railway's management regarding electrification was not so amusing to the magnate. The Metropolitan's directors certainly grasped the fact that their road must "electrify or die"—especially after the newly hatched Central London Railway began to eat away at their earnings. Their dispute with Charles was not over whether to electrify but rather over *how* to electrify. In February 1901, a joint committee of the Metropolitan and the Metropolitan District had advised that their Inner Circle lines be equipped with the Ganz system of electric traction—a system employing alternating current and overhead wires. Charles, on the other hand, favored the direct current, third-rail system in wide use in the United States. Obviously, the Inner Circle, with its shared network of track, could be outfitted with only one of these forms of electric traction. Perks bought time for his partner by helping thwart any early moves on the part of the District to adopt the Ganz system. Shortly after Charles assumed control, the District proposed to lease the Metropolitan Railway and to assume the burden of electrifying the Inner Circle with a third rail. Metropolitan officials swiftly rejected this offer on both counts: They wanted to remain independent and they wanted the Ganz system.

Charles's suspicion of the Ganz system was understandable. It had never been employed on a large scale anywhere in the world. "To take a system which has not been thoroughly tested . . . is a species of business recklessness which I do not wish to try," the magnate stated.[8] Nonetheless, he decided to travel to Budapest, Hungary, in order to inspect the Ganz works and its one-mile-long experimental electric road. Visiting the Hungarian metropolis in August 1901, the financier received assurance from the Ganz officials that their system was the "best and cheapest" in the world. After examining the Ganz facilities for himself, Charles felt instead that he had been sent, in his words, "on a wild goose chase."[9] He left the Hungarian capital more firmly opposed to the Ganz system than ever.

Ultimately, the dispute was referred to the Board of Trade for arbitration. Charles had earlier referred to the Board as an "excellent body" composed of "active, wide-awake gentlemen." His positive assessment received confirmation on December 11, 1901, when the Board ruled in favor of the District and the third-rail system.[10]

Charles had little time to savor his victory. He had been busy during the six-month-long conflict with the Metropolitan. In July, he had organized the Metropolitan District Electric Traction Company with a capital of $5,000,000, acting according to the advice of the financial journalist Robert Porter.[11] The Metropolitan District, the Charing Cross, Euston and Hampstead Railway, and any other acquired lines were to be folded into this new firm—a holding company.

The Metropolitan District Electric Traction Company boasted an impressive roster of investors, including two descendants of U.S. presidents—Thomas Jefferson Coolidge, Jr., and Charles Francis Adams, II. The bulk of the subscribers hailed from Boston, Baltimore, and New York. Conspicuous by their absence from the subscription lists were the Philadelphians Peter Widener and William Elkins and the Chicagoans Marshall Field and Norman Ream—Charles's traditional sources of capital. Having been outmaneuvered in the Chicago Union Traction deal, these financial heavyweights no longer trusted Charles. The suave, smooth-talking financier at least inspired confidence in his new investors. "I think we are going a long way from home to take chances which do not assure us of a large enough profit to be bothered with," Coolidge, Jr., of Boston's Old Colony Trust Company, confided to an associate. "I think, however, that Mr. Yerkes will put it through and make money on it."[12]

It rapidly became clear that the Metropolitan District Electric Traction Company simply did not possess enough capital to finance Charles's multifarious projects. In December 1901, Charles and Perks began to discuss increasing the traction company's capital to $25,000,000. Their correspondence inevitably turned to a consideration of their personal profit. Charles suggested that he and Perks be awarded a kind of security known as a contingent (or deferred) certificate. "We propose Traction Company issue same amount deferred certificates as the amount money paid in and give you and me one half," he wrote to Perks. According to this plan,

Charles and Perks would receive $6,250,000 of the $12,500,000 worth of contingent certificates to be issued. These certificates guaranteed their holder any profits remaining after the 5 percent dividend had been paid out. Perks liked the general idea of the scheme, but pointed out that the Metropolitan District Electric Traction Company did not have the legal authority to issue such certificates.[13] The solution was clear: An entirely new firm with a capital of $25,000,000 had to be organized—one possessing the requisite legal authority.

Charles had barely managed to scrape together the capital for the Metropolitan District Electric Traction Company. To raise the new firm's additional $20,000,000, the magnate had no choice but to seek the assistance of the eminent banker Edgar Speyer. A German-born Jew, the thirty-nine-year-old Speyer was a senior partner in the London office of his family's international banking house. The journalist T. P. O'Connor described him as a "small, well-shaped man, with a very striking face, brilliant black eyes, olive skin, regular features, a small black moustache, a very soft expression." According to O'Connor, the boyish Speyer looked like he "ought still to be an Oxford undergraduate instead of one of the great financial forces of the age." A lover of the arts possibly even more than of finance, the banker was a founder of the Whitechapel Art Gallery and a chairman of the Queen's Hall Concert Board. During World War I, Speyer fell victim to the period's virulent anti-German hysteria. After refusing to pen "a loyalty letter," he was accused of trading with the enemy and worse. Weary of the attacks, Speyer and his family moved to New York. In 1921, the British government revoked his naturalization.[14]

Speyer agreed to undertake the financing of the new company but only after "most careful examination" of Charles's transportation plans. In April 1902, the banker helped incorporate the mighty Underground Electric Railways Company of London, Limited, with a capital of $25,000,000. "The bankers practically control the enterprise," Speyer later reported. He made certain that this was the case. He and the bankers in the Old Colony Trust Company laid down the law to Charles. They demanded the right to nominate a majority of the new firm's board for the following ten years. Charles agreed to this condition reluctantly, having long been accustomed to choosing his own directors—directors that he could control. Speyer also reserved for himself a slice of the contingent certificates, forcing Perks and a dismayed Charles to make do with less—$625,000 less, to be exact. "You see I was compelled to give way, although I felt that it was an unfair kind of trade," the magnate explained to Perks. "We were certainly entitled to that."[15] Perhaps most galling to Charles, he was put on a $60,000 salary like some common employee. The businessman hadn't collected a regular paycheck in probably over forty years—when he had been a teenaged clerk for James P. Perot and Brother!

Charles naturally resented having to share the spotlight with the young upstart Speyer. Thomas Jefferson Coolidge, Jr., tactfully urged the magnate to accept the situation. "It may not be easy for a man of your active temperament and one-man-power method to get along smoothly at all times with our English friends," Coolidge purred, "but I hope you will do your best, as you have in the past, to keep things smooth and easy with them."[16]

With Speyer's strong financial backing, Charles was now in a position to carry out his tremendous designs. "He wants the electrification of London and the transformation of its underground system to be his last great work—the work by which he will be remembered," T. P. O'Connor said of the magnate. Charles had told a group of his investors that he wanted to build a monument to himself in London and that he was "working for the glory as much as for money."[17] By mid-1902, it was evident that this monument would be a colossal one. Charles's plans had expanded to include four railway companies possessing the authority to construct some twenty-four miles of tube line: his initial London acquisition, the Charing Cross, Euston and Hampstead, the Brompton and Piccadilly, the Great Northern and Strand, and the Baker Street and Waterloo.

The last firm—the Baker Street and Waterloo—had an especially interesting history, having been financed by the rather unsavory Whitaker Wright. A native of Cheshire, England, Wright had migrated as a young man to the United States, where he made and lost a fortune. Returning to England in 1889, he embarked upon a high-flying career as a speculator and company promoter. In what was perhaps his most audacious venture, he organized the grandly titled London and Globe Finance Corporation and attracted some of England's most prominent men as investors. The London and Globe collapsed in 1900, after having expended $3,250,000 to construct half of the Baker Street and Waterloo's proposed five-mile route. Found guilty in 1904 of defrauding his investors, Wright was sentenced by an English court to seven years of penal servitude. Shortly after, while conferring with a legal adviser, the disgraced promoter swallowed a potassium cyanide capsule and dropped dead.[18]

Charles planned to operate the four underground lines as a system—a system tied together by means of the District Railway. "The object is to let the District road act as a sort of terminal for all the others," he explained. "As the District runs fourteen miles into the heart of London, it is intended to have connecting links and transfer stations for all the other roads."[19]

Displaying its usual bravado, the New York *World* had crowned Charles "DICTATOR OF LONDON RAPID TRANSIT." One man, however, emerged to challenge the magnate's claim to this title—John Pierpont Morgan himself. The mighty banker was then at the very height of his legendary career. "When he meets Kaisers and Kings it is on a footing of more than equality," an unabashed admirer wrote. "They wear the gilt and tinsel of Royalty, he wields actual power, uncurbed by ministers or Parliament, answerable only to his own conscience."[20]

Having been born in 1837, he was an exact contemporary of Charles, yet the trajectories of the two men's careers could not have been more different. The young Morgan entered into partnership with Charles's friend Anthony Drexel in 1871, embarking upon a promising future the very year of Charles's downfall. Early on, Morgan set himself up as a financial savior—a protector of imperiled railroads in particular. He developed a distaste for the waste and inefficiency of competition, and became a champion of combination—or cooperation, as he preferred to call it. Late in his life, he orchestrated a series of colossal mergers, including the gargantuan U.S. Steel—the world's first billion-dollar corporation. Morgan had a well-deserved reputation as an indomitable opponent. "In the pursuance of his career many a man has had to fall before him," one observer remarked. Most recently, in 1901, he had bested Edward Harriman in a bitter battle for control of the Northern Pacific Railroad.[21]

Charles respected Morgan. "Mr. Morgan is a great man," he once asserted, "and will carry through anything that he undertakes." The feeling was not mutual, however, as Thomas Jefferson Coolidge, Jr., discovered early in 1902. "I saw Mr. Morgan Sr., not long since," Coolidge reported to Edgar Speyer's brother James, "and he confirmed what his son had told me, that Mr. Morgan would have no connection with any enterprise of which Mr. Yerkes had the management. He was very emphatic in regard to this. He added that he was quite ready to trade with Mr. Yerkes and have negotiations with him but did not care to invest in his company."[22] Morgan was a close friend of Peter Widener and so knew about Charles's Chicago adventures. The banker believed that Charles lacked character and, for him, character was paramount. "Money cannot buy it," he declared in 1912, "because a man I do not trust could not get money from me on all the bonds in Christendom."[23]

Morgan made his move on the London traction scene late in 1900. Upon the urging of his son, he decided to back a proposed underground line linking the bustling theater and shopping district around Piccadilly Circus with northeast London. Charles was informed of Morgan's intentions as early as June 1901. The news did not particularly surprise him. "It appears to be just such a scheme . . . as Mr. Morgan might be interested in," he blandly told a reporter.[24]

In its final incarnation, the proposed Morgan tube system posed a serious threat to Charles's growing underground empire. Portions of the Morgan tube were slated to parallel the District Railway, already a financially weak venture. The tracks of the Morgan scheme would also have run directly underneath Charles's Brompton and Piccadilly Circus Railway. The magnate was not about to let Morgan have his way. "Millions will be spent by us and the most strenuous opposition will be made," he publicly warned, "to prevent any attempt by the friends of Mr. Morgan to establish a road which will compete with ours."[25]

The forty-three-year-old Clinton Dawkins served as Morgan's general in this "Homeric contest." The very British, Oxford-educated Dawkins had left a promising foreign-service career in 1900 to become a Morgan partner. A tireless worker, he plunged into the fray with zeal. He formed an uneasy partnership with the London United Electric Tramways Company. The owner of ninety miles of trolley line, the London United was seeking parliamentary authority to build a tube from the southwestern suburb of Hammersmith to Piccadilly Circus. This plan nicely complemented Morgan's proposed tube between Piccadilly Circus and northeast London. Dawkins and Sir George White, the London United's chairman, agreed to combine their resources and package their two schemes as one. When Dawkins was done, he had given Morgan potential control of a twenty-mile-long route of electric tube running from the southwestern suburbs, through the central district, and into northeast London. But first Dawkins had to push this grandiose project through Parliament—a project encompassed in two bills, one backed by the Morgan group and the other by the London United.[26]

The clash of titans moved from the corporate boardroom to another, more public, arena: the "pestilent atmosphere of a committee-room at Westminster." Appearing before a committee of the House of Lords, Dawkins assured his hearers of the financial solidity of J. S. Morgan and Company. When asked about his opponent, the Morgan partner said that he had heard reports on the conditions under which Yerkes's capital had been raised. He then smiled a smile conveying "the intimation that the conditions were never likely to be realized."[27]

In late April 1902, it was Charles's turn to make his case before the House of Lords committee. The magnate hoped to secure from Parliament a connecting link between his Brompton and Piccadilly Circus and his Great Northern and Strand railways. The resulting seven-mile-long line would have zigzagged in an east-west direction under some of London's most crowded thoroughfares, occupying what one British politician called "perhaps the most profitable route for locomotion in the world."[28] The combined project, to be called the Great Northern, Piccadilly and Brompton Railway, would have been most severely injured by the Morgan tube.

Ever the consummate actor, Charles portrayed himself as a would-be benefactor of the London public. "I have got to a time when I am not compelled to go into this business," he declared, "but seeing the way things are in London, I made up my mind that this would be my last effort."[29] Though his health had begun to fail, the businessman still possessed a razor-sharp intellect. This fact became abundantly clear when a counsel for the Morgan interests attempted to grill Charles regarding his underground plans. "Mr. Yerkes was the essence of coolness, caution and resource, proving as difficult and delicate a witness to handle as the leader of the Parliamentary bar ever tackled," a reporter noted. "All the ordinary forensic ruses proved futile in dealing with Mr. Yerkes, who would not be hustled and could not be confused." Charles left the committee room with a grim smile on his face. He had won that round.[30]

The next round, however, went to Morgan. The House of Lords committee approved both the Morgan scheme and the Great Northern, Piccadilly and Brompton Railway, even though portions of their respective routes paralleled each other. During a crucial test on July 16, the House of Commons considered the London United's bill. Proving that politics makes for strange bedfellows, John Burns, the fiery Labour MP, championed Charles's interests on the floor of the House of Commons in the course of the debate. Burns argued that the "American line engineered by Mr. Pierpont Morgan was unnecessary for this reason: it gave competition where it was not needed." Despite Burns's plea, the House sent the London United's measure to second reading in an overwhelming 250–69 vote.[31]

Charles took the news calmly, or he at least affected a stoical air. "In any event our intentions will undergo no alterations," he coolly asserted after the vote. Betraying his true feelings, he went on to express amazement at Morgan's behavior. "What induces Morgan to think there is money in his scheme passes comprehension," the magnate frankly wondered. "He has done a number of reckless things in his life and this is entitled to a high place among them. I would not buy his franchise if offered it unless to burn it."[32] Charles had clearly lost a measure of respect for "the great man."

Parliament adjourned on July 30 for its annual summer recess, without having decided the fate of the Morgan tube. Characteristically, Charles took advantage of this two-month delay. In its July 16 vote, the House of Commons had given the magnate a small opening, and he proceeded to squeeze through it. The House had required that Morgan and his associates build the "whole scheme of railways comprised in the Bill," or rather bills, including the London United Tramway's section between Hammersmith and Piccadilly Circus. It was all or nothing. Well aware of this fact, Charles directed Edgar Speyer to purchase a "commanding interest" in the London United Electric Tramways. Irked by Dawkins's "slighting" treatment of him, Sir George White, the London United's chairman, agreed to give Charles this priceless gift—a gift that meant mastery over Morgan. With Charles in control, the London United would never construct its portion of the Morgan tube. As a result—thanks to the House of Commons' "all or nothing" policy—the entire Morgan underground scheme was torpedoed.[33]

Charles's "coup," as he triumphantly termed it, wasn't revealed to the public until October 21, 1902, when the London United's counsel unexpectedly withdrew his company's bill from Parliamentary consideration. Learning of the "coup" from newspaper reports, Morgan wired Dawkins for information: "Is there any truth in story printed [in] American papers about Yerkes having got control London United Electric Railways thus making your scheme impossible." A still stunned Dawkins quickly responded:

> The owners of the London United Electric Tramways Company who were our associates in the through line of Tube railways without giving us any notice suddenly announced yesterday before the House of Commons Committee that they had sold control in the London United Electric Tramways Company to Speyer Brothers who represent Yerkes and therefore abandoned their section of the total length of Tube Railway.... Their proceedings were of course an act of gross treachery and were described to the Committee by the man who had been their own counsel up to that morning as a conspiracy.

Dawkins considered introducing new bills for a tube line during the next session of Parliament, but decided against the idea since, as he informed Morgan, "it will involve beginning our work afresh."[34]

Charles savored what was very possibly the greatest triumph of his career, considering the caliber of his opponent. As he modestly put it, "things seem to be coming our way." On November 18, his Great Northern, Piccadilly and Brompton Railway plan received the royal assent.[35] His victory over Morgan was complete.

Charles's audacious maneuver provoked a heated, one-and-a-half-hour debate in the House of Commons. One MP expressed doubt "whether for a long time, if ever, such a very dirty transaction was ever done by parties coming before Parliament." He indignantly declared that Parliament itself "had been tricked in this matter." Another MP maintained that the Morgan tube had been destroyed by a "Stock Exchange ramp"—"a game in which it was proposed to make the London roads pawns on the chequer board of Wall Street."[36] Bowing to an outraged Parliament, King Edward VII would eventually appoint a commission to investigate all aspects of the London traffic problem.

As for Morgan, he had suffered his second defeat in England in less than a month. Acting against his wishes, the British government had granted a subsidy to the Cunard steamship line—a line not belonging to the banker's newly organized transatlantic shipping trust. Morgan would never forget Charles's coup. In a telegram to Dawkins, he had characterized it as "the greatest rascality and conspiracy I ever heard of." Nine years later, an editor at the Harper's publishing house would ask Theodore Dreiser's agent for the last part of *The Financier*. The editor apparently wanted to see whether the book covered Charles's tussle with Morgan, a subject that he considered "wholly inadvisable."[37] Morgan, after all, happened to be one of Harper's chief creditors.

26   *The American Invaders*

English commentators could not help but be struck by the spectacle of two Americans vying for control of London's underground system. The conflict was indicative of a larger trend. Charles's scrape with Morgan happened to be one of the most "sensational incidents in a vast campaign"—a campaign waged by Americans seeking new markets overseas. By 1902, the so-called American invasion of England was in full swing. American capital, foodstuffs, manufactures, and even cultural products had begun to pour into the British market. Already, the balance of trade between the two nations had swung sharply in U.S. favor.[1]

Times had indeed changed. In 1820, the English author Sydney Smith had disparagingly asked who, "in the four quarters of the globe," read an American book or drank out of American glasses or ate from American plates or wore American coats or gowns? Over eighty years later, with the "Americanization of the world" seeming a distinct possibility, British intellectuals were reduced to asking what had gone wrong. Charles had his own ideas. He believed that the English people, with their "adherence to tradition," were enslaved by the "fetters of an obsolete past," and, as a result, they left the door open to American "enterprise and broad-gauge methods." He was especially critical of Parliament because of its "propensity . . . to take part in almost everything." The magnate also didn't like the work habits he observed in England. "If you pass through London or adjacent places on a Saturday afternoon," he remarked, "you will be perfectly amazed by the number of men playing ball. There is in reality little doing in a business sense from Friday evening to Monday morning. . . . I will not deny that this is an enjoyable way to live. But it is a bit startling to a busy, hustling American—startling to us of the strenuous life over here."[2]

Charles, however, had some nice things to say about English ways. While deploring the intrusiveness and inertia of Parliament, he did appreciate its "businesslike" manner and, above all, its fairness. After his experiences with the Chicago City Council, the financier found the boodle-free British Parliament to be a refreshing change of pace. Charles had kind words, too, for the "integrity and honor" of the British businessman. "His high standard is a thing for admiration the world over," he asserted.[3]

London may not have been the most ideal environment for Charles the businessman, but it certainly was a paradise for Charles the art connoisseur and "gentleman of leisure." "Mr. Yerkes' greatest hobby while in London was the collecting of pictures, tapestries and all forms of works of art," the magnate's private secretary Francis Vouillon stated. Following a long day of toil in his Hamilton House office on the Thames Embankment, Charles liked to walk the few blocks to Bond Street and wander through the various art galleries there. While in London, he secured the painting of a lifetime: Turner's celebrated *Rockets and Blue Lights*. He paid $78,750 for it—the highest amount ever spent for a single painting up to that point.[4]

Charles led a relatively reclusive existence in London, rarely entertaining and avoiding the public spotlight. He, however, did regularly attend the dinners of the Pilgrims, a newly organized society catering to Americans in London.[5] Charles never possessed a permanent London home, and instead migrated from one ultra-expensive hotel to another—hotels like Claridge's, the Carlton, the Cecil, and the Savoy. At one point, he maintained suites in three hotels simultaneously. Charles wanted his accommodations to project a certain image, one conveying financial solidity *and* sobriety. Extravagance was out of the question. Back in 1900, he had instructed Henry C. Davis to book himself into a first-class hotel, and "while not extravagantly comfortable, a place where he [Charles] could come or anyone else and have accommodations for a meeting or for entertaining people."[6]

The American invaders—Charles among them—gravitated to certain hotels, most especially the Cecil, that were particularly welcoming to U.S. tourists. When the invasion reached its height in the summer months, the lounges of these hotels were absolutely swarming with Americans. According to one English observer of this phenomenon, "there is such a volume of American accent, American vivacity, and American dressing as would be apt to convince a foreigner dropping suddenly into the scene that London was the chief city of America."[7]

Never entirely comfortable with the British way of life, Charles found a refuge in Americanized hotels like the Cecil. He also continued to associate with American women. The American invaders, after all, were not only men. There was, for example, Gladys Buchanan Unger, a San Francisco native in her early twenties. Gladys's mother Minnie and her step-father Arthur Jule Goodman—"a clever black-and-white artist"—had taken her as a young child to England. A Hartford, Connecticut, native, Goodman had studied art in Paris and worked as an illustrator in the United States before moving permanently to Europe. Taking up residence in the artists' colony of St. John's Wood, a London suburb, he struggled to scrape together a living for himself and his new family. It was apparently in Paris at the home of an unidentified American that Charles first encountered Gladys Unger and her mother. Charles resolved to finance the young Gladys's artistic education, possibly impressed by her evident painting ability.

Though barely in her teens, Gladys was already a veteran artist. She claimed to have begun her training in painting and drawing when only three years old. Probably thanks to Charles's patronage, Gladys was able to attend the elite Paris art school Academie Julien. Here she came in contact with some of the most famous painters of the era, including Benjamin Constant. On Constant's advice, she submitted her miniature *Rose* to the Paris Salon of 1902 and was rewarded with an honorable mention.

Painting, though, was not Gladys's greatest passion. She dreamed, above all else, of becoming a playwright. "I wrote my first play at the mature age of eleven," Gladys would later recall, "and even in those early days I had my aspirations, and I must admit heart-burnings too. The play in question was a three-act Christmas Pantomime with lyrics, if you please. I sent it to Sir Henry Irving for production at the Lyceum. Alas! My first effort never saw the light." She had better luck in 1903, when the actor Seymour Hicks agreed to produce her one-act play *Edmund Kean,* the product of an older and wiser woman. This "sad but intensely dramatic little stage story" won rave reviews and even attracted the notice of King Edward VII, who subsequently "commanded" Gladys to craft another play for a Windsor Castle performance. In the course of a prolific career, Unger would write over forty plays and several screenplays. In 1936, she co-scripted George Cukor's *Sylvia Scarlett*—a film that boasted the first teaming of Katherine Hepburn and Cary Grant.[8]

The youthful playwright triumphed socially as well as artistically. She set herself up in style in a beautiful Charles Street home located in the heart of London's fashionable West End. The house was "crammed with the most exquisite works of art," according to one source. The tall, raven-haired Gladys signaled her wealth in other ways as well. She wore beautiful dresses and expensive jewelry and tooled around London in a motor brougham. Before long, she was entertaining in her home "the leading lights of the Bohemian world." By 1905, Gladys had gained social prominence, with her name even being listed in the *Royal Blue Book*— the English equivalent of the *Social Register.* Charles's financial support had helped make possible Gladys's artistic and social success. In 1902, he had agreed in writing to provide her with an annual income of $5,000 for the rest of her life.[9]

The "remarkably beautiful" actress Doris Keane was another rumored "beneficiary of the bounty of Charles T. Yerkes." Born in Holland, Michigan, Doris spent much of her childhood in Evanston, Illinois. The trajectory of her early career was similar to that of Gladys Unger, with the paths of the two young women eventually converging. According to one account, Charles took an interest in Doris out of a sense of familial obligation, the latter's mother being a distant relative of the magnate. Charles was said to have encouraged Doris's acting ambitions, sending her to a drama school in New York and then to Europe. It was in Paris where Doris and Gladys apparently met. The two talented women became fast friends and soon they were confiding to each other their dreams. Gladys vowed to some day write a play just for the budding actress Doris. It took over two decades but Gladys did finally fulfill her promise to Doris, who had since achieved fame on both the American and European stage. Unger's play *Starlight* was tailor-made for Keane: It chronicled the life and loves of a great actress.[10]

Among the women Charles associated with in London, Emilie Busbey Grigsby undoubtedly stood highest in his estimation. The exact nature of their relationship was never entirely clear. Charles may have been her lover or he may have merely been an "elderly platonic infatuate." Theodore Dreiser clearly believed that the former was the case: In *The Titan* and *The Stoic,* "Berenice Fleming"—Emilie—is portrayed as the mistress of "Frank Cowperwood"—Charles. Interestingly, the publisher Mitchell Kennerly objected to this depiction of his friend Emilie and warned Dreiser that she might sue him. Edgar Lee Masters, the lawyer-poet, subsequently assured a worried Dreiser that such a suit would probably fail, the evidence tending "to prove to most people with their eyes open that Emily and Charles were not playing authors or parchesi when they visited with each other." There was no doubt about one thing, at least: Charles harbored strong feelings for Emilie. "I think that

Mr. Yerkes in her had the great passion of his life," an acquaintance of Emilie asserted. "He just worshiped her, that's all."[11]

The amazing odyssey that was Emilie's life began in Kentucky in 1876. In an earlier era, she might have been a Southern belle. Her paternal grandfather was a slaveholder on a large scale and owned farms in both Mississippi and Kentucky. The cellar of his home near Winchester, Kentucky, was rumored to have been a dungeon in which he temporarily kept slaves destined to work on his Mississippi plantation. Older African Americans in the Winchester area were said to believe that the place was haunted, with groans and the clanking chains of the slaves supposedly being audible on stormy days.[12]

Despite coming from a slave-holding background, Lewis Braxton Grigsby—Emilie's father—joined the Union side during the Civil War. His teen-aged bride, the former Susan Burbridge, may have influenced this decision. Susan was the daughter of a brother of the Union general S. E. Burbridge. Her maternal grandfather happened to be James Fisher Robinson, who during the Civil War would serve thirteen tumultuous months as the Unionist governor of Kentucky. Though pro-Union, Robinson did not believe that the slaves should be emancipated, fearing that such an action, in his words, "would result either in the reversion of the blacks to savagery or to their annihilation by whites."[13] Even after Lincoln signed the Emancipation Proclamation, Robinson continued to uphold the Union cause and gloried in the fact that a divided Kentucky had managed to send fifty-one regiments—44,000 soldiers—to the U.S. Army by January 1863. Colonel Lewis Braxton Grigsby had himself organized one of these regiments—the Twenty-fourth Kentucky Infantry—and was in command of it during the brutal battle of Shiloh in April 1862.

Following the war, Lewis went into business with ex-Governor Robinson, opening the Phoenix Hotel in Lexington. The venture failed after a time and Lewis returned with his wife to his hometown of Winchester, where he dabbled in law and politics. These seem to have been fairly contented times for Lewis and Susan. According to one observer, "they were among the most prominent people in the county and moved in the highest circles." Illness ended this happy interlude. Shortly after the birth of his son Braxton in 1877, Lewis relocated his family to Denver upon doctor's orders. It was hoped that Denver would offer a more favorable climate for the ailing Lewis, who had been diagnosed with Bright's (kidney) disease. The hope proved to be a vain one, for the sick man died not long after arriving in the Colorado city.[14]

The death of her husband marked a turning point in Susan's life. Lewis had left no estate worthy of mention, putting Susan and her two children in an extremely difficult position. In the nineteenth century, employment opportunities were quite limited for women, thanks to a rigid system of separate spheres. Susan nonetheless "started on her own path" in Denver. She and her family eventually returned to Winchester and were supported for a time by Lewis's relatives there. Finding Winchester to be too small, Susan ultimately moved to Lexington, but not before sending her children away to school. In Lexington, the attractive widow began associating with a "sporting crowd" drawn to the area's racetracks. Sporting subcultures like this "defended and promoted male sexual aggressiveness and promiscuity," in the words of the historian Timothy Gilfoyle. Above all, they championed prostitution. Susan was said to have been so popular with Lexington's sporting element that three racehorses were named for her, including the 1884 Kentucky Derby winner.

Plagued by money troubles, Susan made a momentous decision in the early 1890s: She resolved to open a brothel in Cincinnati. She told her friend Albert "Blackie" Edwards of her plan. "I advised her not to," Edwards recalled, "but she said her children were both in college, and as it took money to educate them, she was determined to take the step, and she did."[15] Gilfoyle has shown that many madams of the era took this step for the same reason that Susan had—out of "pure necessity."

With the proceeds of her "establishment" on Elm Street in Cincinnati, Susan was able to finance her children's education: Emilie in an Ursuline convent and Braxton at St. Mary's Seminary in Dayton, Ohio. Now in his late teens, Braxton was said to be "a fine-looking fellow, and certainly framed by nature for a woman's eye." He knew all about his mother's Elm Street "resort," having apparently frequented the place himself. "Brax was a horse of another color," a friend maintained, "for in our college days he often told about meeting people in his mother's resort on Elm street and gave us pen pictures of orgies he held there with his mother's knowledge. She seemed to have no objection to his presence in her place and he boasted of the inexpensiveness of his evenings spent there because of his mother being the proprietress."[16]

Braxton may have been simply spinning a yarn for the amusement of his college chums. But he at the very least seems to have known of his mother's profession. The same cannot be said for the teen-aged Emilie at that point. Since her childhood, she had been sheltered from the world. After a few years of schooling at the Catholic Nazareth Academy in Winchester, Emilie had been sent to the Ursuline convent in Brown County, Ohio—forty-eight miles east of Cincinnati. Her stay at this convent would be the crucial formative experience of her life.

Established in 1846 by the English-born Ursuline nun Julia Chatfield, the Brown County Convent existed apart from the mainstream of contemporary American life. The Ursulines had created "an elegant little French world out in the middle of the woods," in the words of a former resident. It was also almost exclusively a woman's world—a tight-knit community of between thirty and sixty nuns and less than 100 female students living in a cluster of red-brick buildings set amid a pastoral landscape of trees and lakes.

Emilie thrived in this environment. Dedicated teachers, the Ursulines exposed Emilie and her fellow students to culture in many of its forms. The boarders learned not only American and European history, but also Roman Catholic history. They were encouraged to write poems and plays about celebrated Catholic women and urged to express their creativity in other ways as well. The nuns, of course, did not neglect moral instruction, making certain to impress upon their students the evils of materialism and extravagant display.[17]

When she left the Brown County Convent, Emilie was a woman empowered—a refined and cultured woman certain of her fundamental self-worth. But she was also a conflicted woman. Emilie suspected that the nuns had been right when they spoke of the folly of material desires. Yet she craved wealth and, above all, social position. Ironically, the nuns may have unwittingly fortified her ambitions if the story is true that they informed her of Susan's secret life, telling Emilie that this was her "cross to bear."[18] This shocking bit of news would have merely increased Emilie's desire for social status—status that would prove to the world she was not like her mother. As for wealth, she would have wanted enough money to ensure that she did not suffer a fate similar to Susan's.

Emilie emerged from the Brown County cocoon as a strikingly attractive woman. "The girl to me was a poem," the New York society woman Ellen Dunlap Hopkins said of her. "I think she was the most beautiful woman I ever saw. Her eyes were brown. Her hair had the reddish gleam of gold. Her face sad in expression: her complexion like alabaster. Her form was beautiful. She was not more than five feet five inches in height, but she wore usually long clinging soft white robes that seemed to give her great height." In addition to possessing a "face like a flower," the "proud and cold" Emilie had "the manner of an empress" and a disposition "like a diamond."[19]

Charles fell instantly under the spell of this fascinating woman. He met her through Braxton, who had drifted to New York City and into Charles's orbit. When the magnate first set eyes on Emilie in 1892 or 1893, she was only sixteen years old. According to a friend of Braxton, Charles's son (Charles Edward) also became infatuated with the Kentucky woman and "it was only a few months before the engagement of young Yerkes to Emilie was whispered about." This anonymous source went on to tell an incredible, not entirely believable, tale. "It was not a great while . . . before the son saw disaster in the cards," Braxton's friend claimed, "and while Emilie is said to have deeply loved him she began giving herself up to both the attentions and the riches of the big provider. As soon as the son, in spite of faithless assurances, learned that his worst fears were realized, an estrangement sprang up between him and his father, which lasted a long while. It was not until his ardor had cooled with passing months and the best endeavors had been made by his father at a reconciliation that the sire and son were again on speaking terms."[20]

Whatever the truth of this account, Charles certainly did lavish his affection—and money—on Emilie. In 1896 or 1897, the magnate began building a splendid palace for the "poem girl" at 660 Park Avenue—only a few blocks away from his Fifth Avenue mansion. Completed in 1898, the white granite-faced, five-story home sprawled 100 feet—one-half of a block—on ritzy Park Avenue. Extensive in width, the structure had a depth of only twenty feet. The home's interior bore no small resemblance to the inside of the museum-like Yerkes mansion. It boasted a central hall, a staircase covered in a lush green carpet, and room upon room cluttered with rare and astronomically expensive artifacts. In a certain guest room, for instance, there were fifteen panels of needlework tapestry, each one of which cost $15,000. "It is a jewel of a home," Ellen Hopkins gushed, "a rare and exquisite creation, fit for the beautiful woman who designed it. In fact, it is not a home. It is a museum, and the lavishness of money poured out to make it shows that the man who is said to have given the money was madly in love."[21]

Sensation-seeking journalists later dubbed Emilie's residence the "House of Mystery," partly because of a supposedly secret room located on the fourth floor. This room, the myth-makers asserted, could only be reached by an elevator hidden behind secret panels. In fact, as a defender of Emilie pointed out, this room—a music room—was "the most public part of the house." It was the apartment adjoining the music room that especially intrigued visiting reporters. One scribe described this space as resembling a "nun's cell": "It contained a narrow white iron bed, a crucifix on the wall and a prie-dieu before it." Another journalist theorized that this room was a replica of Emilie's Brown County Convent cell and served as "a retreat into which she could retire for rest and quiet as the gaiety of worldly life palled on her."[22]

Emilie had not forgotten the lessons of her Brown County days. The nuns had implored her to try and "reclaim" her mother and Emilie had obediently set about this task. By then, Susan had sold her Cincinnati brothel after suffering continual police harassment. "Blackie" Edwards had advised Susan to tell Cincinnati's Chief of Police Philip Deitsch that she was the widow of a Union colonel and to appeal to him for protection on those grounds. But she never mustered up the courage to approach Deitsch. Invited by Emilie to come to New York, Susan lived with her daughter and her son at the Grenoble Hotel until the Park Avenue mansion was ready for occupancy. Emilie ultimately succeeded in converting her mother to Catholicism, and in 1898 the two made a pilgrimage to the Vatican, where they received the blessing of the pope.

Though important to her, religion was not then at the top of Emilie's agenda. More than anything else, she wanted to scale the precipitous heights of New York high society. Her assault began in earnest in late 1900. "Mrs. S. B. Grigsby and Miss E. B. Grigsby . . . are to make a bid for society here this Winter," the gossip rag *Town Topics* announced. "The daughter is, apparently, the holder of the family funds, which are large."[23] Charles, the not-so-secret source of these "family funds," willingly bankrolled the Grigsbys' campaign, though he had only recently derided as "foolish" the person who aspired to be a "star" in society. Storming the very citadel of New York's Four Hundred, Emilie purchased a box in the "grand circle" of the Metropolitan Opera House—a realm where the city's social leaders, people with names like Whitney and Morgan, held sway.

Emilie used her beauty, her charm, her wealth—and her intelligence —to win the friendship of certain important Gotham socialites, including Ellen Dunlap Hopkins, founder of the New York School of Applied Design for Women. Hopkins found the Kentucky woman to be more than just a pretty face. "In intellect she is extremely bright, but it is the polish of the modern woman wedded to the sadness of a woman of a deep religious type," the society woman said of Emilie. "She is really a religious type of girl." Dunlap's "poem girl" cultivated such a pious image, often telling acquaintances that she "was just taking a final look about the world before retiring for the rest of her life into a convent."[24]

In 1901, Emilie extended her social campaign overseas, following in Charles's wake. She quickly attracted the attention of European observers, who began calling her "the American princess," because of the fact that she traveled like royalty. In fact, she probably had a larger retinue than many kings and queens. Emilie often engaged private railroad cars and at times entire trains to transport her small army of servants and her "vast amount" of baggage. She of course stayed in the costliest hotels, occupying their finest rooms at prices that "would stagger many an American millionaire."

Becoming unhappy with hotel life, Emilie rented a "quaint little house," known as "The Chalet," situated at Maidenhead on the Thames. Charles appeared at many of the parties she held there, and was sometimes observed soothingly stroking Emilie's hand. The American beauty liked to entertain people with her sensual dancing, but such exhibitionism was not always appreciated. While attending a stodgy gathering held at the home of an upper-crust acquaintance of Charles, Emilie broke away from the group when dancing was proposed and "holding her soft, clinging dress tightly about her, proceeded to swing and sway gracefully around in a circle, to the somewhat horrified surprise of the entire party."[25]

Literary London was more receptive to Emilie's peculiar charms. The elderly George Meredith, author of *The Egoist* and other novels, seems to have been quite captivated by "the flying Ariel American." Supposedly, when he first saw Emilie, Meredith exclaimed that he had "at last met the heroine of the *Ordeal of Richard Feverel*." Emilie treated her "great, dear Master" with respect and affection. She once dispatched anonymously to Meredith two "great cases" filled with melons, peaches, chocolates, and other "very sweet confectionery things."

Something of a literary groupie, Emilie also focused her sights on none other than the sixty-year-old Henry James, the great American expatriate author. An admirer of James's fiction, she fancied herself as resembling Milly Theale, the doomed American heroine of *The Wings of the Dove*. The bald-headed, rotund, and "hopelessly celibate" James probably didn't entirely mind Emilie's attentions, but he drew the line when rumors began to get out alleging that he had proposed to "Grigsbina," as he once called her. "There is a Miss Grigsby whom I barely know to speak of, who has been in London two or three June or Julys," an embarrassed James informed his curious brother William in May 1904. "She is, I believe, a Catholic, a millionaire and a Kentuckyan, and gives out that she is the original of the Milly of my fiction *The Wings of the Dove*, published before I had ever heard of her apparently extremely silly existence. I have never written her so much as three words save two or three times, at most, to tell her I wouldn't come up from Rye to lunch or dine with her (I've never done it!)."[26]

James probably didn't know that Emilie was herself an author. Few people knew this fact, her 1904 novel *I: In Which a Woman Tells the Truth About Herself* having been published anonymously by D. Appleton and Company. Emilie wanted this anonymity, undoubtedly fearing the reaction of her patron to a certain character in the book. Though a fictional work, *I* reveals much about its author. The book's confessional tone is set immediately with an introductory warning to the reader: "It is not the portrait of an ideal woman which results, but of a woman of the world, not quite the basest of her kind but farther yet from the best. Let those who read, discern, and let those who are without sin first cast a stone."[27]

In *I*, Emilie tells the story of Sidney, a "homely" young woman who gradually awakens to her sexual power. Spurred on by her mother, a beautiful but cold woman, and by a need to be in control of her destiny, the bookish Sidney leaves behind her carefree ways and enlists in the battle of the sexes. She attends a dinner party in a low-cut dress, which she likens to a suit of armor, and thrills to her newfound sense of strength. "I loved my hands because they were so fine of touch and tint," she relates, "and my long, firm, untired limbs, which could dance all night and hardly know it; in fine, I loved the body of me with a hearty, animal relish and yet I was not strongly sensuous." Sidney describes herself as having become, at age twenty-two, "a subtle and skillful coquette of a particularly refined sort."[28] Though not particularly fond of the idea of marriage, she eventually weds her sickly boyhood friend Irving Lloyd, a Boston architect.

The great financier and "railroad king" G. Ross Kimball soon enters Sidney's life and gives the story its chief dramatic thrust. A potential client of her husband, the suave, handsome and wealthy Kimball intrigues Sidney, and, while dancing with him, she has a fantasy: "For a moment as his arm encircled my body, my bare arm in its whiteness resting upon his black sleeve, his eyes straying over my shoulders, I seemed to myself to have slipped my black satin sheath and to be whirling in some shameless, unthinkable Walpurgis night revel." This "hideous delusion" quickly passes, but Sidney resolves "to play the game," to use her charms to entice Kimball into awarding her husband a commission. "Success and distinction were vital elements in my scheme of life," she had explained earlier.[29]

Kimball does indeed employ Irving, appointing him as the architect for his new residence. When not helping her husband design the mansion, Sidney spends her time flirting with Kimball. She is increasingly drawn to the masterful businessman and art connoisseur. He also is attracted to her, and lavishes money on her during a European trip. The drama reaches a climax during a house-warming party for Kimball's new mansion. The financier reveals his true colors when he leads Sidney to a secret, mirrored chamber he had constructed specially for her in the home's octagonal tower. When she realizes what Kimball wants, Sidney recoils in horror. Taking the hint, the businessman lets her go—but not before saying a few parting words. "You have the mind, the soul of the courtezan without her courage," a contemptuous Kimball tells her. "It is courage which fails you now, not principle which guides you. Another thing, you are absolutely cold, incapable of love."[30]

The novel concludes on a moralistic note. Kimball exacts revenge on Sidney by wrecking her husband's career. Unable to find work in Boston, a shattered Irving moves with his wife to Florida and to a new livelihood as an orange grower. Here, in Borromeo, Florida, Sidney finds redemption. She rejects the "Lilith" side of her nature, bowing out of the "contest for enjoyment, gain, appearance, self-advancement." She turns to religion and a life of nun-like simplicity, and strives to become like Dante's "queen of virtue" Beatrice. "I was enamored of poverty and chastity, of my austere solitude, my ascetic and ordered severity of life," Sidney maintains. "Like a draught of cold pure water this discipline seemed to quench the restless fever in my spirit."[31] Following Irving's death, Sidney agrees to marry the only man that she ever loved—the kindly and devout Dr. Kirke.

Like Sidney, Emilie seems to have possessed Lilith and Beatrice sides to her nature, both of which were constantly at war within her. Emilie loved the luxurious lifestyle made possible by Charles, yet at the same time questioned its real worth. Speaking of Charles, does *I* shed any light on her relationship with him? In the course of a conversation with Dr. Kirke, Sidney explains why she was drawn to Kimball. "He satisfied a certain side of me, but not the side that loves," she asserts. "He appealed to my taste and in a subtle, cynical way to my intellect. Most of all I think to my pride and my love of power. I liked him that he could control men."[32] Emilie may have harbored similar feelings in regard to Charles, but one cannot say for certain.

Emilie's book was a financial success but her New York social campaign ultimately ended in failure. People discovered her mother's secret and they began to wonder about the exact nature of her relationship with Charles. Emilie claimed in defense that the magnate had been a friend of the family or even that he was her illegitimate father, but to no avail. The doors started shutting, and before long Emilie was persona non grata among the New York elite. "I cannot but feel that Miss Grigsby's life is an appalling tragedy," an acquaintance remarked, "for never in all my experience have I met a more beautiful and accomplished women, and to think that from her childhood, she has had to carry the burdens and responsibilities of other people's wrong and misconduct."[33]

27 *The Final Struggle*

Ever since his boyhood Charles had zealously—even ferociously—pursued what William James called the "Bitch-Goddess Success." Yet, like Emilie Grigsby, he seems to have possessed rather contradictory feelings regarding wealth. The Quaker voice within him was never entirely silenced.

Charles, though, could not be called a religious man, at least in a traditional sense. One most likely false account portrayed the financier as still in close touch with his Quaker roots, and depicted him on occasional Sundays visiting a Society meeting house in an old section of New York City. Even more implausibly, the story claimed that Charles continued to use the old-fashioned Quaker "thee" and "thy" in private conversation with his family.

Charles was not one for religious orthodoxy. He didn't like rules, yet he laid down for himself four commandments: (1) "The worst fooled man is the man who fools himself." (2) "Have one great object in life. Follow it persistently and determinedly. If you divide your energies you will not succeed." (3) "Do not look for what you do not wish to find." 4) "Have no regrets. Look to the future. The past is gone and cannot be brought back."

Charles might have added a fifth commandment—one concerning wealth. In 1901, the journalist T. P. O'Connor asked Charles whether "riches mean happiness." Instead of giving a stock answer, the magnate told a story. "There were," he began, "two men in Philadelphia—Governor Schultz—he was called 'Governor' because he once wanted to be a candidate for the nomination to the Governorship and another man called Alec Benson. Now Governor Schultz was just one of those happy-go-lucky fellows whom everybody loved but who never had a dollar to his name; while Benson was one of those 'near' men that just thought of nothing but accumulating money. He went back to his office after his supper—which he took at six o'clock—and worked there till midnight; and he was there again next morning, and, in short, he thought of nothing but money, money, money, all the time."

"Well, Schultz got a little queer before he died," Charles continued, "and one night an old friend of his went to visit him. He lived in a small, unostentatious, indeed, rather poor, house. But he turned to his friend and he said: 'Do you see that wall-paper?'—it was a very common and cheap wall-paper—'do you know that it is pure gold?' The friend agreed that it was pure gold. 'Do you see that counterpane?'—it was some poor, common stuff, just an ordinary counterpane—'that is cloth of gold.' The friend agreed that it was cloth of gold. 'And just look at this little slipper,' and then he showed his friend an ordinary down-at-heel slipper. 'Feel how heavy it is; it is solid gold, ten ounces to the inch.' And poor Governor Schultz died in the conviction that he was surrounded by, and lived in, halls of gold."

"And three days after, Alec Benson died," Charles concluded, "and he left millions; but for weeks before his death he was crying all day and all night because he thought he had lost all his money, and was going to die of hunger. Now there were the deaths of a pauper and a millionaire, and they supply the answer to your question as to whether riches mean happiness."[1]

———————

Like Alec Benson, Charles would have difficulty achieving peace of mind in his last days. He had always prided himself on his "perfect health," and he had worked hard to maintain it by exercising regularly and by adhering to a diet free of stimulants like tobacco, tea, and coffee. His health, however, began to break down during his London adventure, with his appearance eventually betraying the effects of his illness.

The businessman was later diagnosed with Bright's disease, or nephritis—inflammation of the kidneys. In its late stages, the malady severely impairs the filtering functions of the kidneys, causing waste products to accumulate in the blood. Its symptoms include fatigue, loss of appetite, fever, and body aches. According to Henry Loomis, a turn-of-the-century expert on nephritis, "the patient [afflicted with Bright's disease] feels that he is growing old, and is unable to apply himself with accustomed energy to work."[2]

Just as his health began to decline, Charles was forced to confront a specter from his past. In April 1903, the Chicago Union Traction Company collapsed under the weight of its massive financial burden, and fell into the hands of a receiver. In a letter to a trust company executive, the banker Charles Dawes outlined Union Traction's problems. "The Chicago Union Traction company faces the greatest difficulties," Dawes wrote. "It must first secure its franchises, and it must then, by a proper reorganization, secure the basis for a credit necessary to the rehabilitation of its property."[3]

Union Traction's plight had been seriously aggravated by the fact of its having guaranteed the bonds of the Chicago Consolidated Traction Company—in accordance with Charles's demands. As it turned out, the latter firm could not meet the interest payments on its $6,750,000 bond debt, so the Union Traction Company had to come—albeit reluctantly—to the rescue. According to rumor, the irate owners of the bankrupt Union Traction now planned to "get even" with Charles. They supposedly intended to petition the receiver for permission to discontinue paying interest on the Consolidated Traction bonds. This action, if approved, would have been disastrous to Charles. He had pledged most of his $4,494,000 in Consolidated Traction bonds as security for loans. The banks would have almost certainly demanded additional collateral if the Consolidated bonds stopped receiving interest. It was an open question whether Charles could have met these calls for more collateral.

The magnate had good reason to believe the rumors: J. P. Morgan, after all, was now one of the principal owners of the Chicago Union Traction Company. In May 1903, Charles hurried back to Chicago from London in a desperate attempt to protect his interests in the former metropolis. His mission ended in success. The Union Traction receiver Rafael Govin agreed to continue the firm's policy of subsidizing the Chicago Consolidated Traction Company. Interest on the Consolidated Traction bonds would still be paid.[4]

Chicago wasn't done with Charles yet—far from it. In October 1903, two stockholders sought a receiver for the Lake Street Elevated Railroad Company, blaming the unhealthy financial state of the 'L' on the "reckless extravagance and fraudulent conduct of Charles T. Yerkes and his associates." And then, in late 1904, the attorney Henry S. Robbins began a long battle in the federal courts for control of the Chicago Consolidated Traction Company. Robbins alleged that the Consolidated's lines had been built with the money or upon the credit of the old North and West Chicago companies, and that therefore the owners of these last two firms were legally entitled to a share of the Consolidated's stock. In a direct hit at Charles, the attorney also petitioned for a cancellation of the $6,750,000 in Consolidated Traction bonds.[5]

The Robbins suit especially worried Charles because it threatened to wipe away roughly one-quarter of his entire fortune. In December 1904, the financier returned to New York and thrashed out the legal situation with Rafael Govin and the lawyer Joseph Auerbach. "Mr. Yerkes asked me to help him in the fight that was being waged against the Consolidated Traction bonds," Govin later recalled, "and I said that I would to the extent of my ability and I did so." Charles must have increasingly felt like a hunted man. According to Henry Robbins, the magnate sailed back to London under an assumed name—"Colonel Richards"—in order to escape a process server in the Consolidated Traction case.[6]

The financier's London activities also began to draw fire. Some English commentators expressed the fear that Charles's Underground Electric Railways Company might be another Chicago Union Traction in the making. For example, Harry Edwin Haward, comptroller of the London County Council, warned that "somewhat similar concerns have been a failure in Chicago"—an obvious reference to Union Traction. Between 1903 and 1905, the Underground company managed to scrounge up over $50,000,000 in additional funds to finance its vast designs. The job wasn't easy. The public failed to show "a great eagerness to come in," and, as a result, Charles and Edgar Speyer were forced to resort to some desperate expedients to secure money. They, for example, offered existing shareholders the "privilege" of subscribing for $25,000,000 worth of an exotic security called a profit-sharing note. In the end, Charles and his banker confederates secured the money they needed—an amazing achievement when one takes into account the unsettled nature of the economy during those years.[7]

In June 1905, Charles told his old partner DeLancey Louderback that "things were going finely with his London scheme, and that it would be a great enterprise." By then, the electrification of the Metropolitan District was nearly complete: The smoke-choked tunnels of the Inner Circle would soon only be an unpleasant memory. The magnate had tapped James R. Chapman to usher in "this great wind of change." The laconic Chapman—the brilliant engineer who had introduced the trolley to Chicago's North and West sides—prosecuted his London task with his usual "relentless efficiency." He was aided by five able American assistants, a quintet of men who "carried their offices" in their bowler hats.

"All of these men had contempt for office work, and forms of any kind were anathema," a witness remembered. "They had no physical office except a hut in the depot or room in a house and a male shorthand typist whom they called the 'boy.'"[8]

Chapman and his crew were also responsible for the electrification of Charles's three underground roads. Work had progressed fairly smoothly on these lines, which were nearing completion by late 1905. The fact that London's blue clay "cut like cheese" materially expedited the process. In 1903, the writer Eric Barton provided a graphic description of the construction of one tube line by means of a Greathead shield. "The shield," Barton asserted, "is a great circular iron structure, in the face of which men are at work hacking away with pickaxes at the earth in front of them, while others shovel the displaced clay or ballast into trucks for removal to the surface. At intervals the shield, which is provided on its outer face with cutting edges, is forced forward a couple of feet by means of powerful hydraulic jacks, and one of the iron rings which form the tunnel is placed in position, segment by segment, and then bolted together. It is rather an eerie sight in the dimly lighted tunnel—the gangs of stalwart navvies plying pickaxe and spade unceasingly day and night, while the iron shield slowly, resistlessly forces its way, like a great scientific mole, through the bowels of the earth, and the slowly lengthening tube of iron approaches daily, in obedience to calculations of the most marvelous precision and accuracy, nearer to its unseen goal."[9] *Punch* would brand Charles "the Moleonnaire."

The Chelsea Power Station provided what Charles called "the key to the situation in London." This huge generating plant—larger than St. Paul's Cathedral—had been constructed to supply electricity to the Metropolitan District Railway *and* to Charles's three underground roads. This gargantuan structure loomed on the banks of the Thames, forming, in the words of the historians T. C. Barker and Michael Robbins, "Yerkes' monument, the symbol of his determination to unify and determine the shape of London's passenger transport." The Chelsea Power Station was also a symbol of Charles's need to have the biggest and best of everything. The facility's four 275-foot-high chimneys and its eight 5,500-kilowatt turbine generators were said to be among the largest of their kind in the world. Not everyone was likely to be impressed, however, including the American expatriate artist James McNeill Whistler. He feared the "Chelsea monster" would mar the beauty of that stretch of the Thames. Whistler told the journalist Ralph Blumenfeld that the persons guilty of erecting the power station "ought to be drawn and quartered."[10] Whistler's mother surely wouldn't have approved of such sentiments.

Charles's health took a sharp turn for the worse in June 1905, following a short trip to the United States. Specialists were called in, and they told Charles that he didn't have long to live. They said that his life might be prolonged for eighteen months at most, but only if he retired from business. The nephritis had reached an advanced stage. "The face is generally pale with a slight yellow hue," a contemporary doctor described the appearance of a patient with a severe form of nephritis. "There is a weary, listless expression; the eyelids are slightly swollen; the temporal arteries are tortuous; the skin of the body is dingy, dry, and scaly, and there is but little tendency to sweat, and stripes remain where the skin is scratched." In those days of comparative medical ignorance, physicians treated this kidney ailment rather crudely. Nephritis sufferers were dressed warmly, given frequent tepid baths, and subjected to a "mixed diet, consisting of light, nourishing, easily digested, and non-irritating food." Charles, for example, was restricted to a liquid and vegetarian diet.

For much of the summer, Charles was confined to his bed in the Savoy Hotel, attended by a small army of physicians. The willful man struggled against his fate. In early August, his condition improved enough so that he could sit up in bed. He often attempted to dress himself but usually failed in the endeavor, "his strong will giving way under stress of pain and weakness." He also made a valiant effort to get back to business, and, defying doctors' orders, had a telephone placed near his pillow. Once, an official of the District Railway visited him bearing an important document. Overruling the nurse's objections, Charles welcomed the official into the room and asked to see the document. After apparently examining the paper for several minutes, the magnate handed it back. "I'm sorry, but I cannot see," he confessed. An optometrist was called and diagnosed the malady "as not of the eyes but of the brain."[11] James R. Chapman was a witness to Charles's decline. "I am indebted to Mr. Yerkes for my career," the engineer would later say, "and the saddest recollection of my life is the fight that he made against failing intellect and his efforts to hide from those around him what was so evident to all of us."[12]

In the advanced phases of nephritis, the buildup of toxins in the blood severely disturbs the functions of all of the body's organs, including the brain. Delusions and hallucinations are two of the resulting symptoms when the brain is affected. Charles betrayed evidence of a nephritis-impaired mind even before this latest flare-up of the disease. While staying at one London hotel, he was said to have spent his evenings peppering the room's furnishings with shot from an air rifle while lounging on a sofa. His behavior became even more erratic during the summer of 1905.

He began to fear that his servants were conspiring to poison him and consequently forced his valet Arnold Held to taste his food for him before every meal. Charles was so certain of his suspicions that he signed a codicil cutting Held and his other servants out of his will for "good and sufficient reasons."

Charles staged a remarkable rally in late August when he was finally able to leave his bed. "He used to get up a little bit in the evening and a little bit in the morning," Mary Lightford Spotswood, Charles's nurse, recalled, "and he used to lie down a good deal—he used to sit up in his chair and he was fed there. He was not able to take any drives or walks just at that time." By August 26, the businessman had almost fully recovered—or so it seemed. According to a journalist who saw him then, "his skin was clear and healthy and he seemed in every way to have returned to his old-time vigor and strength." He was well enough to be sent to France for rest and relaxation. Doctors of the era believed that a "change of air, food, and surroundings" was particularly beneficial for nephritis sufferers.[13]

While vacationing at Bellevue-Upon-Seine, Charles spent a good deal of his time "puttering around in an automobile," in his words. It was no small irony that the traction king had become a devotee of the automobile—the invention destined to supplant the streetcar. "He loved motoring," Charles's private secretary said of his boss, "and experimented with cars of many makes. He drove an electric machine himself."

Charles's stay in the French countryside had a beneficial effect on his health. In a September 30 letter to an English friend, the magnate admitted having had "a rough time of it" but now pronounced himself "much recuperated." He proceeded to reflect upon his illness. "For the first time in my life, I was completely worked out," Charles confessed, "and have had a lesson taught me, suggesting two things—one, that I am not as young as I was twenty years ago, and the other, that a person can undertake too much. However, I am all right now—not quite as strong as I would like to be, but gaining I think every day. They tell me it will take months to bring me back to my old self, but I do not feel that. However, I intend to go very slowly and to watch myself closely. Fortunately I have good people to take my place, which gives me much comfort."[14] The magnate knew that his recovery was only a temporary one.

Despite his vow to "go very slowly," Charles returned to London in late October in order to chair a shareholders' meeting of the Underground Electric Railways company. The businessman had nothing but good news for the firm's owners. He reported that rapid progress was being made in the building of the tube lines. Construction expenditures were expected to be shy of the original cost estimates—"something which was not often met with" in such ventures. The electrification of the Metropolitan District Railway was said to have produced "splendid results," meaning increasing receipts. Charles understandably failed to mention the fact that these increases had fallen far short of expectations.

A few days later, the magnate gave what proved to be his last newspaper interview. In explanation of his "mysterious illness," Charles claimed that he merely "had been working too hard, and broke down." "I kept it quiet because I saw visions of 'scare heads' in the newspapers," he maintained, "and guessed that I should be accused of brain fever or something of that sort." The American also had a few words of criticism for the London commuter. "Londoners are the worst people to get a move on I ever knew," he asserted. "To see them board and get off a train one thinks they had a hundred years to do it in; still, they are doing better, and in the end I shall work them down to an allowance of thirty seconds."

"When my scheme is complete," Charles had declared during the interview, "the Londoner will be able to get from one end of the city to the other or all around it for 2 pence."[15] He would not live to see the completion of his great "scheme." In November 1905, the financier journeyed back to the United States in order to die, his illness having flared up again. The *Chicago Daily News* foreign correspondent Edward Price Bell saw Charles shortly before his final voyage home. "His face was then like marble," Bell remembered, "his eyes were uncommonly bright, and his manner was intensely restless." "I always like to go back to the United States," Charles had told Bell in the course of their meeting. "That is the country for great original enterprise. America will beat England in practical things and eventually it may lead in matters of the mind and the spirit."

When his steamer reached New York City, Charles was too weak to disembark under his own power. He was carried off the ship on a stretcher and then whisked away in an automobile to "the gilded and storied labyrinth" of the Waldorf-Astoria.[16] The businessman would spend his last days in a hotel rather than in his home. Mary Yerkes occupied the Fifth Avenue mansion and she was unwilling to yield it to her dying husband.

Since about 1900, Charles and Mary had lived apart, though the magnate continued to support his wife financially. Emilie Grigsby was rumored to be the cause of the separation. In truth, the marriage had long been dead. Lonely, embittered, and drinking heavily, Mary ultimately turned for comfort to a younger man, the twenty-eight-year-old Wilson Mizner. "Six feet three inches in height, broad of shoulder and deep of chest, with a quick eye and a ruddy complexion, he is . . . just the man to captivate any woman," an admirer said of Mizner. Mary was captivated by more than Mizner's physical appearance. She found him to be "charming," "full of youth and strength," and artistic. Mizner offered Mary what she most needed—hope. "He came at a time when I was looking at life through eyes that were filled with tears," she recalled.

Mizner, though, was not what he seemed. The scion of a famous California family, he was a cynical, wise-cracking, womanizing fortune-seeker. He had made some money—though not exactly a fortune—during the Klondike gold rush by catering to the miners' need for whiskey and women. In early 1905, he headed for the bright lights of Broadway but instead ended up sidetracked on Fifth Avenue.[17] Here, at 864 Fifth Avenue—the home of Mary Yerkes—Mizner stood a better chance of striking it rich than he ever had in the Klondike.

Charles knew about Mary's involvement with Mizner—he had hired detectives to tail her. As he lay dying in his palatial suite in the Waldorf Astoria, the magnate "constantly talked about the necessity of a new will being made"—a new will cutting off his wife. Emilie Grigsby was also on Charles's mind. The attending physician eventually agreed to let Emilie help care for him—as she had done during his illness in London. According to one commentator, "only her presence seemed to keep him at peace." Emilie's grief was said to have been "profound and distressing."[18]

Sources differ as to whether a reconciliation ever took place between Charles and Mary. There is no doubt that Mary visited her husband on about December 12, but what happened at that meeting is unclear. Clarence Knight, an attorney of the magnate, said that Mary "kissed him and they had a short conversation." J. E. Janvrin, Mary's physician, offered a more detailed story of the encounter. "Yerkes was penitent in his last days," Janvrin claimed. "When he summoned Mrs. Yerkes to his bedside, two weeks before his death, he was a changed man in spirit. He told her that he was sorry for the wrong he had done her and that he wanted to be forgiven. Mrs. Yerkes, touched by his distress, did forgive him." According to Mary herself, Charles made her promise, in the presence of his brother, that she would be "buried in the cemetery beside him." Mary's story has a problem, however: None of Charles's brothers were still living. William Randolph Hearst's *New York American* published the most sensational (and almost certainly apocryphal) version of the meeting—a version that had Emilie and Mary bumping into each other and verbally clashing near Charles's deathbed.[19]

There is in fact evidence that Mary never forgave Charles. Just before the businessman lost consciousness forever in late December, Mary apparently made a final pilgrimage to her husband's bedside. One of her sisters accompanied her on this visit. "Mr. Yerkes was too feeble to speak but opened his eyes when we entered," Mary's sister related. "Mrs. Yerkes started toward him but I said 'It is too late now.' With that, she turned and walked into an ante-room. I went with her. A short time after that Mr. Yerkes passed away. As we were leaving the hotel she said, 'I think I did right. He treated me shamefully.'"[20]

At 2:20 P.M. on December 29, 1905, Charles Tyson Yerkes, Jr., finally surrendered to the one enemy even he couldn't outfox. News of his death captured headlines around the globe. In London, the magnate was widely hailed as a public benefactor. "Rapid transit was the ideal he worked for," the *Westminster Gazette* observed, "and he became a street railway king in this respect not only in American cities but in London as well. We owe much to the man who revolutionized our old-fashioned methods of going to and fro."[21]

American views of the man were more divergent. The Chicago rabbi Emil Hirsch saw Charles's career as an illustration of the following biblical verse: "What shall it profit a man if he gain the whole world and lose his own soul?" "He used his millions as his desires led him to do," Hirsch said of Charles. "According to the materialistic view of life he was justified. It was up to him to sell his genius at the highest possible price, if morality is nothing and religion is nothing as you say it is. For Yerkes there was no law but his own."

The *Chicago Record Herald* pronounced the magnate's life to have been an "awful wreck." "The perversion of character, the complete absence of any guiding moral purpose and of a decent respect for the opinion of mankind leaves a heritage of shame to the nearest of kith and kin and a taint upon every item in the vast fortune," the *Record Herald* declared. "Out of the wreck we can make nothing but a warning."[22]

Most editorial writers did not share this exceptionally harsh judgment. "Mr. Yerkes' notable career has come to an end and all animosities should be buried in his grave," the *Chicago Tribune* advised. "While Chicagoans may regret that he was not more devoted to the public welfare than he was, they must admit his great ability and acknowledge that he contributed something to the progress of the city." Even Victor Lawson's *Chicago Daily News* conceded that Charles had achieved "great results"—though his methods and motives may have been dubious. "The day of the people, which is at hand, requires masterful men who are scrupulous men as well," the *News* asserted. "Great winnings are not the true test of genius."[23]

Hearst's *New York American* played on the theme of Yerkes the plunderer and Yerkes the builder. "Yerkes was a pirate, a buccaneer, an Ishmaelite," the *American* maintained. "His hand was against the hand of any man who opposed his ambition for wealth and for success in the game he played. . . . With an indomitable will, a brilliant mind and a complete indifference to any weak scruples of conscience, he founded his fortune by looting the city of Chicago, and then moved upon London, the metropolis of the world. . . . But, while Yerkes was rolling up this enormous fortune through all the devices of watered stock, doubtful bond issues and other expedients by which corporation managers turn the product of a printing press into money, he was building up Chicago."[24]

For the Chicago *Economist*, Charles's achievements in the rapid transit field were what really mattered and should be "set against his alleged criminal acts." The financial newspaper argued that it was "much more to the credit of a man to be dishonest and at the same time accomplish something for the community than to be merely negatively dishonest, absorbing everything that comes his way and doing no good to others."[25]

The *Daily Inter Ocean* went farther than the *Economist* in its defense of the magnate. The newspaper saw Charles's bad public image as a sign of the times. It was the high tide of the Progressive era, and businessmen were on the defensive, Ida Tarbell and other journalists having exposed the dark side of the American myth of success. "It is a penalty of the times that a man of Charles T. Yerkes' success should be misrepresented and misunderstood by millions of the American people," the *Inter Ocean* lamented. "Mr. Yerkes suffered this penalty to the full. And yet, while turning a face of iron to his enemies, fighting his assailants and detractors without asking quarter or expecting any, and striking at his antagonists with a mailed fist, he had a heart full of human kindness and human charity for all who sought him in the human spirit."[26]

All observers could at least agree on one thing about Charles Tyson Yerkes: He had led a remarkable life. Writing a month after the financier's death, a New York *World* editorialist suggested that the "Yerkes affair" would make a great novel. The project, however, would be a difficult one. "The tale is too intricate and various and melodramatic for any living novelist who writes the English speech," the editorialist warned.[27] Theodore Dreiser eventually accepted the challenge and produced a masterful trilogy based on the career of Charles Tyson Yerkes—*The Financier* (1912), *The Titan* (1914), and *The Stoic* (1947). In many ways, however, Charles's real life was far stranger than the fictionalized one depicted by Dreiser.

Epilogue

On New Years Day, 1906, Charles's body was laid to rest in Brooklyn's Greenwood Cemetery as a cold wind blew. A small party of friends and relatives had gathered under the iron gray skies for the burial ceremony. A contingent of eight detectives was also in attendance. The Methodist Episcopal minister Jacob Hughes uttered a short prayer as the casket was being put into place, but his words "were unintelligible to the group behind the wall of detectives." Standing at the entrance of the imposing Grecian tomb beside the steps "piled high" with roses, the black-clad Mary Yerkes lost her composure for a brief moment. She swayed forward, pressed a handkerchief to her eyes, and clutched the arm of a woman companion as Hughes closed his prayer. The massive bronze double doors of the mausoleum were then shut and the mourners hurriedly left the cemetery in a procession of six carriages. "New York has seldom witnessed a more forsaken funeral," a *World* correspondent declared.[1]

A day later, the contents of Charles's will were revealed. He had left $500,000 each to his son Charles Edward and his daughter Elizabeth, and $200,000 to Mary. The people of New York City turned out to be the biggest beneficiaries of the Yerkes will. Charles had decided to bequeath his Fifth Avenue home, with its collection of rarities, to the city of New York, intending for it to be used as a public art gallery. The Sir Richard Wallace Collection—given as a gift to the city of London—served as a model for the proposed Yerkes Galleries. Mary Yerkes had inspired the other major provision in the will—one creating a hospital in the Bronx "open to the public without regard to creed, race or color." The facility was to provide its services free of charge to those of inadequate means.

The building of this hospital had long been Mary's "most cherished desire," and after nearly fifteen years of lobbying her husband, she had finally gotten her wish.[2]

However, it remained to be seen whether there was enough money in the Yerkes estate to finance an art gallery and a hospital. Observers initially estimated Charles's fortune at $22,000,000, but, with the magician dead, the illusion of great wealth swiftly vanished. "His [Charles's] affairs were always so intermingled and muddled up that you could never tell what his income was," Louis Owsley, the executor of the Yerkes estate, confessed. In fact, much of the magnate's fortune consisted of securities of doubtful value. Complicating matters, Charles, in his last years, had gone on a wild spending spree: He had borrowed millions of dollars to fund his extravagant lifestyle, his art purchases, and his transit operations. The bills came due after the businessman's death, and, as a result, the Yerkes estate was besieged by an army of creditors.

The Yerkes Galleries were an early casualty of this onslaught. In April 1910, Charles's marvelous collection of art objects was put on the auction block in order to raise money for the beleaguered estate. The sale was a major social event attended by the "comic opera lords and ladies" of New York high society—the very people who had snubbed Charles and his wife. The auction proved to be record-breaker in terms of prices paid and reaped over $2,000,000 for the estate. "No such art sale ever took place in America," the New York *Sun* truthfully asserted.[3]

By 1912, it had become evident that the hospital plan would also need to be scrapped, the Yerkes fortune having shrunk to less than $5,000,000. Mary Yerkes did not live to witness the final abandonment of her dream project. Her final years were unhappy ones. Only a month after her husband's death, she had married Wilson Mizner—a rash decision that she quickly came to regret. She realized all too soon that the shady Californian was merely interested in her money. "Just another idol shattered," Mary sadly informed a reporter shortly after her wedding. "That's what all this money has done for me. Robbed me of all my real friends, made me doubt them all, suspect and fear them." Mary divorced Mizner in May 1907. She expended her last energies battling Louis Owsley in the law courts, charging him with mismanagement of the Yerkes estate. During this legal struggle, she exhibited a tenacity of purpose and a strength of will reminiscent of her husband. In April 1911, Mary Adelaide Yerkes died of heart disease, and was buried beside Charles in his Greenwood Cemetery tomb. "Oh, I know that there are those who think and talk about the Grigsby woman, but Charley Yerkes loved me just the same," Mary had insisted.[4]

The "Grigsby woman" long outlived Mary. Shortly after auctioning off most of the contents of her Park Avenue home in 1912, Emilie Grigsby moved to England—a country that she found to be more civilized than the United States. In England at least, her every step would not be chronicled in the newspapers. She purchased a cottage sixteen miles west of Hyde Park, christened it "Old Meadows," and set herself up as a hostess. Her friends included such luminaries as the novelist D. H. Lawrence, the poet Rupert Brooke, and Princess Mary. During World War I, Emilie often entertained British officers and indeed considered herself to be the "mascot of the High Command." Though her health began to deteriorate in the 1930s, she survived until 1964, attaining the age of eighty-eight. To the very end, the never-married Emilie had kept Charles's love letters. Acting according to her instructions, Emilie's maid burned these letters after her death. The "poem girl's" ashes were scattered in the rose garden of Old Meadows.[5]

"I hope when I leave the world I shall leave an impress on it, something accomplished, something lasting done," Charles once had said. The Loop Elevated in Chicago, the three underground lines in London—which opened in 1906 and 1907—and the Yerkes Observatory were all products of this fervent desire of his—a desire for immortality.

In 1935, the International Astronomical Union named a crater on the moon after Charles Tyson Yerkes. The crater lies on the edge of the Sea of Crises not far from Palus Somni—the Marsh of Sleep.[6]

NOTES

Chapter 1. The Inner Light

1. *The Press* (Philadelphia), February 14, 1872, p. 6, col. 5; "Charles T. Yerkes the younger," February 10, 1872, Convict Reception Registers, 1869–72, Eastern State Penitentiary, Record Group 15, Pennsylvania State Archives, Pennsylvania State Historical and Museum Commission, Harrisburg, Pa.; *Chicago Daily News*, June 9, 1886, p. 1, col. 1; Norman Johnston, *Eastern State Penitentiary: Crucible of Good Intentions* (Philadelphia: University of Pennsylvania Press, 1994), 48–49; quoted in ibid., 110.

2. *Evening Bulletin* (Philadelphia), December 30, 1905, p. 6, col. 6; Charles Dickens, *American Notes* (London: Oxford University Press, 1957), 97–98; William Harbeson, "Yesteryear in Our Town," in *Philadelphia Architecture in the Nineteenth Century* (Philadelphia: University of Pennsylvania Press, 1953), 5.

3. George G. Foster, "Philadelphia in Slices," *Pennsylvania Magazine of History and Biography* 93 (January 1969): 28; Thomas Hamilton, *Men and Manners in America* (New York: Russell and Russell, 1968), 180; William Chambers, *Things As They Are in America* (New York: Negro Universities Press, 1968), 305–6.

4. Frederick Marryat, *Diary in America* (Bloomington: Indiana University Press, 1960), 172; quoted in Ellis Paxson Oberholtzer, *Jay Cooke: Financier of the Civil War* (Philadelphia: George W. Jacobs Company, 1907), 47.

5. E. Digby Baltzell, *Philadelphia Gentlemen* (New York: The Free Press, 1958), 174–77; quoted in Ellis Paxson Oberholtzer, *Philadelphia: A History of the City and Its People*, vol. 2 (Philadelphia: S. J. Clarke Publishing Company, 1912), 253; Hamilton, 205–6.

6. David R. Johnson, "Crime Patterns in Philadelphia, 1840–70," in *The Peoples of Philadelphia*, ed. Allen F. Davis and Mark H. Hiller (Philadelphia: Temple University Press, 1973), 90–97; Foster, 35.

7. Josiah Granville Leach, *Chronicle of the Yerkes Family* (Philadelphia: J. B. Lippincott Company, 1904).

8. Rufus Jones, *The Later Periods of Quakerism*, vol. 1 (New York: Macmillan and Company, 1921), 441; on the inner light, see Jones, 448, and Howard Brinton, *Friends for 300 Years* (New York: Harper and Brothers, 1952), 31–58. Bliss Forbush, *Elias Hicks: Quaker Liberal* (New York: Columbia University Press, 1956), 68–69; ibid., 131; H. Larry Ingle, *Quakers in Conflict* (Knoxville: University of Tennessee Press, 1986), 248; Leach, 60. Also see Robert W. Doherty, *The Hicksite Separation* (New Brunswick, N.J.: Rutgers University Press, 1967), 248.

9. Leach, 120–21; E. Digby Baltzell, *Puritan Boston and Quaker Philadelphia* (New York: The Free Press, 1979), 437–38.

10. Sidney George Fisher, *A Philadelphia Perspective: The Diary of Sidney George Fisher During the Years 1834–1871*, ed. Nicholas B. Wainwright (Philadelphia: Historical Society of Pennsylvania, 1967), 30.

11. Russell Weigley, "'A Peaceful City:' Public Order in Philadelphia from Consolidation through the Civil War," in *The Peoples of Philadelphia*, ed. Allen F. Davis and Mark H. Hiller (Philadelphia: Temple University Press, 1973), 156.

12. Sam Bass Warner, *The Private City* (Philadelphia: University of Pennsylvania Press, 1968), 132–52.

13. *A. McElroy's Directory for 1839* (Philadelphia: Isaac Ashmead and Company, 1839), 283; quoted in Richard J. Webster, *Philadelphia Preserved* (Philadelphia: Temple University Press, 1968), 308.

14. *A. McElroy's Directory for 1839*, 283; Estate of Samuel P. Shoemaker, March 13, 1858, Philadelphia Register of Wills; Warner, 50.

15. Charles Godrey Leland, *Memoirs* (New York: D. Appleton and Company, 1893), 8; Joseph Elfreth, *The Elfreth Book of Letters*, ed. Susan Winslow Hodge (Philadelphia: University of Pennsylvania Press, 1985), 28; Chambers, 307.

16. Oberholtzer, 46; Leland, 8; Death Certificate of Elizabeth Yerkes, December 8, 1842, Philadelphia City Archives; Charles D. Meigs, *Medical Examiner* 6 (January 21, 1843): 3.

17. Eleanor M. Tilton, *Amiable Autocrat* (New York: Henry Schuman, 1947), 172–73.

18. Leach, 120; Minutes of Green Street Monthly Meeting (Philadelphia), September 18, 1845, and October 23, 1845, Quaker Monthly Meeting Records, Friends Historical Library, Swarthmore College, Swarthmore, Pa.

19. Ingle, 249; quoted in *Chicago Chronicle*, December 30, 1905, p. 4, col. 6.

20. *Chicago Inter Ocean*, June 10, 1898, p. 2, col. 6.

21. Balwant Nevaskar, *Capitalists Without Capitalism* (Westport, Conn.: Greenwood Publishing Corporation, 1971), 120; Frederick Tolles, *Meeting House and Counting House* (Chapel Hill: University of North Carolina Press, 1948), 47; ibid., 46–62; Richard Huber, *The American Idea of Success* (New York: McGraw-Hill Book Company, 1971), 17; ibid., 25; Leland, 32; Ruth Miller Elson, "American Schoolbooks and 'Culture' in the Nineteenth Century," *Mississippi Valley Historical Review* (December 1959): 411–34; *Chicago Journal*, January 29, 1898, p. 4, cols. 5–6; *Daily Inter Ocean*, December 30, 1899, p. 12, cols. 1–2.

22. Franklin Spencer Edmonds, *History of the Central High School of Philadelphia* (Philadelphia: J. B. Lippincott Company, 1902), 27; David Labaree, *The Making of an American High School* (New Haven: Yale University Press, 1988), 70; Edmonds, 64; ibid., 169; Labaree, 27, 32; Edmonds, 70; *Philadelphia Public Ledger*, February 10, 1852, p. 2, col. 3; *32nd Annual Report of the Controllers of the Public Schools of the City and County of Philadelphia for the Year Ending June 30, 1850* (Philadelphia: Crissy and Markley, 1850), 84–103; *34th Annual Report of the Controllers of the Public Schools of the First District of Pennsylvania for the Year Ending June 30, 1852* (Philadelphia: Crissy and Markley, 1852), 103; Edmonds, 169.

23. Edmonds, 38–39; Labaree, 26, 32; Edmonds, 138–39; Labaree, 20.

24. Ibid., 49; ibid., 332; ibid., 60, 163; ibid., 85–87; Ezra Otis Kendall, *Uranography* (Philadelphia: E. H. Butler and Company, 1855), 31–32, 40, 205–6, 282–83; Bessie Zaban Jones and Lyle Gifford Boyd, *The Harvard College Observatory* (Cambridge, Mass.: Belknap Press, 1971), 48.

25. Elias Loomis, "Astronomical Observatories in the United States," *Harper's New Monthly Magazine* 13 (June 1856): 29–31; George Ellery Hale, "The Possibilities of Large Telescopes," *Harper's Magazine* 15 (April 1928): 639.

Chapter 2. The Spoils of War

1. Ellis Paxson Oberholtzer, *Jay Cooke: Financier of the Civil War* (Philadelphia: George W. Jacobs Company, 1907), 58; William Strauss and Neil Howe, *Generations* (New York: William Morrow, 1991), 206–16; Matthew Josephson, *The Robber Barons* (New York: Harcourt, Brace & World, 1962), 5; quoted in Strauss and Howe, 211.

2. "Charles T. Yerkes," in *Biographical Dictionary and Portrait Gallery of Representative Men of Chicago and the World's Columbian Exposition* (Chicago: American Biographical Publishing Company, 1892), 154–57; *New York Tribune*, August 4, 1901, Supplement, p. 5, col. 4; *Chicago Tribune*, March 23, 1890, p. 25, col. 2.

3. *Philadelphia Public Ledger*, July 14, 1854, p. 2, cols. 1–2; Graduation Report, July 13, 1854, Oversize Collection: Charles Yerkes, Chicago Historical Society; *36th Annual Report of the Controllers of the Public Schools of the City and County of Philadelphia for the Year and a Half Ending December 31, 1854* (Philadelphia: Crissy and Markley, 1855), 132; ibid., 137; *Chicago Tribune*, March 23, 1890, p. 25, col. 2; *Daily Inter Ocean*, December 30, 1899, p. 12, cols. 1–2; quoted in Alfred Chandler, Jr., *The Visible Hand: The Managerial Revolution in American Business* (Cambridge, Mass.: Harvard University Press, 1977), 39.

4. *Chicago Tribune*, March 23, 1890, p. 25, col. 2; "James P. Perot and Brother," R. G. Dun Co. PA 132/P. 425, R. G. Dun Co. Credit Ledgers, Baker Library, Harvard University; George W. Van Vleck, *The Panic of 1857* (New York: AMS Press, Inc., 1967), 74.

5. J. Thomas Scharf and Thompson Westcott, *History of Philadelphia*, vol. 1 (Philadelphia: L. H. Everts and Company, 1884), 726; quoted in James L. Hutson, *The Panic of 1857 and the Coming of the Civil War* (Baton Rouge: Louisiana State Press, 1987), 25; "James P. Perot and Brother," R. G. Dun Co. PA 132/P. 425, R. G. Dun Co. Credit Ledgers, Baker Library, Harvard University.

6. *Chicago Times-Herald*, August 11, 1896, p. 9, col. 4; Henry Clews, *Fifty Years in Wall Street* (New York: Irving Publishing Company, 1908), 6; Thomas C. Cochran, "Philadelphia: The American Industrial Center, 1750–1850," *Pennsylvania Magazine of History and Biography* 106 (July 1982): 327.

7. Richard J. Webster, *Philadelphia Preserved* (Philadelphia: Temple University Press, 1976), 312; *Philadelphia Public Ledger*, November 14, 1851, p. 2, col. 3.

8. Quoted in Robert Edwin Wilkinson, "A Study of Theodore Dreiser's *The Financier*" (Ph. D. diss., University of Pennsylvania 1965), 15; *Chicago Tribune*, March 23, 1890, p. 25, col. 2; ibid., April 18, 1886, p. 26, col. 3.

9. Webster, 45–46; Ellis Paxson Oberholtzer, *Philadelphia: A History of the City and Its People*, vol. 2 (Philadelphia: S. J. Clarke Publishing Company, 1912), 178; George G. Foster, "Philadelphia in Slices," *Pennsylvania Magazine of History and Biography* 93 (January 1969): 28.

328   *Notes to Pages 18–23*

10. Scharf and Westcott, vol. 3, 2108; "The History of the Philadelphia Stock Exchange," Philadelphia Stock Exchange website (http://www.phlx.com/exchange /phlxhistory.pdf); *Philadelphia Inquirer*, January 23, 1866, p. 5, col. 1; William Worthington Fowler, *Ten Years in Wall Street* (Hartford, Conn.: Worthington, Dustin and Company, 1870), 42.

11. Scharf and Westcott, vol. 3, 2109; *Philadelphia Inquirer*, August 31, 1865, p. 2, col. 3; Oberholtzer, 188–89; *Chicago Tribune*, March 23, 1890, p. 25, col. 2.

12. Granville Leach, *Chronicle of the Yerkes Family* (Philadelphia: J. B. Lippincott Company, 1904), 194; *Philadelphia Evening Bulletin*, December 24, 1859, p. 1, col. 1; *McElroy's Directories* 1839, 1840, 1846, 1848, 1851; Susannah Guttridge Gamble, 1850 Census, District of Penn, Philadelphia County, Pa., National Archives; Charles T. Yerkes, Jr., 1860 Census, Twentieth Ward, Philadelphia, Pa., National Archives.

13. Fowler, 144; *Philadelphia Inquirer*, November 8, 1860, p. 8, cols. 3–4; ibid., February 23, 1861, p. 8, col. 3.

14. *Philadelphia Inquirer*, February 22, 1861, p. 8, col. 2; ibid., March 5, 1861, p. 8, col. 3.

15. *Philadelphia Inquirer*, April 15, 1861, p. 5, cols. 1–2; Alexander McClure, *Old Time Notes of Pennsylvania*, vol. 1 (Philadelphia: John C. Winston Company, 1905), 467.

16. Scharf and Westcott, vol. 1, 756; *Philadelphia Inquirer*, April 17, 1861, p. 1, col. 6; ibid., April 19, 1861, p. 8, col. 5; ibid., April 27, 1861, p. 3, col. 1; ibid., p. 2, col. 4.

17. *Philadelphia Inquirer*, January 23, 1866, p. 5, col. 1; Vernon Parrington, *Main Currents in American Thought*, vol. 3 (New York: Harcourt, Brace and Company, 1930), 31; *Philadelphia Inquirer*, September 5, 1862, p. 1, cols. 1–2; ibid., September 11, 1862, p. 1, col. 1; J. Matthew Gallman, *Mastering Wartime: A Social History of Philadelphia During the Civil War* (New York: Cambridge University Press, 1990), 16–21.

18. Discharge Papers, Ninth Regiment, Pennsylvania Volunteer Militia, September 28, 1862, Oversize Collection: Charles Yerkes, Chicago Historical Society; *Philadelphia Inquirer*, August 8, 1862, p. 8, col. 3; Gallman, 16; Samuel Bates, *History of the Pennsylvania Volunteers 1861–5*, vol. 5 (Harrisburg, Pa.: D. Singerly, State Printers, 1871), 1147–48, 1168; *Philadelphia Inquirer*, February 5, 1862, p. 3, col. 4.

19. Stephen Sears, *Landscape Turned Red* (New York: Ticknor and Fields, 1983), 295–96; Leach, 158 and 171; for a description of the Home Guard uniform, see *Philadelphia Inquirer*, April 24, 1861, p. 2, col. 3; ibid., September 29, 1862, p. 2, cols. 2–3; *Pennsylvania: A Guide to the Keystone State* (New York: Oxford University Press, 1940), 195–201.

20. McClure, vol. 1, 570–71; Governor Curtin quoted in William Allan Blair, "'A Source of Amusement:' Pennsylvania Versus Lee, 1863," *Pennsylvania Magazine of History and Biography* 115 (July 1991): 323.

21. Certificate of Appointment to 31st Regiment, Pennsylvania Volunteer Militia, June 30, 1863, Oversize Collection: Charles Yerkes, Chicago Historical Society; Bates, 1222–31, 1245; *Philadelphia Inquirer*, July 4, 1863, p. 3, col. 3.

22. Blair, 338; Bates, 1231; descriptions of Yerkes's military collection is found in *Catalogue De Luxe of the Ancient Rugs, Sculptures, Tapestries, Costly Furni-*

ture and Other Objects Belonging to the Estate of the Late Charles T. Yerkes, vol.
2 (New York: The American Art Association, 1910).

23. *Chicago Daily News*, June 9, 1886, p. 1, col. 1; *Philadelphia Inquirer*, March
17, 1863, p. 6, col. 2; ibid., November 28, 1862, p. 7, cols. 3–4; Robert Tomes, "The
Fortunes of War," *Harper's New Monthly Magazine* 29 (July 1864): 230; *Philadelphia Inquirer*, August 1, 1867, p. 3, col. 2.

24. Leach, 120; Fritz Redlich, *Molding of American Banking*, vol. 2 (New York:
Hafner Publishing Company, Inc., 1951), 11; Lorenzo Sabine, "Suggestions to
Young Cashiers on the Duties of Their Profession," *The Bankers' Magazine* 4 (July
1855): 515.

25. *The Bankers' Magazine* 14 (December 1864): 505; *Chronicle of the Union
League of Philadelphia 1862 to 1902* (Philadelphia, 1902), 58; ibid., 94; *Philadelphia Inquirer*, June 19, 1863, p. 5, col. 2; photograph in Leach.

26. *The Bankers' Magazine* 14 (April 1865): 861; Webster, 46 and 83; the building's purchase price is listed in Schedule B-1, Bankrupt's Inventory, In the Matter
of Charles T. Yerkes, Jr., Bankrupt, National Archives—Mid-Atlantic Region,
Philadelphia, Pa.; *Philadelphia Public Ledger*, January 27, 1865, p. 4, col. 2.

27. "Charles T. Yerkes, Jr.," June 1, 1866, R. G. Dun/PA 143/P. 33, R. G. Dun
Credit Ledgers, Baker Library, Harvard University; Scharf and Westcott, vol. 2,
823; *Philadelphia Public Ledger*, April 11, 1865, p. 4, col. 1.

28. *Philadelphia Public Ledger*, April 17, 1865, p. 1, col. 1; ibid., p. 4, col. 1; ibid.,
April 24, 1865, p. 1, cols. 2–5; *Chicago Times-Herald*, May 21, 1897, p. 5, col. 2.

Chapter 3. Addition, Division, and Silence

1. Vernon Louis Parrington, *Main Currents in American Thought*, vol. 3 (New
York: Harcourt, Brace and Company, 1930), 23; *The Sun* (New York), March 4,
1872, p. 1, col. 1; ibid., September 17, 1872, p. 1, col. 2.

2. *Philadelphia Inquirer*, March 8, 1870, p. 4, col. 3; *The Press* (Philadelphia),
June 24, 1872, p. 1, col. 1.

3. P.A.B. Widener, *Without Drums* (New York: G. P. Putnam's Sons, 1940), 21;
Chicago Tribune, April 18, 1886, p. 26, cols. 3–4; *Philadelphia Inquirer*, October
23, 1866, p. 3, col. 1; ibid., January 2, 1867, p. 2, col. 1; *Philadelphia Public Ledger*,
December 6, 1871, p. 3, cols. 6–7.

4. *New York Herald*, November 1, 1871, p. 10, cols. 2–3; *The Sun* (New York),
September 17, 1872, p. 1, col. 1; *Philadelphia Inquirer*, January 2, 1867, p. 8, col. 3;
ibid., April 2, 1867, p. 1, col. 2; ibid., April 4, 1867, p. 8, col. 4.

5. *Chicago Tribune*, April 18, 1886, p. 26, col. 3; *The Sun* (New York), September 17, 1872, p. 1, col. 1.

6. McClure, vol. 2, 255–67; *The Sun* (New York) September 14, 1872, p. 2, cols.
5–6; *The Press* (Philadelphia), July 29, 1872, p. 1, col. 2; ibid., June 29, 1872, p. 1,
col. 1.

7. *The Sun* (New York), August 21, 1872, p. 1, cols. 1–7; ibid., p. 3, cols. 1–3.

8. Testimony of Charles H. Fitler, Report of Register in the Claim of James
Platt Holden, filed May 5, 1875, In the Matter of Charles T. Yerkes, Jr., Bankrupt,
Case Number 1434, U.S. District Court, Eastern District of Pennsylvania,
National Archives—Mid-Atlantic Branch, Philadelphia, Pa.; Matthew Josephson,

The Robber Barons (New York: Harcourt, Brace and World, 1962), 146; *Philadelphia Inquirer*, September 30, 1869, p. 7, col. 1.

9. *Chicago Tribune*, December 3, 1899, p. 1, cols. 1–2; Petition of Bankrupt for Discharge, September 18, 1873, In the Matter of Charles T. Yerkes, Jr., Bankrupt, Case Number 1434, U.S. District Court, Eastern District of Pennsylvania, National Archives—Mid-Atlantic Branch, Philadelphia, Pa.; *Chicago Tribune*, April 18, 1886, p. 26, col. 4; William Worthington Fowler, *Ten Years in Wall Street* (Hartford, Conn.: Worthington, Dustin, and Company, 1870), 46–49; "C. T. Yerkes Jr. and Co.," August 1, 1871, R. G. Dun and Company PA 222/P. 409, R. G. Dun Credit Ledgers, Baker Library, Harvard University; "C. T. Yerkes Jr. and Co.," August 3, 1871, R. G. Dun and Company/PA 143/P. 33, ibid.; Testimony of Charles T. Yerkes, Jr., June 18, 1873, Report of Examiner, John Sparhawk et al. vs. Francis Drexel, Anthony J. Drexel et al., Equity Case Number 56, April Session 1872, U.S. District Court, Eastern District of Pennsylvania, National Archives—Mid-Atlantic Branch, Philadelphia, Pa.; Answer of Defendants, December 3, 1872, John Sparhawk et al. vs. The First National Bank of Philadelphia et al., Equity Case Number 29, April Session 1872, ibid.; Testimony of Charles T. Yerkes, Sr., October 24, 1873, John Sparhawk et al. vs. The Kensington National Bank, Equity Case Number 20, October Session 1872, ibid.

10. William Harbeson, "Yesteryear in Our Town," in *Philadelphia Architecture in the Nineteenth Century* (Philadelphia: University of Pennsylvania Press, 1953), 10; undated (November–December 1872) auction notice in *Philadelphia Evening Bulletin*, found in Case Number 1434, U.S. District Court, Eastern District of Pennsylvania, National Archives—Mid-Atlantic Branch, Philadelphia, Pa.; quoted in Jeffrey Roberts, "Railroads and the Downtown: Philadelphia, 1830–1900," in *The Divided Metropolis*, ed. William Cutler and Howard Gillette, Jr. (Westport, Conn.: Greenwood Press, 1980), 49.

11. Ibid.; *Chicago Journal*, June 6, 1899, p. 4, col. 2; Carter Harrison, Jr., *Stormy Years* (Indianapolis: Bobbs-Merrill, 1934), p. 148; Certificate of Election, First Troop Philadelphia City Cavalry, January 3, 1870, Oversize Collection: Charles Yerkes, Chicago Historical Society; E. Digby Baltzell, *Puritan Boston and Quaker Philadelphia* (New York: The Free Press, 1979), p. 240; E. Digby Baltzell, *Philadelphia Gentlemen* (New York: The Free Press, 1958), p. 55.

Chapter 4. Trial by Fire

1. *Philadelphia Public Ledger*, January 1, 1870, p. 4, col. 2; P.A.B. Widener, *Without Drums* (New York: G. P. Putnam's Sons, 1940), 21; Alexander McClure, *Old Time Notes of Pennsylvania*, vol. 2 (Philadelphia: John C. Winston Company, 1905), 251–52; "Joseph Marcer," 1870 Census, Twentieth Ward, Philadelphia, Pa.; Testimony of Charles T. Yerkes, Jr., October 22, 1872, Report of Joseph Mason, Register, as to Distribution of Proceeds of Sale of Pyne Collieries, In the Matter of Charles T. Yerkes, Jr., Bankrupt; *Philadelphia Public Ledger*, December 6, 1871, p. 3, cols. 6–7; ibid., December 7, 1871, p. 3, col. 7.

2. H. W. Schotter, *The Growth and Development of the Pennsylvania Railroad Company, 1846–1926* (Philadelphia: Allen, Lane and Scott, 1927), 94–97; James Arthur Ward, *J. Edgar Thomson: Master of the Pennsylvania* (Westport, Conn.: Greenwood Press, 1980), 150–53; *Philadelphia Inquirer*, November 23, 1871, p. 2, col. 1; Detailed Statement of Applicant, September 18, 1873, Petition of

Charles T. Yerkes, Jr., for Discharge of Bankruptcy, In the Matter of Charles T. Yerkes, Jr., Bankrupt; Philadelphia Inquirer, December 16, 1871, p. 2, col. 5; "Charles T. Yerkes," in *Biographical Dictionary and Portrait Gallery of Representative Men of Chicago and the World's Columbian Exposition* (Chicago: American Biographical Publishing Company), 157.

3. Donald Miller, *City of the Century* (New York: Simon and Schuster, 1996), 15–16; ibid., 154–59; *Philadelphia Inquirer,* October 16, 1871, p. 6, col. 1.

4. *Philadelphia Inquirer,* October 10, 1871, p. 6, col. 1; ibid., October 11, 1871, p. 6, col. 1; Detailed Statement of Applicant, Petition of Charles T. Yerkes, Jr., for Discharge of Bankruptcy, In the Matter of Charles T. Yerkes, Jr., Bankrupt.

5. Testimony of Anthony Drexel, June 11, 1873, Report of Examiner in Sparhawk et al. vs. Drexel, U.S. Circuit Court, Eastern District of Pennsylvania, National Archives—Mid-Atlantic Region, Philadelphia, Pa.; Testimony of Charles T. Yerkes, Jr., June 18, 1873, ibid.; Vincent Carosso, *The Morgans: Private International Bankers, 1854–1913* (Cambridge, Mass.: Harvard University Press, 1987), 141; J. Thomas Scharf and Thompson Westcott, *History of Philadelphia, 1609–1884,* vol. 3 (Philadelphia: L. H. Everts and Company, 1884), 2102.

6. *Philadelphia Public Ledger,* December 6, 1871, p. 3, cols. 6–7; Testimony of David Jones, December 5, 1873, Report of Examiner in Sparhawk et al. vs. the Kensington National Bank, U.S. Circuit Court, Eastern District of Pennsylvania, National Archives—Mid-Atlantic Region, Philadelphia, Pa.; *Philadelphia Inquirer,* October 14, 1871, p. 6, col. 1; ibid., October 16, 1871, p. 6, col. 1.

7. *Philadelphia Public Ledger,* December 6, 1871, p. 3, cols. 6–7; Commonwealth vs. Charles T. Yerkes, Jr., Grand Jury Bill of Indictment, November 16, 1871, Philadelphia City Archives.

8. Testimony of Charles T. Yerkes, Sr., October 31, 1873, November 7, 1873, Report of Examiner in Sparhawk et al. vs. the Kensington National Bank; Answer of Francis A. Drexel et al., filed December 2, 1872, Sparhawk et al. vs. Drexel, U.S. Circuit Court, Eastern District of Pennsylvania, National Archives—Mid-Atlantic Region, Philadelphia, Pa.; *Philadelphia Public Ledger,* December 6, 1871, p. 3, cols. 6–7; Testimony of David Jones, December 5, 1873, Report of Examiner in Sparhawk et al. vs. the Kensington National Bank.

9. Ibid.; Testimony of Anthony Drexel, June 11, 1873, Report of Examiner in Sparhawk et al. vs. Drexel; Testimony of Charles T. Yerkes, Jr., November 17, 1873, Report of Examiner in Sparhawk et al. vs. Richards and Thompson, U.S. Circuit Court, Eastern District of Pennsylvania, National Archives—Mid Atlantic Region, Philadelphia, Pa.

10. Testimony of George Fox, May 30, 1873, Report of Examiner in Sparhawk et al. vs. Richards and Thompson; Testimony of Joseph Yerkes, July 2, 1873, ibid; Testimony of David Jones, December 5, 1873, Report of Examiner in Sparhawk et al. vs. the Kensington National Bank, *Philadelphia Public Ledger,* December 6, 1871, p. 3, cols. 6–7.

11. Testimony of Samuel Richards, June 23, 1873, Report of Examiner in Sparhawk et al. vs. Richards and Thompson, Testimony of George Fox, May 30, 1873, ibid.; Testimony of Joseph Yerkes, July 2, 1873, ibid; *New York Herald,* November 1, 1871, p. 10, col. 2; "Charles T. Yerkes, Jr., and Co.," August 3, 1871, R. G. Dun/PA 143/P. 33, R. G. Dun Credit Ledgers, Baker Library, Harvard University; "Charles T. Yerkes, Jr., and Co.," November 21, 1871, ibid.; *Chicago Tribune,* December 3, 1899, p. 1, col. 1.

Chapter 5. Trial by Jury

1. Answer of Francis Drexel, filed December 2, 1872, Sparhawk et al. vs. Drexel, U.S. Circuit Court, Eastern District of Pennsylvania, National Archives—Mid-Atlantic Branch, Philadelphia, Pa.; Testimony of George Fox, May 30, 1873, Examiner's Report, Sparhawk et al. vs. Richards and Thompson, U.S. Circuit Court, Eastern District of Pennsylvania, National Archives—Mid-Atlantic Branch, Philadelphia, Pa.

2. Testimony of Charles T. Yerkes, Jr., November 19, 1873, ibid.; *Philadelphia Inquirer*, October 23, 1871, p. 6, cols. 1–2; ibid., November 13, 1871, p. 6, col. 1; ibid., December 16, 1871, p. 2, col. 5.

3. *New York Herald*, November 1, 1871, p. 10, col. 3; *Philadelphia Inquirer*, November 23, 1871, p. 2, col. 1; *Philadelphia Evening Bulletin*, October 20, 1871, p. 4, col. 2; *Philadelphia Inquirer*, October 23, 1871, p. 3, col. 3; *Philadelphia Public Ledger*, October 23, 1871, p. 1, col. 6.

4. Alexander McClure, *Old Time Notes of Pennsylvania*, vol. 1 (Philadelphia: The John C. Winston Company, 1905), 294; Howard Gillette, Jr., "'Corrupt and Contented': Philadelphia's Political Machine, 1865–1887" (Ph.D. diss., Yale University, 1970), 93–94; *New York Sun*, October 2, 1872, p. 2, col. 7; *Philadelphia Public Ledger*, December 31, 1905, p. 17, cols. 1–2.

5. *Philadelphia Evening Bulletin*, October 26, 1871, p. 8, col. 1; ibid., October 26, 1871, p. 8, col. 1.

6. *Philadelphia Age*, October 30, 1871, p. 1, col. 4; *Philadelphia Inquirer*, October 30, 1871, p. 2, col. 6; *Philadelphia Evening Bulletin*, October 27, 1871, p. 4, col. 1; *Philadelphia Inquirer*, November 1, 1871, p. 8, col. 1.

7. *Philadelphia Evening Bulletin*, November 3, 1871, p. 7, cols. 1–2; *Chicago Tribune*, May 22, 1891, p. 1, cols. 3–4; Commonwealth of Pennsylvania vs. Joseph F. Marcer and Charles T. Yerkes, Jr., Grand Jury Bill of Indictment, November 1, 1871, Philadelphia Court of Quarter Sessions, Philadelphia City Archives; *Philadelphia Inquirer*, November 2, 1871, p. 4, col. 2; ibid., November 6, 1871, p. 2, col. 1.

8. *Philadelphia Inquirer*, November 14, 1871, p. 2, col. 3; *Philadelphia Evening Bulletin*, November 10, 1871, p. 8, col. 1; Indenture between Charles T. Yerkes, Jr., and Joseph Pile, October 24, 1871, In the Matter of Charles T. Yerkes, Jr., Bankrupt, U.S. Circuit Court, Eastern District of Pennsylvania, National Archives—Mid-Atlantic Branch, Philadelphia, Pa.; Statement of Joseph Pile to Assignees of Yerkes's Estate, February 9, 1872, ibid.

9. *Philadelphia Inquirer*, November 23, 1871, p. 2, col. 1; ibid., November 22, 1871, p. 2, col. 6; ibid., November 30, 1871, p. 2, col. 4; *Philadelphia Evening Bulletin*, December 29, 1871, p. 7, col. 1.

10. *Philadelphia Inquirer*, November 23, 1871, p. 2, col. 1; Alexander McClure, *Old Time Notes of Pennsylvania*, vol. 2 (Philadelphia: The John C. Winston Company, 1905), 247–49; *New York Tribune*, December 5, 1871, p. 1, col. 4.

11. J. Thomas Scharf, *History of Philadelphia, 1609–1884*, vol. 3 (Philadelphia: L. H. Everts and Company, 1884), 1824; George Norris, *Ended Episodes* (Chicago: The John C. Winston Company, 1937), 81.

12. *Philadelphia Inquirer*, December 1, 1865, p. 2, col. 3; ibid., March 2, 1867, p. 3, col. 3; ibid., December 6, 1871, p. 7, col. 1; *New York Herald*, December 8, 1871, p. 9, col. 1; *Philadelphia Evening Bulletin*, December 5, 1871, p. 5, col. 2.

13. *Philadelphia Inquirer*, December 6, 1871, p. 7, col. 1; *Philadelphia Evening Bulletin*, December 5, 1871, p. 5, col. 2; *Philadelphia Public Ledger*, December 6, 1871, p. 3, col. 6.

14. Ibid.; *Philadelphia Inquirer*, December 6, 1871, p. 7, col. 1; *Philadelphia Evening Bulletin*, December 5, 1871, p. 5, col. 2.

15. *Philadelphia Public Ledger*, December 6, 1871, p. 3, cols. 6–7; *Philadelphia Evening Bulletin*, December 5, 1871, p. 5, cols. 2–3; *New York Herald*, November 1, 1871, p. 10, col. 3; *Philadelphia Inquirer*, December 6, 1871, p. 7, cols. 1–2; ibid., December 16, 1871, p. 2, col. 5.

16. Scharf, 1824; *Philadelphia Public Ledger*, December 6, 1871, p. 3, col. 7; *Philadelphia Inquirer*, ibid., p. 7, col. 2; "Charles T. Yerkes," in *Biographical Dictionary and Portrait Gallery of Representative Men of Chicago, and the World's Columbian Exposition* (Chicago: American Biographical Publishing Company, 1892), 157.

17. *Philadelphia Public Ledger*, December 7, 1871, p. 3, col. 7; *Philadelphia Inquirer*, December 7, 1871, p. 7, col. 1; *Philadelphia Public Ledger*, December 14, 1871, p. 1, col. 5.

Chapter 6. Judgment Day

1. *The Sun* (New York), October 1, 1872, p. 1, cols. 1–2; *Philadelphia Public Ledger*, December 31, 1905, p. 17, cols. 1–2; *The Sun* (New York), March 18, 1872, p. 1, col. 1.

2. William Paine, "Pennsylvania Frauds! How State Officials Teach a Political Arithmetic!" undated pamphlet, Wisconsin State Historical Library, Madison, Wis.; *The Sun* (New York), October 8, 1872, p. 1, cols. 1–2; *Philadelphia Public Ledger*, December 31, 1905, p. 17, cols. 1–2; *The Press* (Philadelphia), August 29, 1872, p. 8, cols. 1–3; *Philadelphia Evening Bulletin*, February 14, 1872, p. 5, col. 1.

3. *The Press* (Philadelphia), February 12, 1872, p. 6, col. 2; *Philadelphia Inquirer*, February 12, 1872, p. 2, cols. 1–3; *Philadelphia Public Ledger*, February 12, 1872, p. 3, cols. 6–7.

4. George Norris, *Ended Episodes* (Philadelphia: The John C. Winston Company, 1937), 13, 15; *Philadelphia Public Ledger*, February 12, 1872, p. 3, cols. 6–7; *The Press* (Philadelphia), February 12, 1872, p. 6, cols. 1–2.

5. *Philadelphia Public Ledger*, February 12, 1872, p. 3, cols. 6–7; *Philadelphia Inquirer*, February 12, 1872, p. 2, cols. 1–3; McClure, vol. 2, 415–16.

6. *Philadelphia Public Ledger*, February 12, 1872, p. 3, cols. 6–7; *The Sun* (New York), February 15, 1872, p. 2, col. 5; *The Press* (Philadelphia), February 12, 1872, p. 6, cols. 1–2.

7. *Philadelphia Public Ledger*, December 31, 1905, p. 17, cols. 1–2; "Charles T. Yerkes the younger," February 10, 1872, Convict Reception Registers 1869–72, Eastern State Penitentiary, Record Group 15, Pennsylvania State Archives, Pennsylvania Historical and Museum Commission, Harrisburg, Pa.

Chapter 7. Buried Alive

1. *The Press* (Philadelphia), February 14, 1872, p. 6, col. 5; Paine pamphlet; *Philadelphia Evening Bulletin*, March 21, 1872, p. 4, col. 1; *Philadelphia Public*

Ledger, December 31, 1905, p. 17, cols. 1–2; McClure, vol. 2, 272–74; Gustave de Beaumont and Alexis de Tocqueville, *On the Penitentiary System in the United States and Its Application in France* (Carbondale: Southern Illinois University Press, 1964), 55; Charles Dickens, *American Notes* (London: Oxford University Press, 1957), 102; ibid., 99.

2. Norman Johnston, *Eastern State Penitentiary: Crucible of Good Intentions* (Philadelphia: University of Pennsylvania Press, 1994), 36; quoted in Philip Stevick, *Imagining Philadelphia* (Philadelphia: University of Pennsylvania Press, 1996), 58; for a good description of the prison entrance, see Johnston, 39–40.

3. *The Press* (Philadelphia), February 14, 1872, p. 6, col. 5; "Charles T. Yerkes the younger," February 10, 1872, Convict Reception Registers 1869–73, Eastern State Penitentiary, Record Group 15, Pennsylvania State Archives, Pennsylvania Historical and Museum Commission, Harrisburg, Pa.; Johnston, 49; *Philadelphia Public Ledger*, July 21, 1865, p. 1, col. 2; *Chicago Tribune*, October 22, 1887, p. 12, cols. 3–5.

4. *Philadelphia Inquirer*, September 5, 1872, p. 2, col. 3; Michael John Cassidy, *Warden Cassidy on Prisons and Convicts* (Philadelphia: Patterson and White, 1897), 31; ibid., 21; *The World* (New York), January 8, 1906, p. 2, col. 3; *Philadelphia Inquirer*, December 30, 1905, p. 2, cols. 1–2.

5. *Philadelphia Inquirer*, September 5, 1872, p. 2, col. 3; *Philadelphia Public Ledger*, December 31, 1905, p. 17, col. 2; Johnston, 49–52; Eastern State Penitentiary's regulations quoted in Harry Elmer Barnes, *The Evolution of Penology in Pennsylvania* (Montclair, N.J.: Patterson Smith, 1968), 299–300.

6. *New York Tribune*, February 28, 1872, p. 5, cols. 3–4; Alexander McClure, *Old Time Notes of Pennsylvania*, vol. 2 (Philadelphia: The John C. Winston Company, 1905), 343; Gordon C. Rhea, *The Battle of the Wilderness May 5–6, 1864* (Baton Rouge: Louisiana State University Press, 1994), 382–83; Noah Andre Trudeaux, *The Last Citadel* (Boston: Little, Brown and Company, 1991), 347–50; Louis J. Weichmann, *A True History of the Assassination of Abraham Lincoln and of the Conspiracy of 1865* (New York: Alfred A. Knopf, 1975), 234–35, 283, 294.

7. *Philadelphia Evening Bulletin*, February 14, 1872, p. 5, col. 1; ibid., February 23, 1872, p. 4, col. 2; *Philadelphia Inquirer*, April 2, 1872, p. 2, col. 1; Paine pamphlet.

8. Matthew Josephson, *The Politicos 1865–1896* (New York: Harcourt, Brace and Company, 1938), 160; Ellis Paxson Oberholtzer, *A History of the United States Since the Civil War*, vol. 3: *1872–8* (New York: Macmillan Company, 1926), 12; Don Seitz, *Horace Greeley: Founder of the New York Tribune* (Indianapolis: Bobbs-Merrill Company, 1926), 1–3; Rosebault, 199.

9. Elihu Washburne to Ulysses S. Grant, June 15, 1872, in *The Papers of Ulysses S. Grant*, vol. 23, ed. John Y. Simon (Carbondale: Southern Illinois University Press, 2000), 240; *The Press* (Philadelphia), August 7, 1872, p. 4, cols. 3–4; McClure, 346; *The Sun* (New York), October 1, 1872, p. 1, col. 1.

10. *Chicago Daily News* (morning), June 9, 1886, p. 1, cols. 3–4; letter quoted in *Philadelphia Evening Bulletin*, September 11, 1872, p. 2, col. 5.

11. *Philadelphia Inquirer*, September 5, 1872, p. 2, col. 3.

12. *Philadelphia Inquirer*, July 10, 1872, p. 3, col. 1; ibid., September 25, 1872, p. 2, col. 5; Erwin Stanley Bradley, *The Triumph of Militant Republicanism* (Philadelphia: University of Pennsylvania Press, 1964), 412; Elihu Washburne to Ulysses S. Grant, June 15, 1872, in *The Papers of Ulysses S. Grant*, vol. 23, ed. John

Y. Simon (Carbondale: Southern Illinois University Press, 2000), 240; Orville Babcock to Simon Cameron, August 16, 1872, Simon Cameron Papers (microfilm), Library of Congress; *Philadelphia Inquirer*, September 27, 1872, p. 8, col. 1.

13. McClure, 347; *The Press* (Philadelphia), September 28, 1872, p. 8, col. 2; *Philadelphia Evening Bulletin*, September 28, 1872, p. 8, col. 1; *Philadelphia Inquirer*, September 28, 1872, p. 1, col. 6; *The Sun* (New York), September 28, 1872, p. 1, col. 5.

14. *The Press* (Philadelphia), September 28, 1872, p. 8, col. 2; Pardon of Charles T. Yerkes, Jr., September 27, 1872, Department of State, Secretary of Commonwealth Pardon Book, Record Group 26 (microfilm roll 613), Pennsylvania State Archives, Pennsylvania Historical and Museum Commission, Harrisburg, Pa.; *Philadelphia Inquirer*, September 28, 1872, p. 1, col. 6; *The Sun* (New York), September 28, 1872, p. 1, col. 5.

15. *New York Times*, October 3, 1872, p. 12, cols. 4–5.

16. *The Press* (Philadelphia), September 30, 1872, p. 4, col. 3; *Philadelphia Evening Bulletin*, September 28, 1872, p. 4, col. 1; *The Sun* (New York), October 2, 1872, p. 2, col. 1; Bradley, 413; *Philadelphia Inquirer*, February 12, 1872, p. 4, col. 2.

Chapter 8. Starting Over

1. Henry Adams, *The Letters of Henry Adams*, vol. 6, ed. J. C. Levenson et al. (Cambridge, Mass.: The Belknap Press of Harvard University Press, 1988), 480; *Chicago Tribune*, October 27, 1901, p. 41, col. 3; *Chicago Journal*, January 29, 1898, p. 4, col. 1.

2. *Philadelphia Inquirer*, September 5, 1872, p. 2, col. 3; "Charles T. Yerkes, Jr., and Co.," August 25, 1873, R. G. Dun Co./PA 143/P. 33, R. G. Dun Company Credit Ledgers, Baker Library, Harvard University.

3. Ibid.; Davis and Thayer vs. New Hampshire Electro Gold Mining Company, March 1874, Grafton County Circuit Court, North Haverhill, N.H.; Ernest Poole, *The Great White Hills of New Hampshire* (New York: Doubleday and Company, 1946), 187–88; Federal Writers' Project, *New Hampshire* (Boston: Houghton Mifflin Company, 1938), 403–4.

4. Detailed Statement of Applicant, Petition of Bankrupt for Discharge, September 18, 1873, Estate of Charles T. Yerkes, Jr. In Bankruptcy (Case 1434), U.S. District Court, Eastern District of Pennsylvania, National Archives—Mid-Atlantic Region, Philadelphia, Pa.; *Journal of the Select Council of the City of Philadelphia from January 1, 1873 to July 1, 1873* (Philadelphia: E. C. Markley and Son, 1873), 286–87; Approval of Discharge, October 3, 1873, In the Matter of Charles T. Yerkes, Bankrupt, U.S. District Court, Eastern District of Pennsylvania, National Archives—Mid-Atlantic Region, Philadelphia, Pa.

5. Ellis Paxson Oberholtzer, *Jay Cooke: Financier of the Civil War* (Philadelphia: George W. Jacobs Company, 1907), 422–23; *Philadelphia Public Ledger*, September 20, 1873, p. 1, cols. 5–6; ibid., September 22, 1873, p. 4, col. 1; *Chicago Tribune*, April 18, 1886, p. 26, cols. 3–4; "C. T. Yerkes, Jr., and Co.," January 23, 1874, R. G. Dun Co./PA 222/P. 409, R. G. Dun Company Credit Ledgers, Baker Library, Harvard University.

6. Ibid.; the Philadelphia Stock Exchange regulations are quoted in In Re Charles T. Yerkes, Jr., A Bankrupt, July 14 1885, U.S. Circuit Court, Eastern District of Pennsylvania, National Archives—Mid-Atlantic Region, Philadelphia, Pa.; "Charles T. Yerkes, Jr., and Co.," December 9, 1884, R. G. Dun Co./PA 143/P. 419, R. G. Dun Company Credit Ledgers, Baker Library, Harvard University; Report of Register as to Petition of Assignees for Leave to Receive Principal of Judgment against John P. Bell, September 30, 1881, In the Matter of Charles T. Yerkes, Jr., In Bankruptcy, U.S. District Court, Eastern District of Pennsylvania, ibid.; "Charles T. Yerkes, Jr., and Co.," December 4, 1881, R. G. Dun Co./PA 143/ P. 359, R. G. Dun Company Credit Ledgers, Baker Library, Harvard University.

7. George Rogers Taylor, "The Beginnings of Mass Transportation in Urban America, Part II," *Smithsonian Journal of History* 1 (Fall 1966): 31; ibid., 47; Sidney George Fisher, *A Philadelphia Perspective: The Diary of Sidney George Fisher During the Years 1834–1871,* ed. Nicholas B. Wainwright (Philadelphia: Historical Society of Pennsylvania, 1967), 316; George Rogers Taylor, "The Beginnings of Mass Transportation in Urban America, Part I," *Smithsonian Journal of History* 1 (Summer 1966): 36–38; Charles Cheape, *Moving the Masses: Urban Public Transit in New York, Boston, and Philadelphia, 1880–1912* (Cambridge, Mass.: Harvard University Press, 1980), 157–58; Sam Bass Warner, *Streetcar Suburbs* (Cambridge, Mass.: Harvard University Press, 1978), 21–31; Lewis Mumford, *The City in History* (New York: Harcourt, Brace and World, 1961), 429; ibid., 529; ibid., 541; ibid., 483; Fisher, 316; *Philadelphia Inquirer,* August 17, 1865, p. 2, col. 2.

8. *Philadelphia Public Ledger,* April 9, 1859, p. 1, cols. 3–4; ibid., May 10, 1859, p. 1, col. 4; ibid., October 13, 1859, p. 1, col. 3; *Philadelphia Inquirer,* November 28, 1862, p. 7, cols. 3–4; Testimony of Charles T. Yerkes, Jr., May 28, 1873, In the Matter of Charles T. Yerkes, Jr., Bankrupt, U.S. District Court, Eastern District of Pennsylvania, National Archives—Mid-Atlantic Region, Philadelphia, Pa.; *Daily Inter Ocean,* October 18, 1899, p. 3, cols. 1–3.

9. Fisher, 345, 522; Burton Hendrick, "Great American Fortunes and their Making: Street Railway Financiers," *McClure's Magazine* 30 (November 1907): 37; *Philadelphia Inquirer,* March 1, 1861, p. 4, col. 1.

10. *Philadelphia Public Ledger,* February 11, 1930, p. 1, cols. 3–4; ibid., p. 6, cols. 2–6; Frederic Speirs, "The Street Railway System of Philadelphia: Its History and Present Condition," *Johns Hopkins University Studies in Historical and Political Science,* 15th Series (Baltimore: Johns Hopkins Press, 1897), 30–31; Cheape, 164–65; Harold Cox and John Meyers, "The Philadelphia Traction Monopoly and the Pennsylvania Constitution of 1874: The Prostitution of an Ideal," *Pennsylvania History* 35 (October 1968): 410–13; *Philadelphia Public Ledger,* February 17, 1930, p. 3, col. 4; Howard Gillette, Jr., "Corrupt and Contented: Philadelphia's Political Machine, 1865–1887" (Ph.D. diss., Yale University, 1970), 214; "Charles T. Yerkes, Jr., and Co.," December 2, 1881, R. G. Dun Co./PA 143/P. 359, R. G. Dun Company Credit Ledgers, Baker Library, Harvard University.

11. Peter A. B. Widener, *Without Drums* (New York: G. P. Putnam's Sons, 1940), 22; *Chicago Tribune,* August 28, 1887, p. 9, col. 7; Hendrick, 34; Widener, 19–20.

12. Widener, 24; *Philadelphia Public Ledger,* November 7, 1914, p. 1, col. 4; ibid., p. 4, cols. 1–2; *Town Topics* (New York), December 4, 1890, p. 9, col. 1; Widener, 15–18; *Chicago Tribune,* August 28, 1887, p. 9, col. 7; Widener, 23.

13. *Philadelphia Public Ledger*, November 8, 1903, p. 1, col. 4; ibid., p. 14, col. 6; Hendrick, 34–35; Josiah Granville Leach, *Genealogical and Biographical Memorials of the Reading, Howell, Yerkes, Watts, Latham, and Elkins Families* (Philadelphia: J. B. Lippincott Company, 1898), 255–56.

14. *Town Topics* (New York), August 13, 1903, p. 9, col. 2; *Chicago Tribune*, August 28, 1887, p. 10, col. 1; Chicago *Herald*, August 28, 1887, p. 1, col. 3; Hendrick, 35–36.

15. *Philadelphia Inquirer*, August 3, 1881, p. 2, col. 1; Kemble quoted in Robert Harrison, "The Hornets' Nest at Harrisburg: A Study of the Pennsylvania Legislature in the Late 1870s," *Pennsylvania Magazine of History and Biography* 103 (July 1979): 351.

16. Harrison, 350; Gillette, 208; ibid., 218; Edward Sculley Bradley, *Henry Charles Lea* (Philadelphia: University of Pennsylvania Press, 1931), 195; Cheape, 162–65; ibid., 48–49.

17. *Philadelphia Inquirer*, May 2, 1876, p. 2, col. 5; *Philadelphia Public Ledger*, February 17, 1930, p. 3, cols. 3–4; Cox and Meyers, 410–11; Cheape, 164–65; Gillette, 219–20; *Chicago Tribune*, May 12, 1895, p. 33, col. 1; *Philadelphia Inquirer*, February 11, 1880, p. 2, col. 6; *Philadelphia Public Ledger*, February 11, 1880, p. 1, col. 8; *Chicago Tribune*, August 28, 1887, p. 10, col. 1; Gillette, 220; *Philadelphia Inquirer*, September 30, 1880, p. 5, col. 4.

18. *The World* (New York), January 8, 1906, p. 2, col. 3; *Philadelphia Public Ledger*, December 31, 1905, p. 17, cols. 1–2; *Philadelphia Inquirer*, December 30, 1905, p. 2, cols. 1–2; *The World* (New York), January 4, 1906, p. 2, cols. 1–2; D. H. Louderback to Theodore Dreiser, March 8, 1913, Theodore Dreiser Papers, Van Pelt Library, University of Pennsylvania, Philadelphia, Pa.; *Daily Inter Ocean*, December 30, 1899, p. 12, cols. 1–2.

19. For an obituary of Mary Adelaide Moore's father, see *Philadelphia Public Ledger*, October 13, 1900, p. 2, col. 6; for Mary Moore's age, see 1860 U.S. Census (microfilm), 20th Ward, Philadelphia, Pa., National Archives—Great Lakes Region, Chicago, Ill.; *The Evening Bulletin* (Philadelphia), January 2, 1906, p. 2, col. 3; *New York Evening World*, June 14, 1913, p. 3, col. 1; *Chicago Record-Herald*, April 3, 1911, p. 1, col. 6; *New York American*, February 26, 1906, p. 2, cols. 3–5; Harper quoted in Donald Osterbrock, *Yerkes Observatory, 1892–1950* (Chicago: University of Chicago Press, 1997), p. 1.

Chapter 9. The Phoenix

1. Harper Leech and John Charles Carroll, *Armour and His Times* (New York: D. Appleton-Century Company, 1938), 106; Theodore Dreiser, *Sister Carrie* (New York: Viking Penguin, 1981), 16; Theodore Dreiser, "An Address to Caliban," *Esquire* (September 1934): 20; Frank Norris, *The Pit* (Columbus, Ohio: Charles E. Merrill Publishing Company, 1970), 62–63.

2. *The Lakeside Annual Directory of the City of Chicago 1883* (Chicago: The Chicago Directory Company, 1883), 4–5; *Chicago Tribune*, July 8, 1888, p. 17, col. 2; Bessie Louise Pierce, *As Others See Chicago* (Chicago: University of Chicago Press, 1933), 228.

3. Charles Dennis, *Eugene Field's Creative Years* (Garden City, N.Y.: Doubleday, Page and Company, 1924), 42; Pierce, 250–52; *Chicago Tribune*, September

23, 1887, p. 9, col. 3; Henry Fuller quoted in Donald Miller, *City of the Century* (New York: Simon and Schuster, 1996), 17; Norris, 23.

4. *Chicago Tribune,* November 10, 1895, p. 6, col. 2; Pierce, 251–52; Miller, 243; Bessie Louise Pierce, *A History of Chicago,* vol. 3 (New York: Alfred A. Knopf, 1957), 533; Hamlin Garland, *Rose of Dutcher's Coolly* (Lincoln: University of Nebraska, 1969), 181; *As Others See Chicago,* 276–77.

5. *Chicago Tribune,* July 8, 1888, p. 17, cols. 2–3; ibid., p. 17, col. 5; Pierce, 51; Thomas Lee Philpott, *The Slum and the Ghetto: Immigrants, Blacks and Reformers in Chicago, 1880–1930* (Belmont, Calif.: Wadsworth Publishing Company, 1991), 14–16; Agnes Sinclair Holbrook, "Map Notes and Comments," in *Hull-House Maps and Papers* (New York: Thomas Y. Crowell and Company, 1895), 5; Pierce, 55; *Chicago Tribune,* April 18, 1886, p. 26, col. 4; F. Cyril James, *The Growth of Chicago Banks,* vol. 1 (New York: Harper and Row, 1969), 488; Wayne Andrews, *Battle for Chicago* (New York: Harcourt, Brace and Company, 1946), 75–76; *As Others See Chicago,* 227; ibid., 251.

6. *History of Chicago,* vol. 3, 79; William Ferris, *The Grain Traders: The Story of the Chicago Board of Trade* (East Lansing: Michigan State University Press, 1988), 8–9; Norris, 40; *Chicago Tribune,* January 21, 1887, p. 1, col. 6.

7. Stead, 71; quoted in Stanley Buder, *Pullman: An Experiment in Industrial Order and Community Planning* (New York: Oxford University Press, 1967), 29; Arthur Meeker, *Chicago, With Love* (New York: Alfred A. Knopf, 1955), 34.

8. Frederic Cople Jaher, *The Urban Establishment* (Champaign: University of Illinois Press, 1982), 532; Meeker, 31–32; Poole, 240; *Chicago Daily News* (morning), September 30, 1891, p. 1, col. 6; "Charles T. Yerkes. Jr., and Company," June 23, 1884, R. G. Dun Co. PA 43/P. 359, R. G. Dun Credit Ledgers, Baker Library, Harvard University; *Chicago Daily News* (morning), June 11, 1886, p. 1, col. 2; ibid., June 21, 1886, p. 1, col. 1

9. *Philadelphia Public Ledger,* March 16, 1883, p. 1, col. 7; *New York Times,* November 9, 1886, p. 5, col. 4; *Chicago Tribune,* January 21, 1887, p. 1, col. 6; *Chicago Daily News,* June 17, 1886, p. 1, col. 2.

10. *Chicago Tribune,* May 13, 1883, p. 20, col. 3; ibid., April 18, 1886, p. 26, col. 4; *The World* (New York), January 8, 1906, p. 2, col. 3; *Evening World* (New York), June 14, 1913, p. 3, col. 1.

11. *Chicago Times-Herald,* August 25, 1895, p. 7, col. 1.

Chapter 10. Mass Transit

1. *Chicago Tribune,* August 19, 1880, p. 6, cols. 2–5; ibid., August 21, 1880, p. 7, col. 6; Chicago *Daily Inter Ocean,* December 26, 1897, p. 9, col. 1; *Chicago Tribune,* January 29, 1882, p. 5, col. 2; George Hilton, *The Cable Car in America* (Berkeley, Calif.: Howell-North Books, 1971), 15; Chicago *Daily Inter Ocean,* December 21, 1897, p. 7, col. 1.

2. *Chicago Daily News,* April 17, 1886, p. 5, col. 1; Chicago *Daily Inter Ocean,* December 26, 1897, p. 9, col. 1.

3. *Chicago Tribune,* December 17, 1885, p. 3, col. 1; Homer Harlan, "Charles Tyson Yerkes and the Chicago Transportation System" (Ph.D. diss., University of Chicago, 1975), 44–45; Slason Thompson, *Life of Eugene Field* (New York:

D. Appleton and Company, 1927), 99; Chicago *Daily Inter Ocean*, December 26, 1897, p. 9, col. 1.

4. Hilton, 21; ibid., 25; ibid., 15; ibid., 27; *Chicago Tribune*, January 29, 1882, p. 5, cols. 1–4.

5. Robert Ferguson, *Enigma: The Life of Knut Hamsun* (London: Hutchinson, 1987), 81–82; *Chicago Daily News*, April 17, 1886, p. 5, col. 1; Hilton, 149; Holmes quoted in ibid., 157.

6. Charles Cheape, *Moving the Masses: Urban Public Transit in New York, Boston, and Philadelphia 1880–1912* (Cambridge, Mass.: Harvard University Press, 1980), 164–69; *Philadelphia Inquirer*, October 25, 1881, p. 2, col. 4; Hilton, 251; *Chicago Tribune*, December 3, 1899, p. 1, cols. 1–2.

7. *Chicago Tribune*, April 27, 1884, p. 14, col. 3; ibid., May 5, 1884, p. 8, col. 2; ibid., August 9, 1885, p. 17, col. 1; ibid., June 24, 1884, p. 12, col. 2; ibid., June 30, 1884, p. 6, cols. 5–6.

8. Ibid., December 3, 1899, p. 8, cols. 5–6; ibid., August 17, 1887, p. 1, col. 4; ibid., April 8, 1886, p. 1, col. 3; *Chicago Times*, March 17, 1889, p. 9, col. 4.

9. *Chicago Tribune*, December 16, 1885, p. 2, col. 1; Chicago *Herald*, December 15, 1887, p. 3, col. 3; *Chicago Tribune*, March 8, 1889, p. 1, col. 4; ibid., March 12, 1892, p. 8, col. 1; Mark Hirsch, *William Whitney: Modern Warwick* (New York: Dodd, Mead and Company, 1948), 207–22; Burton Hendrick, "Great American Fortunes and Their Making: Street Railway Financiers," *McClure's Magazine* 30 (November 1907): 39–43; *Chicago Tribune*, March 27, 1886, p. 1, col. 4.

10. *Chicago Tribune*, May 12, 1895, p. 33, cols. 3–4; *Chicago Journal*, January 29, 1898, p. 4, col. 4; *Chicago Tribune*, August 3, 1890, p. 5, col. 4; ibid., May 12, 1895, p. 33, col. 4.

11. Ibid., September 8, 1888, p. 8, col. 1; ibid., April 4, 1886, p. 9, cols. 3–4; Bessie Louise Pierce, *A History of Chicago*, vol. 3 (Chicago: University of Chicago Press, 1957), 348–49; Ellis Paxson Oberholtzer, *A History of the United States Since the Civil War* III (New York: Macmillan Company, 1926), 144–45; Matthew Josephson, *The Politicos 1865–1896* (New York: Harcourt, Brace and Company, 1938), 135–36.

12. Clarence Barron, *More They Told Barron* (New York: Harper and Brothers, 1931), 125–28; *Chicago Tribune*, October 13, 1895, p. 36, cols. 1–2; ibid., April 4, 1886, p. 9, col. 4.

13. Ibid., October 27, 1901, p. 41, col. 3; a copy of the lease is found in North Chicago City Railway Company Corporate Record (February 18, 1859–July 26, 1899), 274–84, Chicago Surface Lines Collection, Chicago Historical Society; "extremely clever piece of financiering" quote from *Ninth Biennial Report of the Bureau of Labor Statistics of Illinois* (Springfield, Ill.: Phillips Brothers, 1897), 57; North Chicago City Railway Company Corporate Record, 268–69; *New York Times*, October 3, 1872, p. 12, col. 5.

Chapter 11. Tunnel Vision

1. *Chicago Tribune*, March 27, 1886, p. 1, col. 4.

2. John Tebbel, *An American Dynasty* (New York: Greenwood Press, 1968), 4; Ernest Poole, *Giants Gone* (New York: Whittlesey House, 1943), 56.

3. Lloyd Wendt, *Chicago Tribune: The Rise of a Great American Newspaper* (Chicago: Rand McNally and Company, 1979), 279; *Town Topics* (New York), April 22, 1897, p. 7, col. 2; *Chicago Tribune*, June 10, 1886, p. 2, col. 7.

4. *Chicago Tribune*, April 18, 1886, p. 26, cols. 3–4.

5. *Chicago Times*, June 10, 1886, p. 1, cols. 1–2; Carter Harrison, Jr., *Growing Up With Chicago* (Chicago: Ralph Fletcher Seymour, 1944), 268; *Chicago Tribune*, March 6, 1887, p. 20, cols. 1–4; ibid., October 27, 1890, p. 1, cols. 4–5; ibid., March 26, 1892, p. 2, cols. 2–3; ibid., November 2, 1886, p. 2, col. 3; Charles Faye to Victor Lawson, February 10, 1898, Victor Lawson Papers, Newberry Library, Chicago, Ill.; Harrison, 268.

6. Stephen Longstreet, *Chicago 1860–1919* (New York: David McKay Company, Inc., 1973), 201–3; Richard Lindberg, "The Evolution of an Evil Business," *Chicago History* 22 (July 1993): 38–53; Carter Harrison to Major Clifton Williamson, undated, Carter Harrison Papers, outgoing letters 1873–1921, Newberry Library.

7. *Chicago Record*, July 17, 1893, p. 1, col. 4; Carter Harrison, Jr., *Stormy Years: The Autobiography of Carter H. Harrison* (Indianapolis: Bobbs-Merrill Company, 1935), 15; ibid., 36; Claudius Johnson, *Carter Henry Harrison I* (Chicago: University of Chicago Press, 1928), 189; *Chicago Tribune*, March 29, 1885, p. 10, col. 1.

8. *Chicago Daily News* (morning), June 9, 1886, p. 1, col. 5; Chicago *Council Proceedings 1886–1887* (Chicago: J. McCann and Company, 1887), 111.

9. *Chicago Tribune*, June 8, 1888, p. 1, cols. 1–2; *Chicago Daily News* (morning), June 9, 1886, p. 1, col. 5; *Proceedings*, 126–31.

10. *Chicago Times*, June 9, 1886, p. 1, cols. 1–2.

11. Wayne Andrews, *Battle for Chicago* (New York: Harcourt, Brace and Company, 1996), 134; Donald Miller, *City of the Century* (New York: Simon and Schuster, 1996), 474–75; Mother Jones quoted in ibid., 475; Melville Stone, *Fifty Years a Journalist* (Garden City, N.Y.: Doubleday, Page and Company, 1921), 173; John J. McPhail, *Deadlines and Monkeyshines: The Fabled History of Chicago Journalism* (Englewood Cliffs, N.J.: Prentice, 1962), 70–71; Slason Thompson, *Life of Eugene Field* (New York: D. Appleton and Company, 1927), 109; Stone, 11; ibid., 16; ibid., 33–38; ibid., 50–53; ibid., 115–16; ibid., 118; Charles Faye to Victor Lawson, November 27, 1897, Victor Lawson Papers, Newberry Library; *Chicago Daily News* (morning), June 9, 1886, p. 1, cols. 1–4.

12. Ibid., June 10, 1886, p. 1, cols. 3–4; Stone, 118; *Chicago Journal*, January 29, 1898, p. 6, col. 1.

13. *Chicago Daily News* (morning), June 16, 1886, p. 1, col. 3; Chicago *Herald*, December 18, 1889, p. 1, col. 3; *Chicago Tribune*, June 10, 1886, p. 1, cols. 5–6; Johnson, 83; *Chicago Tribune*, April 26, 1888, p. 4, col. 3; DeLancey Louderback to Theodore Dreiser, March 8, 1913, Theodore Dreiser Papers, University of Pennsylvania, Philadelphia, Pa.

14. Frank J. Piehl, "Our Forgotten Streetcar Tunnels," *Chicago History* 4 (Fall 1975): 133–35; Robert David Weber, "Rationalizers and Reformers: Chicago Local Transportation in the Nineteenth Century" (Ph.D. diss., University of Wisconsin, 1971), 284; *Chicago Tribune*, May 27, 1884, p. 8, col. 2; Chicago *Herald*, June 20, 1886, p. 5, cols. 3–4; *Chicago Journal*, January 29, 1898, p. 6, col. 5.

15. *Chicago Tribune*, April 8, 1886, p. 1, col. 3; *Chicago Daily News* (morning), June 9, 1886, p. 4, col. 1; *Chicago Times*, June 10, 1886, p. 1, cols. 1–2.

16. *Proceedings*, 163; *Chicago Tribune*, June 15, 1886, p. 1, cols. 3–4; *Chicago Daily News* (morning), June 21, 1886, p. 1, col. 1; *Town Topics* (New York), June 17, 1897, p. 15, col. 2; *Daily Inter Ocean*, June 11, 1886, p. 5, col. 4; *Chicago Tribune*, June 6, 1886, p. 9, cols. 5–6; *Chicago Daily News* (morning), June 16, 1886, p. 4, col. 2; ibid., June 19, 1886, p. 2, col. 2.

17. *Proceedings*, 194–97; *Chicago Tribune*, June 30, 1886, p. 4, col. 3; ibid., July 7, 1886, p. 1, cols. 1–2; *Chicago Daily News* (morning), July 7, 1886, p. 1, cols. 1–3; *Daily Inter Ocean*, March 18, 1898, p. 7, col. 2; Joel Tarr, "William Kent to Lincoln Steffens: Origins of Progressive Reform in Chicago," *Mid-America: An Historical Quarterly* 47 (1965): 56.

18. *Proceedings*, 199–201; *Chicago Daily News* (morning), July 13, 1886, p. 1, cols. 1–3; *Chicago Tribune*, March 3, 1891, p. 2, col. 5; *Chicago Tribune*, July 20, 1886, p. 1, col. 5.

Chapter 12. Getting a Grip

1. Thomas Lawson, *Frenzied Finance* (New York: Greenwood Press, 1968), 33; David M. Young, *Chicago Transit: An Illustrated History* (DeKalb: Northern Illinois University Press, 1998), 59 60; for Yerkes's early Philadelphia financiering, see Testimony of Joseph Gillingham, May 9, 1873, In the Matter of Charles T. Yerkes, Jr. Bankrupt, U.S. District Court, Eastern District of Pennsylvania, National Archives—Mid-Atlantic Branch, Philadelphia, Pa.; Milo Roy Maltbie, "The Street Railways of Chicago," *Municipal Affairs* (1901): 464.

2. Robert David Weber, "Rationalizers and Reformers," (Ph.D. diss., University of Wisconsin-Madison, 1971), 290–92; *Chicago Daily News* (morning), May 7, 1887, p. 5, col. 3; ibid., May 19, 1887, p. 6, col. 4.

3. *The North Chicago Street Railroad Company and Its Lines* (1889 pamphlet), 6; Chicago *Herald*, November 6, 1887, p. 9, cols. 4–6; *Philadelphia Inquirer*, October 25, 1881, p. 2, col. 4; Chicago *Herald*, March 25, 1888, p. 32, cols. 1–2.

4. *Chicago Tribune*, March 27, 1888, p. 2, col. 2; *Chicago Daily News* (morning), March 27, 1888, p. 1, col. 4.

5. Donald Miller, *City of the Century* (New York: Simon and Schuster, 1996), 309; Harold Mayer and Richard Wade, *Chicago: Growth of a Metropolis* (Chicago: University of Chicago Press, 1969), 128; Miller, 319; Mayer and Wade, 215.

6. *Chicago Daily News* (morning), August 27, 1889, p. 2, col. 6; George Hilton, *The Cable Car in America* (Berkeley, Calif.: Howell-North Books, 1971), 241; Chicago *Herald*, August 31, 1887, p. 3, col. 5; *Chicago Daily News* (morning), September 5, 1889, p. 1, col. 3; Hilton, 66–67.

7. Chicago *Herald*, August 31, 1887, p. 3, cols. 4–5; Hilton, 80; *Chicago Daily News* (morning), September 5, 1889, p. 1, col. 3; Henry Fuller, *The Cliff-Dwellers* (New York: Harper and Brothers, 1893), 14; *Chicago Daily News* (morning), July 2, 1888, p. 1, col. 8.

8. *Chicago Record*, November 28, 1894, p. 4, col. 7; *Chicago Journal*, January 29, 1898, p. 6, col. 5; C. B. Fairchild, *Street Railways: Their Construction, Operation and Maintenance* (New York: Street Railway Publishing Company, 1892), 88; History of Lakeview, Document #14, Chicago Community Documents, vol. 3, part 1, Chicago Historical Society; *Chicago Tribune*, March 8, 1889, p. 1, col. 4;

Hilton, 80; *The North Chicago Street Railroad Company and Its Lines,* 12–13; ibid., 8.

9. *Chicago Daily News* (evening), March 27, 1889, p. 1, col. 5; ibid., March 21, 1889, p. 2, col. 1.

10. Emily Clark and Patrick Ashley, "The Merchant Prince of Cornville," *Chicago History* 21 (December 1992): 4–19; *A History of the Yerkes System of Street Railways in the City of Chicago* (1897 pamphlet); *Daily Inter Ocean,* February 6, 1898, part 2, p. 2, col. 3.

11. Charles Yerkes vs. Samuel Gross, filed August 17, 1899, Case Number 200798, Cook County Archives, Chicago, Ill.; History of Hamlin Park, Document #2, Chicago Community Documents, vol. 3, part 1, Chicago Historical Society; Young, 52; *Chicago Tribune,* May 6, 1888, p. 18, col. 5; quoted in Mayer and Wade, 138.

12. *Chicago Times,* August 6, 1887, p. 5, col. 7; Chicago *Herald,* August 11, 1887, p. 2, col. 3.

13. Chicago *Herald,* August 28, 1887, p. 1, col. 3; ibid., August 10, 1887, p. 3, col. 5; ibid., August 26, 1887, p. 2, col. 3; ibid., August 30, 1887, p. 3, cols. 3–4; ibid., September 13, 1887, p. 3, col. 5; ibid., August 24, 1887, p. 3, col. 5; ibid., November 1, 1887, p. 1, col. 7.

14. Chicago *Herald,* September 1, 1887, p. 3, col. 4; ibid., August 31, 1887, p. 3, cols. 4–5; *Chicago Times,* May 27, 1894, p. 12, col. 2; *Chicago Tribune,* March 8, 1889, p. 1, col. 4.

15. Chicago *Herald,* December 5, 1887, p. 1, col. 1; ibid., August 11, 1887, p. 2, col. 3; *Chicago Times,* November 13, 1887, p. 13, col. 6; Maltbie, 474–79; *Chicago Tribune,* July 17, 1890, p. 8, col. 2; *Daily Inter Ocean,* June 3, 1899, p. 2, col. 2.

Chapter 13. Strike!

1. Robert Ferguson, *Enigma: The Life of Knut Hamsun* (London: Hutchinson, 1987), 81–82; *Chicago Tribune,* April 8, 1894, p. 35, col. 2; Ferguson, 83–85; *Chicago Tribune,* January 20, 1888, p. 8, col. 4; Holmes quoted in George Hilton, *The Cable Car in America* (Berkeley, Calif.: Howell-North Books, 1971), 157.

2. *Chicago Tribune,* April 8, 1894, p. 35, col. 4; Ferguson, 83; George T. Bryant, "The Gripman Wore a Sheepskin Coat," *Chicago History* 1 (Spring 1970): 50; *Chicago Tribune,* March 4, 1888, p. 25, col. 4; ibid., April 8, 1894, p. 35, cols. 1–2.

3. *Chicago Daily News* (evening), March 27, 1889, p. 1, col. 5; *Chicago Daily News* (morning), July 3, 1888, p. 6, col. 1; John R. Commons, *History of Labour in the United States,* vol. 2 (New York: Macmillan Company, 1918), 197–99; ibid., 413–22; Richard Oestreicher, "Terence Powderly, the Knights of Labor, and Artisanal Republicanism," in *Labor Leaders in America,* ed. Melvyn Dubofsky and Warren Van Tine (Urbana: University of Illinois Press, 1987), 45–49.

4. George Schilling to Terence Powderly, April 16, 1888, George Schilling Letterbooks (vol. 1), George Schilling Papers, University of Chicago Department of Special Collections; Schilling quoted in Paul Avrich, *The Haymarket Tragedy* (Princeton, N.J.: Princeton University Press, 1984), 36; *Chicago Tribune,* July 8, 1888, p. 17, col. 5; ibid., April 9, 1888, p. 6, col. 2; Eugene Staley, *History of the Illinois State Federation of Labor* (Chicago: University of Chicago Press, 1930), 97–98; Avrich, 21.

5. *Chicago Tribune*, October 5, 1888, p. 1, cols. 1–2; ibid., July 22, 1888, p. 10, col. 4.

6. *Chicago Daily News* (morning), September 27, 1888, p. 1, col. 6; Homer Harlan, "Charles Tyson Yerkes and the Chicago Transportation System" (Ph.D. diss., University of Chicago, 1975), 54; *Chicago Tribune*, October 1, 1888, p. 1, cols. 3–4.

7. *Chicago Tribune*, July 27, 1890, p. 5, col. 1; *Chicago Evening Post*, July 26, 1890, p. 1, col. 5; *Chicago Daily News* (morning), October 4, 1888, p. 1, col. 6; ibid., October 6, 1888, p. 1, col. 1.; ibid., October 28, 1888, p. 2, col. 7.

8. *Chicago Daily News* (morning), October 6, 1888, p. 1, cols. 1–4; *Chicago Tribune*, October 6, 1888, p. 1, cols. 1–7; ibid., October 7, 1888, p. 9, cols. 1–7; *Real Estate and Building Journal* quoted in Harlan, 85–86; *Chicago Herald*, October 12, 1888, p. 2, col. 3.

9. *Chicago Journal*, January 29, 1898, p. 6, col. 3; *Chicago Daily News* (morning), October 9, 1888, p. 1, col. 2; *Chicago Tribune*, October 9, 1888, p. 1, col. 2; John A. Roche biography, John A. Roche Collection, Chicago Historical Society; *Chicago Daily News* (morning), October 8, 1888, p. 1, col. 3.

10. *Chicago Daily News* (morning), October 9, 1888, p. 1, col. 2; *Chicago Tribune*, October 9, 1888, p. 1, cols. 2–5; *Chicago Mail*, October 8, 1888, p. 1, cols. 1–2; *Chicago Tribune*, October 28, 1888, p. 2, col. 7.

11. *Chicago Herald*, October 10, 1888, p. 2, col. 3; *Chicago Daily News* (morning), October 10, 1888, p. 1, cols. 1–5.

12. *Chicago Daily News* (morning), October 11, 1888, p. 1, cols. 1–2; *Chicago Tribune*, October 11, 1888, p. 2, col. 1; *Chicago Daily News*, October 12, 1888, p. 1, col. 1.

13. George Schilling to Terence Powderly, October 8, 1888, microfilm reel 27, Terence Powderly Papers, Northern Illinois University, DeKalb, Ill.; *Chicago Times*, October 12, 1888, p. 2, col. 2; *Chicago Tribune*, October 8, 1888, p. 1, cols. 3–6.

14. Avrich, 221, ibid., 267; Michael Schaack, *Anarchy and Anarchists* (Chicago: F. J. Schulte and Company, 1889), 688; *Chicago Daily News* (morning), October 12, 1888, p. 1, col. 1; ibid., October 15, 1888, p. 1, col. 5; *Chicago Tribune*, October 13, 1888, p. 1, col. 5; *Chicago Daily News* (morning), October 31, 1888, p. 4, col. 2; *Chicago Mail*, October 11, 1888, p. 1, col. 7.

15. *Chicago Daily News* (morning), October 13, 1888, p. 1, cols. 1–3; *Chicago Tribune*, October 13, 1888, p. 1, col. 5; ibid., October 14, 1888, p. 10, col. 3.

16. Mayor John Roche to Charles T. Yerkes, October 13, 1888, John Roche Letterbook 1887–88, John Roche Collection, Chicago Historical Society; *Chicago Herald*, March 25, 1889, p. 1, col. 3.

17. *Chicago Herald*, October 15, 1888, p. 1, cols. 1–6; *Chicago Tribune*, October 15, 1888, p. 1, cols. 4–7.

18. *Chicago Tribune*, October 16, 1888, p. 1, cols. 5–6; ibid., October 17, 1888, p. 1, col. 3; ibid., October 18, 1888, p. 6, col. 3; *Chicago Daily News* (evening), January 22, 1889, p. 1, col. 7; *Chicago Daily News* (morning), September 22, 1890, p. 2, col. 3; John Harlan et al., *Report of the Special Committee of the City Council of Chicago on Street Railway Franchises and Operations of March 28, 1898* (Chicago: John F. Higgins, 1898), 77–79; *Chicago Tribune*, October 28, 1888, p. 13, cols. 3–4.

Chapter 14. Reaching for the Stars

1. Richard Storr, *Harper's University: The Beginnings* (Chicago: University of Chicago Press, 1966), 32–35; ibid., 47; Paul Shorey, "William Rainey Harper," in *Dictionary of American Biography*, vol. 8, ed. Dumas Malone (New York: Charles Scribner's Sons, 1932), 289; Storr, 74.

2. William Rainey Harper to Charles Hutchinson, January 30, 1892, University of Chicago Presidents' Papers 1889–1925, Box 65, Folder 11, University of Chicago Department of Special Collections; Thomas Goodspeed, *The University of Chicago Biographical Sketches*, vol. 1 (Chicago: University of Chicago Press, 1922), 95–96; William Rainey Harper to Frederick T. Gates, n.d., University of Chicago Presidents' Papers 1889–1925, Box 70, Folder 48, University of Chicago Department of Special Collections; Charles Yerkes to Herman Kohlsaat, April 1, 1892, ibid., Box 70, Folder 47.

3. Helen Wright, *Explorer of the Universe* (New York: E. P. Dutton and Company, Inc., 1966), 16; ibid., 27; ibid., 30; Donald Osterbrock, *Yerkes Observatory, 1892–1950* (Chicago: University of Chicago Press, 1997), 3; Donald Miller, *City of the Century* (New York: Simon and Schuster, 1996), 311; Wright, 47.

4. Osterbrock, 4–5; Wright, 64–69; Henry C. King, *The History of the Telescope* (New York: Dover Publications, 1955), 320–22; Wright, 84.

5. Wright, 75–76; Hale quoted in Pamela Hodgson, "The Scoundrel and the Scientist," *Chicago History* 19 (Fall–Winter 1990–91): 85.

6. Wright, 93–94; George Hale to William Rainey Harper, September 23, 1892, University of Chicago Presidents' Papers 1889–1925, Box 37, Folder 1, University of Chicago Department of Special Collections; George Hale, *The Legacy of George Ellery Hale*, ed. Helen Wright, Joan Warnow, and Charles Weiner (Cambridge, Mass.: MIT Press, 1972), 19; Storr, 86.

7. Wright, 94–98; Osterbrock, 1; *Daily Inter Ocean*, October 12, 1892, p. 1, col. 7; *Chicago News Record*, October 12, 1892, p. 3, col. 3; *Chicago Tribune*, October 12, 1892, p. 1, col. 1; Hale quoted in Wright, 95–96; George E. Hale to William Rainey Harper, September 23, 1892, University of Chicago Presidents' Papers 1889–1925, Box 37, Folder 1, University of Chicago Department of Special Collections.

8. Hale to Harper, September 23, 1892, University of Chicago Presidents' Papers 1889–1925, Box 37, Folder 1, University of Chicago Department of Special Collections; Hale, 193; ibid., 19; *Daily Inter Ocean*, October 12, 1892, p. 1, col. 7; ibid., p. 7, col. 5; *Chicago Evening Journal*, July 31, 1890, p. 5, col. 5; *Chicago Evening Post*, October 11, 1892, p. 1, col. 1.

9. Wright, 98; *Chicago Evening Post*, October 11, 1892, p. 1, col. 2; *Chicago Tribune*, October 13, 1892, p. 9, col. 1; *Chicago Daily Globe*, October 12, 1892, p. 1, col. 5; Yerkes quoted in Hodgson, 88.

10. *Chicago Evening Post*, October 11, 1892, p. 1, col. 1; *Daily Inter Ocean*, October 13, 1892, p. 4, col. 1; Edwin Frost, *An Astronomer's Life* (Boston: Houghton Mifflin Company, 1933), 97–98.

11. *The World* (New York), January 7, 1906, p. 3, col. 3; *Chicago Sunday American*, January 21, 1906, p. 1, col. 2; Wright, 99–101; George Hale to William Rainey Harper, January 15, 1893, Correspondence of the Secretary of the University of Chicago Board of Trustees, Box 1, Folder 3, University of Chicago Department of

Special Collections; Brashear quoted in Hodgson, 83; ibid., 92; George Hale to William Rainey Harper, January 9, 1894, University of Chicago Presidents' Papers 1889–1925, Box 37, Folder 1, University of Chicago Department of Special Collections.

12. Wright, 132; George E. Hale, "The Dedication of the Yerkes Observatory," *Astrophysical Journal* 6 (November 1897): 358–59; Wright, 51.

13. Charles Yerkes to William Rainey Harper, December 5, 1892, University of Chicago Presidents' Papers 1889–1925, Box 70, Folder 48, University of Chicago Department of Special Collections; Warner and Swasey to William Rainey Harper, January 4, 1893, Correspondence of the Secretary of the University of Chicago Board of Trustees, Box 1, Folder 3; *Chicago Tribune,* March 30, 1893, p. 10, col. 4; University of Chicago Board of Trustees *Minutes* 1890–96, 85, University of Chicago Department of Special Collections; *The Legacy of George Hale,* 20; Charles Yerkes to William Rainey Harper, January 19, 1893, Correspondence of the Secretary of the University of Chicago Board of Trustees, Box 1, Folder 3.

14. Warner and Swasey to William Rainey Harper, March 25, 1893, Correspondence of the Secretary of the University of Chicago Board of Trustees, Box 1, Folder 3; George E. Hale, "The Yerkes Observatory of the University of Chicago: 1) Selection of the Site," *Astrophysical Journal* 5 (March 1897): 172; Charles Yerkes to William Rainey Harper, February 4, 1893, Correspondence of the Secretary of the University of Chicago Board of Trustees, Box 1, Folder 3; Osterbrock, 15; University of Chicago Board of Trustees *Minutes* 1890–96, 98.

15. John Johnston to William Rainey Harper, February 24, 1893, Correspondence of the Secretary of the University of Chicago Board of Trustees, Box 1, Folder 3; Warren Furbeck to William Rainey Harper, March 15, 1893, ibid; George E. Hale, "The Yerkes Observatory of the University of Chicago: 4) The Forty-Inch Telescope, Dome and Rising-Floor," *Astrophysical Journal* 6 (June 1897): 41–42; *Chicago Tribune,* August 24, 1893, p. 2, col. 4.

Chapter 15. Crashing the Party

1. William Dean Howells quoted in James Gilbert, *Perfect Cities* (Chicago: University of Chicago Press, 1991), 100; Francis Lederer, II, "Competition for the World's Columbian Exposition: The Chicago Campaign," *Journal of the Illinois State Historical Society* 65 (Winter 1972): 382–83; *Chicago Tribune,* July 21, 1889, p. 4, col. 2; ibid., August 23, 1889, p. 4, col. 1.

2. Lederer, 385; *Chicago Tribune,* September 29, 1889, p. 12, col. 7; *Daily Inter Ocean,* September 13, 1889, p. 8, cols. 1–2.

3. *Chicago Tribune,* November 27, 1892, p. 30, cols. 5–6; Lederer, 393; *Chicago Daily News* (morning), April 5, 1890, p. 1, col. 1; *Chicago Tribune,* April 5, 1890, p. 1, col. 1; *Chicago Times,* April 5, 1890, p. 1, col. 2; *Daily Inter Ocean,* April 5, 1890, p. 2, col. 1.

4. *Chicago Times,* April 5, 1890, p. 1, col. 2; *Daily Inter Ocean,* April 5, 1890, p. 1, col. 7; *Chicago Daily News* (morning), April 5, 1890, p. 1, col. 1.

5. Lyman Gage, *Memoirs of Lyman Gage* (New York: House of Field, Inc., 1937), 76; Charles Dennis, *Victor Lawson: His Time and His Work* (Chicago: University of Chicago Press, 1935), 161; *Chicago Daily News* (morning), April 5, 1890, p. 1, col. 3.

6. Stephen Longstreet, *Chicago 1860–1919* (New York: David McKay Company, Inc., 1973), 55; *Chicago Tribune*, September 13, 1889, p. 5, col. 5.

7. Frank and Marguerite Cassell, "The White City in Peril: Leadership and the World's Columbian Exposition," *Chicago History* 12 (Summer 1983): 15–17; World's Columbian Exposition Board of Directors Minutes, June 28, 1890, Records of the World's Columbian Exposition vol. 43, 76–79, Chicago Historical Society; *Chicago Evening Journal*, April 5, 1890, p. 2, col. 2.

8. World's Columbian Exposition Board of Directors Minutes, July 1, 1890, Records of the World's Columbian Exposition vol. 43, 80–82, Chicago Historical Society; *Chicago Evening Journal*, July 1, 1890, p. 1, cols. 2–3.

9. Cassell, 23–24; *Chicago Tribune*, July 29, 1890, p. 1, col. 3; ibid., July 30, 1890, p. 1, col. 2; ibid., p. 5, col. 1.

10. *Chicago Tribune*, August 20, 1890, p. 2, cols. 1–5; ibid., May 30, 1890, p. 1, col. 1; ibid., February 21, 1891, p. 1, cols. 1–2; ibid., March 28, 1891, p. 2, cols. 3–4; Ferdinand Peck to James W. Ellsworth, April 15, 1891, Box 7, Folder 48, James W. Ellsworth Collection, World's Columbian Exposition Collection, Chicago Public Library.

11. *Chicago Tribune*, March 29, 1891, p. 2, col. 7; Edwin Lefevre, "What Availeth It," *Everybody's Magazine* 24 (June 1911): 839; *Chicago Tribune*, October 23, 1891, p. 1, col. 5.

12. Harriet Monroe, *A Poet's Life* (New York: Macmillan Company, 1938), 117–18; ibid., 129; Thomas Hines, *Burnham of Chicago* (New York: Oxford University Press, 1974), 110; David Burg, *Chicago's White City of 1893* (Lexington: University Press of Kentucky, 1976), 100–109; *Chicago Tribune*, October 22, 1892, p. 1, col. 1; ibid., p. 13, col. 3.

13. Monroe, 130–31; Hines, 111–16; Henry Adams, *The Education of Henry Adams* (Boston: Houghton Mifflin Company, 1973), 339; Theodore Dreiser, *Newspaper Days* (Philadelphia: University of Pennsylvania Press, 1991), 308–9; Bessie Louise Pierce, *As Others See Chicago* (Chicago: University of Chicago Press, 1933), 348; ibid., *A History of Chicago*, vol. 3 (Chicago: University of Chicago Press, 1957), 511.

14. John Allwood, *The Great Exhibitions* (London: Studio Vista, 1977), 182; *Chicago Tribune*, January 10, 1894, p. 3, cols. 2–3; *Street and Electric Railways 1902: U.S. Bureau of Census Special Report* (Washington: U.S. Government Printing Office, 1905), 33–34; *Daily Inter Ocean*, August 14, 1898, p. 30, cols. 1–3; *Chicago Tribune*, August 22, 1890, p. 3, col. 3; Harry Keegan, History of Lakeview, Document 20, Chicago Community Documents, Chicago Historical Society; Donald Miller, *City of the Century* (New York: Simon and Schuster, 1996), 496–97; Perry Duis, *Challenging Chicago* (Urbana-Champaign: University of Illinois Press, 1998), 213–15; Lloyd Lewis and Henry Justin Smith, *Chicago: The History of Its Reputation* (New York: Harcourt, Brace and Company, 1929), 178; Carter Harrison, Jr., *Stormy Years* (Indianapolis: Bobbs-Merrill Company, 1935), 36; *Chicago Tribune*, January 20, 1893, p. 11, col. 4; *Chicago Times*, October 30, 1893, p. 1, col. 3.

15. Ray Stannard Baker, *American Chronicle* (New York: Charles Scribner's Sons, 1945), 31; Barbara Tuchman, *The Proud Tower* (New York: Bantam Books, 1966), 286; Dennis Downey, "William Stead and Chicago: A Victorian Jeremiah in the Windy City," *Mid-America* 68 (October 1986): 154; Baker, 1.

16. Melville Stone, *Fifty Years a Journalist* (Garden City, N.Y.: Doubleday, Page and Company, 1921), 201; Baker, 27; Joseph O. Baylen, "A Victorian's 'Crusade' in Chicago, 1893–1894," *Journal of American History* 51 (December 1964): 424; Downey, 159–60.

17. *Chicago Evening Post,* June 13, 1891, p. 1, col. 1; Stone, 201–2; William Stead to Melville Stone, January 12, 1894, Melville Stone Papers, Newberry Library, Chicago.

18. *Chicago Tribune,* January 17, 1894, p. 7, col. 5; Baker, 30.

19. William Stead, *If Christ Came to Chicago* (Chicago: Laird and Lee, 1894), 107–10.

20. Baker, 31; Downey, 166.

Chapter 16. Current Events

1. Harold L. Platt, *The Electric City* (Chicago: University of Chicago Press, 1991), 59–65; Frank Rowsome, Jr., *Trolley Car Treasury* (New York: Bonanza Books, 1956), 65–68; Harold Passer, *The Electrical Manufacturers 1875–1900* (Cambridge, Mass.: Harvard University Press, 1953), 230–32; Rowsome, 80.

2. Rowsome, 81–83; John Anderson Miller, *Fares, Please!* (New York: D. Appleton-Century Company, 1941), 62–63; Paul Israel, *Edison: A Life of Invention* (New York: John Wiley and Sons, 1998), 375; George W. Hilton and John F. Due, *The Electric Interurban Railways in America* (Stanford, Calif.: Stanford University Press, 1960), 6–7; David Nye, *Electrifying America* (Cambridge, Mass.: MIT Press, 1990), 88–89; Passer, 234.

3. Rowsome, 84–88; Frank J. Sprague, "Birth of the Electric Railway," *Transit Journal* 78 (September 15, 1934): 317–21; Holmes quoted in *Chicago Tribune,* August 17, 1890, p. 26, col. 1.

4. *Street and Electric Railways* (New York: Arno Press, 1976), 5; *Chicago Tribune,* February 27, 1891, p. 7, col. 4; Testimony of Edmund Cummings, November 2, 1906, Transcript of Testimony, 1810–12, North and West Chicago Street Railroad Companies vs. Chicago Consolidated Traction Company, Case Number 27508, U.S. Circuit Court, Northern District of Illinois, Eastern Division, National Archives—Great Lakes Region, Chicago, Ill.

5. *Chicago Tribune,* January 21, 1894, p. 1, col. 7; George Hilton, *The Cable Car in America* (Berkeley, Calif.: Howell-North Books, 1971), 155–56; John McKay, *Tramways and Trolleys* (Princeton, N.J.: Princeton University Press, 1976), 51–67.

6. *Chicago Tribune,* November 29, 1893, p. 6, col. 4; ibid., January 24, 1899, p. 5, col. 1.

7. Passer, 225–30; *Chicago Tribune,* April 23, 1892, p. 1, col. 1; ibid., April 15, 1892, p. 1, col. 1; ibid., April 19, 1892, p. 9, col. 3; *Chicago Times,* June 19, 1892, p. 21, col. 3; *Chicago Tribune,* June 1, 1892, p. 1, col. 1; ibid., January 24, 1899, p. 5, col. 1.

8. *Chicago Tribune,* November 23, 1890, p. 5, cols. 2–3; ibid., January 27, 1892, p. 9, col. 6; ibid., March 9, 1892, p. 3, col. 2; ibid., March 6, 1890, p. 3, col. 1; ibid., May 31, 1890, p. 3, cols. 1–2; ibid., June 3, 1890, p. 3, col. 3; ibid., July 24, 1893, p. 10, col. 1; *Chicago Evening Post,* November 23, 1893, p. 1, col. 7; ibid., December 7, 1893, p. 3, col. 5.

9. *Electric Railway Journal,* April 18, 1914, p. 901, cols. 1–2; *Chicago Tribune,* April 11, 1914, p. 3, col. 5; *Chicago Evening Post,* January 8, 1894, p. 1, cols. 5–6.

10. Testimony of DeLancey Louderback, July 3, 1906, Transcript of Testimony, 551–52, North and West Chicago Street Railroad Companies vs. Chicago Consolidated Traction Company, U.S. Circuit Court, Northern District of Illinois, Eastern Division, National Archives—Great Lakes Region, Chicago, Ill.; *The Economist* (Chicago) *Street Railway Supplement* (1896): 38; *Chicago Tribune,* October 10, 1894, p. 9, cols. 1–2; Louderback Testimony, 547–55.

11. *Chicago Tribune,* August 11, 1895, p. 31, col. 2; Louderback Testimony, 557–94.

12. *Chicago Tribune,* May 19, 1895, p. 44, col. 3; State of Illinois, Bureau of Labor Statistics, *Ninth Biennial Report, 1896* (Springfield, 1896), 59; *Chicago Tribune,* August 11, 1895, p. 31, col. 2; ibid., October 10, 1894, p. 9, cols. 1–2.

13. *Chicago Tribune,* April 2, 1895, p. 9, col. 1; *Ninth Biennial Report, 1896,* 86.

14. *Chicago Tribune,* May 19, 1895, p. 44, col. 5; ibid., May 4, 1894, p. 4, col. 4; ibid., May 25, 1894, p. 4, col. 4; *Western Electrician,* January 19, 1901, p. 47, col. 2; *Chicago Journal,* March 29, 1895, p. 1, col. 3; *Western Electrician,* January 6, 1900, p. 12, col. 1.

15. Harold Mayer and Richard Wade, *Chicago: Growth of a Metropolis* (Chicago: University of Chicago Press, 1969), 206–8; *Chicago Tribune,* May 19, 1895, p. 44, col. 1; ibid., July 13, 1895, p. 4, col. 4; ibid., August 19, 1895, p. 2, col. 7; *Street Railway Review,* October 15, 1899, 718–19; Joseph Schumpeter, *Can Capitalism Survive?* (New York: Harper Colophon Books, 1978), x; ibid., 22–23; *Daily Inter Ocean,* December 12, 1897, p. 44, cols. 2–3.

Chapter 17. An Elevating Prospect

1. Testimony of DeLancey Louderback, July 3, 1906, Transcript of Testimony, 633, North and West Chicago Street Railroad Companies vs. Chicago Consolidated Traction Company, U.S. Circuit Court, Northern District of Illinois, Eastern Division, National Archives—Great Lakes Region, Chicago, Ill.; Brian J. Cudahy, *Cash, Tokens, and Transfers: A History of Urban Mass Transit in North America* (New York: Fordham University Press, 1990), 67.

2. C. B. Fairchild, *Street Railways: Their Construction, Operation and Maintenance* (New York: Street Railway Publishing Company, 1892), 191.

3. *Chicago Tribune,* April 12, 1891, p. 9, col. 2; ibid., July 11, 1889, p. 1, col. 1.

4. Brian Cudahy, *Destination: Loop* (Brattleboro, Vt.: The Stephen Greene Press, 1982), 19–20; *Chicago Tribune,* April 12, 1891, p. 9, col. 2.

5. *Destination: Loop,* 10–11; Bruce Moffat, *The 'L': The Development of Chicago's Rapid Transit System, 1888–1932* (Chicago: Central Electric Railfans' Association, 1995), 21–25.

6. Ibid., 56; John Anderson Miller, *Fares, Please!* (New York: D. Appleton-Century Company, 1941), 77; *Chicago Tribune,* December 30, 1888, p. 10, col. 1.

7. Ibid.; Moffat, 57; Benjamin Butler to John Elliott, November 3, 1890, Benjamin Butler Collection, Chicago Historical Society.

8. *Chicago Tribune,* February 16, 1892, p. 1, col. 5; ibid., December 30, 1892, p. 1, col. 6; ibid., February 2, 1893, p. 7, col. 5.

9. Ibid., July 24, 1892, p. 1, col. 2.

10. Ibid., March 2, 1890, p. 3, col. 2; ibid., March 8, 1890, p. 3, col. 1; ibid., October 6, 1893, p. 1, col. 1; ibid., October 25, 1893, p. 3, col. 4; *Chicago Evening Post,* October 25, 1893, p. 1, col. 1.

11. *Chicago Tribune,* December 30, 1887, p. 6, col. 7; *Chicago Globe,* May 4, 1893, clipping found in Ambler Scrapbooks, Chicago Historical Society.

12. *Chicago Tribune,* July 24, 1891, p. 2, col. 7; ibid., August 23, 1891, p. 3, col. 2; ibid., February 16, 1894, p. 4, col. 5.

13. *Street Railway Journal,* October 8, 1904, 541–42, cols. 1–2; *Western Electrician,* May 25, 1895, p. 252, col. 1; ibid., April 17, 1897, p. 217, col. 1; Moffat, 14–19; *Western Electrician,* January 6, 1900, p. 12, col. 1.

14. *Destination: Loop,* 24; *Chicago Tribune,* November 15, 1894, p. 12, cols. 3–4.

15. Ibid., September 6, 1894, p. 4, col. 7; *Daily Inter Ocean,* September 25, 1894, p. 26, col. 1.

16. *Chicago Evening Post,* June 13, 1894, p. 1, col. 1.

17. *Chicago Tribune,* May 25, 1894, p. 12, col. 2.

18. Moffat, 167; *Chicago Tribune,* September 22, 1892, p. 2, col. 7; ibid., May 16, 1894, p. 8, col. 1; ibid., May 29, 1894, p. 8, col. 1.

19. *Chicago Evening Post,* June 5, 1894, p. 1, col. 3; *Chicago Tribune,* May 26, 1894, p. 1, col. 5.

20. *Chicago Herald,* June 8, 1894, p. 1, cols. 5–6.

21. *Chicago Tribune,* July 4, 1894, p. 4, col. 1; ibid., April 9, 1895, p. 1, cols. 3–4; *Daily Inter Ocean,* July 4, 1894, p. 8, col. 1; *Street Railway Gazette,* July 7, 1894, p. 1; Ziegler vs. Lake Street Elevated Railroad Company et al., *Federal Reporter* 69 (September–November 1895): 176–84.

22. *Street Railway Gazette,* July 28, 1894, p. 38; *Chicago Tribune,* November 1, 1894, p. 4, col. 4; *New York World,* January 8, 1906, p. 2, col. 3; *Chicago Chronicle,* December 30, 1905, p. 4, col. 1.

23. *Chicago Tribune,* December 28, 1894, p. 4, col. 4; Robert David Weber, "Rationalizers and Reformers: Chicago Local Transportation in the Nineteenth Century" (Ph.D. diss., University of Wisconsin-Madison, 1971), 251; *Chicago Tribune,* January 3, 1895, p. 1, col. 2.

24. Weber, 252; *Chicago Tribune,* January 4, 1895, p. 4, col. 4; ibid., September 27, 1895, p. 9, col. 4; Lincoln Steffens, "Enemies of the Republic," *McClure's Magazine* 22 (November 1903–April 1904): 593–94.

25. *Chicago Times-Herald,* September 14, 1895, p. 3, col. 1; *Chicago Tribune,* November 15, 1894, p. 4, col. 4; ibid., July 29, 1894, p. 8, col. 4.

26. Ibid., September 6, 1894, p. 4, col. 7; Moffat, 139; *Chicago Tribune,* January 21, 1897, p. 4, col. 6; ibid., April 18, 1895, p. 8, col. 1; ibid., April 23, 1895, p. 4, col. 4.

27. *Daily Inter Ocean,* March 16, 1898, p. 6, cols. 2–3; *Chicago Tribune,* November 23, 1894, p. 1, col. 1; ibid., February 9, 1893, p. 9, col. 7.

28. *Destination: Loop,* 21; *Chicago Journal,* August 11, 1894, p. 1, col. 5.

29. *Chicago Evening Post,* June 26, 1895, p. 2, col. 1; John Franch, "Opposite Sides of the Barricade," *Chicago History* 24 (Summer 1995): 48.

30. *Chicago Times-Herald,* June 13, 1895, p. 7, col. 3; *Chicago Tribune,* November 10, 1895, p. 6, col. 2; ibid., April 18, 1895, p. 8, col. 1; *Daily Inter Ocean,* March 16, 1898, p. 6, cols. 2–3; Moffat, 170.

31. *Chicago Tribune,* November 10, 1895, p. 6, col. 2.

32. Ibid., June 10, 1904, p. 5, cols. 1–2; Wayne Andrews, *Battle for Chicago* (New York: Harcourt, Brace and Company, 1946), 120; ibid., 12; ibid., 189–90; Nigel Nicolson, *Mary Curzon* (New York: Harper and Row, 1977), 12.

33. Andrews, 187; *Chicago Times-Herald*, October 24, 1895, p. 9, col. 4.

34. *Chicago Tribune*, October 23, 1895, p. 1, col. 5; ibid., November 9, 1895, p. 1, col. 7; *Chicago Journal*, November 15, 1895, p. 1, col. 3.

35. *Chicago Times-Herald*, October 25, 1895, p. 12, col. 2; *Chicago Tribune*, November 10, 1895, p. 6, col. 2; *Chicago Times-Herald*, November 16, 1895, p. 9, col. 3; ibid., November 24, 1895, p. 1, col. 1; *Chicago Tribune*, November 28, 1895, p. 6, col. 3.

36. *Chicago Times-Herald*, March 15, 1896, p. 4, col. 5.

37. Ibid., March 13, 1896, p. 1, col. 1; Moffat, 173; *Chicago Times-Herald*, April 11, 1896, p. 1, cols. 3–4.

38. *Chicago Times-Herald*, October 4, 1897, p. 5, col. 3; *Chicago Tribune*, October 4, 1897, p. 1, cols. 3–5; Moffat, 174.

39. *Chicago Tribune*, January 8, 1896, p. 8, col. 5; ibid., March 4, 1896, p. 9, col. 4; Louderback Testimony, 636; *Chicago Times-Herald*, January 13, 1898, p. 4, col. 6; ibid., January 14, 1898, p. 10, col. 1; *Chicago Tribune*, April 17, 1896, p. 9, col. 4; Charles Faye to Victor Lawson, January 10, 1898, Victor Lawson Papers, Newberry Library, Chicago; *Chicago Tribune*, September 11, 1896, p. 9, col. 4.

40. Louderback Testimony, 633; ibid., 635; *Chicago Times-Herald*, October 2, 1897, p. 10, col. 3; *Chicago Tribune*, September 5, 1897, p. 38, col. 5.

41. Charles Faye to Victor Lawson, May 6, 1898, Lawson Papers.

Chapter 18. Business and Pleasure

1. *Chicago Tribune*, May 2, 1888, p. 7, col. 2; ibid., June 25, 1893, p. 14, col. 7; ibid., May 2, 1888, p. 7, col. 2; *Chicago Journal*, January 29, 1898, p. 6, col. 2.

2. *Chicago Times-Herald*, August 25, 1895, p. 7, col. 1; *Chicago Sunday American*, December 31, 1905, p. 2, col. 4.

3. *Chicago Sunday American*, December 31, 1905, p. 2, col. 2; ibid., p. 2, col. 5; Harry Keegan interview, History of Lakeview, Document #20, Chicago Community Documents, vol. 3, part 1, Chicago Historical Society.

4. *Chicago Times-Herald*, August 25, 1895, p. 7, col. 1; *Chicago Tribune*, January 23, 1889, p. 1, col. 5.

5. DeLancey Louderback to Theodore Dreiser, March 8, 1913, Box 68, Folder 3736, Theodore Dreiser Papers, Van Pelt Library, University of Pennsylvania, Philadelphia, Pa.; *Chicago Record*, April 28, 1893, p. 3, cols. 3–4; Joseph Leiter to Governor John Riley Tanner, June 3, 1897, Joseph Leiter Letterbook, Box 160A, Levi Leiter Papers, Series II General Estate Papers, 1881–1969, Chicago Historical Society; Testimony of LeGrand W. Perce, November 16, 1906, transcript of record, 2054, North and West Chicago Street Railroad Companies vs. Chicago Consolidated Traction Company (Case Number 27508), U.S. Circuit Court, Northern District of Illinois—Eastern Division, National Archives—Great Lakes Region, Chicago, Ill.; Testimony of DeLancey Louderback, July 3, 1906, transcript of record, 583–84.

6. Edwin Lefevre, "What Availeth It," *Everybody's Magazine* 24 (June 1911): 846; *Chicago Herald*, November 19, 1887, p. 4, col. 4.

7. *Chicago Times-Herald,* February 13, 1897, p. 14, col. 1; Testimony of Azariah T. Galt, December 11, 1906, transcript of record, 2725–27, North and West Chicago Street Railroad Companies vs. Chicago Consolidated Traction Company (Case Number 27508), U.S. Circuit Court, Northern District of Illinois—Eastern Division, National Archives—Great Lakes Region, Chicago, Ill.; Testimony of Hugh McBirney, November 7, 1906, transcript of record, 1880–83, ibid.; Frank Vanderlip, *From Farm Boy to Financier* (New York: D. Appleton-Century Company, 1935), 55; David M. Young, *Chicago Transit: An Illustrated History* (Dekalb: Northern Illinois University Press, 1998), 24; *Chicago Tribune,* January 11, 1893, p. 8, col. 1; Dugald C. Jackson and David J. McGrath, *Street Railway Fares* (New York: McGraw-Hill Book Company, 1917), 32–33; William Mann, *Fads and Fancies of Representative Americans* (New York: Arno Press, 1975), 45; *Chicago Evening Post,* April 17, 1895, p. 1, col. 1.

8. *Chicago Record,* November 10, 1894, p. 1, col. 1; Lefevre, 84.

9. *Chicago Times-Herald,* August 15, 1897, p. 21, col. 4; *New York American,* February 26, 1906, p. 2, col. 6.

10. *Catalogue from Collection of Charles T. Yerkes* (privately printed, 1893); *Chicago Tribune,* November 3, 1890, p. 6, col. 6; ibid., December 3, 1899, p. 1, col. 2.

11. F. G. Stephens, "Mr. Yerkes' Collection at Chicago: The Old Masters—I," *Magazine of Art* 18 (1895): 96–101; *Chicago Journal,* January 29, 1898, p. 4, col. 6; Ruth Butler, *Rodin: The Shape of Genius* (New Haven: Yale University Press, 1993), 399; *Chicago Tribune,* March 20, 1892, p. 40, col. 2; ibid., March 27, 1892, p. 40, col. 1; ibid., April 3, 1892, p. 39, col. 3; ibid., April 10, 1892, p. 31, col. 1; ibid., June 5, 1892, p. 5, col. 6; Wesley Towner, *The Elegant Auctioneers* (New York: Hill and Wang, 1970), 195–96; *Chicago Tribune,* October 1, 1893, p. 27, col. 3; *Chicago Journal,* September 23, 1893, p. 5, cols. 1–2.

12. *Chicago Tribune,* November 12, 1893, p. 34, col. 5; Harriet Monroe, *A Poet's Life* (New York: Macmillan Company, 1938), 117; Ernest Samuels, *Bernard Berenson: The Making of a Legend* (Cambridge, Mass.: The Belknap Press of Harvard University Press, 1987), 29–30; *The Letters of Bernard Berenson and Isabella Stewart Gardner,* ed. Rollin Van N. Hadley (Boston: Northeastern University Press, 1987), 236; ibid., 325–26; *A Monthly Journal Devoted to Art in the Household,* December 1890, p. 2, col. 3; ibid., December 1891, p. 2, col. 1.

13. *Catalogue DeLuxe of the Ancient Rugs, Sculptures, Tapestries, Costly Furniture and Other Objects Belonging to the Estate of the Late Charles T. Yerkes* (New York: The American Art Association, 1910); Butler, 399–401; Henry Adams, *The Letters of Henry Adams,* vol. 4 (Cambridge, Mass.: The Belknap Press of Harvard University Press, 1988), 313.

14. *Town Topics* (New York), March 1, 1906, p. 15, col. 1.

15. *New York American,* February 26, 1906, p. 2, cols. 3–7; Towner, 195; *Chicago Times-Herald,* August 15, 1897, p. 21, col. 6; *Catalogue DeLuxe; M.A.P.* (London), June 8, 1901, p. 562, cols. 1–2.

16. Monroe, 117; Helen Wright, *Explorer of the Universe* (New York: E. P. Dutton and Company, Inc., 1966), 132; Charles Yerkes to Ada Rehan, December 1, 1891, Ada Rehan Papers, Van Pelt Library, University of Pennsylvania, Philadelphia, Pa.

17. Lefevre, 840; Ernest Poole, *Giants Gone* (New York: Whittlesey House, 1943), 240; Theodore Dreiser, *Newspaper Days* (Philadelphia: University of Pennsylvania Press, 1991), 82.

18. *Chicago Evening Post*, February 13, 1892, p. 1, col. 5; *Chicago Tribune*, November 23, 1893, p. 5, col. 4; *New York World*, January 8, 1906, p. 2, col. 3; *Baker's Biographical Dictionary of Musicians* (New York: Schirmer Books, 1992), 818–19; *The Lakeside Annual Directory of the City of Chicago 1899* (Chicago: The Chicago Directory Company, 1899); Respondents' Answer, April 17, 1922, In the Matter of the Application for Letters of Administration of the Goods, Chattels, and Credits of Frank V. Burton, Deceased, Surrogate's Court, 9th Judicial District–Orange County, Goshen, New York. I am indebted to Paul Hadley for this last item.

19. DeLancey Louderback to Theodore Dreiser, March 8, 1913, Box 68, Folder 3736, Theodore Dreiser Papers, Van Pelt Library, University of Pennsylvania, Philadelphia, Pa.; *Chicago Sunday American*, December 31, 1905, p. 1, col. 4; *Town Topics* (New York), August 3, 1893, p. 13; ibid., August 17, 1893, p. 11; *New York American*, February 26, 1906, p. 2, col. 2.

Chapter 19. The Temptation of Governor Altgeld

1. *Chicago Tribune*, June 25, 1893, p. 14, col. 7; ibid., July 9, 1899, p. 13, col. 1.

2. *Illinois Senate Journal*, 39th General Assembly, 1st Session, 144; Robert David Weber, "Rationalizers and Reformers: Chicago Local Transportation in the Nineteenth Century" (Ph.D. diss., University of Wisconsin-Madison, 1971), 255.

3. Samuel McConnell, "Memoirs," Typescript, Box 2, Folder 5, Harry Barnard Papers, Illinois State Historical Library, Springfield; Weber, 316–17; *Chicago Times-Herald*, July 28, 1895, p. 25, col. 1.

4. *Illinois Senate Journal*, 233–34; *Chicago Tribune*, March 1, 1895, p. 2, col. 1; ibid., March 7, 1895, p. 5, col. 3; *Daily Inter Ocean*, July 4, 1895, p. 3, col. 3; *Chicago Tribune*, July 4, 1895, p. 2, col. 4; *Chicago Record*, July 4, 1895, p. 4, col. 1.

5. *Chicago Times-Herald*, July 28, 1895, p. 25, col. 1.

6. For an excellent biography of Altgeld, see Harry Barnard, *"Eagle Forgotten": The Life of John Peter Altgeld* (Indianapolis: Bobbs-Merrill Company, 1938); Wayne Andrews, *Battle for Chicago* (New York: Harcourt, Brace and Company, 1946), 139.

7. Governor John Peter Altgeld to Lambert Tree, December 24, 1894, Lambert Tree Papers, Newberry Library, Chicago.

8. Barnard, 147–50; Adolf Kraus, *Reminiscences and Comments* (Chicago: Toby Rubovits, Inc., 1925), 108; Joel Tarr, "J. R. Walsh of Chicago: A Case Study in Banking and Politics, 1881–1905," *Business History Review* 40 (Winter 1966): 451–66; Walter Fisher to President Theodore Roosevelt, February 19, 1904, Theodore Roosevelt Papers, Library of Congress; Fred D. P. Snelling Statement, May 25, 1922, Box 1, Folder 11, Waldo Browne Papers, Illinois State Historical Library, Springfield, Ill.; Barnard, 348–49; *Chicago Record*, May 3, 1895, p. 7, col. 4; Notes on Interview with F. D. P. Snelling, May 1937, Box 2, Folder 8, Harry Barnard Papers.

9. *Illinois House Journal*, 39th General Assembly, 1st Session, 681–82; Ernest Poole, *Giants Gone: Men Who Made Chicago* (New York: Whittlesey House, 1943), 204–5; *Chicago Record*, July 7, 1893, p. 4, col. 7; Poole, 205; Carter Harrison, Jr., *Stormy Years* (Indianapolis: Bobbs-Merrill Company, 1935), 65; Geoffrey Cowan, *The People v. Clarence Darrow* (New York: Times Books, 1993), 29–30.

10. *Chicago Daily News* (morning), December 18, 1889, p. 1, col. 7; Theodore Dreiser, *The Titan* (New York: New American Library, 1965), 440.

11. Weber, 294; *Chicago Times-Herald*, April 21, 1897, p. 2, col. 2; George Schilling to Mayor Edward Dunne, April 28, 1905, George Schilling Letterbook 1903–5, George Schilling Collection, University of Chicago Department of Special Collections.

12. *Chicago Times-Herald*, January 23, 1898, p. 2, col. 7; ibid., p. 3, col. 1.

13. Samuel McConnell, "Memoirs," Typescript, Box 2, Folder 21, Waldo Browne Papers.

14. Clarence Darrow, *The Story of My Life* (New York: Charles Scribner's Sons, 1932), 105–7; *Chicago Times-Herald*, May 15, 1895, p. 5, cols. 1–2.

15. Ibid., June 15, 1895, p. 1, col. 7; *Chicago Tribune*, May 15, 1895, p. 4, col. 2; *Peoria Journal*, June 13, 1895, p. 4, col. 1; *Chicago Times-Herald*, May 15, 1895, p. 5, col. 3; ibid., p. 2, col. 1.

16. *Chicago Evening Post*, May 15, 1895, p. 3, col. 5; *Chicago Times-Herald*, April 22, 1897, p. 3, col. 2.

17. *Chicago Tribune*, May 15, 1895, p. 2, col. 3; Forrest Crissey, *Tattlings of a Retired Politician* (Chicago: Thompson and Thomas, 1904), 41–56; *Chicago Times-Herald*, June 17, 1895, p. 2, cols. 3–4.

18. Ibid., June 15, 1895, p. 2, col. 3; Brand Whitlock, *Forty Years of It* (Cleveland: Press of Case Western Reserve University, 1970), 97.

19. "Recollections of A. L. Yantis," Box 2, Folder 8, Harry Barnard Papers; *Chicago Tribune*, July 4, 1895, p. 2, col. 2; Whitlock, 99–100.

20. *Chicago Times-Herald*, June 17, 1895, p. 2, cols. 3–4; *Peoria Herald*, June 15, 1895, p. 1, col. 3; *Illinois House Journal*, 1142–43.

21. *Peoria Herald*, June 15, 1895, p. 1, col. 1; *Chicago Tribune*, June 15, 1895, p. 1, col. 7; *Chicago Times-Herald*, June 15, 1895, p. 2, col. 4; *Peoria Journal*, June 15, 1895, p. 4, col. 2.

Chapter 20. On the Brink

1. *Chicago Times-Herald*, July 10, 1896, p. 3, cols. 1–5; Willis Abbot, *Watching the World Go By* (New York: Beekman Publishers, 1974), 161–66; Frank Cyril James, *Growth of Chicago Banks*, vol. 2 (New York: Harper and Brothers, 1938), 638–40; Carter Harrison, Jr., *Stormy Years* (Indianapolis: Bobbs-Merrill Company, 1935), 70.

2. Martin Ridge, *Ignatius Donnelly: The Portrait of a Politician* (Chicago: University of Chicago Press, 1962), 4–5, 17, 129–30, 262–64; ibid., 196; ibid., 295–96.

3. Ibid., 362; Thomas Lawson, *Frenzied Finance* (New York: The Ridgway-Thayer Company, 1905), 177–78.

4. *Chicago Times-Herald*, August 11, 1896, p. 9, col. 4.

5. Harper Leech and John Charles Carroll, *Armour and His Times* (New York: D. Appleton-Century Company, 1938), 295; *Chicago Herald*, September 21, 1893, p. 16, col. 4.

6. *Chicago Times-Herald*, February 6, 1897, p. 1, col. 1; *Chicago Tribune*, September 27, 1896, p. 38, col. 6; *Chicago Journal*, November 30, 1896, p. 7, col. 1.

7. *Chicago Evening Post*, September 2, 1896, p. 6, col. 7; *Chicago Tribune*, July 21, 1896, p. 10, col. 4; ibid., July 19, 1896, p. 35, col. 6.

8. Ibid., July 22, 1896, p. 9, col. 4; ibid., July 31, 1896, p. 10, col. 4; *Chicago Journal*, September 7, 1896, p. 6, col. 1; *Chicago Times-Herald*, August 5, 1896, p. 3, col. 2; *Chicago Journal*, August 5, 1896, p. 2, col. 1.

9. *Chicago Times-Herald*, August 5, 1896, p. 1, col. 1.

10. Ibid.; *The Daily News* (London), October 2, 1900, p. 7, col. 5; Edwin Lobdell, "Random Recollections," 32, unpublished MS, Edwin Lobdell Collection, Chicago Historical Society.

11. Ibid.; Edwin Lefevre, "What Availeth It," *Everybody's Magazine* 24 (June 1911): 839; *Chicago Times-Herald*, August 5, 1896, p. 3, col. 4.

12. Charles McArthur Destler, *Henry Demarest Lloyd and the Empire of Reform* (Philadelphia: University of Pennsylvania Press, 1963), 346; *Chicago Journal*, August 26, 1896, p. 2, col. 2; *Chicago Evening Post*, August 25, 1896, p. 1, col. 5.

13. *Chicago Times-Herald*, February 6, 1897, p. 1, col. 1; Harold Irwin Cleveland, "Fifty-Five Years in Business: The Life of Marshall Field," *System* 11 (January–May 1907), 54–55.

14. *Chicago Tribune*, February 6, 1897, p. 3, cols. 5–6; *Chicago Times-Herald*, February 6, 1897, p. 1, col. 1; Leech and Carroll, 297; ibid., 293.

15. *Chicago Tribune*, September 2, 1896, p. 5, col. 4; ibid., September 4, 1896, p. 9, col. 4; ibid., November 3, 1896, p. 9, col. 4.

16. *Chicago Evening Post*, October 1, 1896, p. 1, col. 3; Frank Cyril James, *Growth of Chicago Banks*, vol. 1 (New York: Harper and Brothers, 1938), 646; Leech and Carroll, 292; *Chicago Times-Herald*, July 26, 1896, p. 14, col. 7.

17. *Chicago Journal*, November 30, 1896, p. 7, col. 1; ibid., November 6, 1896, p. 8, col. 2; ibid., November 7, 1896, p. 10, col. 3; ibid., November 30, 1896, p. 7, col. 1.

18. Ibid., February 6, 1897, p. 9, col. 1; *Financial Times*, November 13, 1896; *Daily Inter Ocean*, December 16, 1898, p. 2, col. 4.

19. George Bushnell, "The Buzz Saw Reformer," *Chicago History* 18 (Fall 1989): 93; Lincoln Steffens, "Chicago: Half Free and Fighting On," *McClure's Magazine* 21 (October 1903): 368–69; Elizabeth Kent, *William Kent, Independent*, unpublished 1950 MS, 152; Sidney Roberts, "The Municipal Voters' League and Chicago's Boodlers," *Journal of the Illinois Historical Society* 53 (1960): 143; Bushnell, 96.

20. *Chicago Journal*, February 5, 1897, p. 6, col. 2; *Chicago Tribune*, February 6, 1897, p. 3, col. 5.

Chapter 21. The Franchise War

1. *Chicago Tribune*, March 11, 1897, p. 4, col. 3; ibid., February 18, 1897, p. 12, col. 1.

2. Ibid., February 19, 1897, p. 1, col. 1; *Chicago Times-Herald*, February 19, 1897, p. 1, col. 7; *Chicago Tribune*, January 14, 1897, p. 6, col. 4.

3. *Chicago Journal*, March 10, 1897, p. 3, col. 2; *Chicago Tribune*, March 11, 1897, p. 1, col. 1; ibid., March 11, 1897, p. 4, cols. 2 and 4.

4. *Chicago Tribune*, March 11, 1897, p. 4, col. 3.

5. *Chicago Times-Herald*, March 14, 1897, p. 5, cols. 3–4; *Chicago Tribune*, March 21, 1897, p. 2, col. 4.

6. Harold Ickes, *The Autobiography of a Curmudgeon* (New York: Reynal and Hitchcock, 1943), 82–83; ibid., 93; Carter Harrison, Jr., *Stormy Years* (Indianapolis: Bobbs-Merrill Company, 1935), 113; Ickes, 90.

7. *Chicago Times-Herald*, March 30, 1897, p. 4, col. 6.

8. Harrison, 47; Edward A. Kantowicz, "Carter Harrison II: The Politics of Balance," in *Chicago Mayors: The Chicago Political Tradition*, ed. Paul Green and Melvin Holli (Carbondale: Southern Illinois University Press, 1987), 20.

9. Harrison, 107; *Daily Inter Ocean*, March 2, 1899, p. 1, cols. 1–2; Harrison, 100; *Chicago Evening Post*, March 27, 1897, p. 6, col. 5; Joel Tarr, *A Study in Boss Politics: William Lorimer of Chicago* (Urbana: University of Illinois Press, 1971), 84.

10. *Chicago Journal*, April 14, 1897, p. 1, col. 7.

11. *Chicago Times-Herald*, April 15, 1897, p. 1, col. 7; *Chicago Tribune*, April 15, 1897, p. 3, col. 5; *Chicago Times-Herald*, April 15, 1897, p. 2, col. 1; Chester McArthur Destler, *Henry Demarest Lloyd and the Empire of Reform* (Philadelphia: University of Pennsylvania Press, 1963), 429; *Chicago Journal*, April 14, 1897, p. 1, col. 1; *Chicago Tribune*, May 22, 1897, p. 3, col. 4.

12. *Chicago Times-Herald*, April 19, 1897, p. 4, col. 5; Elizabeth Kent, "William Kent, Independent," unpublished 1950 MS, 157–58; Ickes, 83.

13. *Chicago Times-Herald*, April 22, 1897, p. 3, col. 1; Charles Yerkes to Carter Harrison, Jr., April 22, 1897, Carter H. Harrison, Jr., Papers, Newberry Library.

14. William Rainey Harper to Charles Yerkes, April 19, 1897, Box 3, Folder 13, William Rainey Harper Papers, University of Chicago Department of Special Collections; *Chicago Tribune*, April 23, 1897, p. 7, col. 1; Yerkes quoted in John Franch, "Storming the Gates of Heaven," *Sky and Telescope* 90 (September 1995): 30.

15. *Chicago Journal*, April 15, 1897, p. 1, col. 1; ibid., May 8, 1897, p. 2, cols. 3–4; ibid., May 7, 1897, p. 1, col. 5; ibid., May 8, 1897, p. 1, cols. 1–2.

16. Edward Price Bell, "Seventy Years Deep," unpublished MS, 310–11, Edward Price Bell Papers, Newberry Library, Chicago, Ill.; *Chicago Record*, May 13, 1897, p. 1, col. 7; *Chicago Journal*, May 12, 1897, p. 1, cols. 6–7; *Chicago Times-Herald*, May 13, 1897, p. 3, col. 1.

17. *Chicago Journal*, May 14, 1897, p. 1, col. 1; *Chicago Record*, May 19, 1897, p. 3, col. 1; *Chicago Journal*, May 20, 1897, p. 9, col. 3.

18. John Franch, "Storming the Gates of Heaven," *Sky and Telescope* 90 (September 1995): 30; Helen Wright, *Explorer of the Universe* (New York: Dutton, 1966), 130–31.

19. *Chicago Times-Herald*, May 30, 1897, p. 30, col. 2; Victor Lawson to C. S. Tisdel, May 27, 1897, Victor Lawson Papers, Newberry Library, Chicago, Ill.; Victor Lawson to Edward C. Curtis, ibid.

20. *Chicago Times-Herald*, May 27, 1897, p. 2, col. 3; Sidney Eastman, "Corruption in Illinois," 1897 MS, pp. 4–6, Sidney Eastman Collection, Chicago Historical Society; Note 214, Box 133, Folder 7235, Theodore Dreiser Collection, Van Pelt Library, University of Pennsylvania, Philadelphia, Pa.

21. Sidney Eastman to Herman Kohlsaat, May 27, 1897, Sidney Eastman Collection, Chicago Historical Society; *Chicago Tribune*, June 9, 1897, p. 2, cols. 2–3; *Chicago Times-Herald*, June 4, 1897, p. 6, col. 2.

22. *Chicago Tribune*, June 6, 1897, p. 2, col. 1; Harrison, Jr., 145–46.

23. *Chicago Record*, June 5, 1897, p. 1, col. 7; *Chicago Tribune*, June 6, 1897, p. 2, col. 1.

24. Ibid., June 10, 1896, p. 3, col. 1; Robert P. Howard, *Mostly Good and Competent Men: Illinois Governors, 1818–1988* (Springfield: *Illinois Issues*, 1988), 201; Victor Lawson to Charles Faye, November 18, 1897, Victor Lawson Papers, Newberry Library, Chicago, Ill.; Howard, 200.

25. Medill quoted in Tarr, 86.

Chapter 22. The Battle of His Life

1. *Chicago Times-Herald*, October 22, 1897, p. 1, col. 6; John Franch, "Storming the Gates of Heaven," *Sky and Telescope* 90 (September 1995): 30.

2. *Chicago Tribune*, October 21, 1897, p. 8, cols. 1–2; George Hale to William Rainey Harper, September 2, 1899, Box 37, Folder 2, University of Chicago Presidents' Papers 1889–1925, University of Chicago Department of Special Collections.

3. *Chicago Record*, October 22, 1897, p. 6, col. 1; *Chicago Tribune*, October 22, 1897, p. 3, cols. 1–3; *Chicago Times-Herald*, October 22, 1897, p. 1, cols. 6–7; ibid., p. 2, col. 1; *Daily Inter Ocean*, October 22, 1897, p. 6, col. 1.

4. *Chicago Times-Herald*, October 23, 1897, p. 3, cols. 1–2.

5. *Daily Inter Ocean*, November 22, 1897, p. 6, col. 1.

6. *Town Topics* (New York), January 25, 1894, p. 14, col. 2; ibid., June 17, 1897, p. 15, col. 2; *Chicago Times-Herald*, November 19, 1897, p. 2, col. 2; *Town Topics* (New York), November 2, 1899, p. 7, cols. 1–2; *Chicago Evening Post*, November 20, 1897, p. 6, col. 5; *Chicago Times-Herald*, December 29, 1898, p. 6, col. 3.

7. *Chicago Tribune*, February 18, 1895, p. 12, col. 1; Charles Faye to Victor Lawson, February 10, 1898, Victor Lawson Papers, Newberry Library, Chicago, Ill.

8. *Chicago Evening Post*, April 6, 1898, p. 1, col. 5; *Chicago Times-Herald*, June 10, 1897, p. 2, col. 1; Carter Harrison, Jr., *Stormy Years* (Indianapolis: Bobbs-Merrill Company, 1935), 150.

9. Ibid., 148–49.

10. Ibid., 152; *Chicago Tribune*, January 20, 1898, p. 1, col. 5; ibid., November 18, 1898, p. 3, col. 1; *Chicago Chronicle*, November 16, 1898, p. 7, col. 5; Harrison, 166; *Chicago Times-Herald*, November 25, 1898, p. 10, col. 1.

11. *Chicago Tribune*, July 19, 1898, p. 9, col. 2; *Chicago Journal*, December 6, 1898, p. 2, col. 3; *Daily Inter Ocean*, December 6, 1898, p. 1, col. 1.

12. *Chicago Journal*, December 6, 1898, p. 2, col. 2; *Chicago Daily News*, December 7, 1898, p. 1, col. 7; *Chicago Journal*, December 7, 1898, p. 4, col. 1; *Chicago Chronicle*, December 8, 1898, p. 1, col. 7.

13. *The World* (New York), December 8, 1898, p. 1, col. 1; ibid., December 9, 1898, p. 1, cols. 5–6; ibid., December 11, 1898, p. 6, col. 2; *Chicago Journal*, December 8, 1898, p. 2, cols. 2–3.

14. *Chicago Chronicle*, December 9, 1898, p. 1, col. 7; *Daily Inter Ocean*, December 9, 1898, p. 2, cols. 1–2; ibid., p. 2, col. 7; *Chicago Journal*, December 9, 1898, p. 2, col. 2.

15. *Chicago Journal*, December 6, 1898, p. 2, col. 3; *The World* (New York), December 11, 1898, p. 2, col. 8; *Chicago Journal*, December 8, 1898, p. 2, col. 1; *Chicago Daily News*, December 8, 1898, p. 1, col. 7.

16. *The World* (New York), December 13, 1898, p. 1, cols. 7–8; *Chicago Tribune*, December 13, 1898, p. 2, cols. 5–6; ibid., col. 3; ibid., p. 1, col. 7; Lloyd Wendt and Herman Kogan, *Bosses in Lusty Chicago* (Bloomington: Indiana University Press, 1943), 193–95.

17. *Chicago Chronicle*, December 13, 1898, p. 3, cols. 2–3; *Chicago Tribune*, December 18, 1898, p. 6, col. 1; Wendt and Kogan, 196.

18. *Chicago Daily News*, December 14, 1898, p. 1, col. 7.

19. *Chicago Chronicle*, December 20, 1898, p. 2, col. 1; *Chicago Tribune*, December 20, 1898, p. 1, col. 7.

20. Ibid., p. 2, col. 1.

21. *Chicago Daily News,* December 20, 1898, p. 3, col. 5; *Chicago Times-Herald,* December 20, 1898, p. 1, col. 7; ibid., p. 2, col. 1; *The World* (New York), December 9, 1898, p. 6, col. 2; *Chicago Tribune,* December 20, 1898, p. 2, col. 2.

22. Harrison, 157–59; Elizabeth Kent, "William Kent, Independent," unpublished 1950 MS, 136; Wendt and Kogan, 199.

23. *Chicago Journal,* June 6, 1899, p. 4, col. 2.

Chapter 23. End Game

1. Adams A. Goodrich Testimony, 326–27, 334, found in Claim of Charles Leeds, In Re Estate of Charles T. Yerkes, Case Number 297950, Probate Records, Cook County Archives, Chicago, Ill.; *Chicago Journal,* June 2, 1899, p. 1, col. 5; ibid., January 29, 1898, p. 4, col. 3.

2. *Chicago American,* December 31, 1905, p. 2, col. 2; *Chicago Journal,* January 29, 1898, p. 4, cols. 2–3; *Chicago Daily News,* December 14, 1898, p. 1, col. 7; *Chicago Tribune,* July 9, 1899, p. 13, col. 1.

3. Ibid., July 26, 1898, p. 12, col. 1; Nigel Nicolson, *Mary Curzon* (New York: Harper and Row, 1977), 100–101; Harper Leech and Charles Carroll, *Armour and His Times* (New York: D. Appleton-Century Company, 1938), 310–13; Nicolson, 101; Leech and Carroll, 317–20.

4. *Chicago Times-Herald,* July 24, 1898, p. 37, col. 4; *Chicago Tribune,* August 15, 1898, p. 1, cols. 3–4; Jean Strouse, *Morgan: American Financier* (New York: Perennial, 2000), 545; Joseph Leiter to William B. Walker, undated, Joseph Leiter Letterbook, Box 160A, Series II, General Estate Papers, 1881–1969, Levi Leiter Papers, Chicago Historical Society.

5. Joseph Leiter to J. H. Hoadley, undated, ibid.; Joseph Leiter to Thomas Fortune Ryan, August 16, 1898; *Chicago Journal,* July 25, 1898, p. 1, cols. 1–2; *Chicago Tribune,* May 13, 1899, p. 5, col. 1; *New York Herald,* April 16, 1899, p. 7, cols. 2–3; Joseph Leiter to Thomas Fortune Ryan, March 6, 1899, Joseph Leiter Letterbook, Box 160 A, Series II, General Estate Papers, 1881–1969, Levi Leiter Papers, Chicago Historical Society.

6. *Chicago Tribune,* March 25, 1899, p. 1, col. 1; Testimony of Henry Crawford, October 30, 1906, 1701–2, Transcript of Record, North and West Chicago Street Railroad Companies vs. Chicago Consolidated Traction Company, Case 27,508, U.S. Circuit Court, Northern District of Illinois—Eastern Division, National Archives—Great Lakes Branch, Chicago, Ill.; Testimony of B. G. Burke, October 17, 1906, 1443–4, ibid.; *The Economist* (Chicago), May 13, 1899, p. 577, col. 1.

7. *Chicago Times-Herald,* May 11, 1899, p. 5, col. 5; *Chicago Tribune,* February 13, 1899, p. 7, cols. 3–4; Carter Harrison, Jr., *Stormy Years* (Indianapolis: Bobbs-Merrill Company, 1935), 207.

8. Directors' Records, Chicago Consolidated Traction Company, February 15, 1899–July 1, 1910, May 25, 1899 meeting, vol. 40, 88–95, Chicago Surface Lines Collection, Chicago Historical Society.

9. Arthur Young to Jesse Spalding, November 20, 1899, 1144–46, North and West Chicago Street Railroad Companies vs. Chicago Consolidated Traction

Company, Case 27,508, U.S. Circuit Court, Northern District of Illinois—Eastern Division, National Archives—Great Lakes Branch, Chicago, Ill.

10. Testimony of Henry Crawford, October 30, 1906, 1732, ibid.; *Chicago Tribune,* September 28, 1899, p. 1, col. 4; Harrison, Jr., 207–8.

11. *Chicago Tribune,* December 22, 1899, p. 9, col. 1; North Chicago City Railway Company, Directors' Minutes December 5, 1899–June 18, 1908, April 16, 1900 meeting, vol. 76, 8–10, Chicago Surface Lines Collection, Chicago Historical Society.

12. *Chicago Tribune,* April 23, 1903, p. 2, cols. 4–6; ibid., April 24, 1903, p. 3, cols. 1–3; *Chicago Times-Herald,* February 13, 1897, p. 14, cols. 1–2; Bion Arnold, *Report on the Engineering and Operating Features of the Chicago Transportation Problem* (New York: McGraw Publishing Company, 1905), 62–64; *Chicago Daily News,* May 14, 1903, p. 4, cols. 1–2; *Chicago Chronicle,* May 19, 1903, p. 3, col. 1.

13. *Chicago Tribune,* December 9, 1895, p. 8, col. 6; ibid., December 3, 1899, p. 1, col. 2.

14. *Chicago American,* December 31, 1905, p. 2, cols. 3–4; Melville Stone, *Fifty Years a Journalist* (Garden City, N.Y.: Doubleday, Page and Company, 1921), 118; *The Economist* (Chicago), June 3, 1899, p. 671, col. 3.

15. Harold Mayer and Richard Wade, *Chicago: Growth of a Metropolis* (Chicago: University of Chicago Press, 1969), 250–52; *Chicago Journal,* January 29, 1898, p. 4, col. 4; *The Daily Telegraph* (London), December 30, 1905, p. 6, col. 2.

16. Arnold, 64; Bessie Louise Pierce, *A History of Chicago,* vol. 3 (Chicago: University of Chicago Press, 1957), 56; Mayer and Wade, 256. The historian Sam Bass Warner argues that the streetcar helped create cities and suburbs segregated by income. See Warner, *Streetcar Suburbs* (Cambridge, Mass.: Harvard University Press), 153–66.

17. Lewis Mumford, *Sticks and Stones* (New York: Dover Publications, 1955), 143–44.

18. Arnold, 31–32; Maury Klein, *The Life and Legend of Jay Gould* (Baltimore: Johns Hopkins University Press, 1986), 494–96; *Chicago Journal,* January 29, 1898, p. 4, col. 1; Carter Harrison, Jr., *Growing up With Chicago* (Chicago: R. F. Seymour, 1944), 286.

19. Edward Price Bell, "Seventy Years Deep," unpublished autobiography, 245, Edward Price Bell Collection, Newberry Library, Chicago; Edward Price Bell Diary, entry dated September 15–16, 1904, ibid.

20. Bell, "Seventy Years Deep," 295; *Chicago Record,* December 30, 1898, p. 2, col. 1; ibid., p. 2, col. 2; ibid., December 31, 1898, p. 1, col. 7; ibid., January 27, 1899, p. 2, col. 3; *Chicago Tribune,* October 5, 1901, p. 3, col. 1.

21. Bell, "Seventy Years Deep," 312.

22. Ibid., 308, 319–20.

Chapter 24. London

1. *Chicago Tribune,* July 9, 1899, p. 13, cols. 1–2.

2. Housman et al. vs. Owsley, referee's opinion, 1910, 5–6, in Theodore Dreiser Papers, Box 271, Folder 10390, Van Pelt Library, University of Pennsylvania, Philadelphia, Pa.

3. Housman et al. vs. Owsley, brief for plaintiffs, 1910, 10–11, in Dreiser Papers, Box 271, Folder 10389; ibid., pp. 19–20.

4. Housman et al. vs. Owsley, referee's opinion, 5–6; Housman et al. vs. Owsley, brief for defendants, 1910, 15, in Dreiser Papers, Box 271, Folder 10388.

5. Roy Porter, *London: A Social History* (Cambridge, Mass.: Harvard University Press, 1995), 306; Ebenezer Howard, *Garden Cities of Tomorrow* (Cambridge, Mass.: MIT Press, 1965), 42; Jonathan Schneer, *London 1900: The Imperial Metropolis* (New Haven: Yale University Press, 1999), 4.

6. Schneer, 9; Patricia Garside, "West End, East End: London, 1890–1940," in *Metropolis 1890–1940*, ed. Anthony Sutcliffe (London: Mansell Publishing, 1984), 235; Sidney Low, "The Tangle of London Locomotion," *The Nineteenth Century and After* 52 (December 1902): 928; Frank Sprague, "The Rapid-Transit Problem in London," *The Engineering Magazine* 22 (October 1901): 3–4.

7. Stephen Inwood, *A History of London* (New York: Carroll and Graf Publishers, Inc., 1998), 568; T. C. Barker and Michael Robbins, *A History of London Transport*, vol. 2: *The Twentieth Century to 1970* (London: George Allen and Unwin, Ltd., 1974), 15–16; William Dean Howells, "London Films," *London 1066–1914*, vol. 3: *Literary Sources and Documents*, ed. Xavier Bacon (East Sussex: Helm Information, 1997), 460; Inwood, 563.

8. Samuel George Burgess, Memorandum of Evidence, *Royal Commission on London Traffic*, vol. 3 (1905), 266.

9. Charles Booth, "Life and Labour of the People in London," in *London 1066–1914*, vol. 3, 316; G. F. Millin, "The Future of London Railways," *Contemporary Review* 78 (July 1900): 104.

10. Millin, 105–6; Alan Jackson and Desmond F. Croome, *Rails Through the Clay* (London: George Allen and Unwin Ltd., 1962), 27–28; Millin, 106–7.

11. T. C. Barker and Michael Robbins, *A History of London Transport*, vol. 1: *The Nineteenth Century* (London: George Allen and Unwin, Ltd., 1963), 312–13; Inwood, 561–62; Jackson and Croome, 52–53; *Chicago Daily News*, January 2, 1901, p. 9, col. 4.

12. Housman et al. vs. Owsley, brief for plaintiffs, 20–23; ibid., referee's opinion, 6–8.

13. Ibid., 13; ibid., brief for defendants, 25.

14. Jackson and Croome, 65.

15. *Chicago Tribune*, September 6, 1900, p. 2, col. 7; *Chicago Daily News*, June 8, 1901, p. 1, col. 4; Housman et al. vs. Owsley, brief for plaintiffs, 27–28.

16. Ibid., 28–30.

17. *Chicago Tribune*, July 26, 1900, p. 1, col. 3; *New York Herald* (Paris edition), July 27, 1900, p. 5, col. 3.

18. Ibid.

19. Housman et al. vs. Owsley, referee's opinion, 17; Hugh Prince, "North-West London 1864–1914," in *Greater London*, ed. J. T. Coppock and Hugh C. Prince (London: Faber and Faber Ltd., 1964), 134–35.

20. Housman et al. vs. Owsley, brief for plaintiffs, 33.

21. Ibid., referee's opinion, 17–18.

22. Denis Crane, *The Life-Story of Sir Robert W. Perks, Baronet, M.P.* (London: Robert Culley, 1909), 27–28; ibid., 184; ibid., 44.

23. *Railway Times*, October 27, 1900, p. 471, col. 2.

24. Owen Covick, "R. W. Perks, C. T. Yerkes and Private Sector Financing of Urban Transport Infrastructure in London 1900–1907," unpublished paper presented to 2001 Conference of the Association of Business Historians, Portsmouth, United Kingdom, June 29–30, 2001. I wish to thank Owen Covick for this paper. *Chicago Record,* September 29, 1900, p. 3, col. 5; Housman et al. vs. Owsley, brief for plaintiffs, 40; *Chicago Tribune,* September 29, 1900, p. 2, col. 2.

25. Ibid.; *Chicago Tribune,* October 14, 1900, p. 4, col. 1; *Philadelphia Public Ledger,* October 13, 1900, p. 2, col. 6; *Chicago Chronicle,* October 18, 1900, p. 1, col. 3.

26. Housman et al. vs. Owsley, brief for plaintiffs, 20–21.

Chapter 25. Building a Monument

1. Ralph Blumenfeld, *R. D. B's Diary, 1887–1914* (London: W. Heineman, 1930), 77. Charles was not entirely out of the Chicago streetcar business. He controlled until his death the Suburban Railway—forty-eight miles of trolley road in the western suburbs of Chicago. *Chicago Daily News,* June 8, 1901, p. 1, col. 4; Frank J. Sprague, "The Rapid-Transit Problem in London," *Engineering Magazine* 22 (October 1901): 4.

2. Stephen Inwood, *A History of London* (New York: Carroll and Graf Publishers, Inc., 1998), 528; T. C. Barker and Michael Robbins, *A History of London Transport,* vol. 1: *The Nineteenth Century* (London: George Allen and Unwin, Ltd., 1963), 100–101; Inwood, 550; Benson Bobrick, *Labyrinths of Iron: A History of the World's Subways* (New York: Newsweek Books, 1981), 108–9; Barker and Robbins, 113–17.

3. Ibid., 149–50; Inwood, 552; Barker and Robbins, 225–32.

4. Hugh Douglas, *The Underground Story* (London: Robert Hale Limited, 1963), 117; *Chicago Tribune,* September 29, 1900, p. 2, col. 2; T. C. Barker and Michael Robbins, *A History of London Transport,* vol. 2: *The Twentieth Century to 1970* (London: George Allen and Unwin, Ltd., 1974), 55.

5. Sprague, 7–8.

6. Housman et al. vs. Owsley, brief for defendants, 65–67; ibid., brief for plaintiffs, 59–60.

7. Barker and Robbins, vol. 2, 60; *Chicago Daily News,* June 6, 1901, p. 1, cols. 5–6; *Thrice-A-Week World* (New York), June 7, 1901, p. 1, col. 1.

8. Douglas, 148; Barker and Robbins, vol. 2, 75; *The Railway News,* August 3, 1901, p. 175, col. 1.

9. Barker and Robbins, vol. 2, 75; *Chicago Daily News,* August 16, 1901, p. 2, col. 6; Testimony of Charles Tyson Yerkes, October 30, 1901, The Lyttleton Arbitration (1901), Metropolitan Railway vs. Metropolitan District, National Archives of the United Kingdom (Public Record Office) RAIL 1027/132, 108–9. I am in Paul Hadley's debt for the last item.

10. *Thrice-A-Week World,* September 30, 1901, p. 4, col. 6; *New York Herald,* July 25, 1901, p. 9, col. 1; Douglas, 150–51; Barker and Robbins, vol. 2, 75–76.

11. Housman et al. vs. Owsley, brief for defendants, 83.

12. Thomas Jefferson Coolidge, Jr., to Myron Herrick, June 10, 1901, Thomas Jefferson Coolidge Collection, Baker Library, Harvard University. I wish to thank Paul Hadley for this item.

13. Deposition of William Mandelick, September 4, 1912, 10–11, Robert William Perks Claim, In the Matter of the Estate of Charles T. Yerkes, Probate Court of Cook County, Cook County Archives, Chicago, Ill.; ibid., 16–17.

14. Barker and Robbins, vol. 2, 70–71; *M.A.P.*, December 10, 1904, p. 645, col. 1; G. R. Searle, *Corruption in British Politics 1895–1930* (Oxford: Clarendon Press, 1987), 245–46.

15. Edgar Speyer, Memorandum of Evidence, *Royal Commission on London Traffic*, vol. 3, 815; Testimony of Edgar Speyer, June 3, 1904, *Royal Commission on London Traffic*, vol. 2, 905; Deposition of William Mandelick, 23.

16. Coolidge, Jr., to Charles Yerkes, April 15, 1902; Coolidge, Jr., to Yerkes, January 19, 1903. I again thank Paul Hadley for these items.

17. *M.A.P.*, May 10, 1902, p. 474, col. 2; Coolidge, Jr., to Yerkes, April 15, 1902.

18. Alan A. Jackson and Desmond F. Croome, *Rails through the Clay* (London: George Allen and Unwin, Ltd., 1962), 36–39; Barker and Robbins, vol. 2, 52–53; Searle, 36.

19. *Thrice-A-Week World*, September 6, 1901, p. 5, col. 1; ibid., March 12, 1902, p. 3, col. 6.

20. *Town Topics* (New York), October 30, 1902, p. 74, cols. 1–2.

21. Jean Strouse, *Morgan: American Financier* (New York: Perennial, 1999), 10; *Town Topics* (New York), October 30, 1902, p. 74, col. 2.

22. *Thrice-A-Week-World*, June 10, 1901, p. 5, col. 3; Coolidge, Jr., to James Speyer, January 24, 1902. Many thanks to Paul Hadley for the last invaluable reference.

23. Strouse, 13.

24. Barker and Robbins, vol. 2, 77–78; *Thrice-A-Week World*, June 10, 1901, p. 5, col. 3.

25. *Chicago Daily News*, August 28, 1902, p. 4, col. 6.

26. *Thrice-A-Week World*, February 12, 1902, p. 3, col. 6; Strouse, 386–87; Barker and Robbins, vol. 2, 79–80.

27. *M.A.P.*, May 10, 1902, p. 474, col. 2; *Thrice-A-Week World*, April 23, 1902, p. 1, col. 5; ibid., April 28, 1902, p. 2, col. 7.

28. *The Parliamentary Debates*, 4th Series 111(July 11–July 28, 1902), 438.

29. Jackson and Croome, 81–82.

30. *Thrice-A-Week World*, May 5, 1902, p. 2, col. 3.

31. *The Parliamentary Debates*, 4th Series 111(July 11–July 28, 1902), 448–49.

32. *Chicago Daily News*, July 17, 1902, p. 1, cols. 3–4.

33. Jackson and Croome, 82; Charles Harvey and Jon Press, "Sir George White: A Career in Transport, 1874–1916," *Journal of Transport History* 9 (September 1988): 180–81; Barker and Robbins, vol. 2, 82–83; Covick, 22–23; *Daily Inter Ocean* (Chicago), October 22, 1902, p. 5, col. 1.

34. J. P. Morgan to Clinton Dawkins, Private Telegrams vol. X, October 22, 1902; Dawkins to Morgan, October 29, 1902. Again thanks to Paul Hadley for these items.

35. *Daily Inter Ocean*, October 22, 1902, p. 5, col. 1; *Chicago Daily News*, November 18, 1902, p. 1, col. 4.

36. Barker and Robbins, vol. 2, 83; Jackson and Croome, 84.

37. Strouse, 476; *New York Tribune*, October 22, 1902, p. 3, col. 3; Barker and Robbins, vol. 2, 84; Richard Lingeman, *Theodore Dreiser: An American Journey 1908–1945* (New York: G. P. Putnam's Sons, 1990), 79.

Chapter 26. The American Invaders

1. F. A. McKenzie, *The American Invaders* (London: Grant Richards, 1902), 2; ibid., 7–8.

2. Ibid., 1; *Chicago Daily News*, September 26, 1902, p. 1, col. 6; *New York Herald*, July 25, 1901, p. 9, col. 1; *New York Times*, November 30, 1903, p. 10, col. 3.

3. *Chicago Daily News*, May 31, 1901, p. 1, col. 3; *New York Herald*, July 25, 1901, p. 9, col. 1; *Thrice-A-Week World* (New York), September 2, 1901, p. 2, col. 2.

4. *Chicago Daily News*, December 30, 1905, p. 2, col. 5; *M.A.P.*, May 10, 1902, p. 474, col. 2; *New York Tribune*, October 31, 1901, p. 9, col. 3.

5. *Chicago Sunday American*, December 31, 1905, p. 2, cols. 2–3; *Thrice-A-Week World*, July 12, 1901, p. 6, col. 5.

6. *Chicago Sunday American*, December 31, 1905, p. 2, cols. 2–3; Housman et al. vs. Owsley, brief for defendants, 49–50.

7. Elizabeth L. Banks, "American London," in *Living London*, ed. George Sims (London: Cassell and Company, 1902), 111.

8. *New York World*, January 2, 1906, p. 2, col. 1; *New York American*, May 22, 1904; ibid., April 12, 1903.

9. *New York World*, January 2, 1906, p. 2, col. 2; Claim of Gladys Buchanan Unger, filed March 13, 1907, Estate of Charles Tyson Yerkes, Cook County Probate Court, Cook County Archives, Chicago, Ill.

10. *New York American*, January 4, 1906, p. 3, col. 6; *New York Times*, March 15, 1925, section 8, p. 2, cols. 1–2.

11. Leon Edel, *Henry James: The Master 1901–1916* (Philadelphia: J. B. Lippincott Company, 1972), 175; Edgar Lee Masters to Theodore Dreiser, June 11, 1914, Box 73, Folder 4013, Theodore Dreiser Papers, Van Pelt Library, University of Pennsylvania, Philadelphia, Pa.; *Chicago Daily Tribune*, January 3, 1906, p. 2, col. 5.

12. *Lexington* (Kentucky) *Herald*, January 2, 1906, p. 12, col. 5.

13. Ibid.; John David Smith, "James F. Robinson," in *Kentucky's Governors 1792–1985*, ed. Lowell H. Harrison (Lexington: University Press of Kentucky), 76.

14. Ibid., 75; *Lexington Herald*, January 2, 1906, p. 12, col. 5; *The Cincinnati Times-Star*, January 4, 1906, p. 6, col. 2.

15. Ibid.; *New York World*, January 3, 1906, p. 2, col. 5; Timothy Gilfoyle, *City of Eros* (New York: W. W. Norton and Company, 1992), 99; *New York World*, January 3, 1906, p. 2, col. 5; *The Cincinnati Times-Star*, January 4, 1906, p. 6, col. 2.

16. Gilfoyle, 295; *The Cincinnati Times-Star*, January 4, 1906, p. 6, col. 2; *Cincinnati Enquirer*, January 5, 1906, p. 2, col. 4.

17. Trudelle Thomas, "Our Wilderness Home: Images of Home Among the Brown County Ursulines," *Border States: Journal of the Kentucky-Tennessee American Studies Association* 12 (1999): 1–6.

18. *New York American*, January 1, 1906, p. 5, col. 3.

19. *New York World*, January 3, 1906, p. 2, col. 4.

20. Ibid., December 31, 1905, p. 2, col. 5; *Cincinnati Enquirer*, January 5, 1906, p. 2, col. 4.

21. *New York World*, December 31, 1905, p. 2, col. 1; *New York American*, January 1, 1906, p. 5, col. 1; *New York World*, January 3, 1906, p. 2, col. 5.

22. *New York World.*, December 31, 1905, p. 2, col. 2; ibid., January 1, 1906, p. 2, col. 2; *New York American*, January 1, 1906, p. 5, cols. 2–3.

23. *The Cincinnati Times-Star,* January 4, 1906, p. 6, cols. 2–3; *New York American,* January 1, 1906, p. 5, col. 3; *Town Topics* (New York), October 18, 1900, p. 5, col. 2.

24. *Chicago Tribune,* December 3, 1899, p. 1, col. 1; *New York World,* January 3, 1906, p. 2, col. 5; ibid., p. 2, col. 2.

25. *New York American,* January 7, 1906, part 2, p. 49, col. 2; *New York World,* January 3, 1906, p. 2, col. 3.

26. *London Times,* February 12, 1964, p. 15, col. 1; George Meredith to Mrs. J. G. Butcher, September 20, 1901, *Letters of George Meredith,* vol. 3, ed. C. L. Cline (Oxford: At the Clarendon Press, 1970), 140; Edel, 179–80.

27. *Cincinnati Enquirer,* January 3, 1906, p. 2, col. 5; Emilie Grigsby, *I: In Which a Woman Tells the Truth About Herself* (New York: D. Appleton and Company, 1904), foreword.

28. Ibid., 29–30; ibid.

29. Ibid., 96–97; ibid., 81.

30. Ibid., 208.

31. Ibid., 264; ibid., 324.

32. Ibid., 352.

33. *New York World,* January 1, 1906, p. 2, cols. 1–2; *New York American,* January 6, 1906, p. 5, col. 2; ibid., January 1, 1906, p. 5, col. 3.

Chapter 27. The Final Struggle

1. *Atlanta Constitution,* December 8, 1901, p. 22, col. 1; *Washington Post,* January 1, 1906, p. 6, col. 6; *M. A. P.,* June 8, 1901, p. 562, col. 1.

2. *Chicago Sunday American,* December 31, 1905, p. 2, col. 2; *Chicago Daily News,* May 18, 1903, p. 1, col. 3; Henry Loomis, "Chronic Diffuse Interstitial Nephritis," in *A System of Practical Medicine,* vol. 2, ed. Alfred Lee Loomis and William Gilman Thompson (New York: Lea Brothers and Company, 1897), 742.

3. *Chicago Tribune,* April 23, 1903, p. 2, col. 4; Charles Dawes to William Leupp, April 14, 1904, Charles G. Dawes Business Book, January 26–April 30, 1904, Charles Dawes Papers, Northwestern University, Evanston, Ill.

4. *Chicago Tribune,* April 24, 1903, p. 3, col. 1; *Chicago Daily News,* May 15, 1903, p. 1, cols. 3–4; Testimony of Rafael Govin, February 16, 1912, Charles Tyson Yerkes Estate, Probate Records, Cook County Archives, Chicago, Ill.; Testimony of Julien T. Davies, April 17, 1908, 17–18, Guaranty Trust Company of New York vs. Chicago Union Traction Company et al., Case 26727, U.S. Circuit Court, Northern District of Illinois, Eastern Division at Chicago, National Archives—Great Lakes Branch, Chicago, Ill.

5. Bruce G. Moffat, *The 'L': The Development of Chicago's Rapid Transit System, 1888–1932* (Chicago: Central Electric Railfans' Association, 1995), 104–5; Henry Robbins to President of the North and West Chicago Street Railroad Companies, April 13, 1906, Henry S. Robbins Collection, Chicago Historical Society; *Chicago Tribune,* December 5, 1904, p. 3, cols. 1–2.

6. Govin Testimony; *Chicago Daily News,* January 4, 1905, p. 4, col. 1.

7. Testimony of H. E. Haward, July 24, 1903, *Royal Commission on London Traffic,* vol. 2, 250; Alan Jackson and Desmond Croome, *Rails through the Clay*

(London: George Allen and Unwin Ltd., 1962), 91; T. C. Barker and Michael Robbins, *A History of London Transport*, vol. 2 (London: George Allen and Unwin, Ltd., 1974), 113–15; Covick, 24–25.

8. John Pattinson Thomas, "The Seven from Chicago," pamphlet, The London Underground Railway Society, 1970, 120; ibid., 122.

9. *Chicago Daily News*, December 9, 1902, p. 2, col. 4; Eric Barton, "Underground Travelling London," in *Living London*, ed. George R. Sims (London: Cassell and Company, 1903), 150.

10. *Punch*, December 10, 1902, p. 397, col. 1; *Daily Inter Ocean* (Chicago), May 7, 1903, p. 2, col. 4; Barker and Robbins, 107; *Railway Times*, February 11, 1905, pp. 147–48; Jackson and Croome, 103.

11. *Chicago Chronicle*, December 30, 1905, p. 1, col. 3; *Chicago Daily News*, July 14, 1905, p. 3, col. 7; Loomis, 744; *Chicago Daily News*, July 19, 1905, p. 3, col. 6; ibid., August 4, 1905, p. 3, col. 4; ibid., December 30, 1905, p. 2, col. 5.

12. James Chapman recollection, 12–13, Souvenir, Dinner Given by Sir Edgar Speyer to James R. Chapman, February 7, 1910, found in J. Clifton Robinson Papers, Bristol Record Office, Bristol, United Kingdom. I am indebted to Paul Hadley for this item.

13. *Chicago Sunday American*, December 31, 1905, p. 2, col. 2; *New York Times*, October 1, 1909, p. 1, col. 2; Codicil of Will of Charles Tyson Yerkes, filed September 30, 1909, Charles Tyson Yerkes Estate, Probate Records, Cook County Archives, Chicago, Ill.; Deposition of Mary Lightford Spotswood, November 19, 1909, ibid.; *New York American*, August 27, 1905, p. 35, col. 1; Loomis, 746.

14. *Daily Inter Ocean* (Chicago), October 29, 1905, p. 2, col. 5; *Chicago Daily News*, December 30, 1905, p. 2, col. 5; Charles Yerkes to Francis Hopwood, September 30, 1905, Lord Southborough Papers, Bodleian Library. Many thanks to Paul Hadley for this last item.

15. *Railway Times*, October 28, 1905, p. 487, col. 1; Barker and Robbins, 116; *Daily Inter Ocean* (Chicago), October 29, 1905, p. 2, col. 5.

16. *Chicago Daily News*, December 30, 1905, p. 3, col. 5; Henry James, *The American Scene* (New York: St. Martins Press, 1987), 75.

17. *Chicago Sunday American*, February 4, 1906, p. 2, col. 4; *New York American*, February 26, 1906, p. 2, col. 1; Edward Dean Sullivan, "The First of the Playboys: Wilson Mizner and His Times," *Cosmopolitan* (October 1935): 116, 119.

18. *New York Times*, January 4, 1906, p. 1, col. 7.

19. *Chicago Daily News*, December 12, 1905, p. 4, col. 4; *Chicago Record-Herald*, January 2, 1906, p. 3, cols. 1–2; *New York World*, January 7, 1906, p. 3, col. 3; *New York American*, February 26, 1906, p. 2, col. 2; ibid., January 3, 1906, p. 2, col. 2.

20. *New York World*, January 4, 1906, p. 2, col. 2.

21. Ibid., December 31, 1905, p. 2, cols. 5–6.

22. *Chicago Tribune*, January 1, 1906, p. 10, cols. 1–2; *Chicago Record-Herald*, January 3, 1906, p. 8, col. 2.

23. *Chicago Tribune*, December 31, 1905, part 3, p. 4, col. 4; *Chicago Daily News*, December 30, 1905, p. 8, col. 2.

24. *New York American*, January 2, 1906, p. 16, col. 2.

25. *The Economist* (Chicago), January 6, 1906, p. 10, cols. 2–3.

26. *Daily Inter Ocean* (Chicago), December 30, 1905, p. 6, col. 2.

27. *New York World*, February 4, 1906, p. 2, Section E, cols. 3–4.

Epilogue

1. *New York World,* January 2, 1906, p. 1, col. 7; ibid., p. 2, col. 1; *New York Herald,* January 2, 1906, p. 4, col. 6; *New York Times,* January 2, 1906, p. 1, col. 5.

2. *New York Herald,* January 3, 1906, p. 4, cols. 1–2; *The Outlook,* January 13, 1906, pp. 58–59; *New York American,* January 7, 1906, part 2, p. 49, col. 3.

3. Louis Owsley Testimony, Transcript of Record, 145, Charles Sims et al. vs. Louis Owsley, Appellate Division of the Supreme Court, New York; Wesley Towner, *The Elegant Auctioneers* (New York: Hill and Wang, 1970), 234; ibid., 237.

4. *Chicago Tribune,* March 1, 1912, p. 11, col. 3; *Chicago Evening American,* February 26, 1906, p. 2, col. 1; *New York Times,* April 7, 1911, p. 1, col. 4; *Chicago Evening American,* February 26, 1906, p. 1, col. 2.

5. H. K. Fleming, "Theodore Dreiser's Femme Fatale," *St. Petersburg Times,* December 28, 1986, 4D, col. 3; *The Times* (London), February 12, 1964, p. 15, col. 1.

6. *Chicago Times-Herald,* August 25, 1895, p. 7, col. 1.

INDEX

JOHN FRANCH is a freelance writer whose work has appeared in scholarly and popular publications including *Chicago History, Sky and Telescope, Astronomy,* and the *Illinois Historical Journal.*

*The University of Illinois Press
is a founding member of the
Association of American University Presses.*

---

*Composed in 9.5/12 Trump Mediaeval
by BookComp, Inc.
Manufactured by Thomson-Shore, Inc.*

*University of Illinois Press
1325 South Oak Street
Champaign, IL 61820-6903
www.press.uillinois.edu*